Schriften zur
Europäischen Integration und
Internationalen Wirtschaftsordnung

Veröffentlichungen des
Wilhelm Merton-Zentrums für Europäische Integration und
Internationale Wirtschaftsordnung,

herausgegeben von

Professor Dr. Dr. Rainer Hofmann, Universität Frankfurt a. M.
Professor Dr. Stefan Kadelbach, Universität Frankfurt a. M.
Professor Dr. Rainer Klump, Universität Frankfurt a. M.

Band 24

Prof. Dr. Dr. Rainer Hofmann/
Prof. Dr. Christian J. Tams (Hrsg.)

International Investment Law and General International Law

From Clinical Isolation to Systemic Integration?

 **Nomos**

Die Deutsche Nationalbibliothek verzeichnet diese Publikation in
der Deutschen Nationalbibliografie; detaillierte bibliografische
Daten sind im Internet über http://dnb.d-nb.de abrufbar.

Die Deutsche Nationalbibliothek lists this publication in the
Deutsche Nationalbibliografie; detailed bibliographic data
is available in the Internet at http://dnb.d-nb.de.

ISBN 978-3-8329-6729-1

1. Auflage 2011
© Nomos Verlagsgesellschaft, Baden-Baden 2011. Printed in Germany. Alle Rechte,
auch die des Nachdrucks von Auszügen, der fotomechanischen Wiedergabe und der
Übersetzung, vorbehalten. Gedruckt auf alterungsbeständigem Papier.

FOREWORD

On 26-28 April 2006, the Wilhelm Merton Centre for European Integration and International Economic Order organized a symposium on current issues of ICSID law (see Hofmann/Tams (eds.), The International Convention on the Settlement of Investment Disputes. Taking Stock after 40 Years, Nomos, Baden-Baden 2007). Contacts made at this symposium eventually resulted in the organization of the Frankfurt Investment Arbitration Moot Competition (www.investmentmoot.org) which annually attracts student teams from universities all over the world. Moreover, in the framework of this event, meetings of internationally known practitioners in investment arbitration have been organized jointly by Dr *Sabine Konrad*, now Partner with the Frankfurt Office of K&L Gates, and the Wilhelm Merton Centre to offer a venue for an exchange of views on salient issues of international investment law while strictly applying Chatham House rules. Against this background, *Christian J. Tams*, Professor of International Law at Glasgow University, proposed to convene a conference which would focus, from a more academic point of view, on current issues of international investment law, in particular on how it approaches fundamental concepts and notions of general international law, such as the law of treaties, State responsibility, diplomatic protection or State immunity.

Indeed, this conference was held on 12-13 March 2010 and brought together a considerable number of investment law experts, both academics and practitioners. It was opened with a keynote address by Professor Dr *James Crawford SC*, University of Cambridge, who gave a general and quite personal view on the overarching question: namely whether the relationship between international investment law and general international law could be considered as one of *clinical isolation* or one of *systemic integration*. The actual conference allowed younger scholars to present papers on various aspects of this relationship. The ensuing discussions were initiated by comments from more experienced participants, from both academia and practice. The present volume brings together the keynote address as well as these various papers and comments and, it is hoped, will give readers a good insight into the most prominent issues of the relationship between international investment law and general international law.

The directors of the Wilhelm Merton Centre wish to express their sincere gratitude to Professor Dr *Christian J. Tams* for his initiative and his strong and continuous intellectual input and support throughout the project. Furthermore, the organizers of the conference wish to thank Mr *Philipp Donath* and Mr *Jakob*

Kadelbach for their most valuable assistance before, during and after the conference. Finally, the editors of this volume wish to thank all the contributors for their papers and comments, Mr *Gennadi Rudak* for his editorial skills and Mr *Alek Dumanovic* and Mr *Niko Tsolakidis* for their assistance in the editing process.

Frankfurt am Main, 16 February 2011

Rainer Hofmann   Stefan Kadelbach   Rainer Klump

Contents

International Investment Law: Situating an Exotic Special Regime within the Framework of General International Law

Rainer Hofmann[*] *and Christian J. Tams*[**]

Over the last decade, international investment law has risen to prominence. This prominence is reflected in the number of investment arbitrations just as in the publication, now on a regular basis, of new investment law textbooks.[1] With prominence comes interest, and interest leads to scrutiny. And so, over the last decade, general international lawyers have taken an interest in, and have scrutinized this curious 'hybrid'[2] – or even (in the words of the ILC's Fragmentation Study) 'exotic'[3] – branch of international law: have begun to read awards and investment treaties on which they were based, have looked at investment dispute settlement from a comparative perspective, and have evaluated how tribunals approached questions of general international law. By the same token, the actors of international investment law – and tribunals in particular – have applied provisions of general international law and have had to determine whether general legal rules influenced provisions of investment law or whether investment law deliberately deviated from the general framework.

International investment law is by no means the first sub-area of international law that has been 'detected' in this way and whose actors have had to define the relationship between 'their' field and general international law. It shares this fate with many other specialized sub-areas, including some that today are seen as its rivals such as human rights, international environmental law, and international economic law. Just as investment law today, these at some point became rele-

---

[*] Professor Dr Rainer Hofmann, Professor of Public Law, Public International Law and European Law, University of Frankfurt.

[**] Professor Dr Christian J. Tams, Professor of International Law, University of Glasgow.

1 Such as Dolzer/Schreuer, Principles of International Investment Law (2008); Newcombe/Paradell, Law and Practice of Investment Treaties: Standards of Treatment (2009); Griebel, Internationales Investitionsrecht (2008); Subedi, International Investment Law: Reconciling Policy and Principle (2009); Sornarajah, The International Law on Foreign Investment (3rd edn., 2010); see also Douglas, The International Law of Investment Claims (2009).

2 Cf. Douglas, The Hybrid Foundations of Investment Treaty Arbitration, BYIL 74 (2003), 151.

3 Fragmentation of International Law: Difficulties Arising from the Diversification and Expansion of International Law: Report of the Study Group of the International Law Commission, finalized by Martti Koskenniemi, UN Doc A/CN.4/L.682, at para. 8.

vant, and began to be of concern for mainstream international lawyers. Just as investment lawyers today, those specializing in human rights, international environmental law or international economic law were provided with opportunities to comment on the relevance (if any) of general legal concepts within their specialized sub-area. Over time, debates between generalists and specialists have helped bring about a clearer understanding of whether, and how, the curious new sub-areas fitted within the landscape of general international law. And of course, over time, the special sub-areas themselves have begun to influence the mainstream, have to some extent become part of the general legal framework. Consequently, instead of merely positioning them on the map of general international law, it became necessary to analyze how the special sub-areas influenced the discipline as a whole – hence debates (to give just some examples) about the humanization of international law,[4] or about the radiance of the precautionary principle outside the field of environmental law.[5]

That international law as a system should have to define the role of specialized sub-areas within a general legal framework is not surprising. The international legal system has undergone a process of 'functional differentiation' similar to that identified by sociologists as a key feature of modern societies.[6] Functional differentiation brings risks and opportunities: it can be disruptive and destructive; but it can also be a force for professionalization and specialization that enhance knowledge and understanding. International legal debates have typically stressed the first of these aspects: tellingly, they are often conducted within a framework of 'fragmentation', inviting concerns about the loss of unity.[7] And yet, international law accepts functional differentiation to a large extent. Most of its general rules are dispositive and can be contracted out. In fact, the concept of *jus cogens,* which introduces a normative hierarchy and restricts the scope for contracting-out of the general framework, took decades to become accepted and has a rather narrow field of application: there are but few agreed *leges superi-*

---

4   Cf. Simma, International Human Rights and General International Law: A Comparative Analysis, in: Collected Courses of the Academy of European Law, Vol. IV/2 (1993), p. 153; Meron, The Humanization of International Law (2006).
5   Cf. Zander, The Application of the Precautionary Principle in Practice (2010) for a comparative account.
6   For a brief and helpful summary see the ILC's Fragmentation Study (note 3), paras. 5-20.
7   Pierre-Marie Dupuy's general course contains a particularly emphatic plea for unity: see Dupuy, L'unité de l'ordre juridique internationale. Cours général de droit international public, Recueil des Cours 297 (2002), p. 9. Cf. also Koskenniemi/Leino, Fragmentation of International Law. Postmodern Anxieties?, Leiden Journal of International Law 15 (2002), p. 553.

ores.[8] Typically, the possibility of contracting-out is accepted, and the *lex specialis* maxim provides the conceptual tool for recognizing functional differentiation.[9]

Of course, not every special rule contracts out of the general legal framework. Contracting-out cannot be presumed; it must be assessed whether special rules derogate from, or disapply, general rules. Even where special rules do derogate, international law provides the tools to minimize disruption, by favoring mutually supportive readings that seek to 'harmonize ... apparently conflicting norms by interpreting them so as to render them compatible'.[10] That a special sub-system should modify the general legal framework, in other words, is usually permitted, but not specifically encouraged, and different specialized systems have taken different approaches; some are more special than others.

'Clinical isolation' and 'systemic integration' are terms used to describe possible relationships between general international law and special sub-areas. Clearly, however, both denote extremes that will rarely be matched by reality. Tellingly, the former of them, 'clinical isolation', was first used to describe how a special sub-area (WTO law) should <u>not</u> be viewed.[11] In fact, the closer we look, the more obvious it becomes that very few sub-areas are clinically (or hermetically) isolated in any comprehensive sense, let alone form self-contained regimes (however popular the term may be).[12] However, special they remain – in some ways, we can expect them to contract out of aspects of the general legal frame-

---

8   For nuanced assessments see Paulus, Die internationale Gemeinschaft im Völkerrecht (2001), pp. 330 et seq.; Kadelbach, Zwingendes Völkerrecht (1992); and the ILC's Fragmentation Study (note 3), at paras. 324 et seq.

9   See the ILC's Fragmentation Study (note 3), at para. 108: 'Most of general international law may be derogated from by lex specialis.' On lex specialis see notably Article 55 of the ILC's Articles on State Responsibility (2001) and commentary thereto.

10   ILC Fragmentation Study (note 3), at para. 411. Article 31(3)(c) VCLT most clearly expresses this desire for 'systemically integrated' interpretation of norms: cf. Combacau/Sur, Droit international public (8th edn., 2008), at p. 179; McLachlan, The Principle of Systemic Integration and Article 31 (3) (c) of the Vienna Convention, ICLQ 54 (2005), p. 279.

11   Cf. WTO Appellate Body, United States – Standards for Reformulated and Conventional Gasoline, WTO Doc. WT/DS2/AB/R (1996), at p. 17 (noting that the GATT 'is not to be read in clinical isolation from [general] public international law').

12   Special sub-systems of international law are never complete: they typically regulate specific aspects (primary rules, remedies, enforcement mechanisms, etc.), but as they do not exist outside the international legal framework, they fall back on general international law to address issues such as attribution, remedies, succession, treaty interpretation, etc. In the words of the ILC's Fragmentation Study, '[n]o legal regime is isolated from general international law', and 'no regime is self-contained' (note 3, at paras. 193 and 192 respectively). Since its unfortunate launch, in the ICJ's Tehran judgment (ICJ Reports 1980, 3, at para. 86), the term 'self-contained regime' has confused, rather than elucidated, debates.

work, to be <u>not</u> fully systemically integrated; otherwise they would not be necessary. Contracting-out is a question of degree, with '(systemic) integration' and '(clinical) isolation' describing two ends of the specter.

It should be noted – if only in passing – that there is an important 'cultural' dimension to debates about the isolation and integration. Even if special sub-areas of international law are unlikely to be sealed off substantively from the general legal framework, the people applying and interpreting the law may very well work in 'clinical isolation' from general international lawyers, and any encounter between the two groups may well lead to 'clashes of culture'. Some of this may at present be felt in exchanges about whether international investment law takes due account of non-investment concepts – State sovereignty, transparency, public values enshrined by human rights treaties, etc. Again, it is important to note that investment law is by no means the first special sub-area to be witnessing such 'clashes of culture': in fact, the fault lines are not that different from those separating WTO or human rights specialists on the one hand, and generalists on the other. What may be different is the presence of a different group of 'generalists' – those experienced in commercial litigation who view investment arbitration as private dispute resolution to which commercial arbitration rules applied by analogy. However, the premise underlying this approach is now being questioned more openly. While commercial arbitration has shaped arbitration techniques to a surprising extent, investment law has begun to more openly embrace its 'public' character: if anything, the new trend seems to be for investment lawyers to acknowledge the influence of domestic public law on investment law concepts.[13] This 'public turn' indeed would seem an overdue correction, which reflects the relevance of international treaties for investment law in its current 'BIT generation'[14]. It may take time to be fully reflected in the choice of counsel and arbitrators (and in fact, the move into the market by major international law firms may signal a setback[15]), but if we look at the broader societal debate, the public and international dimensions of international investment law now seem to be more fully appreciated than ever before.

13 See notably the contributions to Schill (ed.), International Investment Law and Comparative Public Law (2010).
14 Cf. Reisman/Sloan, Indirect Expropriation and Its Valuation in the BIT Generation, BYIL 74 (2003), p. 115.
15 This point is made by Crawford, International Protection of Foreign Direct Investments – Between Clinical Isolation and Systematic Integration: in this volume, at pp. 20 - 22.

***

The subsequent contributions address aspects of the complex interrelationship between international investment law and general international law. James Crawford keynote speech, with which the volume opens, provides an impressive *tour d'horizon*[16]: it might best be read as a witness account – by one who has seen the sub-area gain in relevance, and who has always appreciated that as it deals with State behavior, investment law 'requires a refined understanding of the way in which the law of obligations is in general applied to states'.[17] The following chapters deal with specific aspects of the interrelation largely within the general spirit of the opening address, but from a specific angle: the focus throughout is on how investment law approaches the general legal framework. Does it accept it as a given, or does it provide its own set of rules? Does it confirm general international law, or does it contract out? And has the specific investment law approach (if any) perhaps even led to a modification of the general legal framework?

These questions are addressed with respect to what are believed to be representative fields of general international law. The law of treaties and the law of State responsibility – as the two areas of general international law in which the international community has agreed on widely recognized sets of 'meta rules'[18] – feature prominently. These indeed seemed obvious candidates, as they are regularly addressed in investment treaty arbitration – based, as it is, on international treaties and involving allegations of wrongful State conduct. More specifically, the pieces and comments by Michael Waibel,[19] Christoph Schreuer,[20] Lars Markert[21] and Antonios Tzanakopoulos[22] address interactions between investment law and the law of treaties, notably questions of treaty interpretation and treaty denunciation. Aspects of State responsibility are addressed in the contributions by Christina Knahr[23] and Pavel Šturma[24] (dealing primarily with issues of attri-

---

16 Crawford (note 15).
17 Crawford (note 15), at pp. 28 - 29.
18 The 1969 Vienna Convention on the Law of Treaties and the 2001 Articles on State Responsibility, respectively.
19 Waibel, International Investment Law and Treaty Interpretation: in this volume, p. 29.
20 Schreuer, International Investment Law: From Clinical Isolation to Systemic Integration. Comments: in this volume, p. 71.
21 Markert, International Investment Law and Treaty Interpretation – Problems, Particularities and Possible Trends: in this volume, p. 53.
22 Tzanakopoulos, Denunciation of the ICSID Convention under the General International Law of Treaties: in this volume, p. 75.
23 Knahr, International Investment Law and State Responsibility: Conditions of Responsibility: in this volume, p. 95.
24 Šturma, International Investment Law and State Responsibility: in this volume, p. 111.

bution of conduct), Florian Franke[25] (focusing on necessity), as well as Steffen Hindelang[26] and Ursula Kriebaum[27] (debating consequences of breaches, and notably the alleged primacy of restitution). Kate Parlett[28] and Stephan Schill[29] analyze interrelationships that may be less obvious: those between investment law on the one hand and diplomatic protection and State immunity on the other. That investment law should interact with these fields is not always appreciated; however, the two pieces make very clear that they are not 'merely parallel regimes'.[30]

Taken together, the various contributions illustrate the varied interactions between general international law and one of its most dynamic sub-areas. This is not a simple story of *en banc* affirmation or complete contracting-out; instead, four forms of interaction would seem to stand out:

(i) In many areas, international investment law accepts the legal framework provided by general international law. It does so at times expressly – e.g. through the 'without prejudice' clause of Article 55 of the ICSID Convention preserving immunity from enforcement. But mostly, it does so because (as noted by Pavel Šturma) there simply do not exist 'many special secondary rules',[31] and general international law applies by default: there are few specific investment law rules on attribution of conduct, on treaty interpretation, etc. Contracting-out therefore remains the exception, most importantly with respect to diplomatic protection, which Article 27 of the ICSID Convention expressly disapplies (though not comprehensively), but also in specific areas of treaty law such as termination.

(ii) Investment law's acceptance of the general legal framework does not always mean there was serious engagement. Drawing on Christina Knahr's analysis, one might say that State responsibility rules on attribution are recited in investment practice without much discussion, almost for the sake of convenience.[32] There is debate between Michael Waibel and his commentators (Christoph Schreuer, Lars Markert) on whether investment tribunals have properly applied the general rules of treaty interpretation, or merely paid lip service to them. In the field of immunity, there has to date been the least interaction, but as Stephan

---

25   Franke, The Custom of Necessity in Investor-State Arbitrations: in this volume, p. 121.
26   Hindelang, Restitution and Compensation – Reconstructing the Relationship in Investment Treaty Law: in this volume, p. 161.
27   Kriebaum, Comments on Restitution in International Investment Law: in this volume, p. 201.
28   Parlett, Diplomatic Protection and Investment Arbitration: in this volume, p. 211.
29   Schill, International Investment Law and the Law of State Immunity: Antagonists or Two Sides of the Same Coin?: in this volume, p. 231.
30   Cf. Parlett (note 28), at p. 227.
31   Šturma (note 24), at p. 115.
32   See also Crawford (note 15), at pp.24 - 25.

Schill argues, this need not remain so; in fact, with enforcement of awards now apparently becoming a more real problem,[33] pressure on immunity rules will increase, and balancing techniques (such as proportionality, on which he relies) may in future inform the application of 'without prejudice' clauses such as that of Article 55 of the ICSID Convention.

(iii) Conversely, even where investment law could be expected to adopt a special approach, general international law is by no means irrelevant. Kate Parlett, Florian Franke and Antonios Tzanakopoulos show how it could inform the interpretation and application of special investment rules – at the micro-level, no doubt, but perhaps crucially, on questions as diverse as continuous nationality, available defences, and the effects of treaty denunciations. Steffen Hindelang seems to go one step further by emphasizing the primacy of restitution over compensation under the general rules on remedies; this in his view (which in turn is criticized by Ursula Kriebaum) should guide investment tribunals as well. All this is evidence for the power of centripetal forces working towards systemic integration.

(iv) By contrast, there is relatively little evidence of investment law modifying general international law. Investment law may have become generally relevant, but at least in the fields analyzed by contributors, its approaches are not easily generalized. As Kate Parlett notes, the ICJ's *Diallo* judgment was cautious to treat investment practice as special, not affecting the general framework of diplomatic protection;[34] by the same token, Michael Waibel and Steffen Hindelang do not argue that the special approach of investment tribunals (adopting, in their view, a particular understanding of treaty interpretation and of remedies) should have a wider impact outside the field of investment law. This reflects a more cautious approach than that informing earlier claims about investment law approaches 'spilling over' into general international law – allegedly overcoming, to take but two prominent examples, restrictive, general rules on standing set out in *Barcelona Traction*[35] or minimalist readings of the minimum standard.[36]

33 See notably the information provided by Schill (note 29), his footnote 65.
34 Cf. ICJ, Case Concerning Ahmadou Sadio Diallo (Republic of Guinea v Democratic Republic of the Congo), Preliminary Objections, ICJ Reports 2007, p. 579, at paras. 40 - 41.
35 Cf. Orrego Vicuña, International Dispute Settlement in an Evolving Global Society – Constitutionalization, Accessibility, Privatization (2004) 42.
36 Cf. Schwebel, The Reshaping of the International Law on Foreign Investment by Concordant Bilateral Investment Treaties, in: Law in the Service of Human Dignity. Essays in Honour of Florentino Feliciano (Charnovitz et al., 2005), 241.

***

From this brief summary, it is clear that the 'exotic' sub-area of international investment law interacts with general international law in manifold ways. In many fields, it does not seek to contract out of the general legal framework in the first place; in others, it provides for special rules that consciously adapt the general legal framework to the specific demands of foreign investment; in still others, the general legal framework influences the interpretation of special rules. On the specter of 'clinical isolation *versus* systemic integration', investment law sits in somewhere the middle, alongside other special sub-areas that over time have had to define their position within the general legal framework. If there is one general message, it would seem to be that those thinking about the interrelationship between investment law and general international law (and writing about it in this volume) are aware of the need for some interaction. General international law allows for contracting out, but special frameworks seeking to disapply the general rules are well advised not to cut off the links completely, to remain open for engagement. This openness does not mean full integration, but implies a common understanding that investment law forms part of the framework provided by general international law. If experience with other special sub-areas is any guide, this common understanding is the best recipe for balancing the competing demands for contracting out and integration.

International Protection of Foreign Direct Investments: Between Clinical Isolation and Systematic Integration

James Crawford[*]

Keynote Address

We have been set up for this conference by my former doctoral student, Professor Christian Tams, because we are given a choice between clinical isolation and systematic integration. The international legal system has *never* been systematically integrated. It has always been a mishmash, a bric-à-brac, as one French scholar had it.[1] This is because it has been composed since the 17th century primarily of states, who are quite capable of doing two things at once (and more than two things), quite capable of contradiction, quite capable of setting up an institution or sending a mission to do "A" and another to do "not-A" at the very same time. The myth of integration is a myth associated with national legal systems, inappropriately transferred to the international sphere.

Obviously the term "clinical isolation" derives from the early WTO jurisprudence.[2] The WTO was at that time in a phase of motion from a rather clinical isolation to something more like systematic integration. At least, the WTO is an entity for which those terms would have had some meaning. Most international lawyers had little or nothing to do with the WTO in its early manifestation, prior to the Marrakech agreement, and most WTO lawyers had nothing to do with international law. I remember there was one international lawyer in Australia who did both,[3] and he was regarded as a very unusual creature indeed. The progress, if that is the right word, of the WTO towards systematic integration has to some

---

[*]   Professor Dr James Crawford SC, Whewell Professor of International Law, University of Cambridge.

1   Jean Combacau, "Le droit international: Bric à brac ou système", 31 Archives de Philosophie du Droit (1986), 85-105.

2   See United States – Standards for Reformulated and Conventional Gasoline, WTO Doc. WT/DS2/AB/R (1996), at 17 where the Appellate Body acknowledged that "the General Agreement [GATT] is not to be read in clinical isolation from public international law"; see also Korea – Measures Affecting Government Procurement, WTO Doc. WT/DS163/R (2000), at para. 7.96.

3   Professor, later Justice Kevin Ryan. See KW Ryan (ed), International Law in Australia (2nd edn, Law Book Co, Sydney, 1984).

extent been a debate about the role of international law in relation to WTO law.[4] A good deal has been made of the law of treaties in respect of the WTO, but of course the Marrakech agreement specifically refers to the Vienna Convention in the context of the interpretation of the WTO agreements.[5] There have been other references, for example to the ILC Articles on State Responsibility, by the Appellate Body and to a lesser extent by panels.[6] At the same time one gets the impression that these references have not amounted to very much. There have been quite a lot of them, but they have been somewhat superficial. So clinical isolation has not been completely discarded, despite criticism of the WTO for its alleged failure to take into account environmental considerations.[7] My sense is that the second generation, if I may put it in generational terms, of the WTO is moving back towards clinical isolation. That is perhaps an exaggeration, but if you look for general international lawyers on the Appellate Body, they are no longer there. A lot depends on the individuals concerned; a lot depends on the sociology of the legal profession in terms of outcomes.

It is useful to acquire a historical perspective on the move to international investment law, because we tend to have short memories. So first I will say something about the history of its development. Then I will introduce a rough sociology of international investment law because that is a significant determinant of what is going on. Finally I will canvass the various areas which could be coupled with international investment law by the word "and", asking whether it is useful to make such linkages.

*   *   *

The historical perspective on investment law involves a number of developments. There had been mixed arbitrations both before and after the First World

---

4   See e.g., J Pauwelyn, Conflict of Norms in Public International Law: How WTO Law Relates to Other Rules of International Law (Cambridge University Press, 2003).

5   Marrakesh Agreement Establishing the World Trade Organisation, Dispute Settlement Understanding, Article 3.2. See also Appellate Body Report, US – Gasoline, WT/DS2/AB/R, at 17 and 23 and Appellate Body Report, Japan – Taxes on Alcoholic Beverages, WT/DS8/AB/R, WT/DS10/AB/R, WT/DS11/AB/R,10.

6   See e.g. EC - Bananas (1999), WT/DS27/AB/R and Brazil - Aircraft,WT/DS46/AB/R.

7   See A Chatterjee, D Bhattacharya and S Banerjee, Guised in Green: Uncloaking the Myth of World Trade Organization's Trade – Environment Harmony (Science Publications, 2009). Cf also A Goyal, The WTO and In ternational Environmental Law: Towards Conciliation (Oxford University Press, 2006).

War. For example, the Venezuelan arbitrations of 1903 produced uncanny similarities to the sort of issues that arise today.[8]

But the modern problem of reconciling investment protection with national sovereignty arose in acute form in the early 1950s. An important case is the *Anglo-Iranian Oil Company Case*,[9] because there international lawyers made a deliberate attempt to internationalize development contracts in the context of the oil industry. The International Court of Justice would have none of it in the preliminary objections phase of the *Anglo-Iranian Case*. It simply said, these contracts are governed by municipal law and they are not internationalized at all.[10] That had consequences in terms of jurisdiction.

But the internationalization movement did not go away. We have all heard about the *lex mercatoria*[11] – that wonderful creation. Lawyers are not often thought of as being imaginative, but it was possible for a group of lawyers to imagine into existence a legal system – a legal system which curiously had no subjects. No one owed any allegiance to it. International law is difficult enough, since all the people I know who owe their primary allegiance (in Hartian terms, have an internal attitude) to international law are either international lawyers or cranks. But there are some who regard it as an important second legal system that can affect them, for good and ill. *Lex mercatoria* does not even have that. It was invented as a way of trying to escape host state law.

In opposition to that were, of course, the new international economic order[12] and the attempt to re-nationalize international economic law against the bogus internationalization of *Texaco* and the like.[13] Then it was realized that the problem was not the application in normal circumstances of the law of the host state, but how to provide security against arbitrary treatment by the host state whether or not in accordance with its domestic law. And that in turn led to the BIT phenomenon. The BIT phenomenon involves — though this is not often emphasized – a rejection of the internationalization of contracts. At the same time it involves

---

8   Mixed Claims Commission (France-Venezuela) – Acquatella, Bianchi et al. Case, X RIAA 2006, at 1-8, first reprinted in J H Ralston (ed), Venezuelan Arbitrations of 1903 (Washington DC, US Government Printing Office, 1904), at 904 et seq.

9   Anglo-Iranian Oil Co. case (jurisdiction), Judgment of 22 July 1952, I.C.J. Reports 1952, p. 93.

10 Ibid., 112.

11 Cf E Gaillard, "Thirty Years of Lex Mercatoria: Towards the Discriminating Application of Transnational Rules", in A J van den Berg, Planning Efficient Arbitration Proceedings: the Law Applicable in International Arbitration (Kluwer Law International, The Hague, 1996), at 582-602; see also K P Berger, The Creeping Codification of the New Lex Mercatoria (2nd edn, Kluwer, 2010).

12 GA Res. S-6/3201 of 1 May 1974, Declaration on the Establishment of a New International Economic Order.

13 Texaco v. the Government of the Libyan Arab Republic (1978) 17 ILM 3.

the application of a real international standard contained in the treaty. The treaty, of course, is a paradigm vehicle of international law and has been for 400 years, so rather than make up international law as you go on the basis of an superficial comparative analysis, we are actually applying a rather simple set of standards to the conduct of states in accordance with their own law; in return for the concession of arbitration and the abolition of the local remedies rule, states got an acceptance of the principle of localization, and the requirement that in addition to international law the law of the host state was the governing law in these cases.[14] Obviously it is more difficult than that because one has to ask what is the cause of action and so on. But nonetheless, the applicable law provision of the ICSID Convention reflects a profound truth about investment law in our time. There is not an international law of corporations; there is not an international law of shareholdings. There are corporations and shares established by the laws of the various states, no doubt common in many respects, but nonetheless distinctive, capable of producing different results, requiring individual study.[15]

*   *   *

Let me give you a pen picture of the profession as it now is in the field of international arbitration. In the 1960s, for a law firm to describe itself as an international law firm would have been to commit prompt suicide. International law was something done in universities, by rather curious people who could not (or at least did not) do real law, and who had never been inside a courtroom in any professional capacity. Nowadays all the big firms describe themselves as international law firms. If we look at their websites, they are all international law firms now. Are there any international lawyers there? Occasionally, but in the senior ranks of the profession, very few. But with investment arbitration and other developments, this is changing. In particular investment lawyers have been professionalized for good and for real.[16] For good in the sense that after all these people are extremely able as lawyers and do treat international law as law. If we believe in law as a discipline, that cannot be a bad thing. But on the other hand, many of them are rather ignorant of international law as it happens in the traditional way between states or in the context of international organizations. The number of

14   Convention on the Settlement of Investment Disputes between States and Nationals of Other States, 18 March 1965, 575 UNTS 159, Article 42(1).
15   See e.g., Barcelona Traction, Light and Power Company, Limited, Judgment, I.C.J. Reports 1970, p.3,at 33, para. 38.
16   See in general D Bishop (ed), The Art of Advocacy in International Arbitration (Huntington NY, Juris, 2004).

people who can pronounce the *Chorzów Factory* case[17] properly is already limited, but there are still fewer people who have actually read it and who understand the very intricate relationship between the Upper Silesia tribunal and the Permanent Court and the way in which that relationship actually did effect the way the case was decided.

The role of the international lawyer old style is as it were the flip side of that particular coin. There is no doubt about what has happened in terms of the development of the rule of law in our time. What has happened is a vast proliferation of the amount of law in existence. There is a wonderful song sung by Hugh Thirlway (who is fond of making up songs about international court cases) which goes "there's too much international law".[18] It is sung in his inimitable way. No doubt those who do it as a profession will tend to think that there cannot be too much of it. But there is probably more international law by volume than there is of any other legal system, except perhaps United States law. It has got to the stage where it is impossible for anyone to know all of it. Those who try to do environmental law and interstate boundary law and law of the sea and investment law and even occasionally human rights, are regarded quite rightly as mad; it is simply becoming impossible to do all these things properly. In the last twenty years, international criminal law has become a specialization of its own with all the consequences thereof. From a due process point of view, it is a good thing that criminal lawyers are now taking it seriously. But that criminal lawyers take it seriously means that they want at least to some degree to replace international lawyers, and it will tend to separate out.

Another factor plays a significant role in this professionalization. It is the increasing influence of the debate about the ethics of practice in investment law.[19] That is having, I think, some good effects, because we have seen examples where people were acting perhaps for impure motives, let us say. A situation in which one day you are presenting an expert opinion on a particular point, the next day you are acting as counsel on the same point of investment law, and the day after that you are sitting as arbitrator in a case which raises that very point, undoubtedly gives rise to difficulties, however much personal integrity the individuals display.[20] The tendency is for these problems, real as they are, to produce the result of the separating out of a caste of international arbitrators, who come

---

17 Case Concerning the Factory at Chorzów, Jurisdiction, Judgment of 26 July 1927, P.C.I.J. Series A – No. 9, p.5.

18 H Thirlway, Case Notes (privately printed, The Hague, 2010) 32.

19 See e.g. IBA Task Force on Counsel Ethics in International Arbitration Survey and IBA Rules of Ethics for International Arbitrators, available at: www.ibanet.org (last accessed 30 September 2010).

20 Ibid., see also S Luttrell, Bias Challenges in International Commercial Arbitration: the Need for a 'Real Danger' Test (Kluwer, The Hague, 2009).

from the international arbitration world in general and who are not international lawyers. I have not done any actual research on this, but I would imagine that the proportion of people on investment arbitration panels who will be regarded as international lawyers outside that particular field is less than it was. Just as the proportion of general international lawyers on the European Court of Human Rights is less than it was. These factors are undoubtedly going to produce the result of a separation out of doctrine and opinion in the field of investment arbitration which will seem distinct from general international law. That is a sociological observation: we will see if it comes to pass. At the same time (I no doubt show my age), it seems to me a pity, because in some very important way investment law, like human rights law is about the state and not just about corporations or individuals. It is about the way in which we bring the state under some measure of control, which is the main aspiration of general international law. In the end the mechanism for the transmission of the law of obligations is still predominantly the state and that is just as true of investment law as it is true of human rights. There are attempts now to produce horizontal human rights so as to make corporations for example bearers of obligation in the field of human rights.[21] That has however been achieved exclusively by soft law instruments.[22] It does not seem to occur to the proponents of the horizontal effect of international law that human rights are a critical standard for the treatment of individuals and not a distinct legal system.

*   *   *

Now I want to say something about the various areas in which international investment arbitration interacts with other fields of general international law.

The first of the subjects in this conspectus is the relationship between international investment law and the general law of treaties. Here at least we are on relatively firm ground, because after all international investment law derives from the law of treaties. It has made it clear, and this has not been much emphasized, just how effective treaties are as a vehicle for doing things in the international system, what a multipurpose vehicle they are. It has produced results

---

21   Report of the International Commission of Jurists on Corporate Complicity & Legal Accountability, 2008, available at: http://www.icj.org/IMG/Volume_1.pdf (last accessed 30 September 2010).

22   See e.g. 1976 OECD Guidelines on Multinational Enterprises as revised in 2000 (2001) 40 ILM 237; UN Secretary-General's Global Compact at www.globalcompact.org (last accessed 30 Spetember 2010) and UN Norms on the Responsibilities of Transnational Corporations and Other Business Enterprises with Regard to Human Rights adopted by the UN Sub-Commission on the Protection and the Promotion of Human Rights, 13 August 2003, UN Doc. E/CN.4/Sub.2/2003/12/Rev.2.

which a classic dualist would not have foreseen. For example in the United Kingdom, treaties are not part of the law of the land in any sense. They are regarded as external promises which are not binding on the crown as a matter of English law unless they have been implemented by parliament. Yet it was possible for the Court of Appeal to say that the result of a treaty in the form of a BIT arbitration was a domestically-enforceable legal obligation to comply with the outcome,[23] despite the fact that the outcome was the result of this activity in outer space, as one member of the House of Lords once described an international organization: a creature from outer space.[24] The law of treaties has been able to generate its own set of obligations for non-states in relation to states. It has been able to generate a set of rights for investors pursuant to treaties for the most part negotiated bilaterally. It has done so without however directly addressing the question what is the legal structure of these relationships. The best attempt to do that is that of Zachary Douglas in his piece on the hybrid character of investment treaty arbitration.[25]

But to say that something is hybrid is really an English way of saying "*sui generis*". Lawyers have a habit of putting labels, especially Latin labels, on things and thinking that this solves the problems. We do this with *ius cogens*. We tend to say "*ius cogens*" to a norm and everyone nods their heads sagely and says "well ok, that is fixed then". Similarly with obligations *erga omnes*.[26] To say something is *sui generis* is to postpone the analysis and not to engage in it. Yet we do not know whether the obligations of states under a BIT give rise to rights in favour of third parties, that is the investors, or whether the investors are simply, so to speak, parasites upon bilateral relations. In the *Mexican Sugar* cases,[27] that issue was important because Mexico sought to rely on the law of countermeasures in respect of an alleged breach by the United States of the NAFTA. Obviously countermeasures could be appropriate, if investment obligations were strictly bilateral. They would not be appropriate, as they are not appropriate in the field of human rights, if investment treaties gave rise to the rights of investors

---

23   Ecuador v. Occidental Exploration & Production Company [2006] EWCA 345 (Comm).

24   Arab Monetary Fund v. Hashim (No. 3) [1991] 2 W.L.R. 729.

25   Z Douglas, "The Hybrid Foundations of Investment Treaty Arbitration", (2004) 74 BYIL 151.

26   C. Tams, Enforcing Obligations Erga Omnes in International Law (Cambridge University Press, 2005).

27   Archer Daniels Midland Company and Tate & Lyle Ingredients Americas, Inc. v. United Mexican States, (Cremades, President; Rovine and Siqueiros, Arbitrators), Award, 21 November 2007, ICSID Case No. ARB(AF)/04/5; Cargill, Incorporated v. United Mexican States, (Pryles, President; Caron and McRae, Arbitrators), Award, 18 September 2009, ICSID Case No. ARB(AF)/05/2 (NAFTA). See also Mexico – Tax Measures on Soft Drinks and Other Beverages, (US v. Mexico), Panel Report, WT/DS308/R, adopted 7 October 2005.

from the beginning. We discussed this rather theoretical question in three cases. The tribunals expressed a range of views on the subject.

A second subject is investment law and state responsibility. One of the encouraging features of the law of state responsibility in the period since 2001, when the ILC completed the second reading of its Articles on State Responsibility, has been the number of occasions where international courts and tribunals have referred to the ILC articles, almost invariably taking them to reflect international law. I think there has been no case in which the ILC articles have been subjected to strong criticism. In one or two cases, especially assurances and guarantees against non-repetition, there have been reservations, e.g. by the International Court, but its reserve mostly takes the form of silence rather than rejection.[28] Many of the articles, including articles which probably did not reflect international law in 2001, have now been treated as doing so, notably Article 16.[29] Another example is Article 41, that residue of "international crimes", which the Court first quoted without acknowledgement in the Advisory Opinion on the Israeli Wall,[30] and subsequently has discussed in a more forthright way.[31]

There are more than 100 cases in which the ILC articles on responsibility have been referred to since 2001 and about half those cases are investment treaty arbitrations. If you look at these cases and do a quality check on the cases, you will find, however, that the references to them are rather variable.[32] Some cases are quite profound engagements with the issues addressed in the ILC articles, as for example for the provisions dealing with problems of time in the law of responsibility, or with aspects of the law relating to attribution. In other cases it has seemed that "a little knowledge is a dangerous thing", and as you would guess from my account of the sociology of the investment arbitration profession, "a little knowledge" is something quite a lot of professionals have.

---

28 See e.g., La Grand (Germany v. United States of America), Judgment, I. C. J. Reports 2001, p. 466; Avena and Other Mexican Nationals (Mexico v. United States of America), Judgment, I. C. J. Reports 2004, p. 12; and Armed Activities on the Territory of the Congo (Democratic Republic of the Congo v. Uganda), Judgment, I.C.J. Reports 2005, p. 168.

29 Application of the Convention on the Prevention and Punishment of the Crime of Genocide (Bosnia and Herzegovina v. Serbia and Montenegro), Judgment of 26 February 2007, unpublished, para. 420.

30 Legal Consequences of the Construction of a Wall in the Occupied Palestinian Territory, Advisory Opinion, I.C.J. Reports 2004, p. 136, p. 200 (para. 159).

31 Application of the Convention on the Prevention and Punishment of the Crime of Genocide (Bosnia and Herzegovina v. Serbia and Montenegro), Judgment of 26 February 2007, unpublished, paras.167 and 170.

32 See further J Crawford, "Investment Arbitration and the ILC Articles on State Responsibility" (2010) 25 ICSID Reports-FILJ 125, which lists the cases in an appendix.

For example, it is rarely pointed out that Parts 2 and 3 of the ILC Articles have no application to investment arbitration. That is specifically intended. Article 33 paragraph 1 says that the provisions dealing with the consequences of breach and invocation apply only between state and state, they do not apply between individuals and states. This does not mean that they are not relevant; they can be used by way of an analogy – but they do not apply directly. That point has rarely been noted.[33]

Article 33 is itself one of the most important provisions of the ILC articles. It is an article which is responsive to the differences in the relationship between state and state, and state and non-state. Obviously invocation in the context of investment arbitration is its own beast. That is also true of remedies. The international law of remedies has historically given priority to restitution and in a modified form that is what the ILC Articles do. Restitution as between a state and a state is what you might get in a context where there are essentially equal relations between the parties concerned. Restitution between individual and state is available only in extreme circumstances. You do not start out with the assumption, as you do between sovereign states, that the individual is entitled to restitution. Obviously the principle of full reparation remains, but this hardly ever involves restitution or anything like it. That aspect of *Texaco* is equally flawed.[34] But because Part 1 of the Articles was able to deal with the question "what is a breach?" independently of the question of the identity of the beneficiary of the obligation, it applies to all types of obligations that a state has. In other words, it is formulated exclusively in terms of duties and not in terms of rights. It was possible to make Part 1 applicable equally to investment arbitration, human rights, the whole of international law. It was only possible to do that by making the conceptual shift from rights to duties, whereas historically the law of responsibility was formulated in terms of rights. It is no accident that the Chapter 1 of Grotius *De iure belli ac pacis* is entitled "What is war, what is right?" Right here means subjective right. Grotius generated a system of rights from a system about war and peace. We have, I hope, moved beyond that.

The next area of this workshop concerns the relationship between investment law and the law of state immunity. The obvious thing to say is that investment law is prior to the questions of enforcement that arise in relation to obligations of states including especially obligations to pay money under BIT tribunal awards. In general there have not yet been catastrophic problems of non-compliance with bilateral investment treaty decisions (except possibly in the Argentine cases).

---

33   But see United Parcel Service of America, Inc. v. Government of Canada, NAF-TA/UNCITRAL Arbitration Rules Proceeding, (Keith, President; Cass and Yves Fortier, Arbitrators), Final Award, 11 June 2007, paras. 45-63.
34   Texaco v. the Government of the Libyan Arab Republic (1978) 17 ILM 3.

The compliance record, while compliance may sometimes take time, is fairly good, and issues of enforcement have not often arisen. There was an important case in the United Kingdom in which a central bank's assets were sought to be frozen or executed against in relation to an ICSID award.[35] The courts held that the State Immunity Act 1978 (UK) did not allow for any form of execution against central bank assets, even if the central bank assets were not held for central bank purposes but for general investment and therefore commercial purposes of the state. That decision was plainly right on the language of the State Immunity Act (although I would point out that the Australian *Foreign States Immunities Act 1985* would have produced another result and possibly a better one[36]). I understand that Kazakhstan subsequently complied with the award without further attempts at execution against it.

However, that is not the aspect of this relationship that I particularly want to emphasize here. What I do think is significant is the coherence between the rules of attribution and the law of state immunity as it relates to the distinction between organs and agencies. In state responsibility terms, this is the distinction between Articles 4 and 5 of the ILC articles, which reflects rather closely the distinction in the law of state immunity between the state and separate entities. That may be an illustration of international law having a systematic coherence, whether deliberately or by accident.

I turn now to three areas of substantive law. I have been talking essentially about the secondary rules – the law of treaties, the law of responsibility and the role of immunity which looks as if it is substantive but is in an important sense procedural. How is international investment law faring in relation to other specializations of law? Are they operating in – if not clinical – then at least in some form of isolation, perhaps messy isolation? I want to say something briefly about human rights, environmental law and the law of diplomatic protection.

As to human rights, these have been influential in affecting the way we formulate propositions of investment law. Although it is often not articulated, any modern formulation of the fair and treatment standard will emphasize non-discrimination; non-discrimination has economic elements, but it seems to me that this emphasis is partly the result of the influence of human rights law. There are investment arbitration cases which will be brought in situations that could equally have been brought before the European Court of Human Rights. There are indeed a number of cases in which the very same dispute was brought both before an investment treaty tribunal and the European Court, although that is a rather untidy way of proceeding.

35 AIG Capital Partners v. Kazakhstan, [2005] EWHC 2239 (Comm), para. 95.
36 Foreign States Immunities Act 1985 (Cth) s.34; and see Australian Law Reform Commission, ALRC 24, Foreign State Immunity (AGPS, Canberra, 1984) 81 (para. 132).

One of the consequences of comparing that situation is that we get a rather favourable view of the remedial possibilities of investment arbitration compared with those of much human rights adjudication. For example the defendants in the *Guinness* trial had been compelled to give testimony to an investigator in relation to a financial transaction and then that evidence had been used against them and they had been sentenced to a rather long jail term. The European Court of Human Rights held that there was a violation of their procedural right not to incriminate themselves, but it also said that that declaration was sufficient redress.[37] They got not a cent or penny from the European Court. A similar violation of due process rights before an investment tribunal would likely have resulted in a substantial award of damages.

As to international environmental law, the tendency of the NGOs in the field of environmental law has been to be very critical of investment arbitration, just as they have been very critical of the WTO. And it is possible to point to decisions that look as if the tribunals had been particular unresponsive to environmental concerns. Depending on your view of the facts, *Metalclad* is such a case.[38] The *Costa Rica* case is another one which has been criticized as insensitive to environmental values in the context of quantification of compensation.[39] Those are the *Shrimp Turtle*[40] equivalents in the field of investment arbitration but they do not amount to much. Generally speaking, investment tribunals have been reasonably sensitive to the regulatory environmental aspects of decisions they face, both within NAFTA and outside.

The law of diplomatic protection is my final example. The law of diplomatic protection has been largely sidelined by BITs; that is to say, the states have sidelined themselves in the field of diplomatic protection by rarely bringing diplomatic protection claims.[41] But the law of diplomatic protection has responded to the challenge in certain ways, e.g. in the ILC articles of 2006 on diplomatic protection.[42] There is considerably greater awareness of the difficulties presented by traditional doctrines of the corporate veil. That raises quite fundamental questions about the relationship between corporations and recovery in the field of re-

---

37   Saunders v United Kingdom (1996) 23 EHRR 313, and cf R v Lyons [2003] 1 AC 976.
38   Metalclad Corporation v. United Mexican States, ICSID Case No.ARB(AF)/97/1, 5ICSID Reports 209.
39   Compañía del Desarrollo de Santa Elena AS v Republic of Costa Rica, Award of 17 February 2000, 5 ICSID Reports 153.
40   Import Prohibitions of Certain Shrimp & Shrimp Products, Appelate Body Reports, WT/DS58/AB/RW.
41   See e.g. Case Concerning Ahmadou Sadio Diallo (Republic of Guinea v. Democratic Republic of the Congo) Preliminary Objections, Judgment of 24 May 2007; and see now especially Merits, Judgment of 30 November 2010.
42   Draft Articles on Diplomatic Protection, adopted at the 58th session of the International Law Commission in 2006.

sponsibility, which I do not think have been fully worked through. Nonetheless, there have been developments in which the availability of direct recourse proceedings on the part of shareholders in the field of investment arbitration is been seen to have consequences in the traditional field of diplomatic protection. Further, the field of diplomatic protection has expanded from the traditional minimum standard of treatment to cover rights generally and the result of the dictum in *LaGrand*,[43] seems to make diplomatic protection an available mechanism in respect of all obligations owed to individuals and not obligations within a stereotyped range.

Obviously, one could say a lot more about each of the areas that I have discussed, but let me take stock. First of all there are clearly developments in the sociology of the legal profession, which are pushing investment arbitration in the direction not of clinical isolation but a separate existence, a *corpus separatum*, as the Latin term would be. On the other hand, investment arbitration remains part of general international law and I for one very much hope that general international lawyers are not going to abandon the field to the commercial arbitration mafia. Of course such decisions are finally made by clients and not by lawyers. One of the things that is obvious from investment treaties, however increasingly refined as they become – and with the new US model BIT they are very refined indeed – is that there are still only partial statements of the law in the particular case. They can only be made sense of, they can only be made to work, when seen in a framework which includes not only the law relating to interpretation and application of treaties, but also the law relating to responsibility and much else. The application of the standards of investment arbitration requires a refined understanding of the way in which the law of obligations is in general applied to states. This is something international lawyers ought to have, because their meat and drink is the application of the law of obligations to states. The result is neither clinical isolation nor systematic integration, but something in between.

---

43   Note 28, 483, para. 42.

International Investment Law and Treaty Interpretation

Michael Waibel[*]

Investment tribunals often profess fidelity to the rules on treaty interpretation contained in the Vienna Convention on the Law of Treaties (VCLT). At first sight, they mention Article 31 and 32 VCLT with reassuring regularity. But first impressions may lead astray. My hypothesis is that many investment awards demonstrate a cavalier attitude to treaty interpretation. The contrast with the interpretative practice of a highly developed and institutionalized adjudicatory body like the WTO dispute settlement body is particularly striking.[1]

Ubiquitous references to the VCLT in investment awards may serve to reassure readers of the award that the tribunal intends to follow well-trodden paths in treaty interpretation. These declarations of fidelity to the foundational principles of treaty interpretation, however, lack practical substance if tribunals soon thereafter pour cold water on their stated intentions. I contend that careful application of the principles of treaty interpretation to the facts is often wanting in investment arbitration. Superficial treaty interpretation risks distorting the parties' intentions and unravelling their treaty bargain.

The interpretative practice of treaty interpretation by investment tribunals has exerted little influence in other areas of international law – which may be surprising given investment arbitration's high profile in recent years. Perhaps as by-product of their cavalier attitude to treaty interpretation, many investment awards do not offer models of careful treaty interpretation for international lawyers working in other areas.[2] The contrast with the radiance of WTO interpretative practice outside WTO law is striking.[3]

My broader claim is that the Vienna Convention on the Law of Treaties provides an appropriate framework for the interpretation of bilateral investment

---

[*]   Dr. Michael Waibel, British Academy Postdoctoral Fellow, Lauterpacht Centre for International Law, University of Cambridge.

[1]   Cf. W. Michael Reisman, Opinion with respect to Selected International Legal Problems in LCIA Case No. 7941 (United States of America v. Canada), 1 May 2009, 8 ('[the VCLT] provisions have become something of a clause de style in international arbitral awards, where they are often briefly referred to or, (as in the Award), solemnly reproduced verbatim, and then largely ignored.').

[2]   There are, of course, a number of important exceptions, e.g. the dissent by Jan Paulsson in HEP v. Slovenia, (Interpretation), 12 June 2009.

[3]   Cf. Isabelle van Damme, Treaty Interpretation by the WTO Appellate Body (Oxford University Press, 2009).

treaties (BITs) and other international agreements in investment arbitration. Specialised principles of treaty interpretation tailored to investment arbitration are not needed. It would be undesirable for investment arbitration to have its own, tailored-made version of the Vienna Convention on the Law of Treaties.

Empirically, there appear to be few distinct patterns of treaty interpretation in investment arbitration, aside from an excessive reliance on the treaty's object and purpose. Relying on the goal of maximising investor protection as a default rule has its pitfalls. Instead, close attention to the treaty's text and the parties' intention, revealed in part through subsequent statements by the state parties, is desirable when evaluating questions such as the territorial and temporal scope of application of BITs. Mechanisms for coordinating interpretations beyond individual cases are currently a significantly underutilized tool in investment arbitration.[4]

A. *Epistemic Treaty Interpreters and the Fragmentation of International Law*

Over the last decade, there has been growing concern about fragmentation in international law.[5] Arguably, the proximate cause of fragmentation is the importation of regime theory from international relations into international law. Despite some beneficial cross-fertilisation, it is doubtful whether on the whole this development has strengthened international law as a legal system. Regime theory encouraged the latent tendency to regard the various functional areas ('regimes') as self-contained, with vociferous claims to uphold the purity of each regime from within.

International law is a product of the human mind. Its tool is language, which explains the constant need for interpretation. At times, one notes an alarming tendency to divide international law into neat conceptual categories. While convenient, such divisions may take on a life of their own. Slicing and dicing international law as we see fit is risky. Excessive compartmentalisation impedes coherence; it emphasises the particular over the universal; it may defeat important policy objectives of the international community by leading to competition and clashes between regimes.

---

4   Cf. the persuasive arguments for re-establishing interpretative balance between states and investment tribunals in Anthea Roberts, 'Power and Persuasion in Investment Treaty Arbitration: The Dual Role of States', 104 AJIL 179-225 (2010).

5   Fragmentation of International Law: Difficulties Arising from the Diversification and Expansion of International Law, Report of the Study Group of the International Law Commission, A/CN.4/L.682 (13 April 2006) and the Addendum on Draft Conclusions of the Work of the Study Group, Finalized by Martti Koskenniemi, A/CN.4/L.682/Add. 1 (2 May 2006).

Another reason for centrifugal tendencies in international law is the growing role of influential epistemic communities. Professor Vagts underscored the importance of interpretative communities early on.[6] In his view, treaty interpretation emerges from the interplay of the various actors, both domestic and international, that make up the interpretive community. This approach shifts the focus from the text itself to the actors concerned with its interpretation. Vagts defined interpretive communities by reference to the following features: ' (1) generic or background consensus – sharing of a language and concerns and participation in the same 'form of life' ; (2) agreement as to the boundaries of the practice community members share ; (3) common recognition of propositions as to what the practice requires as 'truth' within the practice ; (4) minimal consensus as to the existence of a text and a reading of it that is needed to provide a working distinction between interpretation and invention.'[7]

Epistemic communities lend additional impetus to the creation of sub-subsystems of international law disconnected from the larger universe of general international law. The vocabulary, training and the ideology of international lawyers across the various regimes may differ. Lawyers specialising in international investment law today probably have more in common with domestic corporate lawyers than with international human rights lawyers. The latter are most likely closer to the domestic constitutional lawyer. The unity of international law is almost certainly irretrievably lost.

The different speeds of development of the various substantive areas of international law raise the spectre of values of one regime trumping the values of another. An area such as international trade law that benefits from a highly developed dispute resolution mechanisms may eclipse another area, such as the international law of the environment, which lacks a comparable mechanism. Lawyers working in 'underdeveloped' substantive areas of international law may come to resent the 'imperialist' aspirations of another highly developed substantive area such as investment law.

B. The Canon of Interpretation in the Vienna Convention on the Law of Treaties

Treaty interpretation refers to uncovering the meaning of treaty provisions. According to Wittgenstein, 'the meaning of a word is its use in language'.[8] The aim

---

6   Detlev Vagts, 'Treaty Interpretation and the New American Ways of Law Reading', 4 EJIL (1993) 472-505, 480 ff.
7   Ibid., 480.
8   L. Wittgenstein, Philosophical Investigations, para. 43 (G.E.M. Anscombe trans., 1953).

of all treaty interpretation is to unearththat objective meaning, by reference to context and object and purpose.

The aim of the Vienna Convention on the Law of Treaties was to achieve a minimum level of harmonisation in the methods of treaty interpretation for the whole of international law. The Commentary on the ILC Draft Articles on the law of treaties emphasizes that 'statements can be found in the decisions of international tribunals to support the use of almost every principle or maxim of which use is made in national systems of law in the interpretation of statutes and contracts.'[9] The aim was to avoid this diversity.

The holistic school of interpretation advocates a unified approach to treaty interpretation. A leading exponent is Professor Abi-Saab, who regards treaty interpretation as '... one integrated operation which uses several tools simultaneously to shed light from different angles on the interpreted text; these tools should not be seen as watertight compartments or a series of separate sub-operations but, rather, as connected (even overlapping) and mutually reinforcing parts of a whole, of a continuum or a continuous and multifaceted process that cannot be reduced to a mechanical operation and which partakes as much of art (the art of judgment) as of science (the science of law).'[10]

The textual school focuses on the treaty text.[11] The idea that words have a 'plain meaning' is widely shared among international lawyers. Article 31 of the Vienna Convention on the law of treaties endorses this approach by giving priority to literal interpretation.

The VCLT sets out a carefully calibrated hierarchy of interpretative principles. Article 31 is the primary *rule*, whereas Article 32 contains several *supplementary* means of interpretation. Article 31 gives primacy to textual interpretation. The first task of the interpreter is to ascertain in good faith the 'ordinary meaning'. The ordinary meaning is the default rule, unless the parties intended a

---

9   Draft Articles on the Law of Treaties with commentaries 1966, ILC Yearbook, II, 177.
10   G. Abi Saab, 'The Appellate Body and Treaty Interpretation', in G. Sacerdoti, A. Yanovich and J. Bohanes (eds.), The WTO at Ten-The Contribution of the Dispute Settlement System (Cambridge University Press, 2006), 459; cf. also the ILC's travaux preparatoires, advocating a single combined approach, whereby all elements of Article 31 are thrown into the crucible simultaneously, with their interaction yielding the correct interpretation.
11   A. Orakhelashvili, The Interpretation of Acts and Rules in Public International Law (Oxford University Press, 2008), 311 (the essence of the holistic approach 'is about blurring the distinction between law and politics, and about promoting subjectivism in the process of interpretation'); Methanex v. United States stresses the limited relevance of the negotiation history ('the approach of the Vienna Convention is that the text of the treaty is deemed to be the authentic expression of the intentions of the parties; and its elucidation, rather than wide-ranging searches for the supposed intentions of the parties, is the proper object of interpretation.'), Part II. Chapter B, para. 22.

'special meaning' (Article 31 (4) VCLT). The interpreter is further instructed to arrive at the ordinary meaning by interpreting terms 'in their context' and in light of 'its object and purpose.'

Article 31 (2) VCLT defines context: the remaining text of the treaty, including the preamble and annexes, any agreement relating to the treaty made by all the parties in connexion with the conclusion of the treaty and any agreement made by one or more parties under the same conditions, premised on the acceptance by the other parties as an instrument related to the treaty.' Terms in a treaty cannot therefore be interpreted in clinical isolation from each other. The interpreter must look at the treaty, and connected agreements, as a whole. The treaty's object and purpose, as expressed in the treaty itself, may inform interpretation. The interpretative modalities of Article 31 are designed to lead to the ordinary meaning of treaty terms.

In many cases, the task of the interpreter ends here. Article 32 VCLT sets out the limited circumstances in which recourse to supplementary means of interpretation is permissible[12]: (i) the meaning of the treaty after application of Article 31 is 'ambiguous or obscure'; (ii) such interpretation 'leads to a result which is manifestly absurd or unreasonable'; or (iii) to 'confirm the meaning resulting from the application of Article 31'. Conversely, in all other cases, resort to the supplementary means of interpretation is at odds with the VCLT rules on treaty interpretation.

C. Treaty Interpretation in General International Law

The starting point of treaty interpretation is the text. If recourse by the International Court of Justice to *The Oxford English Dictionary* to determine the ordinary meaning of the word 'commerce' has remained an isolated instance,[13] its frequent use by the WTO Dispute Settlement Body caused one of its former members to speak of the *Shorter Oxford Dictionary* as 'one of the covered agreements'.[14]

---

12   W. Michael Reisman, Opinion with respect to Selected International Legal Problems in LCIA Case No. 7941 (United States of America v. Canada), 1 May 2009, 11 (the interpreter is 'first obliged to construe the ordinary meaning of the text in application of Article 31 and to resort to supplementary means only if one of the contingencies specified in Article 32 is met').

13   Oil Platforms (Islamic Republic of Iran v. United States of America), Judgment on Preliminary Exception, ICJ Reports 1996, p. 818, para. 45.

14   Claus-Dieter Ehlermann, 'Six Years on the Bench of the "World Trade Court". Some Personal Experiences as Member of the Appellate Body of the World Trade Organization', Journal of World Trade 36 (2002), 605-639, 616.

A good recent example of treaty interpretation in general international law, where the ICJ engaged in a careful textual analysis, is the *Case Concerning the Dispute Regarding Navigational and Related Rights*.[15] The principle of contemporaneous meaning equates the 'ordinary meaning' of a treaty clause with its meaning at the time the treaty was concluded. The case below shows that the parties' intention as reflected in the treaty is decisive for whether a static or dynamic ordinary meaning is to be preferred.

The case concerned the scope of navigation rights enjoyed by Costa Rica on the San Juan River by virtue of an 1858 treaty with neighbouring Nicaragua. Costa Rica argued that Article 6 of that treaty obliged Nicaragua, alongside rules in general international law on 'international rivers', to grant free navigation rights to Costa Rican boats and their passengers on the river for any commercial purpose, including for the transportation of passengers and tourism.

The Court first observed that the treaty was *lex specialis*, and left no room for (dispositive) customary international law.[16] It then turned to the interpretative dispute on Article 6, centred on the words 'libre navigación ... con objetos de comercio'. The only authoritative version of the treaty was Spanish, and the parties disagreed on the proper translation of that clause into English and French. Nicaragua construed the clause in a material sense to mean 'with articles of trade'. Costa Rica put forward an abstract meaning: 'for the purposes of commerce'.

The Court looked to Article 31 and 32 VCLT, as a reflection of customary international law. It rejected Nicaragua's contention that restrictions on sovereignty ought to be interpreted narrowly.[17] No *a priori* restrictive principle of interpretation was found in international law. The Court restated its general approach to treaty interpretation in the following terms: 'a treaty provision which has the purpose of limiting the sovereign powers of a State must be interpreted like any other provision of a treaty, i.e. in accordance with the intentions of its authors as reflected in the text of the treaty and the other relevant factors in terms of interpretation.'[18] But neither was a general presumption of expansive interpretation warranted.[19]

The Court contrasted the two competing *a priori* meanings of 'con objetos de commercio' – the abstract and the material version. Recourse to context was necessary to decide between the two. The Court rejected Nicaragua's interpreta-

---

15   Case Concerning the Dispute Regarding Navigational and Related Rights (Costa Rica v. Nicaragua), 13 July 2009.
16   Ibid., para. 36.
17   Ibid., para. 48.
18   Ibid.
19   Ibid.

tion on the grounds that it would render the relevant sentence in the treaty meaningless and incomprehensible. It would either lead to a meaning of 'articles of trade with Nicaragua or 'navigation ... with Nicaragua'.[20] In contrast, the Court observed that Costa Rica's interpretation of the words 'con objetos' 'allows the entire sentence to be given coherent meaning.'

The Court relied on three additional arguments to confirm this conclusion. First, the use of the word 'objetos' in another article of the same treaty ('Nicaragua se compromete á no concluir otro (contrato) sobre los expresados objectos').[21] But this inference in favour of the abstract meaning does not convince. The word 'objetos' is used here as a reference to the treaty's subject matter – a completely different context. At best, this use here may provide very limited support in favour of the abstract notion of 'objetos'.

Second, an unratified treaty signed in the previous year used the expression 'artículos de commercio', a term that undoubtedly translated as 'goods of commerce'. On that basis, the Court concluded that the appearance of the expression in another treaty indicated that some limited practice existed between the parties to use this formulation when their intention was to unambiguously refer to physical objects.[22] *E contrario*, therefore the 1858 treaty, by using the modified formulation 'objetos de comercio', presumably refers to some other notion.

Third, both parties translated the contested clause as 'for the purposes of commerce' in the context of an arbitration on the 1858 treaty presided by the US President.[23] Even though such submissions in dispute settlement were not conclusive and binding on the parties, the Court noted that this provided a supplementary indication of the ordinary meaning of the term.

The Court thus accepted Costa Rica's abstract notion as the ordinary meaning of the term in its context. It remained for the Court to interpret the scope of the term 'commerce'. Nicaragua advocated a narrow concept, confined to trade in goods, based on the understanding of the word 'commerce' in 1858.[24] It favoured a static meaning of the term. Costa Rica contended that the term covered all commercial activities, including the transport of passengers for profit and tourism, and even any movement and contact between inhabitants on the Costa Rican side of the river. The Court rejected this broad reading, noting that the phrase operated as a limitation on the navigation rights.[25]

---

20   Ibid., para. 52.
21   Translated by the Court as 'Nicaragua engages not to conclude any other contract for those purposes...'.
22   Case Concerning the Dispute Regarding Navigational and Related Rights, para. 55.
23   Ibid., para. 56.
24   Ibid., para. 58.
25   Ibid., para. 61.

The Court opted for a dynamic interpretation of 'commerce', giving the term its contemporary meaning: 'This [the practice of the Court to interpret clauses in line with their meaning at the time of conclusion] does not however signify that, where a term's meaning is no longer the same as it was at the date of conclusion, no account should ever be taken of its meaning at the time when the treaty is to be interpreted for purposes of applying it.'[26] In relation to treaties concluded for long periods of time or indefinitely, 'the parties' intent upon conclusion of the treaty was, or may be presumed to have been, to give the terms used – or some of them – a meaning or content capable of evolving, not one fixed once and for all, so as to make allowance for, among other things, developments in international law.'[27] This approach to treaty interpretation respects the common intention of the parties, rather than departing from them.

Proceeding along this line of analysis, the Court concluded that 'commerce' encompassed the transportation of persons, which today fell within its ordinary meaning. In contrast, navigation with vessels used for governmental purposes or navigation to provide public services not of a commercial nature are excluded.[28]

D. Treaty Arbitration by the WTO Dispute Settlement Body

Using a very similar approach to the ICJ in *Costa Rica v Nicaragua*, the Appellate Body (AB) of the WTO in *US-Shrimps*[29] relied on the Rio Biodiversity Convention to interpret the concepts of 'sustainable development' and 'exhaustible natural resources'. The AB reasoned on the basis of the evolutionary character of the term.[30] This dynamic interpretation recognized developments in international environmental law since the GATT was drafted. The AB held that the term did not only cover non-living materials, as the negotiating history of GATT Article XX(g) may have suggested, but that exhaustible resources also cover living organisms.

In *US-Gambling*,[31] Antigua challenged several US laws and regulatory actions. It argued their joint effect was a *de facto* prohibition on the Internetgambling by Antiguan suppliers. Antigua argued that the US measures violated the

---

26   Ibid., para. 64.
27   Ibid.
28   Ibid., para. 71.
29   WT/DS58/AB/R, 12 October 1998.
30   Ibid., at para. 130. On the idea of 'evolutionary interpretation' generally see Brigitte Bollecker, 'L'avis consultatif du 21 juin 1971 dans l'affaire de la Namibie (Sud-Ouest africain)' (1971) 17 AFDI 290.
31   WT/DS285/R, 10 November 2004; WT/DS285/AB/R, 7 April 2005.

US' market access violations (Article XVI GATS) and national treatment (Article XVII GATS).

A condition precedent to the application of these disciplines is that gambling services having been scheduled by the United States in its schedule of commitments. Antigua faced the obstacle that the US schedule did not refer to gambling as such. It claimed that gambling services were including under the heading "other recreational services" or alternatively "entertainment services" in the US schedule. The United States argued that it had never intended an activity as sensitive as gambling to be included in its GATS commitments.

Relying on the 1993 Scheduling Guidelines which employ the Central Product Classification system (CPC), the Panel concluded that the US scheduled gambling when it scheduled other recreational services because "gambling and betting services" is a sub-category of "other recreational services".[32] It reached this conclusion even though the US did not indicate in its schedule that it was following the CPC. In addition, the Scheduling Guidelines were voluntary.

The panel found that the United States violated its market access obligation because its measures amounted to a prohibition (a so-called zero quota). The Unites States claimed its measures were qualitative because they targeted one type of gambling (Internet gambling) – rather than limiting the number of service providers or the quantity of gambling services that could be supplied.

The AB criticized the Panel's cavalier approach to treaty interpretation, but reached the same conclusion on the facts.[33] It upheld the panel's conclusion that the United States had scheduled gambling services. It also accepted that the US schedule, other schedules and the definition of services in the GATS were relevant context for interpreting the US services commitments.

The AB also expressed some scepticism on the widespread use of dictionaries by panels to identify the natural meaning of words.[34] They only offered limited value, because dictionary meanings vary, and leave many interpretative questions unresolved. Dictionary meanings need to be contextualized.[35] The AB rejected one dictionary definition among several because it did not fit the context and the object of the purpose of the provision.

The panel report in *EC-Frozen Boneless Chicken Cuts* concerned a dispute on the proper tariff classification of salted chicken meat under the Harmonised System (HS). Brazil challenged the EC's unilateral decision to subject salted

---

32 WT/DS285/R, paras. 6.41 et seq.
33 WT/DS285/AB/R, paras. 158-213.
34 Ibid, para. 166.
35 Cf. US-Offset Act, where the AB warned that 'dictionaries are important guides to, not dispositive statements of, definitions of words appearing in agreements and legal documents' (WT/DS217/AB/R, para. 248); India- Additional Import Duties, WT/DS360/AB/R, para. 167 (dictionaries are only a useful starting point).

chicken cuts to higher tariffs after the WTO agreement entered in force. The EC pointed to decisions by EC courts which, it argued, consistently imposed higher tariffs on salted chicken cuts. The panel accepted the relevance of such decisions and reviewed them under Article 32 VCLT as relevant context but rejected the EC's substantive argument.[36] The EC was the only importing WTO member with any practice of classifying salted chicken cuts. It was an 'agreement relating to the treaty which was made between all parties in connection with the conclusion of the treaty' under Article 31 (2) (a) VCLT and offered several reasons in support this conclusion. Practice by one WTO member could qualify as subsequent practice if it was the only relevant practice.[37]

On appeal, the AB declined to accept this broad concept of subsequent practice. It held that just a few WTO members might establish subsequent practice, provided trade in that good was limited. A single WTO member state, however, was insufficient: 'To our mind, it would be difficult to establish a 'concordant, common and discernible pattern' on the basis of acts of pronouncements of one, or very few parties to a multilateral treaty, such as the WTO Agreement.'[38]

The AB decision in *EC-Hormones* is a leading example of the application of the *dubio mitius* principle in WTO dispute settlement. The panel interpreted the SPS Agreement to the effect that the respondent generally bore the burden of proof that SPS measures complied with the SPS Agreement, unless on international standards. The effect of such interpretation would be to convert the use of such SPS measures to *prima facie* violations of WTO obligations, unless they conformed to international standards.[39]

The AB reversed the panel's allocation of the burden of proof when a WTO member deviates from an international standard. Where there are one or more possible readings of the same provision, the panel cannot simply assume that WTO members opted for the relatively more onerous obligation. The AB relied on the in *dubio mitius rule*. A more burdensome obligation cannot lightly be assumed.[40]

36   WT/DS269/R, paras. 7.81 et seq.
37   Ibid., para. 7.302.
38   WT/DS269/AB/R, para. 259.
39   WT/DS26/R/USA, paras. 8.48 et seq.
40   WT/DS26/AB/R, paras. 154, 165.

Investment tribunals often rely on the principle of effective interpretation.[41] In this context, they often refer to the objective and purpose of bilateral investment treaties. On this basis, many tribunals appear to resolve uncertain BIT terms in favour of investors. Such reliance on vague notions of strengtheninginvestor protection in the BIT's Preamble to construe treaty terms appears often unprincipled. Two particularly contentious areas where an overly broad recourse to effectiveness risks undercutting the treaty parties' intention, as reflected in the treaty text, is in relation to the definition of investment (Article 25 of the ICSID Convention), and the broad reading of the umbrella clause. The cases that follow demonstrate the danger of over-reliance on the object and purpose by investment tribunals.

For example, the *SGS v Philippines* tribunal referred to the preamble's stated desire to create favourable conditions for investment to reach the conclusion that the BIT was intended to provide effective protection for investors: 'The object and purpose of the BIT supports an effective interpretation of Article X (2) [the umbrella clause of the Philippines-Switzerland BIT]. The BIT is a treaty for the promotion and reciprocal protection of investments. According to the preamble it is intended to 'create and maintain favourable conditions for investments by investors of one Contracting Party in the territory of the other.' It is legitimate to resolve uncertainties in its interpretation so as to favour the protection of covered investments.'[42] This is a particularly noteworthy example of excessive reliance on the treaty's object and purpose of protecting foreign investment. The tribunal failed to explain why such interpretative reliance on the vague notion of a favourable regime for foreign investment is 'legitimate', and it also chose to ignore other objects and purposes of the BIT.

In *Ecuador v. Occidental* (No. 2), the tribunal held that the object and purpose of a BIT is 'to provide effective protection for investors'.[43] It used this singular objective to interpret the provisions of the BIT whose meaning was uncertain in favour of the investor. The tribunal reasoned as follows: '[A]n important feature of that protection is the availability of recourse to international arbitration as a safeguard for the investor. In these circumstances it is permissible to resolve uncertainties in its interpretation in favour of the investor.'[44]

---

41   Noble Ventures v. Romania (Award), 12 October 2005, para. 50.
42   SGS Société Générale de Surveillance SA v. Republic of the Philippines (2004) 8 ICSID Reports 515, para. 116.
43   [2007] 1 Lloyd's Rep 352, para. 28.
44   Ibid.

The *Siemens v. Argentina* tribunal eschewed close textual analysis and made liberal recourse to the treaty's objective and purpose: 'The Tribunal considers that the Treaty has to be interpreted neither liberally nor restrictively, as neither of these adverbs is part of Article 31 (1) of the Vienna Convention.'But then the tribunal does precisely that. 'The Tribunal shall be guided by the purpose of the Treaty as expressed in its title and preamble. It is a treaty 'to protect' and 'to promote' investments ... The intention of the parties is clear. It is to create favourable conditions for investments and to stimulate private initiative.'[45]

This interpretative approach betrays a cavalier attitude to treaty interpretation. Rather than engaging in careful textual analysis, the tribunal underscored that the aim of the treaty was to create favourable investment conditions. The dividing line between favouring broad investment protection and construing the ordinary meaning of ambiguous treaty terms in light of an ideological prior of maximal investment protection is thin – tribunals cross it at their peril. In such cases, the interpreter's prior of maximal investment protection as a good onto itself lurks visibly behind such outcome-driven interpretative strategies. The risk is a re-politicization of investment disputes and, in the long-run, losing support among state parties.

The *Softwood Lumber Dispute* before an arbitral panel under the auspices of the London Court of International Arbitration concerned compensatory payments for excessive exports of softwood lumber.[46] The Softwood Lumber Agreement ('SLA') between the United States and Canada provided for an export volume adjustment mechanism, designed to place an upper bound on exports when prices for softwood lumber sank below a set threshold (US $ 355 per thousand board feet). Each Canadian region had a choice between a soft volume cap, a lower export tax with a hard volume cap or volume restraint. Should a region's exports under the soft volume regime exceed the soft volume cap by more than 1 per cent per month, Canada was under an obligation to retroactively levy an additional export tax.

The United States argued that between January and July 2007 Canada failed to apply the export restrictions it had agreed to under the SLA, leading to over shipment of lumber to the United States. The Award on Liability upheld some of the US's claims, leading to this second stage of arbitration on remedies.

The central issue at the remedies stage of that arbitration was whether Canada had to retrospectively compensate the United States for the excessive exports of softwood lumber that occurred prior to the initiation of arbitration, or whether cessation of the breach would suffice. Article XIV:22 SLA provided that if the LCIA found a breach, it shall identify a reasonable time period, up to 30 days

45   Siemens v. Argentina (Jurisdiction), at para. 81.
46   United States v. Canada (LCIA) No. 81010.

from the Award, for curing the breach. If the breaching party 'fails to cure the breach within a reasonable period of time,' the LCIA shall determine 'appropriate adjustments' to the export restrictions to compensate for the breach. Under Article XIV:24, these adjustments apply from the end of the reasonable time period until the breach has been cured.

The question was whether Section 22 of the SLA provided for prospective remedies only, or whether that provision was designed to also remedy past breaches by wiping out all the consequences of the unlawful act. The temporal scope of remedies turned on whether Section 22 was *lex specialis* in relation to Article 31 of the ILC's Articles on State Responsibility ('reparation') – the Canadian view. The tribunal explained that to 'conclude that [Section 22] is only applicable to continuing breaches and not to past breaches, would require a specific express language to that effect'.[47]

The LCIA held that retrospective remedies were appropriate.[48] While it referred to the WTO Dispute Settlement Understanding for comparative purposes, it regarded the SLA as a stand-alone agreement. It cited the ILC Articles on State Responsibility and the *Chorzow Factory* Case to establish a presumption in favour of retrospective remedies and found nothing contrary to this in the SLA. Whether that conclusion is correct is doubtful in view of Section 22's reference to 'cure the breach', rather than 'cure the effects of the breach'.

Section 22 (b) provided for the adjustment of export measures only when the breaching party failed to cure the breach. That such adjustment of export measures was not available in other cases too demonstrates the prospective character of the remedy foreseen by the SLA. Yet the tribunal was adamant that the SLA implied an obligation on the part of Canada to wipe out the consequences of the breach. It found that 'it is at least plausible' that levying an additional charge against certain Canadian regions 'would be a reasonable method to effectively undo the benefits they enjoyed during the six months of the SLA violation and thus restore, as much as possible … the SLA's economic effect to its intended state.'[49] Where the tribunal takes this intention from remains unclear.

The tribunal acknowledged that Section 22 was 'easier to be applied to deal with breaches that still continue at the time the Tribunal has to decide', particularly in relation to 'section (a) in so far as the breaching Party must be given a reasonable period of time up to 30 days 'to cure the breach'.[50] The tribunal exposed itself to the charge that its application of the *lex generalis* in Article 31 ARISWA overrode the ordinary meaning of a *lex specialis* provides that breach

---

47   Ibid., para. 284.
48   Ibid., paras. 318 et seq.
49   Ibid., para. 335.
50   Ibid., para. 285.

is cured by cessation. The SLA's regime for breach is premised on the idea that the parties ought to return to voluntary compliance, underpinned by economic incentives, as soon as possible.

Professor Reisman contends that the Award on Remedies departs from the customary rules of treaty interpretation. The ordinary meaning is said to be distorted by automatic recourse to supplementary means of interpretation, irrespective of whether the application of Article 31 VCLT on its own yielded a clear meaning. Moreover, the award also erroneously subsumes judicial decisions as 'subsidiary means' for interpretation under Article 38 (1)(d) of the ICJ Statute, and equated them to 'supplementary means of interpretation'.[51]

In *Czech Republic v European Median Ventures* before the English courts the Czech Republic sought annulment of an arbitral award.[52] Article 8 (1) of the BIT between the Czech Republic and the Belgian-Luxembourg Economic Union provided for investor-state dispute settlement for '[d]isputes between the Contracting Parties and an Investor of the other Contracting Party *concerning compensation* due by virtue of Art. 3 paragraph (1) and (3) of the Treaty.'[53]

The Czech Republic submitted that the tribunal, composed of Lord Mustill, Julian Lew and Christopher Greenwood, misconstrued its restrictive consent to arbitration. It took the view that only disputes on the *amount of* compensation fell within the tribunal's jurisdiction. Conversely, EMV argued that the formulation also included disputes on *whether* compensation was due.

The tribunal acknowledged that the formulation 'concerning compensation' implied some restriction. It construed that restriction to exclude from its jurisdiction any remedy aside from compensation (such as a restitution claim or a request for a declaration that the contract was still in force). The Czech Republic objected to this conclusion as erroneous, and on grounds of its sparse reasoning and lack of authority.

Simon J referred to Articles 31 and 32 VCLT. In his view, the proper approach to treaty interpretation was to discern the meaning of the treaty text in its context, rather than looking to the treaty's object and purpose. The clause itself was the best reflection of the intention of the parties. Hence the ordinary mean-

---

51 W. Michael Reisman, Opinion with respect to Selected International Legal Problems in LCIA Case No. 7941, United States of America v. Canada, 1 May 2009, 13, strongly criticizes this approach ('the Tribunal fabricates a methodology even further from that of VCLT Article 32').

52 [2007] EWHC 2851 (Comm).

53 Agreement between the Belgian-Luxembourg Economic Union and the Czechoslovak Socialist Republic Concerning the Reciprocal Promotion and Protection of Investment, 25 April 1989 (emphasis added).

ing derived from the text was bound to give the best effect to the intention of the parties.[54]

The court explained that 'the search for a common intention is likely to be both elusive and unnecessary. Elusive, because the contracting parties may never have had a common intention: only an agreement in the form of words'.[55]

The Czech Republic adduced extensive material on the political and economic background of the Czechoslovak-Belgium-Luxembourg BIT, including on Czechoslovakia's stated policy that disputes with foreign investors are to be litigated in domestic courts and consent to arbitration was therefore very narrow. Specifically, the Republic referred to two statements in the negotiations reflected in the Belgian Parliamentary record on the occasion of the BIT's ratification as evidence of a departure from the Belgian-Luxembourg model BIT, as well as four internal Czech negotiation documents preceding the conclusion of BIT negotiations.

The court found that these materials were ambiguous and inconclusive.[56] The court construed its task to 'interpret the Treaty, rather than to interpret the supplementary means of interpretation.' The court reasoned that the parties to the BIT left the scope of the arbitration clause unclear, perhaps intentionally.[57] The existence of material demonstrating that clearer words could have been chosen, and were indeed chosen in other BITs, did not assist the court in interpreting the BIT. Such material was 'mutually self-defeating.'[58]

In interpreting the terms 'concerning compensation' in Article 8 (1), the Court first noted the wide ordinary meaning of the word 'concerning'. The ordinary meaning was not restricted to 'relating to the amount of compensation'.[59] It covered every aspects of its subject, here entitlement and quantum of compensation. The court inferred the inclusion of whether an expropriation occurred in the consent to arbitrate from the cross-reference to Article 3(3).[60] Noting that this inter-

---

54 Czech Republic v. European Median Ventures, para. 16.
55 Ibid., para. 17., citing O'Connell's reservation that 'intention is very often a fiction ... the parties may never really have wanted to come to an agreement and may have deliberately left the area of operation of the treaty opaque.' O. Connell, International Law (1970), 252, and Ian Sinclair ('there can be no common intentions of the parties aside or apart from the text they have agreed upon. The text is the expression of the intention of the parties; and it is to that expression of intent that one must first look.'), I. Sinclair, The Vienna Convention on the Law of Treaties (1981, 2nd edn), 131.
56 Czech Republic v. European Median Ventures, para. 30.
57 Ibid., para. 32.
58 Ibid., para. 39; cf. also Aguas del Tunari v. Bolivia, para. 274 ('spare negotiating history' offering 'little additional insight' on the BIT, 'neither particularly confirming nor contradicting the Tribunal's interpretation).
59 Czech Republic v. European Median Ventures, para. 43.
60 Ibid., para. 47.

pretation gave effect to all words of Article 8, the court also invoked the object and purpose of creating favourable conditions for investment in support of this construction.[61] Additionally, the court emphasised that this interpretation avoided the need for 'parallel or duplicative proceedings'.[62]

The court confirmed its conclusion that the specific form of consent at issue confined the tribunal's authority to the existence and extent of compensation. For instance, it did not cover restitution. The Czech argument that this construction was 'highly improbable' on account of the rarity with which restitution and declarations were used in investment arbitration was to no avail.[63] The court noted that its 'interpretative solution may be unusual', but brushed the Czech concern relating to the unorthodox outcome aside by reference to the 'unusual form of words.'[64]

The subsidiary Czech argument that the BIT assigned the question whether an expropriation had occurred to local courts and inter-state arbitration, also failed.[65] The court relied on the tension between the alleged objective of the BIT to guarantee an effective and valuable right to arbitrate and the supposed unavailability of redress in local courts. Finally, Simon J dismissed two published accounts by academic writers that supported the narrow construction of Article 8 advocated by the Czech Republic. He explained that these studies were based on limited material, and did not benefit from the extensive argument before the court.[66]

Simon J explained that 'in interpreting a BIT the Court is entitled to take into account that one of the objects of the treaty was to confer rights on an investor, including a valuable right to arbitrate.' Despite heavy reliance on the BIT's object and purpose, he cautioned against a rule of interpretation that uncertainties ought invariably to be resolved in favour of the investor, on the basis of the treaty's objective and purpose. The object and purpose was a factor, but without any automaticity that ambiguities should invariably be resolved in favour of investors.

In *HEP v. Slovenia*, the majority construed a treaty between Croatia and Slovenia to oblige Slovenia to supply electricity to HEP from 1 July 2002 onwards, before the treaty had entered in force. In his dissent, Jan Paulsson strongly criticises the majority's mantra-like repetition of the principle of parity that he alleges was used to imply the above obligation to deliver electricity into the treaty

---

61   Ibid., para. 48.
62   Ibid., para. 49.
63   Ibid., para. 51.
64   Ibid., para. 51.
65   Ibid., para. 52.
66   Ibid., para. 53.

without any textual basis, on a retroactive basis.[67] In his view, the treaty's terms were unambiguous. The parties desired to create a clean slate, waiving their respective claims until the entry into force of the treaty.

In his view, the majority's fundamental methodological flaw was to rely on Article 32 VCLT despite the absence of ambiguity. The majority engaged in extratextual analysis and made use of the treaty's alleged object and purpose, in a wide-ranging attempt to discover the parties' true intentions.[68] Such attempt went beyond the legitimate role of arbitrators and risks undoing the treaty bargain concluded by the two state parties. The dissent is a powerful plea for careful adherence to the treaty's text and for the primacy of Article 31 over Article 32 VCLT.

This line of investment arbitration cases demonstrates that the search for a common intention of the parties outside the treaty's text is often elusive. Great care is needed when relying on material other than the preamble or common expressions of intent. And even then, the vague purposes set out in the preamble are secondary to ordinary meaning of a clause on careful textual analysis.

Other investment tribunals steer clear of either restrictive or expansive interpretation as a general canon of interpretation. They adopt an intermediate posture. The tribunal in *Mondev v United States* reasoned that 'there is no principle either of extensive or restrictive interpretation of jurisdictional provisions in treaties. In the end the question is what the relevant provisions mean, interpreted in accordance with the applicable rules of interpretation of treaties.'[69] This appears to be the superior approach, and one that is in line with the VCLT canon of interpretation.

The tribunal in *Plama v Bulgaria* also alerted us to the dangers of stretching the object and purpose analysis too far, recalling Ian Sinclair's admonitions that teleological interpretation based on the object and purpose risks obscuring the intention of the parties as reflected in the treaty's text.[70] But in other respects, it adopts a similar cavalier attitude: its vacuous reference to the 'well known customary rules codified under Article 31' said to support a restrictive interpretation of the umbrella clause.[71] Such a rule of restrictive interpretation is simply nowhere to be found in the VCLT.[72]

---

67 HEP v. Slovenia, (Interpretation), 12 June 2009, Dissent by Arbitrator Jan Paulsson, para. 23.
68 Ibid., para. 39.
69 Mondev v. United States (Award), 11 October 2002, para. 43.
70 Plama v. Bulgaria (Jurisdiction), 8 February 2005, para. 193.
71 Ibid., para. 55.
72 C. Schreuer, Diversity and Harmonization of Treaty Interpretation in Investment Arbitration, (2006) 3 Transnational Dispute Management, at 5.

The tribunal in *Eureko v Poland*, in interpreting the umbrella clause, explained that 'each and every operative clause of the treaty is to be interpreted as meaningful rather than meaningless.'[73] There is no specific reference to the treaty's object and purpose of investor protection. The principle of effectiveness, as formulated here, is rather more limited. It is to give meaning to each and every term of the treaty – a different approach than a treaty tending towards maximal investor protection.

In *Noble Ventures v Romania*, the tribunal also rejected a broad notion of effectiveness. The tribunal dismissed the contention that there was an interpretative presumption that clauses were to be interpreted exclusively in favour of investors[74], relying on an alleged principle of restrictive interpretation. That alleged principle was particularly important for the interpretation of the umbrella clause at the intersection of domestic and international claims.[75] Curiously, the tribunal then elevated contractual into treaty claims generally.[76] Other interpretations, the tribunal reasoned, would deprive that clause of any practical effect. Both the award's fabrication of a rule of restrictive interpretation, as well as their application to the facts at hand, is disappointing.

The poignant criticism in *Aguas del Tunari v Bolivia* certainly applies to *Noble Ventures*: '... the Vienna Convention represents a move away from the canons of interpretation previously common in treaty interpretation and which erroneously persist in various international law decisions today. For example, the Vienna Convention does not mention the canon that treaties are to be construed narrowly, a canon that presumes States cannot have intended to restrict their range of action.'[77]

There is a tendency to conflate effectiveness and the scope of protection of BITs and the ICSID Convention. For example, a BIT with a restrictive definition of investment may perfectly well be construed using effectiveness as an interpretative guide, mindful of the limits of the State's restrictive consent to arbitrate. More generally, a desire to provide a stable framework for investments does not mean that every ordinary commercial transaction amounts to an investment.

To draw inferences on the scope of investment protection from such preambular language is circular. It is a *non sequitur* to conclude from such the typical language in a BIT's preamble on investment protection that an oil hedge, for example, amounts to an investment. This question must be resolved primarily on the basis of the ordinary meaning of the term investment. The intention of in-

---

73 Eureko v. Poland (Partial Award), 19 August 2005, para. 248.
74 Noble Ventures v. Romania (Award), 12 October 2005, para. 52.
75 Ibid., para. 55.
76 Ibid., para. 61.
77 Aguas del Tunari v. Bolivia (Jurisdiction), 21 October 2005, para. 91.

vestment protection set out in the preamble only assists us once we know that we are – in fact – dealing with an investment.

F. Treaty Interpretation by State Parties

There are important precedents for treaty parties playing a substantial role in treaty interpretation. The Free Trade Commission, a representative body of the state parties to the NAFTA, has authority to adopt binding treaty interpretations.[78] In a controversial interpretative note, the FTC interpreted the notions of fair and equitable treatment and full protection and security.[79] The *Methanex* tribunal identified two independent bases for the binding character of the interpretative note, Article 1131 (2) NAFTA, and Article 31 (3) (a) VCLT.[80]

Article 17 of the New Canadian Model BIT provides for a binding report by the state parties on prudential matters, a provision that could acquire particular importance in relation to investment arbitration claims arising from the financial crisis. Moreover, Article 51 creates a Commission with representatives at Cabinet level charged with resolving disputes regarding the implementation and interpretation of the Agreement.[81]

Scholars are divided on how much weight ought to be given to subsequent interpretations by state parties. Professor Schreuer maintains that unilateral assertions by the disputing party on how a treaty provision ought to be interpreted while the arbitration is pending lack much interpretative value. Such statements may be regarded as self-serving, prompted by a desire to influence the tribunal to decide in favour of the State offering the interpretation.[82]

Anthea Roberts advocates a more nuanced approach to interpretative statements by the state parties BITs that are in force, at least insofar as there is subsequent practice. She suggests that the balance between state parties and investment tribunals is at presently askew.[83] States play a dual role – they are potential respondents, but they also retain a legitimate function in treaty interpretation. And they retain some role in treaty arbitration even when they are involved in a pending ISCID arbitration. Roberts argues that mechanisms for coordinating interpretations through referral to the state parties are a significantly underutilized

---

78   NAFTA Article 2000(1) and 1131 (2).
79   FTC Note of Interpretation, 31 July 2001.
80   Methanex v United States, Award, 3 August 2005, para. 23.
81   Model Canadian bilateral investment promotion agreement :
     http://www.international.gc.ca/trade-agreements-accords-commerciaux/assets/pdfs/2004-FIPA-model-en.pdf.
82   Schreuer, Diversity and Harmonization of Treaty Interpretation (note 72), 18.
83   Roberts, Power and Persuasion in Investment Treaty Arbitration (note 4).

tool.[84] According to her, due process concerns are no obstacle to greater involvement of state parties in interpretation.

The WTO at present appears more open, compared to investment arbitration, to taking the views of the state parties into account. The WTO covered agreements establish a series of WTO organs and provide them with the legal capacity to create law. Article IX of the WTO Agreement enables WTO members to adopt joint interpretations of the existing legal framework. Article X provides that members can, through joint action, adopt amendments of the WTO Agreement. The only amendment thus far is of particular policy importance: the TRIPS amendment on public health and essential medicines. In response to widespread concerns about the impact of the Agreement on Trade Related Aspects of Intellectual Property Rights (TRIPS), WTO members formally amended it to expand the scope for compulsory licensing for countries with no local manufacturing capacity.[85]

G. Territorial and Temporal Scope of Application of BITs

While there is a rich jurisprudence on ICSID subject matter jurisdiction, the case law on jurisdiction *ratione tempore* and *ratione loci* is less developed. It may be expected to play a more important role in future cases. Article 28 VCLT contains the general rule that treaties do not apply retroactively. Article 13 of the ILC Articles on State Responsibility reflects the same principle in providing for state responsibility only in cases 'where the State is bound by the obligation in question at the time the act occurs.'

Investment tribunals generally take the view that international investment law as it stands at the time of the alleged breach is to be applied.[86] They also draw a distinction between the intertemporal applicability of jurisdiction and substantive obligations. The *SGS v Philippines* tribunal explained this distinction in the following terms: 'It may be noted that in international practice a rather different approach is taken to the application of treaties to procedural or jurisdictional clauses than to substantive obligations.'[87]

---

84 Contra Schreuer, Diversity and Harmonization of Treaty Interpretation (note 72), 19 ('occasional views expressed by State parties to treaties on the meaning of particular provisions are not a viable method to achieve uniformity of interpretation').

85 Amendment of the TRIPS Agreement, Article 31bis; see also Declaration on the TRIPS Agreement and Public Health, WT/MIN(01)/DEC/W/2, 14 November 2001.

86 Impregilo v. Pakistan (Jurisdiction), 22 April 2005, 12 ICSID Reports 518, para. 311; cf. also Island of Palma Arbitration, II RIAA, 829, 845 (1949); Amco International Finance Corp. v. Islamic Republic of Iran (1987) 15 Iran-US Claims Tribunal Reports 189, 215.

87 SGS v. Philpines (Jurisdiction), 29 January 2004, 8 ICSID Reports 518.

As a result of the general rule on non-retroactivity, a BIT typically only applies to events after the BIT entered into force. Under the default rule, the date of the treaty's entry into force provides the cut-off point for the tribunal jurisdiction *ratione temporis*. The State has limited its consent to arbitration to acts (or omissions) after the BIT's entry into force.[88]

Some BITs depart from this default rule by providing expressly that the BIT's protections apply to existing as well as to future investments.[89] Others remain silent. However, the question of whether there is coverage for existing investments is separate from whether the BIT's substantive protections apply to acts allegedly in violation of the BIT prior to its entry into force.[90] The *Maffezini* tribunal looked to the time when the dispute arose as the decisive criterion:

'The Tribunal is satisfied that in this case the dispute in its technical and legal sense began to take shape in 1994, particularly in the context of the disinvestment proposals discussed between the parties. At that point, the conflict of legal views and interests came to be clearly established, leading not long thereafter to the presentation of various claims that eventually came to this Tribunal ... the critical date here is the date of entry into force of the [Argentine-Spain BIT] ...'

Jurisdiction *ratione temporis* will also tend to be inclusive on account of the doctrines of the continuous act and composite acts. According to Article 14 (2) ILC Articles on State Responsibility with regard to acts of a continuous character, '[t]he breach of an international obligation by an act of a State having a continuing character extends over the entire period during which the act continues and remains not in conformity with the international obligation'. Accordingly, a breach may be found even if the commencement of the continuous act predates the BIT's entry into force. In the words of the *Mondev v United States* tribunal:

'For its part the Tribunal agrees with the parties both as to the non-retrospective effect of NAFTA and as to the possibility that an act, initially committed before NAFTA entered into force, might in certain circumstances continue to be of relevance after NAFTA's entry into force, thereby becoming subject to NAFTA obligations. But there is a distinction between an act of a continuing character and an act, already completed, which continues to cause loss or damage. Whether the act which constitutes the gist of the (alleged) breach has a continuing character depends both on the facts and on the obligation said to have been breached.'[91]

---

88 SGS v. Philippines, Decision on Jurisdiction, 29 January 2004, 8 ICSID Reports 518, paras. 167-168; Tecmed v. Mexico (Award), 29 May 2003, 10 ICSID Reports 134, paras. 63-65.
89 E.g. Article II (2) of the Argentina-Spain BIT.
90 SGS v. Philipppines, para.166; TECMED v. Mexico, 29 May 2003, paras. 53-68.
91 Mondev v. United States (Award), 11 October 2002, para. 58.

The *Mondev* tribunal referred to the 'basic principle' that only obligations binding at the time of the alleged breach could trigger international responsibility – a position adopted by both the VCLT and the ILC Articles on State Responsibility. Note 39 to NAFTA confirmed this position by establishing that 'this Chapter covers investments existing on the date of entryinto force of this Agreement as well as investments made or acquired thereafter'.[92]

According to the tribunal, an example of a continuous act was a creeping expropriation.[93] However, the tribunal highlighted a crucial caveat: 'The mere fact that earlier conduct has gone unremedied or unredressed when a treaty enters into force does not justify a tribunal applying the treaty retrospectively to thatconduct. Any other approach would subvert both the intertemporal principle in the law of treaties and the basic distinction between breach and reparation which underlies the law of State responsibility.'[94] On the facts, the *Mondev* tribunal found no wrongful act after NAFTA's entry into force.[95]

Less relevant are composite acts, because BIT violations will rarely fall into this category. A possible example would be a systematic campaign of nationalizations extending over a period of time. Composite acts finish when the last separable act occurs.[96] Hence it suffices that the last of a series of acts occurs after the treaty entered into force.

The territorial scope of BIT coverage is expected to feature more prominently in future investment cases. This question is likely to loom large in arising out of investment in disputed zones such as the Arctic, in the continental shelf or the exclusive economic zone. Many BITs simply refer to investments "in the territory" of the other party. For that reason, the default rule of Article 29 VCLT on the territorial scope of treaty obligations is important. It limits the treaty's obligation to the state's territory, absent contrary intentions: 'Unless a different intention appears from the treaty or is otherwise established, a treaty is binding upon each party in respect of its entire territory.'

The crucial wording is 'its entire territory.' Consider the example of an investment to upgrade Gibraltar's airport, a facility located on a narrow strip of land between the castle of Gibraltar and the Spanish mainland. Sovereignty over the airport, and Gibraltar at large, is disputed. The Energy Charter treaty refrains from stating whether or not its territorial scope of application includes Gibraltar.

---

92   Ibid., para. 68.
93   Referring to Papamichalopoulos v. Greece, ECHR Ser A No. 260-B (1993); SGS v Philippines, para. 167 (failure to perform a contract is a continuing act).
94   Mondev v. United States (Award), 11 October 2002, para. 70.
95   Ibid., paras. 73-74.
96   Article 15 ILC Articles on State Responsibility: Rudolf Dolzer and Christoph Schreuer, Principles of International Investment Law (Oxford University Press, 2008), 40.

The UK's BITs are also silent on the question. The inclusion of Gibraltar would have likely occasioned a protest and reservation by Spain.

Delimiting the territorial scope of application in such scenarios requires careful interpretation of the BIT. In particular, one needs to consider whether 'in the territory' presupposes the exercise of sovereignty or whether effective control over territory suffices. The rule in *dubio pro investore* derived from the BIT's object and purpose of maximising investor protection, which criticized as an automatic rule earlier, would counsel in favour of an extensive reading that includes disputed territories, even if such approach results in overlap of the territorial scope of application of several BITs.

H. Conclusion

A central reason why WTO panels and the AB are more sophisticated in treaty interpretation than investment tribunals is the imperative embedded in Article 3.2 Dispute Settlement Understanding (DSU): 'Recommendations and rulings of the DSB cannot add or diminish the rights and obligations provided in the covered agreements.' To ensure that recommendations and rulings do not exceed these bounds, Article 3.2 DSU specifies the interpretative method that adjudicating panels and the AB must use: they must reach their interpretations using customary rules of interpretation. There is no comparable command to adhere to the canon of treaty interpretation contained in the VCLT in investment arbitration. Perhaps as a result, arbitral awards display great heterogeneity in the quality of their application of the principles of treaty interpretation.

WTO adjudicating bodies have understood Article 3.2 DSU to be an implicit reference to the relevant provisions of the VCLT which representcustomary international law.[97] The majority view holds that the use of extra-contractual (extra WTO) interpretative elements is permissible when interpreting a covered agreement, even if it is generally denied that non-WTO law is part of the applicable law. Trachtman believes the WTO adjudicators cannot apply non-WTO international law, but allows for the use of general international law in interpretation. Professor Howse and Pauwelyn warn us against the dangers of interpreting the WTO agreement in clinical isolation from public international law as a whole.

When WTO members considered that the WTO adjudicating bodies undid the balance of rights and obligations they had negotiated, they reacted strongly. For example, the majority expressed the view that the AB was acting *ultra vires* in allowing *amici curiae* to participate in the proceedings. WTO members play a

---

97　The leading case is US-Gasoline, WT/DS2/AB/R.

dual role: they are potential respondent states, but also retain a strong interest in correct interpretation. The same principle translates to investment arbitration. But treaty interpretation in investment arbitration suffers from the absence of a similar corrective mechanism.

The phenomenon of fragmentation triggered renewed interest in treaty interpretation. Curiously, interpretation is regarded as both the problem, given the increasing number of epistemic communities in international law, and the solution, for its potential harmonizing effect through systemic interpretation. Whether interpretation can avoid the first, and live up to the high expectations, remains to be seen. In the future, we can expect greater tension between investment and non-investment law before investment tribunals. Arguments about the territorial and temporal scope of application of BITs are also likely.

In these circumstances, the harmonising function of treaty interpretation will be much in demand. However, until corrective mechanisms such as Commissions under the Canadian model BIT become more widespread and a legitimate role for state parties to interpret investment treaties is recognized, two essential ingredients in treaty interpretation in investment arbitration are missing. These mechanisms also safeguard against broad teleological interpretations that have little basis in the treaty's text.

As Professor Reisman notes, fidelity to the ordinary meaning of treaty text is paramount for respecting the expectations of states and investors: 'just as treaties facilitate cooperative behaviour by stabilizing expectations with respect to reciprocal rights and duties, the rules of interpretation of treaties are designed to ensure that those stabilized expectations are respected.'[98] 'Conservative' approaches to treaty interpretation that pay close attention to the text are particularly important in international investment arbitration, a method of dispute settlement without explicit law-making authority and wide-ranging impact on domestic regulatory space.

---

98 W. Michael Reisman, Opinion with respect to Selected International Legal Problems in LCIA Case No. 7941, United States of America v. Canada, 1 May 2009, para. 6.

International Investment Law and Treaty Interpretation – Problems, Particularities and Possible Trends

Comments by *Lars Markert**

One cannot but agree with the thoughtful and interesting analysis of *Michael Waibel* in which he remarks that some investment arbitration awards display a *"cavalier attitude to treaty interpretation"* that does not *"offer models of careful treaty interpretation for international lawyers working in other areas."*[1] Although the principles of international treaty interpretation embodied in Articles 31 and 32 of the Vienna Convention on the Law of Treaties (VCLT)[2] should allow for a uniform approach to interpreting International Investment Agreements (IIAs) and the ICSID Convention, investment arbitral tribunals have not yet developed a consistent methodology.

A. The Need for a Consistent Approach

The current heterogeneity of approaches is problematic, as interpretation of the scope of application of treaty clauses is decisive for determining their legal effect. A methodological and consistent approach to interpretation is especially important in investment arbitration since legal certainty cannot be established by arbitral case law due to the lack of a system of binding precedent. While there might be a developing trend to at least take other tribunals' reasoning on similar issues into account,[3] each tribunal ultimately remains free to give a new meaning to similar or even identical clauses.

---

* Dr Lars Markert, LL.M. (Georgetown), Associate, Gleiss Lutz, Stuttgart.

1 Michael Waibel, International Investment Law and Treaty Interpretation, in Hofmann/Tams, International Investment Law and General International Law – From Clinical Isolation to Systemic Integration? (2011), p. 29.

2 The VCLT will oftentimes not be directly applicable, either because it entered into force after the ICSID Convention or the relevant IIA (see Article 4 VCLT) or important signatory states to IIAs, such as France or the US, are not signatories to the VCLT; see MHS v. Malaysia, Decision on Annulment, 16 April 2009, para. 56.

3 Saba Fakes v. Turkey, ICSID Case No. ARB/07/20, Award, 14 July 2010, para. 96 ("The present Tribunal shares the opinion of the Tribunal in the Bayindir v. Pakistan case that, unless there are compelling reasons to the contrary, it ought to follow solutions established in a series of consistent cases that are comparable to the case at hand, subject to the specificity of the treaty under consideration and the circumstances of the case."); Bayin-

At present, the introduction of new approaches such as preliminary rulings[4] or new bodies like an appellate mechanism[5] or an international investment court[6] does not seem a very realistic means of achieving greater consistency. Before attempting to implement 'external' changes to the investor-state dispute resolution mechanism, one should strive for a pragmatic solution to ameliorate the system 'from within'.[7] This might help to mitigate the criticism that different outcomes on similar issues are a sign of a "legitimacy crisis" of investment arbitration[8] and to prevent a "backlash" against investment arbitration.[9]

When examining interpretation in international investment law, one has to bear in mind that a uniform interpretation by no means implies that different treaty clauses should be assigned the same regulatory content. It is not the similarity of the interpretative result but rather the homogeneity of the interpretative process which should create greater legal certainty and predictability in investment disputes.

dir v. Pakistan, ICSID Case No. ARB/03/29, Award, 27 August 2009, para. 145; Saipem v. Bangladesh, ICSID Case No. ARB/05/7, Decision on Jurisdiction, 21 March 2007, para. 67; Pey Casado v. Chile, ICSID Case No. ARB/98/2, Award, 9 May 2008, para. 119.

4   Christoph Schreuer, Preliminary Rulings in Investment Arbitration, in Appeals Mechanism in International Investment Disputes (Karl Sauvant, ed.) (2008) 207.

5   For critical views see Christian Tams, An Appealing Option? The Debate about an ICSID Appellate Structure, Beiträge zum Transnationalen Wirtschaftsrecht, issue 57 (2006) 42, available at http://www.wirtschaftsrecht.uni-halle.de/Heft57.pdf; Jan Paulsson, Avoiding Unintended Consequences, in Sauvant/Chiswick-Patterson (eds.), Appeals Mechanism in International Investment Disputes (2008), 241, 258-262.

6   Gus van Harten, Investment Treaty Arbitration and Public Law (2007) 180; for more suggestions, see Mariel Dimsey, The Resolution of International Investment Disputes: Challenges and Solutions (2008) 141-221.

7   Lars Markert, The Crucial Question of Future Investment Treaties: Balancing Investors' Rights and Regulatory Interests of Host States, in Bungenberg et al. (eds.), International Investment Law and EU Law (2011), 145, 170.

8   Susan Franck, The Legitimacy Crisis in Investment Treaty Arbitration: Privatizing Public International Law Through Inconsistent Decisions, 73 Fordham L. Rev. (2005) 1521, 1568; Mariel Dimsey, The Resolution of International Investment Disputes: Challenges and Solutions (2008) 35 et seq.; Gus van Harten, Investment Treaty Arbitration and Public Law (2007) 166; UNCTAD, Investor State Dispute Settlement and Impact on Investment Rulemaking, UNCTAD/ITE/IIA/2007/3, New York (2007) 92; Jörn Griebel/Yun-I Kim, Zwischen Aufbruch, Stillstand und Rückschritt – Überlegungen zur Zukunft des internationalen Investitionsrechts, SchiedsVZ (2007) 186, 191.

9   See generally Michael Waibel et al. (eds.), The Backlash against Investment Arbitration - Perceptions and Reality (2010).

B. Two Problematic Interpretative Approaches in International Investment Law

Two particular interpretative approaches seem to exist, which might be responsible for the current inconsistencies in investment arbitration. One, as identified by *Waibel*, is an exaggerated emphasis on the IIAs' preambular language. The other is a general tendency to let policy considerations unduly influence the interpretative approach.

When interpreting IIA provisions, some arbitral tribunals almost reflexively refer to the preamble of the IIA.[10] The preamble describes the aims of the IIA, which normally include the protection and promotion of investments. This aim has caused arbitral tribunals to single-sidedly focus on the protection of the investment in dispute and consequently give procedural and substantive protections in IIAs a particularly wide scope of application. However, this approach does not comport with the interpretative principles embodied in the VCLT. Important as the preambular language might be, it does not constitute the only relevant tool for interpretation. In fact, according to Article 31 of the VCLT, interpretation starts with the wording and the context of the norm, before referring to the object and purpose of the treaty. An isolated focus on the protection of investments could either extend or narrow the scope of application of a provision in an IIA contrary to its wording and systematic context. It would fail to recognize that the promotion of investments is as important as their protection[11] – a fact which calls for a balanced interpretative approach. Overemphasis on the protection of investors could even endanger the overall aim of promoting investments; after all, host states have to be willing to accept investments and provide for a positive investment climate. If investments and their normative framework in international law are perceived to unduly curtail state regulatory autonomy, the willingness of states to promote investments will eventually decline.[12]

---

10 Siemens v. Argentina, ICSID Case No. No. ARB/02/08, Decision on Jurisdiction, 3 August 2004, para. 81; Gus van Harten, Investment Treaty Arbitration and Public Law (2007) 138; Ole K. Fauchald, The Legal Reasoning of ICSID Tribunals – An Empirical Analysis, 19 The European J. of Int'l L. 2 (2008) 301, 323.

11 Saluka v. Czech Republic, UNCITRAL, Partial Award, 17 March 2006, para. 300.

12 Saluka v. Czech Republic, UNCITRAL, Partial Award, 17 March 2006, para. 300 ("The protection of foreign investments is not the sole aim of the Treaty, but rather a necessary element alongside the overall aim of encouraging foreign investment and extending and intensifying the parties' economic relations. That in turn calls for a balanced approach to the interpretation of the Treaty's substantive provisions for the protection of investments, since an interpretation which exaggerates the protection to be accorded to foreign investments may serve to dissuade host States from admitting foreign investments and so undermine the overall aim of extending and intensifying the parties' mutual economic relations.").

The second problematic interpretative approach consists in placing an undue emphasis on policy considerations when interpreting a provision. While policy considerations certainly can and should play a role in investment arbitration, and particularly when drawing on the object and purpose of a treaty, it could be considered an 'undue emphasis' if the result of the interpretative process is predominantly based on and shaped by policy considerations. As one arbitrator described in a dissenting opinion:

> "The majority [of the arbitral tribunal] says, in effect, that one may postulate an outcome and force-fit it into the actual text. Nuances and omissions in the text are of no moment. In the result, the majority retains from Article 31(1) VCLT only the elements that confirm their subjective gloss (perceptions of good faith and object and purpose), ignoring those which are of an objective nature (textual terms and context)."[13]

Such "reverse-engineering"[14] often seems to be triggered by provisions in IIAs which the contractual parties may have adopted without being fully aware of their possible consequences.[15] In such a case, can an arbitral tribunal conclude that the parties could not possibly have wanted to agree on the particular effect of a provision (maybe by reading such intent into the object and purpose of the provision or the treaty)?[16] This is what some arbitral tribunals seem to do when applying the *in dubio mitius rule*.[17] Others, for example, conclude that the appli-

---

13 HEP v. Slovenia, Decision on the Treaty Interpretation Issue, Dissenting Opinion Arbitrator Paulsson, 8 June 2009, para. 47.

14 HEP v. Slovenia, Decision on the Treaty Interpretation Issue, Dissenting Opinion Arbitrator Paulsson, 8 June 2009, para. 7; similarly Thomas Wälde, Interpreting Investment Treaties, in Binder et al. (eds.), International Investment Law for the 21st Century, Essays in Honour of Christoph Schreuer (2009) 724, 730.

15 Thomas Wälde, Interpreting Investment Treaties, in Binder et al. (eds.), International Investment Law for the 21st Century, Essays in Honour of Christoph Schreuer (2009) 724, 736; also John Gaffney/James Loftis, The "Effective Ordinary Meaning" of BITs and the Jurisdiction of Treaty-Based Tribunals to Hear Contract Claims, 8 J. World Investment & Trade 1 (2007) 5, 23 ("[M]any State parties may have not foreseen or intended umbrella clauses to have such effect"); John Boscariol/Orlando Silva, The Widening Application of the MFN Obligation and its Impact on Investor Protection, Int'l Trade L. & Regulation (2005) 61 ("Up until recently, conventional wisdom appeared to hold that [...] the MFN obligation applied primarily to a state's substantive measures regarding investors and investments, rather than[sic] the protections offered by other investment treaties to which that state was party.").

16 See John Gaffney/James Loftis, The "Effective Ordinary Meaning" of BITs and the Jurisdiction of Treaty-Based Tribunals to Hear Contract Claims, 8 J. World Investment & Trade 1 (2007) 5, 21.

17 According to this rule, treaty provisions are to be interpreted restrictively because states could not have constrained their sovereignty on purpose. See e.g. SGS v. Pakistan, ICSID Case No. ARB/01/13, Decision on Jurisdiction, 6 August 2003, para. 171 ("The appropriate interpretive approach is the prudential one summed up in the literature as *in dubio pars mitior est sequenda*, or more tersely, *in dubio mitius*."); El Paso v. Argentina, ICSID

cation of umbrella clauses to contractual relationships might open the floodgates for requests for arbitration[18] or that the application of the most-favored-nation clause to dispute resolution clauses might lead to treaty shopping and therefore to a chaotic situation.[19] These approaches contradict the objective approach of interpretation inherent in the rules of customary international law codified in Articles 31 and 32 VCLT,[20] which the arbitral tribunal in the *Wintershall* case succinctly described as follows:

> "The carefully-worded formulation in Article 31 is based on the view that the text must be presumed to be the authentic expression of the intention of the parties. The starting point of all treaty-interpretation is the elucidation of the meaning of the text, not an independent investigation into the intention of the parties from other sources (such as by reference to the travaux préparatoires, or any predilections based on presumed intention)."[21]

The subjective approach and policy considerations often reflect more the opinion of the person interpreting the agreement than they serve to determine a barely identifiable common intent of the parties.[22] This might not only lead to different interpretations of essentially the same clauses, and thus to legal uncertainty,[23] but may also result in neglecting the actual intent of the parties as ex-

---

Case No. ARB/03/15, Decision on Jurisdiction, 27 April 2006, para. 85; Noble Ventures v. Romania, ICSID Case No. ARB/01/11, Award, 12 October 2005, para. 55.

18   See the examples given in John Gaffney/James Loftis, The "Effective Ordinary Meaning" of BITs and the Jurisdiction of Treaty-Based Tribunals to Hear Contract Claims, 8 J. World Investment & Trade 1 (2007) 5, 21 and Wintershall v. Argentina, ICSID Case No. ARB/04/14, Award, 8 December 2008, para. 89.

19   Maffezini v. Spain, ICSID Case No. ARB/97/7, Decision on Jurisdiction, 25 January 2000, para. 63.

20   Aguas del Tunari v. Bolivia, ICSID Case No. ARB/02/3, Decision on Jurisdiction, 21 October 2005, para. 91; John Gaffney/James Loftis, The "Effective Ordinary Meaning" of BITs and the Jurisdiction of Treaty-Based Tribunals to Hear Contract Claims, 8 J. World Investment & Trade 1 (2007) 5, 22; Mondev v. USA, ICSID Case No. ARB(AF)/99/2, Award, 11 October 2002, para. 43.

21   Wintershall v. Argentina, ICSID Case No. ARB/04/14, Award, 8 December 2008, para. 78; Thomas Wälde, Interpreting Investment Treaties, in Binder et al. (eds.), International Investment Law for the 21st Century, Essays in Honour of Christoph Schreuer (2009) 724, 752 ("Nevertheless – and this is the common position between civil and common law lawyers – interpretation has to start with the text – and not with theories about intention, policy, political desirability nor with evidence, presumptions, or speculations about the 'original intentions' of the drafters.").

22   Renta 4 v. Russia, SCC Case No. 24/2007, Award on Jurisdiction, 20 March 2009, para. 93 ("Speculations relied upon as the basis for purposive readings of a text run the risk of encroachment upon fundamental policy determinations."); Thomas Wälde, Interpreting Investment Treaties, in Binder et al. (eds.), International Investment Law for the 21st Century, Essays in Honour of Christoph Schreuer (2009) 724, 737.

23   Gabrielle Kaufmann-Kohler, Interpretation of Treaties: How Do Arbitral Tribunals Interpret Dispute Settlement Provisions Embodied in Investment Treaties, in Mistelis/Lew (eds.), Pervasive Problems in International Arbitration (2006), para. 13-13, pointing out that different approaches of investment arbitrators might depend on whether they are ex-

pressed in the treaty.[24] Therefore, relying on general policy considerations or a purported intent of the parties not implied in the text of the treaty runs the risk of (inadvertently) falsifying the interpretative outcome.[25]

C. One Proposed Solution to the Interpretative Approach and the Consequences

Waibel's critique of the abovementioned approaches as well as his proposed solution advocating a "*'conservative' approach[ ] to treaty interpretation that pay[s] close attention to the text*"[26] are convincing.

Such an 'objective'[27] interpretative approach does not ask for the intent of the parties but seeks to uncover the intent of the provision.[28] A reflection on the intent of the parties only takes place as a subsidiary means of interpretation because the true intent of the parties should find its expression in the text of the treaty itself.[29] The starting point of the interpretative process must be the particular term in the provision or the provision itself, which is then concretized and

---

perts in public international law or have a commercial arbitration background; similarly Thomas Wälde, Interpreting Investment Treaties, in Binder et al. (eds.), International Investment Law for the 21st Century, Essays in Honour of Christoph Schreuer (2009) 724, 725; Gus van Harten, Investment Treaty Arbitration and Public Law (2007), Chapter 6.

24 Ian Sinclair, The Vienna Convention on the Law of Treaties (1984) 131; Plama v. Bulgaria, ICSID Case No. ARB/03/24, Decision on Jurisdiction, 8 February 2005, para. 193.

25 Wintershall v. Argentina, ICSID Case No. ARB/04/14, Award, 8 December 2008, para. 88 ("[T]here is no room for any presumed intention of the Contracting Parties to a bilateral treaty, as an independent basis of interpretation; because this opens up the possibility of an interpreter (often, with the best of intentions) altering the text of the treaty in order to make it conform better with what he (or she) considers to be the treaty's "true purpose"." [emphasis in the original]).

26 Waibel, International Investment Law and Treaty Interpretation, in Hofmann/Tams, International Investment Law and General International Law – From Clinical Isolation to Systemic Integration? (2011), p. 52; see also Lars Markert, Streitschlichtungsklauseln in Investitionsschutzabkommen [Dispute Settlement Clauses in International Investment Agreements] (2010) 70-82.

27 This term seems preferable to the term 'conservative'.

28 Gabrielle Kaufmann-Kohler, Interpretation of Treaties: How Do Arbitral Tribunals Interpret Dispute Settlement Provisions Embodied in Investment Treaties, in Mistelis/Lew (eds.), Pervasive Problems in International Arbitration (2006), para. 13-12 ("[I]n treaty arbitration more objective criteria will by essence prevail and the subjective element will play a lesser role."), making a distinction to interpreting private law contracts, id. paras. 13-11.

29 Omar E. García-Bolívar, The Teleology of International Investment Law – The Role of Purpose in the Interpretation of International Investment Agreements, 6 J. World Investment & Trade 5 (2005) 751, 772 ("[A]rbitrators and judges cannot go beyond the purpose as mentioned in the text of the agreements, their preambles and the travaux préparatoires; that is, to the point where the negotiators have left the IIA.").

contextualized by the interpretative steps laid out in Articles 31 and 32 of the VCLT.[30] By having recourse to criteria present in the treaty, the objective approach seems to be better suited to achieve a coherent and uniform approach in the interpretation of similar clauses. A departure from an over-emphasis of policy considerations is particularly relevant in the area of investment law. IIA negotiations regularly occur against the backdrop of the conflicting interests of optimal investor protection and unimpeded pursuit of governmental policy.[31] A common intent of the parties – apart from the promotion of investments – is therefore unlikely to be established.[32]

Advocating a textual approach does not mean that the other steps provided for in Articles 31 and 32 of the VCLT should be ignored. They form part of a *"single combined operation"*[33] and in certain instances can even prevail over the wording of a provision.[34] However, the textual or objective approach ensures that arbitral tribunals will first take into account the ordinary meaning of a provision before turning to other interpretative means and balancing them against the wording.

---

30 Aguas del Tunari v. Bolivia, ICSID Case No. ARB/02/3, Decision on Jurisdiction, 21 October 2005, para. 91 ("Interpretation under Article 31 of the Vienna Convention is a process of progressive encirclement where the interpreter starts under the general rule with (1) the ordinary meaning of the terms of the treaty, (2) in their context and (3) in light of the treaty's object and purpose, and by cycling through this three step inquiry iteratively closes in upon the proper interpretation.").

31 Lars Markert, The Crucial Question of Future Investment Treaties: Balancing Investors' Rights and Regulatory Interests of Host States, in Bungenberg et al. (eds.), International Investment Law and EU Law (2011), 145, 146.

32 Jürgen Kurtz, Adjudging the Exceptional at International Law: Security, Public Order and Financial Crisis, Jean Monnet Working Paper No. 6 (2008) 6, available at http://centers.law.nyu.edu/jeanmonnet/papers/08/080601.html; Thomas Wälde, Interpreting Investment Treaties, in Binder et al. (eds.), International Investment Law for the 21st Century, Essays in Honour of Christoph Schreuer (2009) 724, 746. Moreover, a common intent of the parties seems to be much harder to establish in international investment law than would be the case in contract law. While parties to a private law contract usually draft provisions for a concrete two-party relationship, IIAs incorporate abstract norms for a multitude of possible investment situations with regard to which the parties to the treaty may have had different aims. The fact that only one of the two parties of an IIA is involved in an investment dispute in front of an arbitral tribunal makes the determination of the intent of both parties even more difficult to achieve, Gabrielle Kaufmann-Kohler, Interpretation of Treaties: How Do Arbitral Tribunals Interpret Dispute Settlement Provisions Embodied in Investment Treaties, in Mistelis/Lew (eds.), Pervasive Problems in International Arbitration (2006), para. 13 -12.

33 International Law Commission, Draft Articles on the Law of Treaties with Commentaries (1966), Art. 27 [now Art. 31] para. 8, in YBILC (1966 II) 188, 219.

34 See e.g. Berschader v. Russia, SCC Case No. 080/2004, Award, 21 April 2006, paras. 191-192.

One of the consequences of the objective approach can be that it leads to results that – at least in the eyes of one of the parties to the dispute or the interpreting arbitrator – might seem difficult to reconcile with the "object and purpose" of the treaty or the interpreter's ideas of how investment law should work. Yet, the overall harmonization of the interpretative approach and the greater legal certainty and predictability achieved by a uniform textual approach seem to outweigh the pursuit of – sometimes questionable – equitable results in individual cases.[35]

Another consequence of a textual approach to interpretation is that the context of a provision and the principle of effective interpretation ('*effet utile*') gain particular significance. While the principle of effective interpretation is not expressly mentioned in Articles 31 and 32 of the VCLT, it is recognized as embodied in the requirement to interpret a treaty "*in good faith*" pursuant to Article 31 of the VCLT.[36] If one accepts that the scope of a provision should not be 'manipulated' by following a subjective approach construing a presumed intent of contracting parties, it is important that a particular treaty term is given a meaning rather than rendered meaningless. *Crawford* aptly describes the correlation between a textual approach and effective interpretation as follows:

> "[T]reaty language is presumed to have its natural and ordinary meaning in its context. It is stated as a general rule in Article 31(1) of the Vienna Convention on the Law of Treaties of 1969. A corollary is the principle of effet utile: the words of a substantive treaty provision should be given some rather than no effect."[37]

While the principle of effective interpretation is invoked by a number of tribunals and academics in investment arbitration,[38] *Waibel* demonstrates that it is

---

35   Contra Thomas Wälde, Interpreting Investment Treaties, in Binder et al. (eds.), International Investment Law for the 21st Century, Essays in Honour of Christoph Schreuer (2009) 724, 727-728, criticizing decisions with a "very contract-text-focused standard commercial arbitration approach [...]."

36   ILC, Draft Articles on the Law of Treaties with Commentaries (1966), Art. 27 [now Art. 31] para. 6, in YBILC (1966 II) 188, 219 ("[...] in so far as the maxim ut res magis valeat quam pereat reflects a true general rule of interpretation, it is embodied in article 27 [now Art. 31], paragraph 1, which requires that a treaty shall be interpreted in good faith in accordance with the ordinary meaning to be given to its terms in the context of the treaty and in the light of its object and purpose. When a treaty is open to two interpretations one of which does and the other does not enable the treaty to have appropriate effects, good faith and the objects and purposes of the treaty demand that the former interpretation should be adopted." [emphasis in the original]).

37   James Crawford, Treaty and Contract in Investment Arbitration, 24 Arb. Int'l 3 (2008) 351, 355.

38   Noble Ventures v. Romania, ICSID Case No. ARB/01/11, Award, 12 October 2005, para. 50 ("Reference should also be made to the principle of effectiveness (effet utile), which, too plays an important role in interpreting treaties."); Eureko v. Poland, Partial Award, 19 August 2005, para. 248 ("It is a cardinal rule of the interpretation of treaties that each and every operative clause of a treaty is to be interpreted as meaningful rather than meaningless."); Maffezini v. Spain, ICSID Case No. ARB/97/7, Decision on Juris-

sometimes used to introduce a subjective approach 'through the backdoor'.[39] Instead of trying to give meaning to a particular provision, tribunals *"conflate effectiveness and the scope of protection of BITs"*[40] by construing provisions so that either – in light of the BIT's preamble – 'effective' protection is granted to investors or – taking into account the *in dubio mitius* principle – host states retain an 'effective' autonomy to regulate in the public interest. If one does not agree with such subjective interpretative approaches, it is obvious that an overly broad understanding of the principle of effectiveness must be rejected. Instead, the principle of effectiveness should be understood as the interpretative approach that gives a particular provision a meaning rather than rendering it meaningless.[41]

D. Particularities of Interpretation in Investment Arbitration

When examining interpretative approaches in public international law, it is certainly advisable to draw on the experiences and holdings of the ICJ and the WTO panels and Appellate Body. Yet, there are systemic explanations why investment arbitral tribunals do not – and maybe cannot – achieve the same coherence; the particularity of interpretation in investment arbitration is rooted as much in the legal structure of investment law as in its actors.

Turning to the actors first, one can distinguish between arbitrators, parties and their counsel. Considering the arbitrators, probably the least important aspect is a perceived (textual) common law versus a (purpose-oriented) civil law approach leading to different interpretative outcomes. The members of the ICJ and of WTO panels face the same situation and despite different legal backgrounds

diction, 25 January 2000, para. 36; Salini v. Jordan, ICSID Case No. ARB/02/13, Decision on Jurisdiction, 29 November 2004, para. 95; Gaffney/James Loftis, The "Effective Ordinary Meaning" of BITs and the Jurisdiction of Treaty-Based Tribunals to Hear Contract Claims, 8 J. World Investment & Trade 1 (2007) 5, 8; Julien Fouret, Denunciation of the Washington Convention and Non-Contractual Investment Arbitration: "Manufacturing Consent" to ICSID Arbitration?, 25 J. Int'l Arb. 1 (2008) 71, 86; Andrew Newcombe/Lluís Paradell, Law and Practice of Investment Treaties, Standards of Treatment (2009) 114.

39 Michael Waibel, International Investment Law and Treaty Interpretation, in Hofmann/Tams, International Investment Law and General International Law – From Clinical Isolation to Systemic Integration? (2011), pp. 39, 47.

40 Michael Waibel, International Investment Law and Treaty Interpretation, in Hofmann/Tams, International Investment Law and General International Law – From Clinical Isolation to Systemic Integration? (2011), p. 47.

41 ILC, Draft Articles on the Law of Treaties with Commentaries (1966), Art. 27 [now Art. 31] para. 6, in YBILC (1966 II) 188, 219; James Crawford, Treaty and Contract in Investment Arbitration, 24 Arb. Int'l 3 (2008) 351, 355; Eureko v. Poland, Partial Award, 19 August 2005, para. 248.

seem to successfully deal with it. However, in contrast to the latter two institutions, interpretation in investment arbitration seems influenced by the arbitrators' affiliation with either the commercial arbitration or the public international law 'bars'.[42] Some argue that the former might not be as ready to develop sophisticated interpretative solutions, since the commercial arbitration culture focuses more on the effective resolution of the dispute, emphasizing the facts and paying less consideration to public interests and development of the law.[43] On the other hand, a public international arbitrator might overemphasize academic aspects to the detriment of pragmatic solutions.[44] While these differences might be exaggerated,[45] the particular composition of the 'investment arbitration bar' certainly can be identified as one particular cause for inconsistent interpretations.[46] This is even amplified by the fact that the two 'different bars' get mixed and matched each time a new tribunal is constituted, and two tribunals are rarely the same.

The situation is reinforced by another group of actors, namely the parties and their counsel. In investment arbitrations, they will appoint the "party's arbitrator" according to criteria that seemingly best support their case. Given the public nature of awards and the increase in academic texts on investment arbitration, parties and their counsel turn to 'arbitrator profiling' in order to seek suitable academic views and interpretative approaches of given arbitrator candidates.[47] As both parties to the dispute might have very different views as to which interpreta-

---

42 See Thomas Wälde, Interpreting Investment Treaties, in Binder et al. (eds.), International Investment Law for the 21st Century, Essays in Honour of Christoph Schreuer (2009) 724, 725.

43 Jan Paulsson, Avoiding Unintended Consequences, in Sauvant/Chiswick-Patterson (eds.), Appeals Mechanism in International Investment Disputes (2008), 241, 263 ("Some excellent commercial arbitrators seem to have insufficient grounding in public international law."); Thomas Wälde, Interpreting Investment Treaties, in Binder et al. (eds.), International Investment Law for the 21st Century, Essays in Honour of Christoph Schreuer (2009) 724, 725.

44 Jan Paulsson, Avoiding Unintended Consequences, in Sauvant/Chiswick-Patterson (eds.), Appeals Mechanism in International Investment Disputes (2008), 241, 264.

45 See Stephan Wilske et al., International Investment Treaty Arbitration and International Commercial Arbitration – Conceptual Difference or Only a "Status Thing"? 1 Contemp. Asia Arb. J. 2 (2008) 213, 228.

46 Gabrielle Kaufmann-Kohler, Interpretation of Treaties: How Do Arbitral Tribunals Interpret Dispute Settlement Provisions Embodied in Investment Treaties, in Mistelis/Lew (eds.), Pervasive Problems in International Arbitration (2006), para. 13-13. This raises doubts about Waibel's proposition of international investment arbitration lawyers forming an "epistemic community", see Michael Waibel, International Investment Law and Treaty Interpretation, in Hofmann/Tams, International Investment Law and General International Law – From Clinical Isolation to Systemic Integration? (2011), p. 31.

47 Lars Markert, Challenging Arbitrators in Investment Arbitration: The Challenging Search for Relevant Standards and Ethical Guidelines, 3 Contemp. Asia Arb. J. 2 (2010), 237, 255. Where one party-appointed arbitrator's views too obviously support a party's case, the other party might react by challenging the appointed arbitrator, id. 262.

tive approach favors their arguments, they might appoint arbitrators whose views are diametrically opposed, making it difficult for a given tribunal to agree on a uniform interpretative approach.[48] Finally, the pleadings of counsel can greatly influence an arbitral tribunal's reasoning. Not having the same support apparatus as the ICJ or the WTO Appellate Body, investment arbitral tribunals and their awards will be influenced by the ingenuity, quality – or lack thereof – and stringency of counsel's interpretative approaches when deciding cases as they are presented.[49] Taking all these factors into account it is hardly surprising that interpretative approaches of investment arbitral tribunals are more divergent than those of the ICJ or the WTO Appellate Body.

The interpretative task of investment arbitral tribunals is further complicated by the structure of the legal norms to be interpreted. As has been pointed out above, contractual parties to an IIA often might have had very different and even conflicting ideas in mind when signing the IIA. This makes the *"search for a common intention of the parties outside the treaty's text [...] often elusive."*[50] Moreover, only one of the parties to the dispute will have actually been involved in negotiating and drafting the IIA. The dual role of a state as treaty party and respondent[51] justifies a healthy dose of skepticism with respect to the respondent's proposed interpretative approaches and outcomes.[52] In fact, various cases evidence that the investor's home state, when asked about the common intent of the contracting parties to an IIA during an arbitral proceeding, does not necessarily support the respondent state party's view.[53] Finally, the vast universe of IIAs with their similar – but in their details diverging – provisions makes it difficult to

---

48   See the example of the HEP v. Slovenia decision on interpretation and the dissenting opinion by arbitrator Jan Paulsson, supra note 13.

49   Thomas Wälde, Interpreting Investment Treaties, in Binder et al. (eds.), International Investment Law for the 21st Century, Essays in Honour of Christoph Schreuer (2009) 724, 726; Jan Paulsson, Avoiding Unintended Consequences, in Sauvant/Chiswick-Patterson (eds.), Appeals Mechanism in International Investment Disputes (2008) 241, 248 ("There are limits to jura novit curia. [...] And so major issues may be decided in the context of a mediocre debate").

50   Michael Waibel, International Investment Law and Treaty Interpretation, in Hofmann/Tams, International Investment Law and General International Law – From Clinical Isolation to Systemic Integration? (2011), p. 45.

51   On this issue, Anthea Roberts, Power and Persuasion in Investment Treaty Arbitration: The Dual Role of States, 104 Am. J. Int'l L. (2010) 179 et seq.

52   Christoph Schreuer, Diversity and Harmonization of Treaty Interpretation, in Fitzmaurice et al. (eds.), Treaty Interpretation and the Vienna Convention on the Law of Treaties: 30 Years on (2010) 129, 146.

53   See e.g. Tza Yap Shum v. Peru, ICSID Case No. ARB/07/6, Decision on Jurisdiction, 19 June 2009, para. 210; Eureko v. Slovak Republic, PCA Case No. 2008-13, UNCITRAL, Award on Jurisdiction, 26 October 2010, paras. 155-163; Aguas del Tunari v. Bolivia, ICSID Case No. ARB/02/3, Decision on Jurisdiction, 21 October 2005, paras. 258-259.

develop a consistent approach on a particular issue. For the WTO panels and Appellate Body, such task is facilitated by the more coherent WTO regime.

As long as corrective mechanisms such as, for example, the binding state party interpretations[54] alluded to by *Waibel*[55] remain the exception, the structural particularities of investment law make a uniform interpretative approach difficult. Nevertheless, the approach to interpretative issues proposed above can hopefully lead to a noticeable harmonization.

E. Possible Trends in Interpretation in Investment Arbitration

Being in agreement with most of *Waibel's* views, it seems appropriate to take the analysis of interpretation in investment arbitration further and point out two possible future trends.

One trend is the changing interpretative approach to the application of most-favored-nation (MFN) clauses to dispute settlement provisions. The first couple of years after the issue arose were marked by a strong reliance on policy considerations. Very generally speaking, the *"Maffezini"* line of cases determined that in order to protect the investment in accordance with the IIA's preamble, MFN clauses had to be given a wide scope.[56] The followers of *"Plama"* objected,[57] pointing out that the contracting states never (could have) envisaged such wide application of the MFN clause. While a closer look reveals that the strong divergence might have been caused by the dispute settlement provisions at play,[58]

---

54   For a critical view of such a mechanism, Christoph Schreuer, Diversity and Harmonization of Treaty Interpretation, in Fitzmaurice et al. (eds.), Treaty Interpretation and the Vienna Convention on the Law of Treaties: 30 Years on (2010) 129, 148; Lars Markert, The Crucial Question of Future Investment Treaties: Balancing Investors' Rights and Regulatory Interests of Host States, in Bungenberg et al. (eds.), International Investment Law and EU Law (2011), 145, 153.

55   Michael Waibel, International Investment Law and Treaty Interpretation, in Hofmann/Tams, International Investment Law and General International Law – From Clinical Isolation to Systemic Integration? (2011), p. 48.

56   E.g. Maffezini v. Spain, ICSID Case No. ARB/97/7, Decision on Jurisdiction, 25 January 2000, para. 63; Siemens v. Argentina, ICSID Case No. ARB/02/08, Decision on Jurisdiction, 3 August 2004, paras. 102, 103; Gas Natural v. Argentina, ICSID Case No. ARB/03/10, Decision on Jurisdiction, 17 June 2005, paras. 31, 49; National Grid v. Argentina, UNCITRAL, Award on Jurisdiction, 20 June 2006, paras. 92, 93.

57   Plama v. Bulgaria, ICSID Case No. ARB/03/24, Decision on Jurisdiction, 8 February 2005, paras. 198-200; Telenor v. Hungary, ICSID Case No. ARB/04/15, Award, 13 September 2006, para. 91; Berschader v. Russia, SCC Case No. 080/2004, Award, 21 April 2006, para. 206.

58   Okezie Chukwumerije, Interpreting Most-Favored-Nation Clauses in Investment Treaty Arbitrations, 8 J. World Investment & Trade 5 (2007) 597, 643; Ruth Teitelbaum, Who's

more recent decisions place a stronger emphasis on the wording of the MFN clause and its context in the IIA. One tribunal found that an MFN clause that expressly referred only to the standard of fair & equitable treatment was not meant to encompass dispute settlement provisions;[59] another tribunal held that a limited dispute settlement provision, allowing in a subparagraph for unlimited dispute settlement if the parties so agree, could not be expanded by the use of an MFN clause in the absence of such an agreement by the parties.[60] The shift away from policy considerations and the focus on a (con)textual interpretative approach marks a new – or third – generation of decisions on the application of MFN clauses to dispute settlement provisions. It also could signify a general trend toward applying a more objective interpretative approach to particularly disputed issues in investment arbitration.

The second possible interpretative trend – the use of Article 31(3)(c) of the VCLT – has yet to be discovered by investment arbitral jurisprudence. Nevertheless, it could be considered a trend as its current discussion in academic contributions is sure to influence arbitral jurisprudence. Article 31(3)(c) of the VCLT might be seen as the 'secret weapon' to tackle the fragmentation of international law.[61] Properly applied, it could lead to a systemic integration of investment law within the international legal system[62] and attenuate the growing criticism that the protection of investments necessarily leads to a neglect of other important international law standards. Article 31(3)(c) of the VCLT provides that "*any relevant rules of international law applicable in the relations between the parties*" shall be taken into account when interpreting a provision. But does this mean that investment arbitral tribunals deciding on a specific issue of investment law will have to take into account WTO law, human rights and environmental conventions, EU law and all conceivable rules of customary international law?[63] This will very much depend on an interpretation of the interpretative rule con-

Afraid of Maffezini? Recent Developments in the Interpretation of Most Favored Nation Clauses, 22 J. Int'l Arb. 3 (2005) 225, 233.

59   Renta 4 v. Russia, SCC Case No. 24/2007, Award on Jurisdiction, 20 March 2009, paras. 115, 118 et seq.

60   Tza Yap Shum v. Peru, ICSID Case No. ARB/07/6, Decision on Jurisdiction, 19 June 2009, para. 216. Similarly, Salini v. Jordan, ICSID Case No. ARB/02/13, Decision on Jurisdiction, 29 November 2004, para. 118.

61   Cf. Michael Waibel, International Investment Law and Treaty Interpretation, in Hofmann/Tams, International Investment Law and General International Law – From Clinical Isolation to Systemic Integration? (2011), p. 30.

62   Campbell McLachlan, The Principle of Systemic Integration and Article 31(3)(c) of the Vienna Convention, 54 Int'l & Comp. L. Quarterly 2 (2005) 279, 280 et seq.

63   For examples see Anne Van Aaken, Fragmentation of International Law: The Case of International Investment Law, 17 Finnish Yb Int'l L. (2008) 92, 112-124.

tained in Article 31(3)(c) of the VCLT. Without going into too much detail,[64] the terms *"relevant rules"* and *"applicable in relations between the parties"* play a particularly significant role. The latter implies that the rules to be taken into account in interpreting an investment treaty provision must actually be applicable between the two parties to an IIA. Thus, unless the contracting parties to an IIA are also joint parties to particular WTO agreements, human rights or environmental conventions, homogenization cannot take place.

The scope of application of Article 31(3)(c) VCLT widens if norms of customary international law are taken into account. Norms of customary international law also count among the relevant rules of international law to be considered[65] and it is argued that the parties leave every question not specifically addressed in the treaty to be answered by customary international law.[66] Proceeding on the assumption that IIAs – where they are silent on certain issues – are generally supplemented by customary international law, the second prong in the application of Article 31(3)(c) VCLT becomes exceedingly important. The question is: What are *"relevant rules"*?

An example from investment arbitral practice shall illustrate how Article 31(3)(c) VCLT could be used. So-called "local remedies clauses", still contained in some of the older, 'Calvo- or Soviet-type' IIAs, require the investor to first

---

64   For concise analyses see Campbell McLachlan, The Principle of Systemic Integration and Article 31(3)(c) of the Vienna Convention, 54 Int'l & Comp. L. Quarterly 2 (2005) 279; Duncan French, Treaty Interpretation and the Incorporation of Extraneous Legal Rules, 55 Int'l & Comp. L. Quarterly 2 (2006) 253; Thomas Wälde, Interpreting Investment Treaties, in Binder et al. (eds.), International Investment Law for the 21st Century, Essays in Honour of Christoph Schreuer (2009) 724, 769-777; Richard K. Gardiner, Treaty Interpretation (2008) 250-298; Anne Van Aaken, Defragmentation of Public International Law Through Interpretation: A Methodological Proposal, 16 Indiana J. of Global Legal Studies 2 (2009) 483; Anne Van Aaken, Fragmentation of International Law: The Case of International Investment Law, 17 Finnish Yb Int'l L. (2008) 92.

65   Kardassopoulos v. Georgia, ICSID Case No. ARB/05/18, Decision on Jurisdiction, 6 July 2007, para. 208; Campbell McLachlan, The Principle of Systemic Integration and Article 31(3)(c) of the Vienna Convention, 54 Int'l & Comp. L. Quarterly 2 (2005) 279, 312; Conclusion of the work of the Study Group on the Fragmentation of International Law: Difficulties arising from the Diversification and Expansion of International Law (2006) 7 ("ILC, Report on Fragmentation of International Law"), available at http://untreaty.un.org/ilc/texts/instruments/english/draft%20articles/1_9_2006.pdf; Anne Van Aaken, Defragmentation of Public International Law Through Interpretation: A Methodological Proposal, 16 Indiana J. of Global Legal Studies 2 (2009) 483, 498.

66   Campbell McLachlan, The Principle of Systemic Integration and Article 31(3)(c) of the Vienna Convention, 54 Int'l & Comp. L. Quarterly 2 (2005) 279, 311; ILC, Report on Fragmentation of International Law (2006) 7, para. 19 lit. a; George Pinson v. Mexico, Decision No. 1, 19 October 1928, RIAA Vol. V 327, 422 ("Toute convention internationale doit être réputée s'en référer tacitement au droit international commun, pour toutes les questions qu'elle ne résout pas elle-même en termes exprès et d'une façon différente.").

exhaust all available local remedies before instituting arbitral proceedings against the host state.[67] They are comparable to the rule of customary international law prescribing that an investor has to exhaust all local remedies before its home state can extend diplomatic protection by taking up the investor's claim against the host state.[68] However, in customary international law an exception is made to the prerequisite of the exhaustion of local remedies if the latter would constitute undue hardship.[69] This is the case if, *inter alia,* the exhaustion of local remedies is considered as obviously futile,[70] i.e. if remedies are not available or inadequate[71] or if it is obvious that the investor will not be able to achieve the aim of legal protection.[72] In the absence of a specific exception in a local remedies clause contained in an IIA, the question arises whether such clause could be interpreted pursuant to Article 31(3)(c) VCLT, making the customary international law exception applicable as a *"relevant rule of international law applicable in the relations between the parties."* This issue has not yet been decided, but at first sight the comparability of the mechanisms and the interests involved seem to argue in favor of applying the customary 'local remedies exception' when interpreting local remedies clauses in IIAs pursuant to Article 31(3)(c) VCLT.

A related question is then whether Article 31(3)(c) VCLT may be used to apply the 'local remedies exception' to so-called waiting clauses, found in nearly every modern IIA. Waiting clauses usually provide that an investor has to conduct good faith negotiations with the host state or at least "wait" for a period of about six months before the investor is allowed to institute arbitral proceedings.[73]

---

67   Art. 4(2) Denmark-Romania BIT ("If any dispute between an investor of one Contracting Party and the other Contracting Party concerning the amount of compensation continues to exist after the exhaustion of remedies available in the territory of the Contracting Party in which the investment was made, either Party to the dispute shall be entitled to submit the case for conciliation or arbitration [...]."); Art. 6 Netherlands-South Korea BIT; Art. 7(2) Romania-Sri Lanka BIT; Art. 9(1) Jamaica-UK BIT.

68   Interhandel Case, ICJ Reports (1959) 6, 27; Shaw, International Law (6th ed. 2008) 819.

69   Chittharanjan F. Amerasinghe, Local Remedies in International Law (2d ed. 2004) 200; Finnish Shipowners Arbitration, Award, 9 May 1934, RIAA Vol. III 1479, 1496.

70   Biwater Gauff v. Tanzania, ICSID Case No. ARB/05/22, Award, 24 July 2008, para. 343; Christoph Schreuer, Travelling the BIT Route – Of Waiting Periods, Umbrella Clauses and Forks in the Road, 5 J. World Investment & Trade 2 (2004) 231, 238.

71   ILC, Draft Articles on Diplomatic Protection with Commentaries (2006), Art. 15 lit. a, in YBILC (2006 II) 22, 76; Loewen v. USA, ICSID Case No. ARB(AF)/98/3, Award, 26 June 2003, paras. 168 et seq.; Chittharanjan F. Amerasinghe, Local Remedies in International Law (2d ed. 2004) 203.

72   Finnish Shipowners Arbitration, Award, 9 May 1934, RIAA Vol. III 1479, 1543; Panevezys-Saldutiskis Railway Case, Judgment, 28 February 1939, PCIJ Ser. A/B, No. 76, 18.

73   Christoph Schreuer, Travelling the BIT Route – Of Waiting Periods, Umbrella Clauses and Forks in the Road, 5 J. World Investment & Trade 2 (2004) 231, 232; Art. 8(1) UK Model-BIT (2005) ("Disputes [...] which have not been amicably settled shall, after a pe-

Could an exception from the waiting period of six months be made by taking into account the customary 'local remedies exception' when interpreting the waiting clause pursuant to Article 31(3)(c) VCLT? Quite a number of tribunals suggest that compliance with waiting periods is not required if negotiations with the host states were futile.[74] One tribunal even made explicit reference to the 'local remedies exception'.[75] Yet, it seems necessary to take a more detailed look at whether this exception can be considered a *"relevant rule...applicable"* in conjunction with a waiting clause in a BIT. A logical prerequisite for the applicability of the exception as a relevant rule seems to be that there is a similarity of facts which calls for the same or at least similar legal consequences. Or as the *RosInvest v. Russia* tribunal put it

> "When it comes to Article 31(3) (c), [...] '[a]pplicable in the relations between the parties' must be taken as a reference to rules of international law that condition the performance of the specific rights and obligations stipulated in the treaty – or else it would amount to a general licence to override the treaty terms that would be quite incompatible with the general spirit of the Vienna Convention as a whole."[76]

Taking this into account, the purpose of waiting clauses and the local remedies rule at first sight seems comparable insofar as both envisage the possibility for states to redress the wrongs done to an investor before an international proceeding against the state can be initiated.[77] However, the factual situation underlying the two provisions makes comparability appear questionable. Fully implemented, the exhaustion of local remedies rule requires the investor to pass through all available local court instances, which demands a large amount of time, cost and effort. If the local court system does not provide for effective re-

---

riod of three months from written notification of a claim, be submitted to international arbitration..."); Art. 10 German Model-BIT (2009); Art. 8 French Model-BIT (2006).

74 Biwater Gauff v. Tanzania, ICSID Case No. ARB/05/22, Award, 24 July 2008, para. 343; Bayindir v. Pakistan, ICSID Case No. ARB/03/29, Decision on Jurisdiction, 14 November 2005, para. 102; Lauder v. Czech Republic, UNCITRAL, Final Award, 3 September 2001, para. 188; SGS v. Pakistan, ICSID Case No.ARB/01/13, Decision on Jurisdiction, 6 August 2003, para. 184; Ethyl v. Canada, UNCITRAL (NAFTA), Award on Jurisdiction, 24 June 1998, paras. 77, 84.

75 Ethyl v. Canada, UNCITRAL (NAFTA), Award on Jurisdiction, 24 June 1998, paras. 84 ("It is argued, therefore, that no purpose would be served by any further suspension of Claimant's right to proceed. This rule is analogized to the international law requirement of exhaustion of remedies, which is disregarded when it is demonstrated that in fact no remedy was available and any attempt at exhaustion would have been futile.").

76 RosInvest v. Russia, SCC Case No. 079/2005, Award on Jurisdiction, October 2007, para. 39. Similarly Oil Platforms Case, ICJ, Judgment, 6 November 2003, Separate Opinion Judge Higgins, ICJ Reports (2003) 225, 237, para. 46; Richard K. Gardiner, Treaty Interpretation (2008) 260; Duncan French, Treaty Interpretation and the Incorporation of Extraneous Legal Rules, 55 Int'l & Comp. L. Quarterly 2 (2006) 281, 304 et seq.

77 Burlington Ressources v. Ecuador, ICSID Case No. ARB/08/5, Decision on Jurisdiction, 2 June 2010, para. 315.

dress, it constitutes a significant hardship for the investor to nevertheless have to exhaust all means of appeal. In contrast, waiting clauses are mainly directed towards an amicable solution of the dispute. If negotiations remain futile, the investor simply has to wait until the rest of the time limit has expired before initiating arbitral proceedings. In view of the average length of investment arbitration proceedings of 3 years and more,[78] a time limit of normally 6 months does not seem to be unduly burdensome, at least if one considers that this period is usually used to prepare an effective request for arbitration.[79] Therefore, the burden on the investor imposed by the local remedies rule seems different and considerably higher than the one imposed by a waiting clause. Consequently, upon closer inspection it appears difficult to consider this a *"relevant rule"* and to read the 'local remedies exception' in customary international law into a waiting clause by way of interpretation pursuant to Article 31(3)(c) VCLT.

Whether future tribunals will follow this distinction in applying Article 31(3)(c) VCLT remains to be seen. Yet, the examples show that there is certainly a scope of application for Article 31(3)(c) VCLT in international investment law, the boundaries of which still have to be discovered and refined. The successful systemic integration of investment law with other public international law regimes will certainly be aided by a better understanding and a more frequent use of Article 31(3)(c) VCLT.

F. Conclusion

The problem of heterogeneity of arbitral awards in investment arbitration is partly due to the divergent approaches to treaty interpretation. As *Waibel* has shown, a more systematic and objective interpretative approach might provide an adequate remedy. Yet, a closer look at the structure of investment arbitration and its actors reveals that there are a number of particularities which probably will prevent interpretative results from ever reaching the uniformity of the ICJ or WTO system. Nevertheless, the debate about the proper interpretation of MFN-clauses seems to indicate a shift in the interpretative approach from policy considerations towards a more objective and contextual approach. A greater focus on Article 31(3)(c) of the VCLT in the interpretation of IIAs might lead to harmonization with other areas of public international law. Until these potential trends become the norm, treaty interpretation in investment arbitration will certainly remain subject to much interesting debate.

---

78   This is true at least in the case of ICSID proceedings, see Anthony C. Sinclair, ICSID Arbitration: How Long Does it Take? 4 Global Arb. Rev. 5 (2009) 18, 19.
79   Christopher Dugan et al., Investor-State Arbitration (2008) 118.

International Investment Law and General International Law – From Clinical Isolation to Systemic Integration?

Comments by *Christoph Schreuer**

A. *Uniformity and Coherence in Treaty Interpretation*

Much of what we have heard from Michael Waibel was focused on the capacity of the Vienna Convention on the Law of Treaties (VCLT) to achieve coherence in the interpretation of investment treaties. In this context, it is already a major achievement that the principles of interpretation contained in Articles 31-33 of the VCLT are today practically universally accepted. Let us not forget that these principles were at one time hotly contested not least during their drafting in Vienna in 1969.

At the same time, I have rather limited confidence in the capacity of the VCLT to produce predictable results and hence to contribute to uniformity in the interpretation of treaties. Different tribunals, even if they faithfully apply Articles 31-33 of the VCLT, are likely to reach different results. Therefore, the usefulness of the VCLT as a tool for the harmonization of practice in the application of investment treaties is limited. But there is no doubt that the VCLT's provisions on treaty interpretation are a useful starting point. Perhaps they should be regarded not so much as rules that will lead to inescapable results but rather as an intellectual checklist that should be used when applying treaties. Treaty interpretation is not a mechanical process that will automatically lead to the correct result if only the right method is applied. The old adage that treaty interpretation is not a science but an art is still very true today.

B. *Effective and Restrictive Interpretation*

The term «effective interpretation» is somewhat ambivalent. It can mean two quite different things. One meaning is that every treaty provision should be interpreted so as to give it some meaning. In other words it should not be deprived of all effect. This is a perfectly sensible maxim. The other meaning of «effective

*   Professor Dr Christoph Schreuer, Of Counsel Wolf Theiss Rechtsanwälte, Vienna; formerly Professor of Public International Law, University of Vienna.

interpretation» is a purported principle of extensive or expansive interpretation. Under this maxim treaties should be interpreted so as to give them maximum effect. Such a suggestion is of doubtful value and has not been widely accepted in practice.

In international investment law «restrictive» or «effective» methods of interpretation have a particular connotation. Since investment treaties are focused on the rights of investors their restrictive interpretation will tend to favour host States. Conversely, their effective interpretation will typically favour investors. Although tribunals have at times subscribed to one or the other method of interpretation[1] the prevalent and clearly better view appears to be a balanced approach that rejects both these methods. The Tribunal in *Mondev* v. *United States*[2] said:

> 43. In the Tribunal's view, there is no principle either of extensive or restrictive interpretation of jurisdictional provisions in treaties. In the end the question is what the relevant provisions mean, interpreted in accordance with the applicable rules of interpretation of treaties.[3]

C. Object and Purpose

A related issue is the use of a treaty's object and purpose as reflected in its preamble.[4] This method is often seen as favouring the investor.[5] But if we take a closer look at preambles of investment treaties we see that their object and purpose extends beyond the simple protection of investments to the improvement of economic cooperation between States and, perhaps most importantly, to economic development. These different goals are entirely compatible. The Tribunal in *Amco* v. *Indonesia*[6] pointed out that investment protection was also in the longer term interest of host States:

---

1   For examples of tribunals subscribing to a restrictive method of interpretation see: SGS v. Pakistan, Decision on Jurisdiction, 6 August 2003, 8 ICSID Reports 406, para. 171; Noble Ventures v. Romania, Award, 12 October 2005, para. 55. For examples of tribunals favouring an interpretation that gives full effect to investor rights see: SGS v. Philippines, Decision on Jurisdiction, 29 January 2004, 8 ICSID Reports 518, para. 116; Eureko v. Poland, Partial Award, 19 August 2005, 12 ICSID Reports 335, para. 248.
2   Mondev v. United States of America, Award, 11 October 2002, 6 ICSID Reports 192.
3   At para. 43. Footnote omitted.
4   Plama v. Bulgaria, Decision on Jurisdiction, 8 February 2005, para. 193.
5   Noble Ventures v. Romania, Award, 12 October 2005, para. 52; Siemens v. Argentina, Decision on Jurisdiction, 3 August 2004, para. 81.
6   Amco v. Indonesia, Decision on Jurisdiction, 25 September 1983, 1 ICSID Reports 389.

...to protect investments is to protect the general interest of development and of developing countries.[7]

From the perspective of the principles of interpretation as enshrined in the VCLT there is no reason to criticize tribunals for relying on a treaty's object and purpose. The basic rule, as reflected in the first paragraph of Article 31, lists object and purpose as a primary principle of treaty interpretation together with good faith, ordinary meaning and context.

D. Official Interpretations

I am a bit more sceptical than Michael Waibel of the role of States officially interpreting treaties in pending disputes between investors and host States. Obviously, a unilateral assertion by a disputing State party is of limited value. Apart from the fact that the State is likely to have an evident interest in the acceptance of a particular interpretation by the tribunal, arguments presented in litigation are typically drafted by the State's counsel. They do not necessarily reflect the meaning that the States Parties had in mind when concluding the treaty. It is an interesting question whether pleadings on behalf of a State put forward by a private law firm may be regarded as State practice in the sense of the VCLT[8] or for purposes of developing customary international law.

In most cases there will be no available information concerning the circumstances of a BIT's conclusion. BITs are frequently based on model texts with limited negotiations. There are typically no records that can be used by way of *travaux préparatoires*.

In *Aguas del Tunari* v.*Bolivia*[9] the Tribunal sought information from the investor's home State on certain aspects of the BIT's interpretation. But it did not find the information thus obtained helpful.[10] In *CME* v. *The Czech Republic* the two States, parties to the BIT, issued a joint statement on a question of interpretation pending before the tribunal.[11] It is unclear to what extent that statement had an influence on the Tribunal's decision.

---

7   At para. 23. See also Award, 20 November 1984, 1 ICSID Reports 413, at para. 249.
8   Article 31(3)(b) VCLT refers to subsequent practice in the application of a treaty.
9   Aguas del Tunari v Bolivia, Decision on Jurisdiction, 21 October 2005.
10 At paras. 47, 249-263.
11 In CME v The Czech Republic the BIT between the Czech Republic and the Netherlands provided for «consultations» with a view to resolving any issue of interpretation and application of the Treaty. Pursuant to this procedure, the Netherlands and the Czech Republic issued «Agreed Minutes» containing a «common position» on the BIT's interpretation, after the Tribunal had issued a Partial Award. See Final Award, 14 March 2003, 9 ICSID Reports 264 at paras. 87-93, 437, 504.

The NAFTA has a mechanism whereby the Free Trade Commission (FTC), a body composed of representatives of the three States parties, can adopt binding interpretations of the treaty.[12] The FTC has made use of this method in July 2001 in interpreting the concepts of «fair and equitable treatment» and «full protection and security» under Article 1105 of the NAFTA.[13]

Some BITs offer an institutional mechanism to obtain authentic interpretations of their meaning.[14] But this method has serious drawbacks. States are prone to attempt to influence proceedings to which they are parties or are likely to become parties. A mechanism whereby a party to a dispute is able to influence the outcome of judicial proceedings by issuing an official interpretation to the detriment of the other party is incompatible with principles of a fair procedure and is hence undesirable. This is true even if the official interpretation requires also the assent of the other party or parties to the treaty. In addition, a system involving hundreds of separate treaties each with its own mechanism for an official interpretation is unlikely to lead to a harmonization of interpretations and to systemic integration.

---

12 NAFTA Article 2001(1): «The Parties hereby establish the Free Trade Commission, comprising cabinet-level representatives of the Parties or their designees.».
    NAFTA Article 1131(2): «An interpretation by the Commission of a provision of this Agreement shall be binding on a Tribunal established under this Section.»
13 FTC Note of Interpretation of 31 July 2001.
14 See Article 30(3) of the US Model BIT of 2004.

Denunciation of the ICSID Convention under the General International Law of Treaties

Antonios Tzanakopoulos[*]

A. ICSID Denunciation in Context: The Bolivarian Alternative to Free Trade

On 2 May 2007 Bolivia 'denounced' (or, better, withdrew from)[1] the 1965 Washington Convention on the Settlement of Investment Disputes between States and Nationals of other States[2] ('ICSID Convention' or 'Convention'; 'IC-SID' or 'Centre' refers to the International Centre for the Settlement of Investment Disputes created by the Convention). Even if Bolivia became the first state ever to withdraw from the ICSID Convention, its move should hardly have come as an utter shock to those following developments in South America. Even less so should the subsequent withdrawal from the Convention of Ecuador, on 6 July 2009.[3] These unprecedented withdrawals have brought to the forefront a host of legal problems regarding withdrawal from the ICSID Convention and its effects, particularly with respect to consent to ICSID arbitration expressed in a Bilateral Investment Treaty ('BIT').

These legal problems cannot be dealt with in isolation, however. It is also necessary to present the context within which the withdrawals from ICSID have taken place. The roots of the crisis go back to the beginning of this century. It all started with the establishment of ALBA, a 'Bolivarian Alternative for Latin America and the Caribbean' (*Alternativa Bolivariana para la América Latina y el Caribe*). An alternative to what, would be the first question to ask, and the answer is strikingly simple, as unfathomable as it may seem to some: an alternative to the neoliberal model of integration, originally planned as a response to ALCA (*Área de Libre Comercio de las Américas*), the US-sponsored Free Trade Area of the Americas. The 'Bolivarian alternative' envisioned regional integration that was to be founded on solidarity and the promotion and protection of social

---

[*]   Dr Antonios Tzanakopoulos, Lecturer in Public International Law, University of Glasgow.
[1]   Cf on the use of terms A Aust Modern Treaty Law and Practice (2d ed CUP Cambridge 2007) 277.
[2]   See the Notification of 1 May 2007 by the Bolivian Foreign Affairs Ministry addressed to the President of the World Bank in (2007) 46 ILM 973.
[3]   ICSID News Release of 9 July 2009, available at http://www.worldbank.org/icsid.

rights, in particular (but not exclusively) with respect to trade liberalization.[4] Since the first proposals for a 'Bolivarian alternative' in 2001, its establishment in 2004 by an agreement between Venezuela and Cuba,[5] the establishment of a Bank (Banco de ALBA),[6] the adoption of a common currency[7] (*Sistema Unitario de Compensación Regional*, SUCRE),[8] and a number of yearly summits, which also saw the 'Bolivarian Alternative' renamed as the 'Bolivarian Alliance for the Peoples of Our America' (*Alianza Bolivariana para los Pueblos de Nuestra América*; hereinafter: 'ALBA') at the Sixth Summit in 2009,[9] the Organization has now grown to include eight states: Venezuela, Cuba, Bolivia, Nicaragua, Dominica, St Vincent and the Grenadines, Ecuador, and Antigua and Barbuda.[10]

In the context of ALBA, agreements have been concluded to implement the spirit of solidarity and social rights in regional (economic, among others) integration: within the context of *Misión Barrio Adentro*, an oil-for-doctors pro-

---

4　See the statement by the President of Venezuela in What is the ALBA—TCP?, available at http://www.alternativabolivariana.org/modules.php?name=Content&pa=showpage& pid=2080.

5　See the Agreement between the President of the Bolivarian Republic of Venezuela and the President of the Council of State of Cuba for the Application of the Bolivarian Alternative for the Americas (done at Havana on 14 December 2004), available at http:// www.alternativabolivariana.org/modules.php?name=Content&pa=showpage&pid=2079.

6　See the Memorandum of Understanding between the Republic of Bolivia, the Republic of Cuba, the Republic of Nicaragua and the Bolivarian Republic of Venezuela for the Creation of the Bank of the ALBA (done at Caracas on 6 June 2007), available at http://www.alternativabolivariana.org/modules.php?name=Content&pa=showpage&pid= 1996.

7　Or unit of account, currently still a virtual currency, to be precise.

8　See for the constitutive treaty of SUCRE: Ley Aprobatoria del Tratado Constitutivo del Sistema Unitario de Compensación Regional de Pagos Gaceta Oficial No 5.955 Extraordinario (13 January 2010), available at http://150.188.8.226/db/bibpgr/edocs/2010 /5955.pdf; see also M Al Attar & R Miller 'Towards an Emancipatory International Law: The Bolivarian Reconstruction' (2010) 31 Third World Quarterly 347, 354; Al-Jazeera (17 October 2009) 'Bolivia Summit Adopts New Currency', available at http://english.aljazeera.net/news/americas/2009/10/2009101712255748516.html; S Mather 'Venezuela Pays for First ALBA Trade with Ecuador in New Regional Currency' venezuelanalysis.com (7 July 2010), available at http://venezuelanalysis.com/news/5480.

9　See the statement by the Venezuelan Ministry of Communication and Information of 24 June 2009, available at http://www.vtv.gob.ve/noticias-nacionales/19957.

10　Statement by the President of Venezuela (n4). Honduras also joined ALBA in 2008 but withdrew in January 2010: see La Tribuna (13 January 2010) 'Congreso aprueba retiro de la ALBA', available at http://www.latribuna.hn/web2.0/?p=85566, following, conspicuously, a coup which ousted the left-wing Zelaya government: see El Tiempo (13 January 2010) 'El Parlamento de Honduras Ratifica Su Salida de la ALBA', available at http://www.eltiempo.com/archivo/documento/CMS-6939247.

　　The official acronym is ALBA-TCP. The latter stands for 'Peoples' Treaty of Commerce' (Tratado de Comercio de los Pueblos) and complements the official name of the Organization.

gramme has been implemented between Cuba and Venezuela, providing the former with cheap oil and the latter with thousands of doctors in exchange;[11] *Operación Milagro* has consolidated cooperation in the field of healthcare.[12] These first successful experiments were extended to form a general trade-in-kind policy between ALBA states, catering to local needs.[13]

This much is necessary in order to contextualize both statements by ALBA states that they intend to withdraw from the IMF and the World Bank,[14] as well as the actual withdrawal of Bolivia and Ecuador from ICSID. Latin America was always particularly cautious with the ICSID Convention, having voted *en bloc* against the World Bank Board of Governors resolution instructing the Board of Directors to prepare a Convention in 1964,[15] and having waited for many years (and many a regime change) until it saw the first states from the region join ICSID. More broadly, the region having given birth to the Calvo doctrine,[16] and having participated in the attempt to establish a 'new international economic order',[17] has always been imbued with a spirit of defiance and change. In the instance, Latin American states have decided to challenge the virtual monopoly of the neoliberal economic paradigm, in part through questioning the necessity for global participation in a number of its structures. This challenge is taking place –

---

11 Al Attar & Miller (n8) 352; JM Feinsilver 'Médicos por petróleo: La diplomacia médica cubana recibe una pequeña ayuda de sus amigos' (2008) 216 Nueva Sociedad 107, 110 seq. See for another evaluation R Jones 'Hugo Chavez's Health-Care Programme Misses its Goals' (2008) 371 Lancet 1988, which concludes however that '[w]hatever its failings … Barrio Adentro I is providing health care to a sector that previously went largely ignored'.

12 Al Attar & Miller (n8) 352.

13 ibid 354.Cf also the establishment of Petrocaribe, which allows purchase of Venezuelan oil for a number of states (but without allowing access to private entities) on preferential terms, including low interest rates (1%) and the ability to pay, in part, in goods and services: http://www.petrocaribe.org and http://www.pdvsa.com/index.php?tpl=interface.en/ design/biblioteca/readdoc.tpl.html&newsid_obj_id=6213&newsid_temas=111 section IV (Financing). A proposal has been put forward to establish Petroamérica, which would cover the whole of the South American continent: see http://www.petrocaribe.org.

14 See E Gaillard 'The Denunciation of the ICSID Convention' (2007) 237:122 NYLJ 6 (26 June).

15 A Broches 'The Convention on the Settlement of Investment Disputes Between States and Nationals of Other States' (1972) 136 RdC 331, 348.

16 See ibid 373; for a connection between the Calvo doctrine and recent Latin American practice in investment law see OM Garibaldi 'Carlos Calvo Redivivus: The Rediscovery of the Calvo Doctrine in the Era of Investment Treaties' (2006) 3(5) TDM.

17 General Assembly Resolution 3201 (S-VI) of 1 May 1974 (UN Doc A/RES/S-6/3201). For the requiem: TW Wälde 'A Requiem for the "New International Economic Order": The Rise and Fall of Paradigms in International Economic Law' in N Al-Nauimi and R Meese (eds) International Legal Issues Arising under the United Nations Decade of International Law (Nijhoff The Hague 1995) 1301.

appropriately – amidst a global economic and financial crisis that is bound to see more questioning what a few years back had seemed like revered orthodoxy.

The purpose of this brief contribution is not to engage with the political or economic arguments for or against ICSID withdrawal or, more broadly, for a new economic vision, for an alternative. It is rather to approach the question of the legal effects of withdrawal from ICSID under the general international law of treaties. In this, it aims to draw some tentative conclusions about the interface between international investment law and general international law in the specific area of withdrawal from treaties. The context already provided is important in order to situate the discussion. In what follows, the legal problems surrounding ICSID withdrawal are set out. Sections B and C argue that the legal problems identified are due, in large measure, to the tendency for propounding exclusively self-contained interpretations of the ICSID Convention, which cannot yield any clear result. These leave all competing positions plausible, but make none compelling. Section D explores how the general international law of treaties may come to bear on the interpretation of the ICSID Convention provisions on withdrawal and its effects. Section E finally argues that 'residual fallback'[18] on general international law allows for determining the proper effects of withdrawal from the ICSID Convention.

B. The Uncertainty of Self-Contained Interpretation of the ICSID Convention

General rules on treaty termination cannot, however, be the starting-point of the debate. In fact, on the face of it, they might add little to the special rules found in the ICSID Convention itself, which addresses questions of withdrawal and its effects. Withdrawal from the ICSID Convention is allowed under the terms of the Convention. Article 71 provides that '[a]ny Contracting State may denounce this Convention by written notice to the depositary of this Convention. The denunciation shall take effect six months after receipt of such notice.'[19] This express clause (common to many special regimes) is complemented by a curious, at first sight, and much more complex 'survival clause'. Article 72 safeguards 'rights or obligations under this Convention … arising out of consent to the jurisdiction of the Centre', which are not to be affected by denunciation.[20] The provision purports to ensure that those rights and obligations created by consent to the Cen-

---

18   The term is used here in the same sense as in B Simma and D Pulkowski 'Of Planets and the Universe: Self-Contained Regimes in International Law' (2006) 17 EJIL 483.

19   Cf Article 54(a) VCLT and further below Section E.

20   Cf Article 70 VCLT and further below Section E.

tre's jurisdiction, significantly the right to bring a case before an ICSID arbitral tribunal, survive withdrawal from the Convention.

While the general thrust of this provision is clear, its precise interpretation is not. Uncertainties relate to the meaning of the terms 'arising out of consent to the jurisdiction of the Centre'. 'Consent to the jurisdiction of the Centre' is defined in Article 25 as consent of 'the parties to the dispute', ie of a state party to the ICSID Convention on the one hand and of a national of another state party to the Convention on the other. The main focus in the literature has been on the meaning of 'consent' in Articles 25 and 72 of the ICSID Convention. If the term is to have the same meaning under both provisions, then only in cases where consent has been 'perfected', ie has been given in writing by both 'parties to the dispute', does a right 'arising out of consent' exist under the Convention to be safeguarded by Article 72. If, on the other hand, consent of both parties, ie mutual consent, is only required under Article 25, while unilateral consent by one of the parties is sufficient for Article 72 to apply, then a unilateral expression of consent to IC-SID jurisdiction might survive withdrawal from the ICSID Convention and create jurisdiction for the Centre.

The different interpretations do not entail divergent results where jurisdiction depends on an investment contract between investor and host state – in this case, consent is either perfected, or has not been given at all. However, where (as in the vast majority of cases) a state 'consents' to jurisdiction by entering into a BIT, the question is of crucial relevance. If a BIT is understood as constituting consent under the ICSID Convention (and thus as creating a right for the investor to arbitrate under ICSID and an obligation for the state to submit to it), then withdrawal from ICSID will not affect that right for as long as the BIT's provisions remain operable.[21] Given that most BITs provide that BIT protection will survive termination of the BIT for anywhere between five and twenty years,[22] it would appear that ICSID withdrawal has little effect if not accompanied by *en bloc* denunciation of BITs that include ICSID arbitration clauses and the passage of some considerable time. The main question thus is if a withdrawing state's promises to arbitrate under ICSID, which are provided for in various BITs of that

---

21 This is subject to the caveat that the specific provision regarding investor-state arbitration in the BIT will be worded in such a way as to constitute 'unqualified consent': Gaillard (n14) 8; or a 'firm offer': M Nolan and FG Sourgens 'The Interplay Between State Consent to ICSID Arbitration and Denunciation of the ICSID Convention: The (Possible) Venezuela Case Study' (2007) TDM provisional 20 seq.

22 See eg 2004 US Model BIT Article 22(3); UK Model BIT Article 14; Germany Model BIT Article 14(3); Netherlands Model BIT Article 14(3); Switzerland Model BIT Article 11; Turkey Model BIT Article IX(4); South Africa Model BIT Article 12(3); India Model BIT Article 15(2); PRC Model BIT Article 13(4), all available from UNCTAD Investment Instruments Online at http://www.unctadxi.org/templates/DocSearch____780.aspx.

state, are enough to establish the jurisdiction of the Centre even after the notification of withdrawal from the Convention.

Detailed arguments have been put forward with respect to the meaning of 'consent' in the ICSID Convention and in Article 72 in particular.[23] The basic positions are the two already referred to above: one argues that 'consent' has a special meaning in Article 72 of the ICSID Convention, different from that of 'consent of the parties to the dispute' in Article 25, and encompasses a unilateral offer of consent in a BIT, which results in rights (for the investor) and obligations (for the state) being established *under the ICSID Convention* that survive a state's withdrawal from it.[24] The other position is that 'consent' in Article 72 has the same meaning as in Article 25, ie it requires *both* parties to the dispute to have consented to ICSID jurisdiction.[25] To the extent that this is not the case, withdrawal from ICSID constitutes at the same time withdrawal of the unilateral offer to arbitrate provided elsewhere, ie in a domestic law or in a BIT.[26] The result is that, unless the offer has already been taken up – creating an arbitration agreement and thus giving rise to a 'right' and a concomitant state obligation *under the ICSID Convention* – ICSID withdrawal means that investors can no longer accept the withdrawing state's offer of consent to ICSID arbitration expressed in a BIT that continues in force.

At first sight, both interpretations of the term 'consent' in Article 72 of the ICSID Convention are indeed plausible. It makes sense to understand 'consent' as having the same meaning throughout the Convention, and thus to mean *mutual* consent in Article 72, much like it admittedly does in Article 25, the article

23 For a convenient overview of the basic positions see MT Montanes 'Introductory Note to Bolivia's Denunciation of the Convention on the Settlement of Investment Disputes between States and Nationals of Other States' (2007) 46 ILM 969, 970.

24 Depending, however, on the particular wording of the offer in the BIT: see the caveat in n21 above. See generally, among others, Gaillard (n14) 6 seq; Nolan and Sourgens (n21); eidem 'Limits of Consent—Arbitration without Privity and Beyond' in MÁ Fernández-Ballesteros & D Arias (eds) Liber Amicorum Bernardo Cremades (La Ley Madrid 2010) 873; C Tietje et al 'Once and Forever? The Legal Effects of a Denunciation of ICSID' (2008) 74 Beiträge zum Transnationalen Wirtschaftsrecht and (2009) 6(1) TDM; OM Garibaldi 'On the Denunciation of the ICSID Convention, Consent to ICSID Jurisdiction, and the Limits of the Contract Analogy' in C Binder et al (eds) International Investment Law for the 21st Century—Essays in Honour of Christoph Schreuer (OUP Oxford 2009) 251; and cf idem (2009) 6(1) TDM.

25 Primarily C Schreuer 'Denunciation of the ICSID Convention and Consent to Arbitration' in M Waibel et al (eds) The Backlash against Investment Arbitration: Perceptions and Reality (Kluwer Alphen aan den Rijn 2010) 353; idem et al (eds) The ICSID Convention—A Commentary (2d ed CUP Cambridge 2009) 71 seq and, crucially, 1279 seq (hereinafter 'Schreuer Commentary').

26 See idem 'Consent to Arbitration' in P Muchlinski et al (eds) The Oxford Handbook of International Investment Law (OUP Oxford 2008) 830, 835; contra in part Garibaldi (n24) 263-270.

that can be argued to *define* consent as an essential condition for ICSID jurisdiction under the Convention,[27] or in Articles 26[28] and 27 for example,[29] which establish rights and obligations arising out of that consent (the obligations not to resort to any other remedy and not to extend diplomatic protection).[30] On the other hand, Article 72 does not expressly refer to such 'mutual consent' as do Articles 25 to 27 – *a contrario* it is plausible that it may be interpreted as referring to *unilateral* consent,[31] particularly since the Convention generally seems to understand 'consent' as unilateral consent in some instances and as mutual consent in others.[32] Further, provision of consent in a BIT was not really contemplated during the preparation of the ICSID Convention. Preparatory works thus are of limited assistance when trying to decide which of the two interpretations should be preferred. This also impacts on any attempt to ascribe systemic preferences under the ICSID Convention for one or the other interpretation. The issue then cannot be convincingly solved through a self-contained interpretation of the Convention based on the text of the provision, its systematic context or the drafting history.[33] This is further demonstrated in the consideration of the Convention's object and purpose as decisive for the correct interpretation, in Section C below.

C. The Limits of Self-Contained Interpretation

Some streams of the argumentation regarding the effects of ICSID withdrawal seem to focus on the object and purpose of the ICSID Convention as decisive for selecting between the possible interpretations of 'consent' in Article 72 that emerge from the consideration of the text, context, and drafting history.[34] The object and purpose of the Convention is admittedly of crucial importance for the interpretation of the relevant ICSID provisions. Interpretation under the customa-

---

27 Schreuer Commentary 190 [374]-[376]; cf n44 below.
28 ibid 353 [7].
29 ibid 425 [33].
30 ibid 1281-1282 [11].
31 Cf M Paparinskis 'Investment Arbitration and the Law of Countermeasures' (2008) 79 BYIL 264, 305-306 and fn 198.
32 See Garibaldi (n24) 258.
33 For a rather extreme confirmation of this point see K Rastegar 'Denouncing ICSID' in Binder et al (n24) 278, 282 seq. The inadequacy of self-contained interpretation in the instance is treated by the author as a symptom (or yet another expression) of the indeterminacy permeating all (international) law.
34 See for a similar assessment Garibaldi (n24) 255.

ry international law of treaties, as reflected in the Vienna Convention,[35] involves ordinary meaning, context, and object and purpose taken together, as if thrown in a crucible.[36] As such, while object and purpose cannot be relied upon in isolation to interpret a treaty provision, it may allow for deciding between possible interpretations of the terms in their context.[37]

However, there is a tendency on the part of those relying on object and purpose as decisive to assume, without much discussion, that the Convention has a decidedly pro-investor object and purpose, ie that its core objective is the accommodation and broadest possible (even if only procedural) protection of foreign private investors.[38] This then allows teleology-heavy (and investment-specific) interpretation of the Convention provisions on withdrawal. But the object and purpose of the Convention is not so obviously geared towards protecting the investor against the state. The protection was meant to extend to state interests as well. Indeed, a treaty can have many objects and purposes.[39] If object and purpose is usually to be sought in the preamble or some general clause at the beginning of the treaty,[40] it might be worth highlighting how strikingly non-committal the ICSID Convention preamble is. In view of this uncertainty, it is worth examining the object and purpose of the Convention a little bit closer.

The object and purpose of international investment arbitration in general may indeed be to create a stable and positive climate for international private investment, inter alia by removing relevant disputes between host states and foreign investors from the presumably non-neutral domestic fora.[41] However that is ex-

---

35 Article 31 VCLT. See as to customary status generally J-M Sorel 'Article 31—Convention de 1969' in O Corten and P Klein (eds) Les Conventions de Vienne sur le droit des traités—Commentaire article par article (Bruylant Bruxelles 2006) 1289, 1296 [10] seq.

36 See eg R Gardiner Treaty Interpretation (OUP Oxford 2008) 9-10.

37 See also n51 below and accompanying text.

38 See eg Tietje et al (n24) 21 seq; Nolan and Sourgens (n21) 6-7; W Alschner et al Legal Basis and Effect of Denunciation under International Investment Agreements (2010) 27 [65], available at http://www.graduateinstitute.ch. Even C Schreuer 'International Centre for the Settlement of Investment Disputes (ICSID)' in R Wolfrum (ed) Max Planck Encyclopedia of Public International Law (OUP Oxford) [3]-[4], available at http://www.mpepil.com, argues along these lines, relying on the ICSID preamble no less, without however employing such a determination of object and purpose to resolve the question here at hand.

39 ME Villiger Commentary on the 1969 Vienna Convention on the Law of Treaties (Nijhoff Leiden 2009) 427 [11].

40 ibid 428 [13]; see also generally M Gounelle La motivation des actes juridiques en droit international public (Pedone Paris 1979) 38 seq.

41 See eg briefly C Schreuer 'Investment Disputes' in Wolfrum (n38) [3], [15], [21]. As to the claim that investment arbitration 'depoliticizes' investment disputes see generally M Paparinskis 'The Limits of Depoliticization in Contemporary Investor-State Arbitration' in J Crawford & S Nouwen (eds) Select Proceedings of the European Society of Interna-

plicitly neither the purpose of the ICSID Convention nor the expectation of the contracting states.[42] Rather, the ICSID Convention object and purpose in particular is to provide a *facility* for those states that wish to encourage foreign investment by opting, voluntarily, for the settlement of investment disputes by arbitration in the particular shape and form offered by the Centre.[43] This is evidenced by the centrality, in the Convention, of the notion of consent of *both* parties to the submission of disputes to the Centre. Irrespective of how the matter is understood within Article 72, it is clear that under Article 25, consent, the fundamental jurisdictional condition and the 'cornerstone' of the jurisdiction of the Centre,[44] means, 'mutual consent' of the parties to the dispute.[45] Once both parties have given their consent, this cannot be withdrawn unilaterally.[46] The general neutrality of the Convention as between host state and investor is confirmed by the drafters' stated objective to achieve a reasonable balance between the two classes of litigants,[47] as well as by the preamble.[48]

If it is established that the object and purpose of the ICSID Convention in general is not to provide particular procedural benefits to foreign investors against host states, but rather to create a facility that can be used by states to provide such benefits to foreign investors if they so wish, it illuminates the particular provisions of Articles 25(1) and 72 regarding irrevocability of mutually expressed consent. The last period of paragraph 1 of Article 25, which provides that '[w]hen both parties have given their consent, no party may withdraw its consent unilaterally' merely restates the principle that *pacta sunt*, indeed, *servanda*, and extends its reach to cover the agreement to arbitrate under ICSID between a host state and a foreign investor. Article 72 complements this protection by making sure that the agreement to arbitrate, once concluded, cannot be vitiated even through a state's withdrawal from the ICSID Convention. This is, then, the *telos* of the two provisions, in line with the object and purpose of the Convention: to elevate a concluded agreement (or 'perfected consent') to arbitrate under ICSID to a right and an obligation under the Convention, which can-

tional Law (vol 3 Hart Oxford forthcoming), available at http://www.esilen.law .cam.ac.uk/Media/Draft_Papers/Agora/Paparinskis.pdf.

42 Broches (n15) 349, who argues that this is made clear in the preamble.
43 Cf ICSID Convention preamble; Report of the Executive Directors [3], available at http://www.worldbank.org/icsid (hereinafter 'Report'); and Broches (n15) 344, 349.
44 Report (n43) [23].
45 Cf ibid; Broches (n15) 351-2; Schreuer Commentary 190 [374] seq.
46 Cf Article 25(1) and Broches (n15) 353.
47 See Broches (n15) 396. While Broches is referring specifically, in casu, to Articles 53-55, he notes that the drafters' objective of reasonable balance 'extended as well to other parts of the Convention'.
48 See text at n40 above.

not be affected through any unilateral act.[49] In doing this, the two provisions fulfil their part in the creation of a stable and effective facility to be used upon agreement: they establish legal certainty with respect to a private agreement, now elevated to the level of international law.

All this is mentioned for a reason: the ordinary meaning of the terms (or their interpretative radius)[50] is always the outer limit of interpretation. This means that object and purpose of a treaty may help to decide between all the possible 'ordinary meanings' but will not allow interpretations going beyond the interpretative radius.[51] In the context of the particular problem at hand, this means that the object and purpose may help one decide whether 'consent' in Article 72 of the ICSID Convention has the same meaning as it does under Article 25 (ie consent by both parties in writing) or whether it can be read as referring even to a unilateral offer of consent that has not yet been accepted and thus is not 'perfected' (ie no arbitration agreement has been concluded). As already mentioned, both of these interpretations are at least plausible and have been argued with some force.[52]

If the object and purpose of the Convention is indeed solely and unqualifiedly to offer private investors a way out of the dire problems they face when recalcitrant states renege on their promises, then this could lead one to select the latter interpretation: treating consent as such would allow unilateral offers of consent in BITs to establish the jurisdiction of the Centre long after a state has withdrawn from the ICSID Convention. The object and purpose could be used to explain the radically different treatment of the very same term, 'consent', in two provisions (Article 25(1) and Article 72) that seem to complement each other.

If, on the other hand, the object and purpose of the Convention is the neutral one of providing a particular facility for those states that wish to make use of it, and if the specific object and purpose of the two provisions is to make explicit that which should be self-evident, ie that an agreement is binding and cannot be vitiated by unilateral act, then it remains open to a state – or a group of states, for that matter – to change their position or policy as to the usefulness of the facility provided and to withdraw from it, making it impossible to be brought before it except where an agreement has been concluded while the Convention was in force. As should be clear from the discussion in Section A above, several ALBA states have changed their mind with respect to, among other things, the useful-

---

49   See further Section E below.
50   For the term see EP Hexner 'Teleological Interpretation of Basic Instruments of International Organizations' in S Engel (ed) Law, State, and International Legal Order—Essays in Honor of Hans Kelsen (University of Tennessee Press Knoxville 1964) 119, 123. The interpretative radius of a provision signifies the range of possible meanings attributable to it.
51   Cf Villiger (n39) 428 [14]; Gardiner (n36) 190 and 197-198 with further references.
52   See nn23-33 above and accompanying text.

ness of ICSID. Two of them have decided to withdraw, a right that the Convention itself grants them.

The discussion in this section demonstrates that a fully self-contained interpretation of the ICSID Convention, even using the object and purpose to decide between two plausible and possible interpretations of the term 'consent' in Article 72, cannot fully succeed in convincingly resolving the issue. It remains open that 'consent' under Article 72 could be read to mean either 'mutual' or 'unilateral' consent, while considerations on the basis of the object and purpose are relevant, but also arguably open-ended and finally subjective. In such a circumstance, reference and resort to applicable general international law to the extent not abrogated by the ICSID Convention will help decide the matter.

D. Interaction between the ICSID Convention and General International Law

A note on the methodology of bringing in general international law on withdrawal from treaties is required at this juncture. There are two ways in which general international law may impact our understanding of the particular rules under the ICSID Convention, and the interaction between these two ways is not altogether clear. One way in which general international law comes into play is directly, by applying on questions not covered by the special rule.[53] *Lex specialis derogat legi generali* only to the extent that the two come into direct conflict. For the rest, the general rule continues to apply. But the ICSID Convention does include special provisions on withdrawal and its effects. Is this enough to fully displace general international law? An argument could be made that the inclusion of a special provision does have this effect of complete displacement of the application of general law. The ILC's words seem to point to such a conclusion: the principle of *lex specialis*, giving priority to the special norm, is said to apply 'when two norms deal with the same subject-matter',[54] as indeed is the case here. On the other hand, it could be argued that the special rule displaces the general rule not merely by providing on the same subject-matter, but by doing so in 'a different way'.[55] The ILC itself has noted that, most of international law being dispositive, 'special law may be used to *apply*, clarify, update, *or modify as well*

---

53 See succinctly the ILC in its Conclusions of the Work of Study Group on Fragmentation in UN Doc A/61/10 (2006) 409 [9], 412 [15] (hereinafter 'ILC Fragmentation Conclusions').

54 ibid 408 [5].

55 Cf Georges Pinson (France) v United Mexican States [1928] 5 RIAA 327, 422 [50(4)]: 'Toute convention internationale doit être réputée s'en référer tacitement au droit international commun, pour toutes les questions qu'elle ne résout pas elle-même en termes exprès et d'une façon différente' (emphasis added).

as set aside general law'.[56] The question then becomes one of the extent to which the special rule has derogated from the general rule.

The other way is through the principle of 'systemic integration', articulated in Article 31(3)(c) VCLT, which reflects customary international law.[57] Under the principle of systemic integration, or what in domestic law is usually called 'systematic interpretation',[58] general law, even if displaced as to its applicability by the special rule, continues to be relevant for its interpretation.[59] In particular, it may crucially inform the interpretation of a special treaty rule where the treaty rule is unclear,[60] as Article 72 ICSID Convention has shown itself to be. This then falls within the more general principle of 'harmonization', according to which two rules bearing on the same issue should be interpreted harmoniously to the extent possible.[61] Reference to the general rules on withdrawal from treaties and its effects could be called upon to clarify the specific rules in the ICSID Convention.

Which of the two ways one will argue in order to bring general international law into the picture seems largely academic.[62] It could be said that, at the very least, if general international law is displaced by the existence of the special rule, even to the extent that the special rule *does not expressly diverge from general law*, then it comes back into the picture through the 'back door' of 'systemic integration', ie of Article 31(3)(c) VCLT. To the present author the better argu-

---

56   ILC Fragmentation Conclusions (n53) 409 [8].

57   See eg Certain Questions of Mutual Assistance in Criminal Matters (Djibouti v France) [2008] ICJ Rep 177, 219 [112].

58   See V Tzevelekos 'The Use of Article 31(3)(c) of the VCLT in the Case Law of the ECtHR: An Effective Anti-Fragmentation Tool or a Selective Loophole for the Reinforcement of Human Rights Teleology?—Between Evolution and Systemic Integration' (2009-2010) 31 Michigan JIL 621, 633.

59   ILC Fragmentation Conclusions (n53) 413 [18].

60   ibid 414 [20(a)].

61   ibid 408 [4]. Similar principles exist with respect to the interpretation of domestic law 'in harmony' with international law ('consistent interpretation'), as well as within domestic law itself ('systematic interpretation'). In all these cases, the principle could be recast as (or seen as accompanied by) a presumption of non-derogation from the general rule. On consistent interpretation of domestic law and international law the locus classicus is Murray v The Charming Betsy 6 US 64, 118 (1804); see further generally A Tzanakopoulos 'Domestic Courts as the "Natural Judge" of International Law: A Change in Physiognomy' in Crawford & Nouwen (n41), available at http://www.esil-en.law.cam.ac.uk/Media/Draft_Papers/Agora/Tzanakopoulos.pdf; on systematic interpretation within domestic law cf Garland v British Rail [1983] 2 AC 751, 757 (Lord Diplock) and Ex parte Brind [1991] 1 AC 696, 760 (Lord Ackner).

62   The answer would depend on whether one would qualify the relationship between the general rules on withdrawal from treaties and the special rules of the ICSID Convention as one of 'conflict' or one of 'interpretation': ILC Fragmentation Conclusions (n53) 407-408 [2].

ment seems to be that the special rule applies to the extent that it derogates, excludes, or modifies the general rule. For the rest, the general rule applies. Whether that 'applies' is understood as 'informs the interpretation' of the special rule,[63] or merely as 'applies', ie is generally binding on the subjects at hand and has not been contracted out of in the instance, is of no consequence. 'Systemic integration' is to be resorted to when the special and the general rule are not on the exact same subject-matter, but more generally when they are both binding on the subjects at hand and bear some relevance to each other and to the situation in question. In any event, general law on treaty withdrawal will have to come to bear on the understanding of the relevant provisions of the ICSID Convention.

If all this is so, 'residual fallback' to general international law seems not only allowed and justifiable, but also required.[64] Beyond the ICSID Convention, the Vienna Convention on the Law of Treaties also provides for the legal effects of withdrawal from treaties. Article 70(2) VCLT directs the application of paragraph 1 of the same Article (dealing with the effects of termination of a treaty) in the case of withdrawal from a multilateral treaty, as between the withdrawing state and the other parties to the treaty. The Vienna Convention does not apply as such to the ICSID Convention, as the former entered into force long after the latter's entry into force, and as not all parties to the ICSID Convention are also parties to the Vienna Convention. However, the provision of Article 70 VCLT may apply as customary law,[65] and may indeed not be superseded by the relevant special provisions of the ICSID Convention. This is now taken up in Section E.

---

63   ibid: In the second instance mentioned above, the two rules apply simultaneously in that the general informs the interpretation of the special one; in the first instance a choice must be made in accordance with the lex specialis principle.

64   See generally Garibaldi (n24), particularly 263-264. However, reference to general international law is merely made to confirm the textual and contextual interpretation of the term 'consent' in Article 72 ICSID Convention. The general international law referred to is limited to the broad principles of good faith and pacta sunt servanda, and to notions of consent and unilateral acts under general international law, including consent to the jurisdiction of the ICJ. Similar excursions are to be found in Nolan and Sourgens (n21) 23 seq, as well as in Alschner et al (n38) 21 [50]. Curiously, none of these authors considers the VCLT provisions on the effects of termination of and withdrawal from treaties.

65   Even if merely coming to bear under Article 31(3)(c) VCLT, which allows rules of another treaty not 'applicable in the relations between the parties' to inform the interpretation of another treaty rule when they 'have passed into customary international law': ILC Fragmentation Conclusions (n53) 414-415 [21].

E. General International Law on Withdrawal from Treaties

The general regime of treaty law as set out in the Vienna Convention of course recognises the possibility of special withdrawal clauses; however, it also allows us to ascertain some of the special features of Articles 70-72 of the ICSID Convention. Analysing them from the perspective of the residual fallback rule in turn may inform our interpretation.

Article 54(a) of the Vienna Convention on the Law of Treaties provides that a state can terminate or withdraw from a treaty in conformity with the provisions of that treaty. Indeed Article 71 of the ICSID Convention allows a state to withdraw without any requirements except that of a written notification to the depositary, but subjects the effect of withdrawal to a six month time limit after receipt of the notification. Article 70 of the Vienna Convention deals with the effects of termination of or withdrawal from a treaty.[66] The provision, which is reflective of customary international law,[67] provides that withdrawal releases the withdrawing party from any obligation *further* to perform the treaty, but does not affect any right, obligation, or legal situation of the parties (to the treaty) created through the execution of the treaty prior to its termination.[68] But all this of course '[u]nless the treaty otherwise provides'. The rule reflected in Article 70 VCLT being merely a default or dispositive rule,[69] capable of being set aside by agreement of the parties (as, *in casu*, reflected in the treaty), it remains to be seen whether – and to what extent – the ICSID Convention *does* otherwise provide.

Gaillard has noted that Article 72 of the ICSID Convention, dealing with the effects of withdrawal, is nothing but an application of the customary rule reflected in Article 70 VCLT.[70] Indeed, *prima facie*, Article 72 of the Convention merely restates the rule of Article 70 VCLT:[71] 'Notice by a Contracting State pursuant to Articles 70 or 71 shall not affect *rights or obligations under this Convention* of that State or of any national of that State arising out of consent to

---

66   The term 'consequences' in the article's title is synonymous with 'effects': see H Ascensio 'Article 70—Convention de 1969' in Corten and Klein (n35) 2503, 2504 [1].

67   See A Nollkaemper 'Some Observations on the Consequences of the Termination of Treaties and the Reach of Article 70 of the Vienna Convention on the Law of Treaties' in IF Dekker & HHG Post (eds) On the Foundations and Sources of International Law (TMC Asser The Hague 2003) 187; Villiger (n39) 875 [14] (quoting Nollkaemper); Ascensio (n66) 2511-2513 [8]-[10] (at least through crystallization during the Vienna conference, which in the case here contemplated however would raise difficult questions of supervening custom).

68   The provision of paragraph 2 of Article 70 directs to the application of paragraph 1 (dealing with termination) also to instances of withdrawal.

69   Ascensio (n66) 2509 [6].

70   (n14) 6-7.

71   Cf text at n56 above.

the jurisdiction of the Centre given by one of them before such notice was received by the depositary'.[72] These are but rights and obligations 'created through the execution of the treaty prior to its termination'.[73]

On closer inspection, however, there are some differences to the VCLT – viz customary – rule, which is, to that extent, either overridden,[74] or complemented.[75] First of all, Article 72 ICSID Convention thankfully does away with the term 'legal situation', which could create interpretative difficulties. Only rights and obligations under the Convention that arise out of consent to the jurisdiction of the Centre are safeguarded, as long as that consent was provided before withdrawal.

More importantly, Article 72 extends to cover not just rights and obligations of ICSID states parties arisen under the Convention, but also those of private individuals or legal entities. This is in line with the Convention's elevation, in Article 25, of *mutual* consent (ie agreement) between a state and a private entity to resort to ICSID arbitration to the level of an international legal obligation.[76] To that extent, the Convention constitutes the private entity as a subject of international law.[77] This can be well seen when considering an investment contract between a state and an investor that includes an arbitration clause: if the arbitration clause refers to ICSID, the right and obligation to arbitrate under ICSID created by the contract is elevated to the level of an internationally protected right and an international obligation by the ICSID Convention. This international right and obligation created under the Convention survives any withdrawal from the Convention (Article 72) just as it survives any other unilateral attempt to withdraw from the obligation to arbitrate (Article 25).

When considering an ICSID arbitration clause in a BIT, even one where the states parties agree that investors shall have the 'right' to bring investment disputes before an ICSID tribunal, there is evidently no mutual consent of the par-

---

72 As far as the expression 'given by one of them' is concerned, this has served sometimes as a springboard from which to argue that a unilateral offer of consent is enough for the provision to apply. This matter is not taken up here, as the expression quite clearly refers to the withdrawing state or any national of the withdrawing state having given consent. If either of them has given consent to arbitration in the context of an agreement with another investor or state, respectively, then withdrawal from the ICSID Convention by a state does not affect the obligations created for that state or the rights created for any of its nationals under Article 25.

73 Article 70(1)(b) VCLT.

74 On the basis of the lex specialis principle: ILC Fragmentation Conclusions (n53) 408 [5], 409 [8].

75 It could be argued that Article 72 ICSID Convention does not fully derogate from but rather to some extent also complements Article 70 VCLT: cf Ascensio (n66) 2516-2517 [16]. Cf ILC Fragmentation Conclusions (n53) 409 [8].

76 Broches (n15) 352; cf 349-350; see also text at n49 above.

77 Ibid.

ties *to the dispute* to be sanctioned by the Convention. Rather, what there is, if anything, is a right of investors to arbitrate disputes under ICSID that is *created by the BIT*.[78] In this sense, it is the BIT that elevates the private entity to the level of a subject of international law in the instance, and not the ICSID Convention.[79] Once an agreement to arbitrate is concluded, by the private entity availing itself of its right to arbitrate under ICSID (either through a unilateral written notice to the State that it will so avail itself in the future, should any disputes arise, or through the registration of a request for arbitration), only then is a right and an obligation arising out of consent *created under the ICSID Convention*. This is because the ICSID Convention, in Article 25, only constitutes the *mutual* consent of parties to a dispute (to arbitrate it before an ICSID tribunal) as an international right and obligation under the Convention.

This is the extent to which Article 72 'contracts out' of the customary rule as expressed in Article 70 VCLT. For the rest, the latter rule continues to apply,[80] or, in any event, informs the interpretation of the provision. This is because a customary rule, whether identical, non-identical, or in part identical, to a parallel-running treaty rule at the very least may be resorted to, under Article 31(3)(c) VCLT, to assist in the interpretation of the treaty rule.[81]

The distinction drawn between a right created under the ICSID Convention (the right to arbitrate before ICSID created by mutual consent under Article 25) and one created under a BIT is crucial when considered under the prism of the general international law of treaties and Article 70 VCLT. Already the Harvard Draft on the Law of Treaties noted that 'after a treaty has been terminated [or a state has withdrawn from it] ... there can be ... no disturbing of rights vested as a result of performance'.[82] This is also the position under Article 70 VCLT.[83] Even though the understanding of 'vested' or 'acquired' rights under the VCLT refers solely to rights of the parties to the treaty and not to those of private entities,[84] the ICSID Convention, through Article 72, extends the effect also to specified acquired rights of private entities, as argued above.[85] Accordingly, an

---

78   Cf Schreuer in Waibel et al (n25) 365.
79   Cf nn76-77 above.
80   Cf the possibility of complementarity rather than derogation in n75 and Section D above generally.
81   See Section D above and cf eg Gardiner (n36) 278; Villiger (n39) 432-433 [24]-[25].
82   'Draft Convention on the Law of Treaties' (1935) 29 AJIL Supplement 657, 1172. Cf generally Certain German Interests in Polish Upper Silesia [1926] PCIJ Ser A No 7 at 42, which, in another context, considers that the principle of respect for vested rights ... forms part of generally accepted international law'; but see text at nn84-85 below.
83   Villiger (n39) 872-873 [9].
84   ibid 873 [10]; Aust (n1) 304; in detail Ascensio (n66) 2518-2521 [19]-[21].
85   Conversely, survival clauses in BITs do not extend the application of Article 70 VCLT to private entities, but rather aim at compensating for its non application (and the inexis-

agreement to arbitrate under ICSID between a state and an investor in accordance with Article 25 constitutes a 'right vested as a result of performance' (cf Article 70(1)(b) VCLT: 'execution') of the ICSID Convention and cannot be 'disturbed' (cf Article 70(1)(b) VCLT: 'affected') by withdrawal, as Article 72 ICSID Convention confirms. An arbitration clause in a BIT is at best (depending on the wording) a right extended by states reciprocally to nationals of each other, respectively, and as such does not constitute a right vested as a result of performance of the ICSID Convention; it does not 'result from' the Convention.[86]

In this, the general international law of treaties confirms that Article 72 ICSID Convention, interpreted on its terms, and against the background of the customary rule on the effects of withdrawal from treaties, which it confirms and extends, only sanctions rights and obligations created under the Convention, on the terms of the Convention (viz Article 25). These survive withdrawal for eternity. Rights granted under other international instruments cannot come under the ICSID survival clause unless at the same time they would fall within the Convention's provisions for the creation of rights and obligations.

Article 72 ICSID Convention introduces yet another special regulation: while withdrawal is to take effect, in accordance with Article 71, six months after receipt of the relevant notice by the depositary, Article 72 stipulates that only rights arising from consent established before notice was received by the depositary will survive the Convention. Under Article 70 VCLT, rights would continue to accrue (and if they became vested, they would survive) during the period in which withdrawal has not taken effect. In fact some treaties provide specifically for this eventuality, in order to extend Article 70 VCLT protection to individuals: Article 12(2) of the Optional Protocol to the ICCPR for example provides that '[d]enunciation shall be without prejudice to the continued application of the provisions of the present Protocol to any communication submitted … *before the effective date* of denunciation'.[87]

The combined effect of these considerations is that a provision for ICSID arbitration in a BIT will cease being operative – in the sense that it will become incapable of being implemented – from the moment of notification of withdrawal from the ICSID Convention. While a provision for ICSID arbitration in a domestic (investment) law can be withdrawn at the discretion of the enacting state,[88]

---

tence of a doctrine of acquired rights for private entities) through providing protection past termination for a certain period of time so that the investor is not surprised and has enough time to wind up the investment: cf Ascensio (n66) 2521-2522 [22].

86 Cf G Fitzmaurice 'Second Report on the Law of Treaties' (1957) II YILC 16, 67 [205].

87 (emphasis added); the effective date of denunciation is three months after the date of receipt by the depositary in accordance with paragraph 1 of the same article.

88 See L Markert Streitschlichtungsklauseln in Investitionsschutzabkommen (Nomos Baden-Baden 2010) 129.

and thus creates no legal problems on the international level, a similar provision in a BIT constitutes an international obligation of the state party to the BIT, an international treaty (if indeed formulated in a legally binding manner).[89] How is it then possible that a state can, through a unilateral act relating to treaty A in effect modify treaty B?

But there is no unilateral modification of another treaty (the BIT) through withdrawal from ICSID. Rather, the obligation of the state to arbitrate under ICSID (or to offer ICSID as an alternative arbitral forum) in the BIT remains in force. Since it is incapable of being implemented because of a unilateral act of the withdrawing state, the latter's international responsibility for breach of the obligation under the treaty will be engaged, exposing it to all possible reactions under general international law, whether of treaties (eg termination for material breach)[90] or of state responsibility (countermeasures).[91] These remedies accrue to the other state party to the BIT, and not to any private entity that might have benefited from the promise of ICSID arbitration.[92] But this just serves to confirm the traditional position of the individual under general international law, for lack of any special agreement between states to elevate the individual to international subjecthood in a given instance.

F. Conclusion

The effects of withdrawal from the ICSID Convention have been extensively discussed in the specialized investment literature with particular – almost exclusive – focus on the concept of 'consent' in Articles 25 and 72 of the Convention.[93] Between two plausible interpretations, one is selected – but based solely on arguments from the ICSID Convention itself, ie either arguments from its structure and drafting history, or arguments from an assumed object and purpose of the Convention to protect investors. When general international law is considered, this is typically only to clarify the concept of consent to jurisdiction.[94] This contribution, rather than engaging with these arguments, has sought to

---

89   Cf ibid 129-131; on the question of formulation see Schreuer (n26) 835.
90   See Article 60 VCLT. This can refer to important ancillary provisions, such as provisions on dispute settlement: see B Simma & C Tams 'Article 60 – Convention de 1969' in Corten and Klein (n35) 2131, 2145-2146 [21].
91   See Articles 49 seq ILC Articles on the Responsibility of States for Internationally Wrongful Acts (2001) UN Doc A/56/10; (2001) II(2) YILC 26. Cf generally Paparinskis (n31).
92   See also Schreuer (n26) 835-836.
93   See the overview by Montanes (n23) 970 and the works mentioned in nn24-26 above.
94   See n64 above.

demonstrate that the object and purpose of the ICSID Convention cannot be a safe guide in selecting between plausible interpretations, being a facilitative, rather than a protective one. Instead, the analysis was based on the customary rules on the effects of withdrawal from treaties and their relationship to the relevant provision of the ICSID Convention, to which little – if any – attention had been paid. General international law, to the extent it is applicable, either directly as not having been contracted out of, or as 'informing the interpretation' of the special provisions, provides the decisive argument for the correct interpretation of the ICSID Convention provisions on effects of withdrawal. It informs the reading of the ICSID Convention and militates against self-contained interpretation when there is no clear evidence of abrogation from the general regime.

This analysis argued that the general international law of treaties is helpful in understanding the effects of withdrawal from ICSID. This is because the relevant ICSID Convention provisions are a mere application and partial extension of the general rules so as to cover individuals, *in casu* the investors, who are elevated by the Convention to subjects of international law. The interpretation of the general rules clarifies the interpretation of the ICSID Convention rules. From a broader perspective, one might see this as evidence that even where investment law provides special rules, the general international law of treaties might still enter the debate 'through the back door'.

Whether an actual case before an ICSID tribunal would focus on the narrow issue of the meaning of 'consent' on the basis of investment-specific arguments, or whether it would extend to consider the general law on treaty withdrawal, will remain an open question for some time. A few days before the Bolivian withdrawal was to take effect, an investor brought a request for arbitration against it that was registered by the Centre on the basis of a BIT provision.[95] The tribunal would have to decide on its competence to hear a case where the right of the claimant to appear before it had not arisen under the ICSID Convention – if the interpretation of Article 72 here advocated is accepted – but rather, if at all, under the BIT. The proceeding was however discontinued at the request of the claimant.[96] As such, it remains to be seen whether this issue will be finally decided on the basis of an investment-specific approach or by reference to the general international law of treaties. But given the growth, both in size and in boldness, of the ALBA, perhaps another opportunity will arise once the next Latin American state withdraws from the ICSID Convention.

---

95   ETI Euro Telecom NV v Plurinational State of Bolivia (ICSID Case No ARB/07/28). See for details http://www.worldbank.org/icsid.
96   Order of 21 October 2009.

International Investment Law and State Responsibility: Conditions of Responsibility

Christina Knahr[*]

A. Introduction

State Responsibility is undoubtedly one of the core principles of public international law. The principles of state responsibility are outlined in textbooks on public international law and have been analyzed frequently in scholarly articles.[1] The issue of state responsibility, which has also been the focus of attention of the work of the International Law Commission (ILC)[2], has, however, not only been relevant in general public international law, but increasingly also in the specific

[*]   Dr Christina Knahr, MPA, Post-Doctoral Researcher, Department of European, International and Comparative Law, University of Vienna.

[1]   See e.g. I. Brownlie, State Responsibility (1983); J. Crawford, The International Law Commission's Articles on State Responsibility. Introduction, Text and Commentaries (2002); D. Bodansky/J.Crook, Symposium: The ILC's State Responsibility Articles: Introduction and Overview, 96 AJIL 773 (2002); J. Crawford, Revising the Draft Articles on State Responsibility, 10 EJIL 435 (1999); J. Crawford & P. Bodeau, Second Reading of the Draft Articles on State Responsibility: A Progress Report, 1 ILF 44 (1999); J. Crawford & P. Bodeau, Second Reading of the I.L.C. Draft Articles on State Responsibility: Further Progress, 2 ILF 45 (2000); J. Crawford, P. Bodeau & J. Peel, The ILC's Draft Articles on State Responsibility. Toward Completion of a Second Reading, 94 AJIL 660 (2000); J. Crawford, J. Peel & S. Olleson, The ILC's Articles on Responsibility of States for Internationally Wrongful Acts: Completion of the Second Reading, 12 EJIL 963 (2001); D. Caron, The ILC Articles on State Responsibility: The Paradoxical Relationship between Form and Authority, 96 AJIL 857 (2002); W. Czaplinski, UN Codification of Law of State Responsibility, 41 Archiv des Völkerrechts 62 (2003); G. Hafner, The Draft Articles on the Responsibility of States for Internationally Wrongful Acts – The Work of the International Law Commission, 5 ARIEL 189 (2000); S. Wittich, The International Law Commission's Articles on the Responsibility of States for Internationally Wrongful Acts Adopted on Second Reading, 15 Leiden Journal of International Law 891 (2002); C. Tams, All's Well that Ends Well? Comments on the ILC's Articles on State Responsibility, 62 ZaöRV 759 (2002).

[2]   See J. Crawford, First Report on State Responsibility, UN Doc. A/CN.4/490 and Add.1–7 (1998); J. Crawford, Second Report on State Responsibility, UN Doc.A/CN.4/498 and Add. 1 - 4 (1999); J. Crawford, Third Report on State Responsibility, UN Doc. A/CN.4/507 and Add. 1 - 4 (2000); J. Crawford, Fourth Report on State Responsibility, UN Doc. A/CN.4/517 and Add.1 (2001).

field of international investment arbitration.[3] It is the purpose of this contribution to address one aspect of the rules on state responsibility that has proven to be of particular importance in investment arbitration, i.e. the issue of attribution.

In international investment arbitration investors frequently claim that the protection granted to them in bilateral investment treaties (BITs), e.g. fair and equitable treatment, national treatment etc, has been violated by measures set by an organ of the host state or an entity that exercises governmental authority. According to the principles of state responsibility, the state will only be responsible for such actions if the conduct in question is attributable to it.[4] The ILC Articles on State Responsibility[5] contain provisions on attribution in Chapter II of Part One, whereby Article 4 (Conduct of organs of a State), Article 5 (Conduct of persons or entities exercising elements of governmental authority) and Article 8 (Conduct directed or controlled by a State) have been most relevant in investment arbitration. After providing a brief overview of the content of these provisions, the focus of this contribution will lie on an analysis of their application in the practice of arbitration. It will examine how investment tribunals have applied the relevant provisions of the general concept of state responsibility in the specific contexts of investment disputes. It will investigate if this issue is dealt with in a consistent manner or if there are diverging approaches.

B. Principles of Attribution

As indicated above, the provisions of the ILC Articles on State Responsibility concerning attribution most relevant in investment arbitration are Articles 4, 5 and 8. They provide as follows:

---

3   See e.g. K. Hober, State Responsibility and Investment Arbitration, in C. Ribeiro (ed), Investment Arbitration and the Energy Charter Treaty 261 (2006); K. Hober, State Responsibility and Attribution, in P. Muchlinski/F. Ortino/C. Schreuer (eds.), The Oxford Handbook of International Investment Law 549 (2008); A.M. Harb, The Wrongful Acts of Independent State Entities and Attribution to States in International Investment Disputes, 3 (5) TDM (2006); S.M. Perera, State Responsibility – Ascertaining the Liability of States in Foreign Investment Disputes, 6 JWIT 499 (2005).

4   Aricle 2 ILC Articles on State Responsibility provides: "There is an internationally wrongful act of a State when conduct consisting of an action or omission:
     (a) is attributable to the State under international law; and
     (b) constitutes a breach of an international obligation of the State."

5   Articles on Responsibility of States for Internationally Wrongful Acts adopted by the International Law Commission at its Fifty-third Session 2001, reproduced in Report of the International Law Commission on the Work of its Fifty-third Session, UN Doc. A/56/10.

ARTICLE 4
Conduct of organs of a State

1. The conduct of any State organ shall be considered an act of that State under international law, whether the organ exercises legislative, executive, judicial or any other functions, whatever position it holds in the organization of the State, and whatever its character as an organ of the central government or of a territorial unit of the State.

2. An organ includes any person or entity which has that status in accordance with the internal law of the State.

ARTICLE 5
Conduct of persons or entities exercising elements
of governmental authority

The conduct of a person or entity which is not an organ of the State under Article 4 but which is empowered by the law of that State to exercise elements of the governmental authority shall be considered an act of the State under international law, provided the person or entity is acting in that capacity in the particular instance.

ARTICLE 8
Conduct directed or controlled by a State

The conduct of a person or group of persons shall be considered an act of a State under international law if the person or group of persons is in fact acting on the instructions of, or under the direction and control of, that State in carrying out the conduct.

All three provisions share the fact that they aim at attributing the conduct of specific entities to a State. Nonetheless, the content and focus of each of these provisions is clearly distinct. Article 4 follows a structural approach, providing for attribution of the conduct of State organs to a State. What is essential in this context is the status of the entity in question rather than the capacity in which it is acting. According to Paragraph 2, the status is to be determined by the national law of the respective State, an approach that is necessary due to the fact that States are free to determine their internal organizational structure and these structures can consequently vary considerably from State to State. It is, however, the purpose of the entire chapter on attribution of the ILC Articles, and of Article 4 in particular, to ensure that a State cannot escape its international responsibility simply through an internal division into separate legal entities whose actions are not attributable to the State.[6] For purposes of Article 4 it is irrelevant what func-

---

6   See J. Crawford, The International Law Commission's Articles on State Responsibility 93 (2002).

tion the organ exercises, be it legislative, executive or judicial. What is essential is entirely its qualification as an organ of the State.

Article 5, on the other hand, emphasizes the function of an entity as the decisive condition for attribution. Following this functional approach, Article 5 provides for attribution of the conduct of persons or entities that are not organs of a State but that exercise governmental authority. Put simply, Article 5 does not look at what an entity is, but what it does. Thereby this Article ensures that also the conduct of entities that do not have the status of State organs, but nonetheless exercise governmental authority is covered and attributable to the State. According to Article 5, the power to exercise elements of governmental authority has to be awarded to the entity by the national law of the respective State. Therefore, like with the determination of what constitutes a State organ under Article 4, there is no general rule under international law on what exactly constitutes "governmental authority". Rather one has to examine in each situation individually whether in fact an entity's action was done in exercise of governmental authority and thus will be attributable to the State.[7]

Article 8 differs from Articles 4 and 5 insofar as it does not refer to either structure or function of an entity, but that it provides for attribution based on control. Under this Article the conduct of persons or group of persons will be attributable to the State if they act on the instructions of or under the direction or control of the State carrying out the conduct. In this context it is irrelevant whether an entity has the status of a State organ or acts in exercise of governmental authority. What is essential is an element of control of the State over the entity and a real link between the entity conducting the act and the State.[8] Making such a determination will of course require an individual fact-specific examination of the circumstances in each case and cannot be generalized.[9]

It is clear that these provisions are cumulative and a State will only become responsible if one of these conditions is fulfilled.[10] What is equally clear is that each of these provisions emphasizes distinct elements as conditions for attribution. Thus, it seems interesting for purposes of this contribution to examine how investment tribunals address this issue of attribution. What approach do they take? Do they primarily take into consideration whether an entity acts in exercise of governmental authority? Or do they deem the element of control as provided for in Article 8 to be more important? Is one of these principles more relevant in the practice of investment arbitration than the others? The following section of this contribution is intended to shed some light on these questions.

---

7   Ibid, at 101.
8   Ibid, at 110.
9   Ibid.
10   Ibid, at 93.

C. Arbitral Practice

It is very common in international investment arbitration that situations arise where it is disputed whether the conduct of certain entities is attributable to the host State and the State incurs responsibility. Thus, investment tribunals frequently have to address the question of attribution in the cases before them. It would certainly exceed the scope of this contribution to scrutinize all cases where the question of attribution has been controversial in detail[11]. The following section will provide a representative selection of cases that demonstrate the most important aspects that tribunals tend to take into consideration in their reasoning.

I. Application of Article 4 ILC Articles in Investment Arbitration

In *Eureko* v. *Poland*[12] the focus of the tribunal lay on a structural approach when assessing whether the Minister of the State Treasury of Poland was a state organ. For the tribunal it was clear that

"[i]n the perspective of international law, it is now a well settled rule that the conduct of any State organ is considered an act of that State and that an organ includes any person or entity which has that status in accordance with the internal law of that State."[13]

Applying this rule to the facts of the case, the tribunal found that the Minister was

"acting pursuant to clear authority conferred upon him by the Council of Ministers of the Government of Poland in conformity with the officially approved privatization policy of that Government. As such the Minister of the State Treasury engaged the responsibility of the Republic of Poland."[14]

In *Jan de Nul* v. *Egypt* the tribunal was also confronted with the issue of attribution of a particular conduct of an entity to the respondent State. In its analysis it stated that

"An organ is part of the central or decentralized structure of the State, which means that it is a person or entity which is part of the legislative, executive, or judicial powers. To determine whether an entity is a State organ, one must first look to domestic law."[15]

---

11 For a more comprehensive analysis of the cases see e.g. the study by L. Schicho, State Entities in International Law (PhD Thesis, University of Vienna 2010).
12 Eureko v. Poland, Partial Award, 19 August 2005.
13 Ibid., para. 127.
14 Ibid., para. 129.
15 Jan de Nul N.V. and Dredging International N.V. v. Arab Republic of Egypt, ICSID Case No. ARB/04/13, Award, 6 November 2008, para. 160.

Thus the tribunal examined the relevant national law, finding that according to this law, the SCA was not qualified as a State organ under Egyptian law.[16] Further, analyzing the respective provisions, it found that

> "it is clear that the SCA is not part of the Egyptian State, as results from Articles 4, 5 and 10 of the Law No. 30/1975. Indeed, these provisions insist on the commercial nature of the SCA activities and its autonomous budget."[17]

After it concluded that the SCA was not an organ of the State and therefore its actions were not attributable to Egypt under Article 4,[18] the tribunal continued with examining Articles 5 and 8 ILC Articles, which will be discussed in a later section of this contribution.[19]

In *EDF* v. *Romania* the tribunal also made clear that the domestic law of the respondent State was decisive for determining organ status of an entity.[20] Referring to the commentaries to the ILC Articles, the tribunal determined that

> "neither AIBO nor TAROM, both possessing legal personality under Romanian law separate and distinct from that of the State, may be considered as a State organ."[21]

Another case where the tribunal had to address the issue of attribution was *Bayindir* v. *Pakistan*. In this case the tribunal also starting with examining whether the National Highway Authority (NHA) was an organ under the laws of Pakistan. It found that

> "pursuant to section 3(2) of the National Highway Authority Act of 1991 ("NHA Act"), NHA is a "body corporate having perpetual succession and a common seal with power to acquire, hold and dispose of property, and may in its own name sue and be sued" [...]. The fact that there may be links between NHA and some sections of the Government of Pakistan does not mean that the two are not distinct. State entities and agencies do not operate in an institutional or regulatory vacuum. They normally have links with other authorities as well as with the government. Because of its separate legal status, the Tribunal discards the possibility of treating NHA as a State organ under Article 4 of the ILC Articles. The Claimant also asserts, however, that NHA's conduct was in fact the mere execution of decisions taken by government officials. This argument would appear to suggest that the acts incriminated emanate from government officials, who are themselves organs of the State under Article 4 of the ILC Articles. Given that – as already indicated above – NHA is a separate legal entity and that the acts in question are those of NHA as a party to the Con-

---

16   Ibid.
17   Ibid., para. 161.
18   Ibid., para. 162.
19   Jan de Nul N.V. and Dredging International N.V. v. Arab Republic of Egypt, ICSID Case No. ARB/04/13, Award, 6 November 2008, paras. 163-171 and 172, 173.
20   EDF (Services) Limited v. Romania, ICSID Case No. ARB/05/13, Award, 8 October 2009, para. 188.
21   EDF (Services) Limited v. Romania, ICSID Case No. ARB/05/13, Award, 8 October 2009, para. 190.

tract, the Tribunal considers that there are no grounds for attribution by virtue of Article 4."[22]

Another example for a case where the tribunal was confronted with the question whether the conduct of an entity was attributable to the respondent State was *MCI* v. *Ecuador*. In this case, respondent argued that claimant signed the contract in question with an entity, INECEL, which according to respondent was "an autonomous entity that is legally independent of the State."[23] The tribunal did, however, not share respondent's assessment. Rather, it found that the entity in question was to be qualified as an organ of Ecuador and that, consequently, Ecuador incurred responsibility for its actions. The tribunal stated that

> "[...] INECEL, in light of its institutional structure and composition as well as its functions, should be considered, in accordance with international law, as an organ of the Ecuadorian State. In this case, the customary rules codified by the ILC in their Articles on Responsibility of States for Internationally Wrongful Acts are applicable. Therefore, any acts or omissions of INECEL in breach of the BIT or of other applicable rules of general international law are attributable to Ecuador, and engage its international responsibility."[24]

II. Application of Article 5 ILC Articles in Investment Arbitration

In *Helnan* v. *Egypt*[25] a dispute arose out of a contract for the management and operation of a hotel in Egypt between Helnan, the successor to the original contractor Scandinavian, and EGOTH, the Egyptian Company for Tourism and Hotel, the successor to the original contractor EHC. In order to determine whether the conduct of EGOTH was attributable to Egypt, the tribunal applied a functional test, focusing on whether EGOTH acted in the exercise of governmental authority. It concluded that

> "EGOTH was an active operator in the privatisation of the tourism industry on behalf of the Egyptian Government. [...] Even if EGOTH has not been officially empowered by law to exercise elements of the governmental authority, its actions within the privatisation process are attributable to the Egyptian State."[26]

---

22 Bayindir Insaat Turizm Ticaret Ve Sanayi A.S. v. Islamic Republic of Pakistan, ICSID Case No.ARB/03/29, Award, 27 August 2009, para. 119.
23 M.C.I. Power Group L.C. and New Turbine, Inc. v. Ecuador, ICSID Case No. ARB/03/6, Award, 31 July 2007, para. 222.
24 M.C.I. Power Group L.C. and New Turbine, Inc. v. Ecuador, ICSID Case No. ARB/03/6, Award, 31 July 2007, para. 225.
25 Helnan International Hotels A/S v. The Arab Republic of Egypt, Decision on Jurisdiction, 17 October 2006.
26 Ibid., para. 93.

In *Noble Ventures* v. *Romania*[27] the dispute concerned a privatization agreement for the acquisition, management and operation of a steel mill entered into by Noble Ventures and the Romanian State Ownership Fund (SOF). Following political changes in Romania, SOF was replaced by the Authority for the Privatization and Management of the State Ownership (APAPS). After quickly establishing that "since SOF and APAPS were legal entities separate from the Respondent, it is not possible to regard them as *de jure* organs"[28] the tribunal focused on a functional analysis of whether these entities were acting in the exercise of governmental authority in accordance with Article 5 of the ILC Articles. It found that

> "it was not only within the competence of SOF – and APAPS which replaced SOF at the end of 2000 – when acting as the empowered public institution under the Privatization Law, to conclude agreements with investors but also, acting as a *governmental agency*, to manage the whole legal relationship with them, including all acts concerned with the implementation of a specific investment. In the judgment of the Tribunal, no relevant legal distinction is to be drawn between SOF/APAPS, on the one hand, and a government ministry, on the other hand, when the one or the other acted as the empowered public institution under the Privatization Law. All the acts allegedly committed by SOF/APAPS were related to the investment of the Claimant. There is no indication from the parties, and there is no reason to believe, that any act by these institutions was outside the scope of their mandate. Consequently, the Tribunal concludes that SOF and APAPS were entitled by law to represent the Respondent and did so in all of their actions as well as omissions. The acts allegedly in violation of the BIT are therefore attributable to the Respondent for the purposes of assessment under the BIT."[29]

Further, with regard to the argument raised by Romania that a distinction had to be made between governmental and commercial conduct in this context, the tribunal held the view that

> "the distinction plays an important role in the field of sovereign immunity when one comes to the question of whether a State can claim immunity before the courts of another State. However, in the context of responsibility, it is difficult to see why commercial acts, so called *acta iure gestionis*, should by definition not be attributable while governmental acts, so called *acta iure imperii*, should be attributable. The ILC-Draft does not maintain or support such a distinction. Apart from the fact that there is no reason why one should not regard commercial acts as being in principle also attributable, it is difficult to define whether a particular act is governmental. There is a widespread consensus in international law, as in particular expressed in the discussions in the ILC regarding attribution, that there is no common understanding in international law of what constitutes a governmental or public act. Otherwise there would not be a need for specified rules such as those enunciated by the ILC in its Draft Articles, according to which, in principle, a certain factual

---

27 Noble Ventures v. Romania, Award, 12 October 2005.
28 Ibid., para. 69.
29 Ibid., paras. 79, 80.

link between the State and the actor is required in order to attribute to the State acts of that actor."[30]

It concluded that

"the acts of SOF and APAPS which were of relevance in the present case are attributable to the Respondent for the purposes of assessment under the BIT."[31]

In *Jan de Nul* v. *Egypt*, the tribunal, after reaching a conclusion on Article 4 ILC Articles,[32] continued by examining whether the requirements of Article 5 ILC Articles would be fulfilled. Thereby it addressed separately the elements of being "empowered" by the State and to "exercise governmental authority". The tribunal stated that

"[…] for an act to be attributed to a State under Article 5, two cumulative conditions have to be fulfilled: - first, the act must be performed by an entity empowered to exercise elements of governmental authority (i); - second, the act itself must be performed in the exercise of governmental authority (ii)."[33]

In its analysis the tribunal referred to the commentaries to the ILC Articles, providing that

"[t]he fact that an entity can be classified as public or private according to the criteria of a given legal system, the existence of a greater or lesser State participation in its capital, or, more generally, in the ownership of its assets, the fact that it is not subject to executive control — these are not decisive criteria for the purpose of attribution of the entity's conduct to the State. Instead, article 5 refers to the true common feature, namely that these entities are empowered, if only to a limited extent or in a specific context, to exercise specified elements of governmental authority."[34]

The tribunal concluded that

"There is no doubt that the SCA was and still is empowered to exercise elements of governmental authority. […] The SCA is in particular empowered "*to issue the decrees related to the navigation in the canal*" (Article 6 of the Law No. 30/1975) or to "*impose and collect charges for the navigation and passing through the canal*" […]. The Tribunal therefore concludes that the SCA is an entity under Article 5 of the ILC Articles."[35]

In a second step of analysis the tribunal focused on the question if the entity in question exercised governmental authority. In this respect, the tribunal emphasized that rather than performing a general assessment it was important to look at

---

30   Ibid., para. 82.
31   Ibid., para. 83.
32   See supra text at note 15.
33   Jan de Nul N.V. and Dredging International N.V. v. Arab Republic of Egypt, ICSID Case No. ARB/04/13, Award, 6 November 2008, para. 163.
34   Jan de Nul N.V. and Dredging International N.V. v. Arab Republic of Egypt, ICSID Case No. ARB/04/13, Award, 6 November 2008, para. 165.
35   Jan de Nul N.V. and Dredging International N.V. v. Arab Republic of Egypt, ICSID Case No. ARB/04/13, Award, 6 November 2008, para. 166.

the specific actions of the entity vis a vis the investor in the particular circumstances of the dispute. The tribunal stated that

"[...] the fact that the subject matter of the Contract related to the core functions of the SCA, i.e., the maintenance and improvement of the Suez Canal, is irrelevant. The Tribunal must look to the actual acts complained of. In its dealing with the Claimants during the tender process, the SCA acted like any contractor trying to achieve the best price for the services it was seeking. It did not act as a State entity. The same applies to the SCA's conduct in the course of the performance of the Contract. 170. It is true though that the Contract was awarded through a bidding process governed by the laws on public procurement. This is not a sufficient element, however, to establish that governmental authority was exercised in the SCA's relation to the Claimants and more particularly in relation to the acts and omissions complained of. What matters is not the "*service public*" element, but the use of "*prérogatives de puissance publique*" or governmental authority. In this sense, the refusal to grant an extension of time at the time of the tender does not show either that governmental authority was used, irrespective of the reasons for such refusal. Any private contract partner could have acted in a similar manner."[36]

Based on these considerations, the tribunal concluded that

"although the SCA is a public entity empowered to exercise elements of governmental authority, the acts of the SCA vis à vis the Claimants are not attributable to the Respondent in this arbitration on the basis of Article 5 of the ILC Articles, as they were not performed pursuant to the exercise of governmental authority."[37]

In *EDF* v. *Romania* the tribunal also examined the specific actions of the entity in question which according to the claimant led to violations of the BIT. Applying the general requirement of exercise of governmental authority to the specific facts of the case, the tribunal found that

"neither the auctions organised by AIBO nor the exercise by AIBO and TAROM of their rights as shareholders of ASRO and SKY and under the ASRO Contract and the SKY Contract were exercise of delegated governmental authority."[38]

Further, it determined that

"[...] there is a distinction to be made between the legal regime of public property at the airport (such as runways, embarking or disembarking platforms or taxiways), which is held and managed by AIBO under the terms of a concession with the Ministry of Transportation as public assets regulated by public law, and the legal regime of AIBO's private property which is a part of its own patrimony (such as all retail and other commercial spaces at the airport). Regarding the latter, the evidence before the Tribunal shows that AIBO takes decisions within its own corporate bodies, as any other commercial company operating in Romania. [...] 196. The auctions of commercial spaces at the Otopeni Airport [...] fall within the category of the legal regime of AIBO's private property. They were

---

36   Jan de Nul N.V. and Dredging International N.V. v. Arab Republic of Egypt, ICSID Case No. ARB/04/13, Award, 6 November 2008, paras.169, 170.

37   Jan de Nul N.V. and Dredging International N.V. v. Arab Republic of Egypt, ICSID Case No. ARB/04/13, Award, 6 November 2008, para. 171.

38   EDF (Services) Limited v. Romania, ICSID Case No. ARB/05/13, Award, 8 October 2009, para. 194.

[...] acts aiming at the better exploitation by AIBO of commercial spaces, which were part of its private property, and the conduct of its own duty-free business, subject only to its corporate bodies' determinations. 197. Likewise, AIBO's and TAROM's contractual relations with EDF under the ASRO Contract and the SKY Contract were [...] entered into and performed in pursuit of the corporate objects of a commercial company with the view to making profits, as any other commercial company operating in Romania."[39]

Consequently, the tribunal reached the conclusions that the requirements of Article 5 ILC Articles were not fulfilled and thus the alleged actions could not be attributed to the respondent.

Similar to the cases examined above, the tribunal in *Bayindir* v. *Pakistan* also emphasized the need to examine the very specific actions or omissions of the entity in question rather than generally assessing whether it can exercise governmental authority. It stated that

"It is not disputed that NHA is generally empowered to exercise elements of governmental authority. Section 10 of the NHA Act vests broad authority in NHA to take "such measures and exercise such powers it considers necessary or expedient for carrying out the purposes of this Act," including to "levy, collect or cause to be collected tolls on National Highways, strategic roads and such other roads as may be entrusted to it and bridges thereon." Other relevant provisions of the NHA Act are section 12 on "Powers to eject unauthorized occupants" and section 29 on the NHA's "Power to enter" upon lands and premises to make inspections."[40]

According to the tribunal this general empowerment did not suffice.It expressed the view that

"The existence of these general powers is not however sufficient in itself to bring the case within Article 5. Attribution under that provision requires in addition that the instrumentality acted in a sovereign capacity in that particular instance [...]"[41]

Based on the evidence before it the tribunal found that in the specific circumstances of the case the actions were not in exercise of governmental authority and thus not attributable to Pakistan under Article 5 ILC Articles.

In *Salini* v. *Morocco*[42] a dispute arose between two Italian companies, Salini Costruttori S.p.A. and Italstade S.p.A., and the Kingdom of Morocco out of a construction contract. In this case ADM, a limited liability company, issued an invitation to tender for the construction of a highway, which was then awarded to Claimants. During the dispute, the question arose whether certain conduct of ADM was attributable to Morocco. In order to make this determination the tri-

39 EDF (Services) Limited v. Romania, ICSID Case No. ARB/05/13, Award, 8 October 2009, paras. 195-198.
40 Bayindir Insaat Turizm Ticaret Ve Sanayi A.S. v. Islamic Republic of Pakistan, ICSID Case No.ARB/03/29, Award, 27 August 2009, para. 121.
41 Bayindir Insaat Turizm Ticaret Ve Sanayi A.S. v. Islamic Republic of Pakistan, ICSID Case No.ARB/03/29, Award, 27 August 2009, para. 122.
42 Salini Costruttori SpA et Italstrade SpA v. Morroco, Decision on Jurisdiction, 23 July 2001, 6 ICSID Reports 400, 42 ILM 609.

bunal took a structural as well as functional approach, concluding that ADM's conduct was in fact attributable to Morocco. It found that

> "the fact that a State might be able to act by means of a company having its own legal personality is not unusual if one considers the extraordinary expansion of public authority activity. In order to perform its obligations, and at the same time, take into account the sometimes divergent interests that the private economy protects, the State uses a varied spectrum of modes of organisation, among which are particularly semi-public companies, similar to ADM, a company mostly held by the State, which, considering the size of its participation (80%), directs and manages it. All these circumstances imprint a public nature on the said company. Thus, since ADM is an entity, from a structural as well as a functional point of view, which is distinguishable from the State solely on account of its legal personality, the Tribunal, in spite of the observations of July 2, 2001 made by the Kingdom of Morocco, concludes that the Italian companies have shown that ADM is a State company, acting in the name of the Kingdom of Morocco."[43]

III. Application of Article 8 ILC Articles in Investment Arbitration

Aside from Article 4 and 5 ILC Articles it is also Article 8 that has become relevant in a number of investment disputes. Ascertaining the requirements of this Article seems particularly challenging. Frequently it proves difficult to determine whether an entity actually acts "on the instruction of" or "under the direction or control" of the State. Further, it is not sufficient that an entity might generally act under the control of a State. Rather, the requirements of Article 8 will only be fulfilled if in the particular circumstances of a case the specific act in question is performed under the control of the State. This need to scrutinize the particular conduct of an entity in order to determine if it is attributable to a State or not has been emphasized by a number of tribunals. In *Jan de Nul* v. *Egypt* the tribunal stated that

> "International jurisprudence is very demanding in order to attribute the act of a person or entity to a State, as it requires both a general control of the State over the person or entity and a specific control of the State over the act the attribution of which is at stake; this is known as the "effective control" test. There is no evidence on record of any instructions that the State would have given to the SCA in regard to the very specific acts and omissions of the SCA that are complained of in this arbitration. Accordingly, the Tribunal concludes that there can be no attribution of the acts of SCA to the Respondent under Article 8 of the ILC Articles."[44]

In *Nycomb* v. *Latvia*[45], Latvenergo, a company 100% owned by Latvia, entered into a contract with the Claimant for providing a favourable price for elec-

---

43   Ibid., para. 35.
44   Jan de Nul N.V. and Dredging International N.V. v. Arab Republic of Egypt, ICSID Case No. ARB/04/13, Award, 6 November 2008, para.173 (footnote omitted).
45   Nycomb v. Latvia, Award, 16 December 2003, Stockholm Int Arb Rev 2005:1.

tricity. A dispute arose when Latvenergo refused to pay a double tariff guaranteed to the investor. The fact that the company was under the supervision of the Ministry of Economy lead the tribunal to assess that through this element of control the government was certainly aware of the breach of the contract. It concluded that

> "in the circumstances of this case, the Republic must be considered responsible for Latvenergo's actions under the rules of attribution in international law. [...] whether Latvenergo's refusal to pay the double tariff was based on a misunderstanding of the legal situation, or whether it for other reasons ignored the legal framework under which it was operating, its actions concerning the purchase price are attributable to the Republic. Consequently, the Republic must be found responsible for Latvenergo's failure to pay the double tariff."[46]

IV. Application of Articles 4, 5 and 8 cumulatively

The cases examined above already demonstrate that quite frequently tribunals not only examine one of the Articles on attribution. Rather two or even all three Articles are tested. In a number of cases tribunals have expressly stated that all three Articles are equally relevant and that it did not matter based on what provision they would reach a finding on attribution as it would lead to the same result. A case in point is *EnCana* v. *Ecuador*[47] where a dispute arose out of a contract between the Claimant and Petroecuador, a company owned and controlled by the State.

In determining whether the conduct of Petroecuador was attributable to Ecuador the tribunal did not focus solely on either a structural, functional or control test. Rather, it held the view that for purposes of attribution it did not matter whether an assessment on attribution would follow from the functional principle according to Article 5 ILC Articles or from the control according to Article 8 ILC Articles since they would lead to the same result. It found that

> "it is relevant that Petroecuador was [...] subject to instructions from the President and others, and that the Attorney-General pursuant to the law had and exercised authority "to supervise the performance of ... contracts and to propose or adopt for this purpose the judicial actions necessary for the defence of the national assets and public interest". According to the evidence this power extended to supervision and control of Petroecuador's performance of the participation contracts and to their potential renegotiation. Thus the conduct of Petroecuador in entering into, performing and renegotiating the participation contracts (or declining to do so) is attributable to Ecuador. It does not matter for this purpose whether this result flows from the principle stated in Article 5 of the ILC's Articles on Re-

---

46   Ibid., p. 31.
47   EnCana Corp. v. Ecuador, Award, 3 February 2006.

sponsibility of States for Internationally Wrongful Acts or that stated in Article 8. The result is the same."[48]

Also the tribunal in *Eureko* v. *Poland*, after establishing attribution based on the status of the relevant entity as a state organ, made reference to the relevance of the other provisions on attribution. It pointed out that

"Professor Crawford further observed that the principles of attribution are cumulative so as to embrace not only the conduct of any State organ but the conduct of a person or entity which is not an organ of the State but which is empowered by the law of that State to exercise elements of governmental authority. It embraces as well the conduct of a person or group of persons if he or it is in fact acting on the instructions of, or under the direction or control of, that State. [...]"[49]

In *Maffezini* v. *Spain*[50] the tribunal addressed the issue of attribution both in its Decision on Jurisdiction as well as in the Award. In the jurisdictional decision the tribunal also expressed the view that frequently more than one of the principles laid down in the ILC Articles has to be examined in order to determine attribution. It stated that

"[t]he question whether or not SODIGA is a State entity must be examined first from a formal or structural point of view. Here a finding that the entity is owned by the State, directly or indirectly, gives rise to a rebuttable presumption that it is a State entity. The same result will obtain if an entity is controlled by the State, directly or indirectly. A similar presumption arises if an entity's purpose or objectives is the carrying out of functions which are governmental in nature or which are otherwise normally reserved to the State, or which by their nature are not usually carried out by private businesses or individuals. [...] Because of the many forms that State enterprises may take and thus shape the manners of State action, the structural test by itself may not always be a conclusive determination whether an entity is an organ of the State or whether its acts may be attributed to the State. An additional test has been developed, a functional test, which looks to the functions of or role to be performed by the entity. [...]"[51]

In the Award[52] the *Maffezini* tribunal again emphasized that solely looking at one of the principles of attribution would not be sufficient, holding that

"[t]he structural test, however, is but one element to be taken into account. Other elements to which international law looks are, in particular, the control of the company by the State or State entities and the objectives and functions for which the company was created."[53]

---

48   Ibid., para. 154 (footnotes omitted).
49   Eureko v. Poland, supra note 12, para. 132.
50   Maffezini v. Spain, Decision on Jurisdiction, 25 January 2000, 5 ICSID Reports 396, 40 ILM 1129 (2001).
51   Ibid., paras. 77, 79.
52   Maffezini v. Spain, Award, 13 November 2000, 5 ICSID Reports 419, 40 ILM 1148 (2001).
53   Ibid., para. 50.

Following these general remarks on the applicability of all principles, the tribunal reached its conclusion on attribution based on the functional criterion. It found that

> "[b]ecause the acts of SODIGA relating to the loan cannot be considered commercial in nature and involve its public functions, responsibility for them should be attributed to the Kingdom of Spain."[54]

In *Waste Management* v. *Mexico*[55] the tribunal had difficulties establishing whether certain acts of Banobras, an entity partly owned and controlled by Mexican governmental agencies, were attributable to Mexico. It examined whether Banobras could be qualified as a state organ, whether it was acting in exercise of governmental authority and whether it was under the control of Mexico. It found that

> "Banobras' general objective, in the words of the regional director of Banobras in Guerrero, is "to promote and finance activities carried out by the Federal, State, and Municipal Governments of the Country".From the material available to the Tribunal it is doubtful whether Banobras is an organ of the Mexican State within the meaning of Article 4 of the ILC's Articles on Responsibility of States for Internationally Wrongful Acts. Shares in Banobras were divided between the public and private sector, with the former holding a minimum of 66%. The mere fact that a separate entity is majority-owned or substantially controlled by the state does not make it ipso facto an organ of the state. Nor is it clear that in its dealings with the City and the State in terms of the Line of Credit it was exercising governmental authority within the meaning of Article 5 of those Articles. The Organic Law of 1986 regulating Banobras' activity confers on it a variety of functions, some clearly public, others less so. A further possibility is that Banobras, though not an organ of Mexico, was acting "under the direction or control of" Guerrero or of the City in refusing to pay Acaverde under the Agreement:again, it is far from clear from the evidence that this was so."[56]

Although its analysis did not lead to a clear answer the tribunal concluded that

> "[f]or the purposes of the present Award, however, it will be assumed that one way or another the conduct of Banobras was attributable to Mexico for NAFTA purposes."[57]

This blunt assessment of the tribunal that "one way or the other" the conduct of the entity in question would be attributable to the respondent State seems at least questionable. Should it really be possible to conclude that an act is attributable to a State "somehow", "one way or the other" without exactly determining that the requirements of one particular Article is fulfilled? A more precise determination by the tribunal would certainly have been preferable.

---

54   Ibid., para. 83.
55   Waste Management v. Mexico, Award, 30 April 2004, 43 ILM 967 (2004).
56   Ibid., para. 75.
57   Ibid.

D. Conclusion

This contribution aimed at identifying to what extent and in what way certain provisions of the general international law principles on State Responsibility penetrate into the specific contexts of investment arbitration. In particular, the focus lay on the question how investment tribunals apply the principles of attribution as provided for in Chapter II Part One of the ILC Articles on State Responsibility in the disputes before them. The first observation that can be made in this regard is that the principles of attribution are highly relevant in inter-national investment arbitration. The question of attribution is not just a rare exception that arises in unusual cases. Rather, problems associated with this issue occur regularly in disputes brought before investment tribunals. As for the question of prevalence of one particular principle of attribution, the cases examined do not yield a clear picture as to whether one of them is more relevant in investment arbitration than the others. It seems to depend very much on the specific circumstances of each case whether tribunals base their reasoning more on structural, functional or control criteria for establishing attribution. It is, however, noteworthy, and the examination of the relevant case-law has demonstrated, that in the majority of disputes investment tribunals tend not to resort to either a structural, functional or control approach in strict separation. Rather, they frequently look at two or even all three elements provided for in Articles 4, 5, and 8 of the ILC Articles when examining whether the conduct of a particular entity is attributable to the State.

International Investment Law and State Responsibility

Comments by *Pavel Šturma*[*]

A. Introduction

It was my honour and pleasure to take part in the Investment Law Conference in Frankfurt and to comment on the very interesting paper of Christina Knahr. Although I spent a good part of my research and teaching activities in the field of International Economic Law, namely the investment law, I have always been rather a generalist in International Law. Therefore I will approach the subject from a more general and theoretical point of view.

I fully share the view that the State Responsibility is one of the core principles of public international law. It is not only the "necessary corollary" of the equality of States,[1] but also an essential part and condition of the existence of an international legal order.[2] I also agree that both rules on attribution and circumstances precluding wrongfulness are very relevant issues for the theory and practice of international investment law. And in order to fulfil my obligations of a commentator, of course, I will later join a brief comment on these issues. However, from my perspective, I would start from another point. To use the well known and widely recognized work of the International Law Commission, I would start rather from Article 55 on *Lex specialis*. It provides as follows:

> "These articles do not apply where and to the extent that the conditions for the existence of an internationally wrongful act or the content or implementation of the international responsibility of State are governed by special rules of international law."[3]

---

[*]   Professor Dr Pavel Sturma, Professor of Public International Law, Charles University Prague.

[1]   Cf. Ch. de Visscher, La responsabilité des Etats (Leiden, 1924), 90.

[2]   Cf. R. Ago, Third Report on State Responsibility, YILC, 1971, Vol. II(1), 205; P. Reuter, Trois observations sur la codification de la responsabilité internationale des Etats pour fait illicite. In: Le droit international au service de la paix, de la justice et du développement – Mélanges Michel Virally (Paris, 1991), 390; A. Pellet, The Definition of Responsibility in International Law. In: J. Crawford, A. Pellet, S. Olleson (eds.), The Law of International Responsibility (Oxford, 2010), 4-5.

[3]   Articles on the Responsibility of States for Internationally Wrongful Acts, Report of the ILC, 53rd Session, UN Doc. A/56/10, p. 356; YILC 2001, Vol. II(2), …

Indeed, the very subject of our conference is about the relationship between International Investment Law as one of the special subsystems (or boxes) and general international law.[4] Being fully aware that many investment arbitration tribunals do not hesitate to refer, at some occasions, to the Articles on State Responsibility, I have to ask a disturbing question: why, on what legal basis? Is the investment law, or more precisely, the law of investment disputes a proper area for application of the rules of State Responsibility?

To be clear and to avoid any misunderstanding, I do not have in mind the formal legal status of the ILC Articles on State Responsibility. In spite of their non-binding form and a little chance to achieve their transformation into a convention, I do not see any problem to apply them to the extent that they codify general customary norms.[5]

Instead, I have in mind a complex and differentiated nature of relations arising in International Investment Law. They involved both inter-state relations and relations between states and non-sovereign subjects (natural or juridical persons).[6] Just to take any standard BIT: its dispute settlement clauses include both disputes between States Parties and disputes between investors and the host State. These clauses are not mutually exclusive, therefore the application of one does not exclude the other. Moreover, if we stay on the level of the BIT and do not have resort to the Convention on the Settlement of Investment Disputes between States and Nationals of Other States (ICSID Convention, 1965),[7] we cannot exclude a possibility of the diplomatic protection.

Put simply, while the subsidiary application of the general rules on State Responsibility is evident in cases of rare (or almost non-existing) inter-state disputes, it is open to question in case of a typical dispute between a State Party and a national of another State Party. Is it already the moment when secondary rules on State Responsibility start to apply? Or the international wrongful act of the State has not yet been completed because there is still a possibility of a redress? In other words, the operation of arbitration clauses seems to give a chance to

4   See M. Koskenniemi (ed.), Fragmentation of International Law: Difficulties arising from the Diversification and Expansion of International Law. Report of the Study Group of the International Law Commission, UN doc. A/CN.4/L.682 (2006). Cf. also P. Šturma et al., Universality of International Law: What Is the Role of General International Law in the Period of its Fragmentation? In: M. Tomášek (ed.), Czech Law between Europeanization and Globalization (Prague, 2010), 208-225.

5   Cf. A. Pellet, The ILC's Articles on State Responsibility for Internationally Wrongful Acts and Related Texts. In: J. Crawford, A. Pellet, S. Olleson (eds.), The Law of International Responsibility (Oxford, 2010), 86-87.

6   See Z. Douglas, Other Specific Regimes of Responsibility: Investment Treaty Arbitration and ICSID. In: J. Crawford, A. Pellet, S. Olleson (eds.), op. cit., 816-817.

7   Cf. e.g. Ch. Schreuer, L. Malintoppi, A. Reinisch, A. Sinclair, The ICSID Convention, 2nd ed. (Cambridge, 2009).

reach a friendly settlement or to go to arbitration. Is it possible to view this procedural mechanism of dispute settlement as an alternative to the exhaustion of domestic remedies? If so, then the responsibility of the respondent State – under general international law – may generate only when it does not comply with the final award? But what kind of legal relations arises? Is it plausible to view the responsibility of State towards investors under BITs as a special kind of treaty-based liability (*ex contractu*)?

Well, the answer lays in the principle of *lex specialis*. This concept is great, simply because it makes possible many interpretations, from slightly modified versions of State Responsibility for internationally wrongful acts up to the famous concept of international liability.[8] If we return back to more orthodox interpretation according to which the material element of the international wrongful act (i.e. the breach of an international obligation) is controlling, irrespective of the nature of the injured party, many questions still remain. Assuming that the Articles on State Responsibility are *lex generalis* applicable also in cases of investment disputes, the question is: where are *leges speciales*?

When it comes to the ICSID Convention, there are at least some special rules relating to the international responsibility and its implementation.[9] First of all, Article 27 includes the obligation of the Contracting State to desist from giving diplomatic protection or bringing an international claim with respect of a dispute involving one of its nationals that has been submitted to ICSID arbitration, save in the case of non-compliance by the respondent Contracting State with the award. Next, Article 26 provides that the consent to ICSID arbitration shall be considered as the choice of this arbitration with the exclusion of any other means. The Contracting State may condition its consent by the exhaustion of local remedies which implies that the rule of exhaustion does not apply otherwise. Finally, Article 53 requires a Contracting State to desist from appealing against ICSID awards or pursuing other remedy, save those remedies envisaged by the Convention itself.

Leaving aside the ICSID Convention, we have to search in the BITs. They provide most but not all rules applicable. As it was pointed out already in *AAP v. Sri Lanka* (1990),[10]

---

8   Cf. e.g. J. Barboza, International Liability for Injurious Consequences of Acts not Prohibited by International Law and Protection of the Environment, 247 RCADI (1994-III), 301; A. Boyle, State Responsibility and International Liability for Injurious Consequences of Acts not Prohibited by International Law: a Necessary Distinction, 39 ICLQ (1990), 1; P. Šturma, La responsabilité en dehors de l'illicite en droit international économique, 19 Polish YbIL (1993), 91.

9   See Z. Douglas, op. cit., 816-817, 820 ff.

10   Asian Agricultural Products Ltd. v. Sri Lanka, ICSID Case No. ARB/87/3, Award, 27 June 1990, in: 4 ICSID Reports, 257, para. 21.

"...the Bilateral Investment Treaty is not a self-contained closed legal system limited to provide for substantive material rules of direct applicability, but it has to be envisaged within a wider juridical context in which rules from other sources are integrated through implied incorporation methods, or by direct reference to certain supplementary rules, whether of international law character or of domestic law nature..."

It is true that precisely the BITs, which provide a basis for most investment disputes today, contain mostly substantive rules on treatment and protection of foreign investments, i.e. just primary rules. Where are some special secondary rules? With the most liberal interpretation, we can accept two standard clauses on dispute settlement (arbitration clauses), which can be consider as special rules on implementation of the State Responsibility.

Besides these clauses, I am afraid that special secondary rules are missing in BITs. In my view, the standard rule on the adequate compensation in case of nationalization or expropriation has another function in this context, precisely the primary obligation, compliance with which is a condition of the legality of expropriations. Otherwise we have to re-write all the textbooks and the classical case-law deriving from the *Chorzów Factory* case. However, it is not only the famous distinction between the lawful expropriation and unlawful takings which can be derived from this case. At another place the judgment makes distinction between the forms of reparations owed to the investor and the national State:

"The rules of law governing the reparation are the rules of international law in force between the two States concerned, and not the law governing relations between the State which has committed a wrongful act and the individual who has suffered the damage. Rights or interests of an individual the violation of which rights causes damage are always in a different plane to rights belonging to a state, which rights may also be infringed by the same act."[11]

This analysis leads me to the troublesome conclusion that International Investment Law does not have many special secondary rules and the application of general rules on State Responsibility seems to be, to a certain extent, at the discretion of arbitrators. This would not be a big problem as such. However, many arbitrators are not necessarily specialists in general Public International Law. It creates a risk of non-systematic but rather selective application of certain rules on State Responsibility only. And, of course, it happens usually when the interpretation and application of a specific rule is in support of the responsibility of the respondent State.

---

11   Factory at Chorzów, Merits, PCIJ Reports, 1928, Series A, No. 17, p. 28.

B. Principles of Attribution

The above preliminary remarks are to introduce two brief comments on the excellent paper of Dr. Knahr. I agree with her conclusion that many investment tribunals use in their reasoning structural, functional or control criteria for establishing attribution but they do not resort to one of these approaches in strict separation. This is correct and not too surprising. Firstly, the rules on attribution belong to the oldest articles of the ILC work, which are already well-known, widely accepted and far less controversial than some other Articles. This is true for Articles 4, 5 and 8 which are often referred to in various investment treaty arbitrations.

Secondly, the question of attribution arises regularly as the State entities and agencies dealing with foreign investors are different which requires different criteria of attribution. Arbitration tribunals thus, while excluding attribution under Article 4 (such agencies are not organs of the State), come sometimes to a conclusion that such an agency is an entity empowered by the law of that State to exercise elements of the governmental authority.[12] It is interesting that the same analysis as in *Jan de Nul* case was done in *Noble Ventures* v. *Romania*.[13] However, in the first case the tribunal concluded that the SCA, the public entity in question, did not act as a State entity but as any other private contractor.[14] In the second case the tribunal came to the completely different conclusion and declared the acts of Romanian governmental agencies attributable to the Respondent for the purposes of assessment under the BIT.[15] What is particularly striking in this case, the tribunal refused to apply, for the purpose of the attribution of State responsibility, the well-known distinction between commercial acts (*acta iure gestionis*) and governmental acts (*acta iure imperii*).[16]

Thirdly, investment tribunals prefer to have more than one argument, if available, in order to support the conclusion that the States is responsible for certain conduct or omission. It means that tribunals sometimes apply the structural and functional tests[17] or functional and control principles simultaneously.[18]

---

12   Jan de Nul N.V. and Dredging International N.V. v. Arab Republic of Egypt, ICSID Case No. ARB/04/13, Award, 6 November 2008, para. 166.

13   Noble Ventures v. Romania, Award, 12 October 2005.

14   Jan de Nul N.V. and Dredging International N.V. v. Arab Republic of Egypt, ICSID Case No. ARB/04/13, Award, 6 November 2008, para. 171.

15   Noble Ventures v. Romania, ibid., para. 83.

16   Noble Ventures v. Romania, ibid., para. 82.

17   Maffezini v. Spain, Award, 13 November 2000, 5 ICSID Reports 419, 40 ILM 1148 (2001), para. 50.

18   See e.g. EnCana Corp. v. Ecuador, Award, 3 February 2006, para.

However, the principles of attribution are general principles, so they should be applied also in favour of States. In particular, in arbitrations under ICSID Convention the eligible investor has to be a private person. In other words, investor must not be an entity belonging to or acting on behalf of another State Party. Quite interestingly, tribunals do not apply so strict structural, functional and control test. Sometimes, they are satisfied with the general distinction of activities *iure imperii* and *iure gestionis*.[19]

C. Circumstances Precluding Wrongfulness

Here again, the situation is far from being clear. As far as the special secondary rules in BITs are sporadic or missing, the general rules on circumstances precluding wrongfulness are applicable in International Investment Law. Two out of six circumstances (Articles 20 to 25 of the ILC Articles) seem to be of special relevance to the investment disputes, namely Force majeure (Art. 23) and Necessity (Art. 25). Although they are very different in nature, both circumstances offer certain advantages as defenses in investment disputes.

First, *force majeure* appears to be much stronger defense according to Art. 23 of the ILC Articles, "the wrongfulness of an act of a State... *is precluded* if the act is due to *force majeure*, that is the occurrence of an irresistible force or of an unforeseen event, beyond the control of the State, making it materially impossible in the circumstances to perform the obligation".[20] This is in sharp contrast with the merely negative wording of Art. 25, according to which the necessity defense is available only under very exceptional conditions:

> "Necessity *may not be invoked* by a State as a ground for precluding the wrongfulness... *unless* the act: (a) is the only way for the State to safeguard an essential interest again a grave and imminent peril; and (b) does not seriously impair an essential interest of the State or States towards which the obligation exists, or of the international community as a whole".[21]

In others words, the necessity may be invoked at the best and the defense will depend on the proportionality test.

Second, *force majeure* appears to be an older defense used in the international judicial and arbitral practice in the pre-BIT times. The extremely difficult finan-

---

19   Cf. ČSOB v. the Slovak Republic, ICSID Case No.ARB/97/4, Decision of the Tribunal on Objection to Jurisdiction, 24 May 1999, para. 20.
20   Articles on the Responsibility of States for Internationally Wrongful Acts, Report of the ILC, 53rd Session, UN Doc. A/56/10, p. 183.
21   Ibid., p. 194.

cial situation was invoked by the Ottoman Government as the exception of force majeure in the *Russian Indemnity* case (1912).[22] The general principle was accepted but the plea of *force majeure* failed on the facts of the case because the payment of the debt was not materially impossible. In the same way as the above arbitration, States claimed before the Permanent Court of International Justice a material impossibility of the performance of their obligations in the *Serbian Loans* and *Brazilian Loans* cases.[23] The different jurisdictions considered that the States were facing difficulties which, however, were not really material impossibilities, and did not rise to the level of *force majeure*. In other words, the plea of *force majeure* was rejected.[24]

However, the commentary of the ILC considers the situation to be more like a state of necessity.[25] On the other hand, there are also some old cases that put the defense of grave economic difficulties in the light of necessity.[26]

Third, it seems to me that the defense of *force majeure* may have support even in the text of many BITs. Most BITs include a provision on losses suffered as a consequence of war or another armed conflict, emergency, civil disturbances or other exceptional situations. According to such clauses having the nature of primary rules, investors may be entitled to a restitution or compensation only subject to the national treatment or the MFN clause. In other words, if the State invokes *force majeure* on a non-discriminatory basis, it will be in conformity with the BIT. All depends on the interpretation of other exceptional situations. In fact, certain economic and financial crisis may have comparable effects to war or civil disturbances. However, the interpretation of the relevant articles of the BITs under the principle *expressio unius est exclusio alterius* may also lead to the contrary conclusion that *force majeure* cannot be invoked in other than expressly described situations.

Therefore, it would be safer to explore rather the argument of *necessity*, which is indeed used also in some recent investment treaty arbitrations, mostly in cases against Argentina due to the financial crisis of the late 1990s – 2001. It is worth noting that in *CMS Gas Transmissions v. Argentina*, the ICSID Tribunal affirmed in its award of 2005 the customary nature of the circumstance of necessity codified by the ILC Article 25. However, it rejected the argument of Argentina raised on the grounds of its financial crisis on the facts, because Argentina's measures to suspend its obligations were neither temporary, nor the sole means

22   UNRIAA, vol. XI, p. 443.
23   Serbian Loans, 1929, PCIJ, Series A, No. 20, p. 39-40; Brazilian Loans, 1929, PCIJ, Series A, No. 21, p. 120.
24   See S. Szurek, Circumstances Precluding Wrongfulness in the ILC Articles on State Responsibility: Force Majeure. In: J. Crawford, A. Pellet, S. Olleson (eds.), op. cit., 479.
25   Cf. Report of the ILC, GAOR, Fifty-sixth session, Suppl. No. 10 (A/56/10), p. 197.
26   Société Commerciale de Belgique, 1939, PCIJ, Series A/B, No. 78, p. 160.

at its disposal to avert the crisis.[27] Indeed, the threshold of the applicability of the state of necessity (Art. 25) is very high. It is very interesting that the Tribunal next considered the emergency clause in Article XI of the 1991 US-Argentina BIT,[28] which is a primary rule which broadly resembles the principle of necessity.[29] Moreover, having rejected the applicability of necessity and the emergency clause in Article XI, the Tribunal nonetheless considered the consequences of the crisis. According to it, "whilst not excusing liability or precluding wrongfulness from the legal point of view they ought nevertheless to be considered by the Tribunal when determining compensation".[30] The Tribunal did it and used, maybe surprisingly, the argument based on Article 27 (Consequences of invoking a circumstance precluding wrongfulness) of the ILC Articles.[31]

The award of 2005 was criticized and annulled by the Annulment Committee on the ground of a manifest error of law.[32] Clearly, one can agree that the principle of necessity and the emergency clause in the BIT are different in content and function. On the one hand, the necessity is a circumstance precluding wrongfulness, being thus a secondary rule. On the other hand, Article XI of the BIT is an emergency clause of primary nature. If the conditions of the emergency clause had been met, there would be no breach of the BIT and no need to use the plea of necessity. It looks as a strong argument.

However, there are also other similar cases against Argentina in respect of the same financial crisis. Of special interest is the case *LG&E v. Argentina*. Here, it seems that the conditions of necessity were met. Nevertheless, the Tribunal preferred to decide on the basis of the primary rule of Article XI of the BIT:

"Whilst this analysis concerning Article 25 of the Draft Articles on State Responsibility alone does not establish Argentina's defence, it supports the Tribunal's analysis with regard to the meaning of Article XI's requirements that the measures implemented by Argentina had to have been necessary either for the maintenance of public order or the protection of its own essential security interests."[33]

27　CMS Gas Transmission Company v. Argentina, ICSID Case No. ARB/01/08, Award of 12 May 2005, 14 ICSID Reports, 212-213.

28　The same rule (emergency clause) is in Article X of the 1991 US-Czech BIT.

29　Cf. S. Heathcote, Circumstances Precluding Wrongfulness in the ILC Articles on State Responsibility: Necessity. In: J. Crawford, A. Pellet, S. Olleson (eds.), op. cit., 500.

30　CMS Gas Transmission Company v. Argentina, ibid., p. 217-218.

31　See Report of the ILC, GAOR, Fifty-sixth session, Suppl. No. 10 (A/56/10), p. 209: „The invocation of a circumstance precluding wrongfulness in accordance with this chapter is without prejudice to: …
(b) The question of compensation for any material loss caused by the act in question."

32　CMS Gas Transmission Company v. Argentina, ICSID Case No.ARB/01/08, Decision on application for annulment of 25 September 2007, 14 ICSID Reports, 333-334.

33　LG&E Energy Corp., LG&E Capital Corp., LG&E International Inc. v. Argentina, ICSID Case No. ARB/02/1, Decision on Liability of 3 October 2006, para. 258.

It appears that the Tribunal hesitated to establish its argument on the sole basis of necessity. Instead, the necessity corroborates the conclusion drawn from the analysis of the primary rules of the BIT, where two out of three legitimate grounds in Article XI were applicable. To conclude, it appears that the application of circumstances precluding wrongfulness in investment arbitrations may lead to various and sometimes surprising results. Several options seem to be available for a future development:

(1) The strict conditions of Article 25 of the ILC may be weakened and, consequently, a wider applicability of the necessity in cases of financial crisis could be upheld in arbitral awards.

(2) Instead of secondary rules of general international law (such as codified in the ILC Articles), the special primary rules of the BIT could be interpreted and applied in emergency situations. Both *force majeure* and necessity pleas would then become superfluous in investment arbitration cases.

(3) The approach of *lex specialis* could also operate with the cumulative application of the primary BIT rules and some elements of the circumstances precluding wrongfulness, in particular the necessity.

(4) Finally, the often forgotten and misunderstood argument based on Article 27 of the ILC (reservation as to compensation for damage) might perhaps find its right sphere of application. Clearly, Article 27 is rather a saving clause. And the 2001 ILC Articles and commentaries thereto did not provide enough guidance (case law and literary sources) in order to clarify the meaning.[34] To shed more light on the issue, one should take into consideration also the text of and the commentary to the former Article 35 of the first ILC draft Articles of 1996.[35] Except of two cases which involve the exercise of right rather than a simple circumstance precluding wrongfulness (i.e. self-defence and countermeasures), all other circumstances listed in the ILC Articles might preclude responsibility of the acting State subject to or with a reservation to a certain, at least partial, compensation for material loss caused by the act in question. This could be an interesting way out for many tribunals seeking to reach an equitable decision in investment treaty arbitrations.

---

34 It was rightly criticized in scholarly writings, see e.g. Č. Čepelka, Náhrada škody způsobené chováním státu za okolností vylučujících protiprávnost tohoto chování [Compensation for damage caused by acts of State in circumstances precluding wrongfulness]. In: Č. Čepelka, D. Jílek, P. Šturma, Mezinárodní odpovědnost [International Responsibility] (Brno, 2003), 14-20.

35 Report of the ILC on the work of its forty-eight session, GAOR, Supplement No. 10 (A/51/10):"Preclusion of the wrongfulness of an act of a State by virtue of the provisions of articles 29, 31, 32 or 33 does not prejudge any question that may arise in regard to compensation for damage caused by that act."

D. Conclusion

This contribution aimed at giving some comments on three issues of the relationship between International Investment Law and State Responsibility. The first observation focused on the application of *lex specialis*. The ILC Articles on State Responsibility are without any doubts general secondary rules. However, International Investment Law does not reveal many special secondary rules. In particular the BITs include mostly, if not exclusively, primary rules. Therefore the application of general international law on State responsibility seems to be necessary but also difficult in some cases. Of less controversial nature are the principles of attribution provided in Articles 4, 5 and 8 of the ILC Articles (see the second observation). They are frequently interpreted and applied in investment arbitration cases. However, the tribunals do not always make clear distinction between structural, functional and control principles but rather apply them simultaneously. The third observation concerns the circumstances precluding wrongfulness which belong to the most difficult issues of the State responsibility. Here, by contrast, arbitration awards do not yet provide a clear picture. Again, a certain confusion of primary and secondary rules may appear. *Force majeure* is not used in modern cases and even the plea of (financial) necessity is rarely accepted by the arbitration tribunals. They seem to prefer the arguments based on special emergency clauses in the BITs, i.e. special rules of primary character. However, this area may still bring many surprises.

The Custom of Necessity in Investor-State Arbitrations

*Florian Franke**

A. Introduction

The growing multitude of distinct areas of contemporary international law (such as the law of the sea and the law of world trade, amongst others) has been cause for concern in international legal scholarship in recent times. Such academic concern has prompted the International law Commission's report on the fragmentation of international law.[1] Asserting that such fragmentation endangers the unified development of international law, Martti Koskenniemi, the special rapporteur, has promoted resort to general international law as a means to prevent fragmentation.[2] In other words, Koskenniemi asserts that general international law can act as a unifying force on the various distinct areas of international law that threaten to drift apart.

One such discrete area of international law is the law of investment protection which has grown out of the law diplomatic protection over the last fifty years.[3] The threat of fragmentation in this area is particularly high due to the large amounts of case law generated by investment tribunals. Resort to general international law, as propagated by Koskenniemi brings to the fore the defence of necessity – the roots of which reach back to the dawn of inter-state relations. As a

*   Florian Franke, doctoral candidate and research assistant at the Wilhelm Merton Centre for European Integration and International Economic Order, University of Frankfurt.
1   International Law Commission: Fragmentation of international law: difficulties arising from the diversification and expansion of international law - Report of the Study Group of the International Law Commission - Finalised by Martti Koskenniemi, UN Doc A/CN.4/L.682 2006, pp. (hereinafter ILC Report on Fragmentation).
2   Ibid., at p. 255 et seq: "It is that general international law that provides the rudiments of an international public realm from the perspective of which the specialized pursuits and technical operations carried out under specific treaty-regimes may be evaluated. Thus, it is proposed that the Commission should increasingly look for the avenue of "restatement" of general international law in forms other than codification and progressive development - not as a substitute but as a supplement to the latter.
3   Dolzer/Schreuer: Principles of International Investment Law, Edition, Oxford; New York 2008, at pp. 17 - 24.

result of Koskenniemi's guidelines, resort to general international law has given added impetus to the defence of necessity in international investment law.[4]

However, systematic consistency of international law may nevertheless be at risk when the application of those unifying general principles is undertaken in a conceptually flawed way. By applying the defence of necessity in a way inconsistent with its original meaning the unifying effect may in fact cause even greater fragmentation.[5] Inconsistent jurisprudence of international investment arbitrations shows misunderstanding and misapplication by arbitrators. However, such flawed conceptual application must be not be confused with continued development of necessity as a concept. Such development can result in comprehensive and consistent case law which may ultimately result in greater legal certainty for investors.

The following analysis attempts to encourage the development of necessity whilst warning against misapplication. Firstly, the source and substance of the defence of necessity will be examined. Subsequently, a number of important issues relating to the customary international law defence of necessity in investor state arbitrations will be considered. Lastly, this analysis will scrutinise whether such conflicts have led to a fragmented or rather a more fully developed defence of necessity in international investment law.

B. Genesis of Necessity in International Law

From Grotius in 1625,[6] the development of the defence of necessity is one of great interest. Today necessity is part of customary international law and is central to states attempting to excuse their non-compliance with international obligations in certain circumstances.[7] As such, it is not surprising that the defence of

---

4   United Nations Conference on Trade and Development: The Protection of National Security in IIAs, UNCTAD Series on International Investment Policies 2009, UNCTAD/DIAE/IA/2008/5, accessible online at www.unctad.org.

5   McLachlan: Investment Treaties and General International Law, ICLQ 2008, pp. 361 - 401, at p. 391 states general principles are not a "bag of liquorice all sorts in which tribunals may pick and chose at will those doctrines which suit its decisions."

6   "The Jewish law (...), no less than the Roman, acting upon the same principle of tenderness forbids us to kill anyone, who has taken our goods, unless for the preservation of our own lives. This principle was equally applicable to inter-state relations." Grotius: De Iure Belli Ac Pacis Libri Tres, at book II, chapter. 1 XII, cl. 3; the conditions of Grotius concept of necessity were identified by Rodick: The Doctrine of Necessity in International Law, Edition, New York 1928, at p. 6.

7   ILC Special Rapporteur Ago wrote: "... the concept of "state of necessity" is far too deeply rooted in the consciousness of the members of the international community and of individuals within States. If driven out of the door it would return through the window, if need be in other forms; in that case, the only result would be the unhappy one of distort-

necessity was included in the ILC's codification of state responsibility[8] - itself possibly on the verge of becoming an international convention.[9]

Accordingly, a brief illustration of the historic development of necessity in international law culminating in the ILC's codifying work follows. Subsequently, a concise outline of the results of the ILC's studies as presented in the Draft Articles on State Responsibility for Internationally Wrongful Acts of 2001 falls to be undertaken.[10]

I. Development of the Defence of Necessity

For over two hundred years international jurisprudence and scholarship have influenced the development of the defence of necessity in international law. The historical development of the plea of necessity is a vivid example of the development of international law from a regime of co-existence to a system of co-operation.

1. Evolution of the Theoretical Concept

The principle of necessity was designed to "justify actions which otherwise would appear to be outside the pale of the law".[11] The source of the concept stems from the now outdated principle of self-preservation. In the nineteenth century it was believed among scholars that states posses certain 'fundamental rights' defined as 'the right to existence'. These fundamental subjective rights

ing and obscuring other concepts, the precise delimitation of which is no less essential." International Law Commission: Addendum - Eight report on State Responsibility by Mr. Roberto Ago, Special Rapporteur - the internationally wrongful act of the State, source of international responsibility, UN Doc A/CN.4/318/Add.5-7, Yearbook of the International Law Commission 1980, vol. II, Part Two. pp. 13 - 86, (hereinafter Eighth Report Ago), at 80.

8   For an overview of the process see Bjorklund: Emergency Exceptions: State of Necessity and Force Majeure, in: The Oxford Handbook of International Investment Law (eds. Muchlinski/Ortino/Schreuer, 2008), pp. 459 - 523, at pp. 466 - 471.

9   General Assembly, Res.56/83 of 12 December 2001, Responsibility of States for Internationally Wrongful Acts; General Assembly, Res. 59/35 of 2 December 2004, Responsibility of States for Internationally Wrongful Acts; General Assembly, Res. 62/61 of 6 December 2007, Responsibility of States for Internationally Wrongful Act.

10   International Law Commission: Draft Articles on Responsibility for States for Internationally Wrongful Acts, with Commentaries, UN Doc Yearbook of the International Law Commission 2001, vol. II, Part two. pp. 31 - 143, (hereinafter ILC Draft Articles on State Responsibility with Commentaries or DASR).

11   Rodick, The Doctrine of Necessity in International Law, at pp. 2 - 7.

should naturally take precedence over any other right of a foreign state. Flowing from this concept, any conduct of a state in support of its right of self-preservation was deemed juridically legitimate – even if such conduct breached an international obligation.[12] Accordingly, the defence of necessity was understood as a conflict between two subjective rights of states, ultimately resolved by the predominant nature of the right of states to self-preservation.

However, due to its potential for abuse, the defence of necessity was not wholeheartedly endorsed by the 'international community'. Instead, customary international law developed to provide that the doctrine could only justify a state's misconduct in exceptional circumstances, such as when a vital interest of the state was in danger.[13] In the course of the 20th century when, due to the experiences of the two World Wars, the right of self-preservation was abandoned in favour of a more co-operative system of international law, the defence of necessity developed accordingly. What remained was the understanding that the plea of necessity was attached to a conflict. Importantly, however, this new conception of necessity redefined what was formed a right as merely an interest. Consequently, in the event that the interest of a state in its continued existence were to conflict with its international obligations, it could no longer be said that its interest in existence automatically took precedence over any other obligation. The new approach also embodied ideas of proportionality and reasonableness and remained limited to very exceptional circumstances.

2. Codification Work of the ILC

The review of the defence of necessity had initially started in 1925 when the Assembly of the League of Nations' Committee of Experts decided that the law of state responsibility was ripe for codification. In 1930, at the League of Nations Conference for the Codification of International Law, defences did not yet appear in the Committee's Articles. However, in the preparatory work for the conference it was stated that a state shall not be held liable for its breach of an inter-

---

12 Wheaton: Elements of International Law, 6th Edition, London 1929, at pp. 150 et seq; Klüber: Droit Des Gens Moderne De l'Europe, 2nd Edition, Paris 1874, at pp. 75 et seq; Hall: A Treatise on International Law, 8th Edition, Oxford 1924, at pp. 322 et seq; Heffter: Das Europäische Völkerrecht der Gegenwart, 6th Edition, Berlin 1873, at pp. 59 et seq; Rivier: Principles Du Droit Des Gens, Edition, Paris 1896, at p. 277-p. 278; Twiss: The Law of Nations (Considered as Independent Political Communities), Edition, Oxford 1884, at pp. 178 et seq; Hershey: The Essentials of International Public Law and Organisation, 2nd Edition, New York 1927, at pp. 232 et seq; Faatz: "Notwehr" und "Notstand" Im Völkerrecht, Edition, Greifswald 1919, at pp. 25 et seq; Fenwick: International Law, Edition, London 1924, at pp. 142 et seq.
13 Eighth Report Ago, 12.

124

national obligation when the reason for the violation was 'immediate necessity of self-defence'.[14]

With the establishment of the ILC in 1947, the topic of state responsibility for injuries to aliens (including the law of defences precluding or justifying such) returned to the focus of attention. Five years after the ILC started its work García Amador was appointed as the Special Rapporteur for the topic. In his second report issued in 1957 the defence was limited to 'grounds of public interest or of the economic necessity of the State'.[15] However, only one year later García Amador's third report included a definition of the defence of necessity much closer to that found today in Article 25 DASR.[16] The next significant contribution to the text was made by Roberto Ago whose eighth report included a comprehensive analysis of the defence of necessity in international law.[17] During this time the ILC had broadened its focus to cover all breaches of international obligations and not just breaches committed in relation to aliens. Ago's Article 33 essentially embodies the final formulation of the defence as we know it today - systemically setting out in a system of defences precluding the wrongfulness of any violation of an international obligation.[18] Special Rapporteur James Crawford completed the codification project and in 2001 the ILC adopted its Draft Articles on State Responsibility for Internationally Wrongful Acts and recommended that the General Assembly (GA) take note of the Articles.[19] In addition it

14 League of Nations, Bases of discussion, No. 25, reprinted in: International Law Commission: Report on International Responsibility by Mr. F.V. Garcia-Amador, Special Rapporteur, UN Doc A/CN.4/96, Yearbook of the International Law Commission 1956, vol. II. pp. 173 - 231, at p. 208.
15 International Law Commission: International responsibility. Second report by F. V. Garcia Amador, Special Rapporteur, UN Doc A/CN.4/106, Yearbook of the International Law Commission 1957, vol. II. pp. 104 - 130, (hereinafter Second Report García Amador), at p. 129, Article 7(2)(a)
16 International Law Commission: International responsibility. Third report by F. V. Garcia Amador, Special Rapporteur, UN Doc A/CN.4/111, Yearbook of the International Law Commission 1958, vol. II. pp. 47-73, (hereinafter Third Report García Amador), at p. 50:"...the State shall not be responsible for injuries caused to an alien if the measures taken are the consequence of force majeure or of a state of necessity due to a grave and imminent peril threatening some vital interest of the State, provided that the State did not provoke the peril and was unable to counteract it by other means."(Emphasis added).
17 Eighth Report Ago.
18 International Law Commission: Report of the International Law Commission on the work of its Thirty-second session, 5 May - 25 July 1980, Official Records of the General Assembly, thirty-fifth session, Supplement No. 10, UN Doc A/35/10, Yearbook of the International Law Commission 1980, vol. II, Part Two. pp. 13 - 86, (hereinafter 32nd ILC Report), at p. 33, Article 33.
19 International Law Commission: Report of the International Law Commission on the work of its fifty-third session (23 April–1 June and 2 July–10 August 2001), UN Doc A/56/10, Yearbook of the International Law Commission 2001, vol. II, Part Two. pp. 1 - 205, (hereinafter 53rd ILC Report), at 11.

was suggested that the GA examine the Draft Articles with a view to adopting an international convention on the topic.[20] Shortly afterwards the GA took note of the Articles by passing a resolution annexing the Articles with its commentaries.[21] Subsequently the GA has issued further resolutions promoting the conclusion of a convention on the topic.[22] States themselves, however, remain divided on the future of the Articles.[23]

II. The Content of the Defence of Necessity as codified by the ILC in 2001

The DASR have been welcomed in both international jurisprudence and scholarship. The International Court of Justice has stated that Article 25 of the Articles forms part of customary international law.[24] However, whilst certain provisions may do so, it is important to note that the Articles as a whole do not represent customary international law nor do they create contractual obligations for states.

The DASR take a neutral approach to the primary rules of international law – instead focussing on the secondary rules dealing with the consequences of a breach of the primary rule. Hence, the DASR do not contain any requirement for fault or intent and similarly contain no definition of injury, damages or harm.[25] Article 1 DASR states that 'every internationally wrongful act of a State entails the international responsibility of that State'. An internationally wrongful act is defined in Article 2 which provides that conduct that breaches an international obligation is attributable to that state. The obligation breached can be both cus-

---

20 Ibid.
21 General Assembly, Res.56/83 of 12 December 2001, Responsibility of States for Internationally Wrongful Acts.
22 General Assembly, Res. 59/35 of 2 December 2004, Responsibility of States for Internationally Wrongful Acts; General Assembly, Res. 62/61 of 6 December 2007, Responsibility of States for Internationally Wrongful Acts.
23 The working group of the Sixth Committee considered at its meetings on 23 October, and 12 and 19 November 2007 the prospects of the draft Articles. Regarding future action on the Articles, some delegations considered that negotiations on a convention would reopen controversial points and jeopardize the delicate balance built into the Articles. They also pointed out that the ensuing convention might be ratified only by a small number of States. Some other delegations favoured an immediate decision on the future of the Articles, emphasizing that the adoption of a convention would be the most logical and preferable outcome of the work of the ILC and would ensure legal certainty in the field. General Assembly, Sixty-second session, Official Records, Summary record of the 12th meeting, UN Doc A/C.6/62/SR.12, p. 9 et seq.
24 Case Concerning the Gabĉíkovo-Nagymaros Project (Hungary v. Slovakia), Judgment of 25 September 1997, I.C.J. Reports 1997, pp. 7 - 84, (hereinafter Gabĉíkovo-Nagymaros), at 40.
25 Crawford: State Responsibility, in: Max Planck Encyclopaedia of Public International Law (eds. Wolfrum et al.), 2010, accessible online at <www.mpepil.com> , at 12.

tomary or treaty based[26] since international law does not distinguish between responsibility *ex delicto* and *ex contractu*.[27] Further, Article 28 DASR provides that international responsibility of a state gives rise to legal consequences including reparation which can take various forms including restitution, compensation or satisfaction.[28]

In relation to defences, the regime set out in Chapter V containing six defences do not justify the breach of an international obligation itself but can preclude the attribution of this wrongful act to the state. Accordingly the DASR's defences must be distinguished from the grounds for suspension and termination of the obligation itself [29] which are governed by the Vienna Convention on the Law of Treaties.[30] Further, the defences in Chapter V preclude the wrongfulness of the non-compliance of an international obligation only for the period of time in which the defence's elements are fulfilled.[31] Importantly, none of the defences apply if the relevant wrongful act is a breach of a peremptory norm of general international law according to Article 26.[32]

1. Chapter V DASR, Defences

Chapter V of the DASR contains six defences which preclude the wrongfulness of states conduct. Chapter V covers the defences of consent (Art. 20), self-defence in conformity with the UN Charter (Art. 21), countermeasures (Art. 22), force majeure (Art. 23), distress (Art. 24), and necessity (Art. 25). The different defences may easily be divided into two groups - while consent, self-defence and countermeasures are dependent on the prior conduct of the injured state,[33] force majeure, distress and necessity are not.

---

26 ILC Draft Articles on State Responsibility with Commentaries, at Art. 12.
27 Crawford: State Responsibility (MPEPIL), at 12.
28 Ibid., at 28.
29 The ILC stresses that the state defences act rather as a shield than as a sword, see: ILC Draft Articles on State Responsibility with Commentaries, at p. 71, 2.
30 See Part Five VCLT: Invalidity, Termination and Suspension of the Operation of Treaties.
31 Crawford: State Responsibility (MPEPIL), at 21; and see Article 27 (a) DASR; the same opinion was expressed by the ICJ in Gabêíkovo-Nagymaros (1997), at 101.
32 The approach also in corresponds with Article 53 and 64 of the Vienna Convention on the Law of Treaties (VCLT) its Article 53 states: "A treaty is void if, at the time of its conclusion, it conflicts with a peremptory norm of general international law. For the purposes of the present Convention, a peremptory norm of general international law is a norm accepted and recognized by the international community of States as a whole as a norm from which no derogation is permitted and which can be modified only by a subsequent norm of general international law having the same character."
33 ILC Draft Articles on State Responsibility with Commentaries, at Art. 25, 2.

Force majeure (Art. 23) may be invoked by a state in the event that an 'Act of God' (circumstances out with a state's control) makes it impossible for a state to comply with its international obligation.[34] Crucially, force majeure differs from necessity and distress in that it does not involve an element of free choice.[35] Distress (Art. 24) may preclude the wrongfulness of state's conduct if the state in question had 'no other reasonable way' to safeguard human life under its case.[36] Distress can be distinguished from necessity by the element of will. While necessity is characterised as a situation of choosing between compliance with international law and other legitimate interests of the state, the element of free will in distress is nullified by the situation of peril.[37] Moreover, the legally protected interest of distress covers only human life whereas necessity may be invoked for any 'essential interest' of the state.[38] Necessity requires a conflict between adhering to an international obligation and an essential interest of higher weight and urgency.[39]

2. The Elements of Necessity under Article 25

The final version of the ILC's Draft Articles on State Responsibility contains the customary law defence of necessity. Article 25 provides:

1. Necessity may not be invoked by a State as a ground for precluding the wrongfulness of an act not in conformity with an international obligation of that State unless the act:

(a) is the only way for the State to safeguard an essential interest against a grave and imminent peril; and

(b) does not seriously impair an essential interest of the State or States towards which the obligation exists, or of the international community as a whole.

2. In any case, necessity may not be invoked by a State as a ground for precluding wrongfulness if:

(a) the international obligation in question excludes the possibility of invoking necessity; or

(b) the State has contributed to the situation of necessity.

---

34   UNCTAD: The protection of national security in IIAs, at p. 34.
35   ILC Draft Articles on State Responsibility with Commentaries, at Art. 23, 1.
36   Ibid., at Art. 24, 1.
37   Ibid.
38   Ibid., at Art. 25, 2.
39   Martinez: Invoking State Defences in Investment Treaty Arbitration, in: The Backlash Against Investment Arbitration (eds. Waibel/Kaushal/et al., 2010), pp. 315 - 337, at p. 317; ILC Draft Articles on State Responsibility with Commentaries, at Art. 25, 2.

The negative drafting of Article 25 attempts to ensure that the application of the defence of necessity is exceptional. Only if the stringent elements of the Article are met may states rely on the defence. The restrictive conditions are intended to reduce subjectivity. This approach underlines the exceptionality of necessity defence necessary to avoid the possibility of abuse inherent in the defence of necessity.[40]

The preliminary condition for the plea of necessity is an attributable breach of an international obligation by a state. In absence of a breach of an international obligation there is no recourse to Article 25. If the primary international obligation itself, such as compliance with a treaty,[41] sets out conditions for the derogation from the treaty obligation then there is in fact no breach of an international obligation.

C. Implementation Issues Relating to the Defence of Necessity in the Field of Investor-State Arbitration

Investor-state arbitration as a hybrid form of international arbitration has rapidly evolved in the last two decades. The defence of necessity has been invoked by respondent states in a sizable number of proceedings and the application of this defence has raised several important legal questions. Such questions have caused division in international legal scholarship and have produced inconsistent jurisprudence. Problems relating to the application of the defence of necessity arise out of two sources: the treaty basis and the hybrid nature of investor state arbitration.[42]

A number of tribunals have had to confront the defence of necessity under the rules of ICSID[43] and UNCITRAL.[44] In a few cases, annulment committees have

---

40 Ibid., at Art. 25, 2, 14; at 75.
41 See Art. 26 VCLT: "Every treaty in force is binding upon the parties to it and must be performed by them in good faith."
42 Douglas in: BYIL 2003.
43 CMS Gas Transmission Company v. Argentine Republic, ICSID Case No. ARB/01/8, Award of 12 May 2005, Orrego-Vicuña/Lalonde/Rezek, hereinafter CMS (2005); LG&E Energy Corp., LG&E Capital Corp. and LG&E International inc. v. Argentine Republic, ICSID Case No. ARB/02/01, Award of 3 October 2006, Maekelt/Rezek/van den Berg, hereinafter LG&E (2006); Enron Corporation and Ponderosa Assets, L.P. v. Argentine Republic, ICSID Case No. ARB/01/3, Award of 22 May 2007, Orrego-Vicuña/Tschanz, hereinafter Enron (2007); Sempra Energy International v. Argentine Republic, ICSID Case No. ARB/02/16, Award of 28 September 2007, Orrego-Vicuña/Lalonde/Morelli Rico, hereinafter Sempra (2007); Continental Casualty Company v. Argentine Republic, ICSID Case No. ARB/03/9, Award of 5 September 2008, hereinafter Continental Casualty (2008).

reviewed the decisions.[45] The vast majority of the disputes have arisen out of the measures undertaken by the Government of Argentina to enact emergency legislation to overcome its economic crisis of 2001. The unexceptional nature of the facts in this case do not hinder the analysis, but in fact aid its general application. Moreover, the jurisprudence on the Argentina crisis has arisen at the same time as several decisions against African respondent states.[46]

However, the number of cases cited should in no way suggest that there is a comprehensive and well-developed jurisprudence on this topic since the practitioners involved in these tribunals were selected from a small group of arbitrators which has led to curious overlaps and outcomes.[47]

That being said, the management of the aforementioned conflicts may have given rise to a new understanding of necessity in the international law regime of investment protection. In relation to the debate concerning the fragmentation of international law several factors need further analysis. As a result, four facets of the conflict fall to be examined and illuminated. First, necessity invoked against private persons; second, the elements of Article 25 DASR as interpreted by investment tribunals; third, the application of customary law necessity in relation to treaty-based defences; and finally, the duty to pay compensation during the situation of necessity.

---

44   BG Group Plc v. Argentine Republic, UNCITRAL, Award of 24 December 2007, Aguilar Alvarez/Garro/van den Berg, hereinafter BG (2007); National Grid PLC v. Argentine Republic, UNCITRAL, Award of 3 November 2008, Rigo Sureda/Garro/Kessler, hereinafter National Grid (2008).

45   CMS Gas Transmission Company v. Argentine Republic, ICSID Case No. ARB/01/8, Decision on Annulment of 25 September 2007, Guillaume/Elaraby/Crawford, hereinafter CMS Annulment (2007); Sempra Energy International v. Argentine Republic, ICSID Case No. ARB/02/16, Decision on the Argentine Republic's Application for Annulment of the Award of 29 June 2010, Söderlund/Edward/Jacovides, hereinafter Sempra Annulment (2010); Enron Creditors Recovery Corp. and Ponderosa Assets, L.P. v. The Argentine Republic, ICSID Case No. ARB/01/3, Decision on the Application for Annulment of the Argetnite Republic of 30 July 2010, Griffith/Robinson/Tresselt, hereinafter Enron Annulment (2010).

46   Patrick Mitchell v. Democratic Republic of the Congo, ICSID Case No. ARB/99/7, of 1 November 2006, Dimolitsa/Dossou/Giardina, hereinafter Mitchell Annulment (2006), at 55 et seq; Bernardus Henricus Funnekotter and others v. Republic of Zimbabwe, ICSID Case No. ARB/05/6, of 22 April 2009, Guillaume/Cass/Zafar, hereinafter Funnekotter (2009), at 102 et seq.

47   Professor Orrego-Vicuña was presiding over three of the first five cases, which dealt with the issue of necessity (CMS, Enron, Sempra). Those awards are nearly literally identical in the parts concerning necessity defence. Additionally, arbitrators seemed to have changed their mind on the topic, if one considers Professor Rezek sitting in CMS and then in LG&E and van den Berg sitting in LG&E and then in Enron and BG. In those cases, the awards were rendered unanimously. Lalonde and Carro sitting in CMS and Sempra and BG and National Grid respectively, obviously seem to have less convincing counsels.

I. Necessity Invoked against Investors

The defence of necessity is a defence of a state intended to preclude the wrongfulness of an act not in conformity with an international obligation of a state. At first glance, necessity also seems applicable in the international law of investment protection, since the basis for investor-state arbitrations are treaties - instruments of international law. In relation to the DASR, the violation of substantial rights set forth in International Investment Agreements (IIA) is a breach of an international obligation which ultimately results in an internationally wrongful act. The wrongfulness of such act may thus be excluded by invoking necessity under Article 25.

In investment arbitration practice, the defence is in fact regularly raised and tribunals without question have accepted its applicability.[48] Only in one case, *BG*, has the tribunal suggested that 'Article 25 may relate exclusively to international obligations between sovereign States'.[49] In the end, however, the tribunal did not pronounce on the question due to the application of Article 25 being refused on other grounds.[50]

The largely uncritical approach of tribunals is surprising considering that investment arbitration is anything but a traditional international law setting where the competing interests of sovereign states are at stake.[51] But due to arbitration clauses in many IIAs investors can commence arbitration proceedings and seek recourse against states. In the course of such proceedings the investor, either a natural or a legal person, confronts the state on equal legal footing. On the basis of international law, this is unusual since individuals have traditionally been considered objects of international law, rather than subjects like states.[52] As such, the nature of the legal relationship between investor and state may feasibly not allow recourse to a defence deriving from international law - the law regulating conduct of sovereign states.

Moreover, the international obligations contained in IIAs are owed between the contracting states. The single investor is not party to the IIA and thus neither debtor nor creditor in relation to the international obligations in question. However, the investor is *in concreto* beneficiary of the IIA because it can start arbitration concerning a particular dispute without assistance from contracting states. In

---

48   For an overview see UNCTAD: The protection of national security in IIAs, at pp. 45 et seq.

49   BG (2007), at 408.

50   Ibid., at 411, by quoting LG&E, the tribunal decided that the "very restrictive conditions" of Article 25 were not met, because measures adopted by Argentina were illicit.

51   Bjorklund, in: Handbook of Investment Law, at p. 463, see also McLachlan in: ICLQ 2008, at p. 390

52   Brownlie: Principles of Public International Law, p. 65.

light of their relative legal relationship, it seems unclear how the respondent state may invoke defences which derive from another legal relationship (the IIA) which, moreover, is concluded on a level of law to which individuals do not regularly have access.

The comparative analysis of circumstances where necessity is invoked in legal relations between individuals and states, outlined below, is followed by an analysis of the legal relations between investors and respondent states.

1. Necessity in Relations between Private Persons and States

Two trends in international legal relations have increased necessity's impact on the relationship between states and individuals. In the first the state descends to the level of private law[53] and in the second the individual ascends to the level international law.

Firstly, recent state practice indicates the tendency for states to act internationally not only as a sovereign (*acta iure imperii*) but also rather frequently under private law on equal footing with individuals (*acta iure gestionis*). Public-private partnerships (PPP) and concession agreements serve as examples. Through such instruments states descend to the legal level of private persons and do not act in their capacity as subjects of international law. The applicable law in those disputes is in fact domestic law.[54] However, public international law also plays an important role in those relations[55] because they often involve public interests, such as development of natural resources or infrastructural undertakings, and the private parties of the contracts are often powerful multi national enterprises (MNE) with arguably as much power as states.

In the field of governmental loans (which can be classified as a state's civil law engagement) states regularly invoked the plea for necessity, often in the

---

53   The term 'private law' is used in the following to describe legal relationships that take place on equal footing between the related subjects. It may be distinguished from public law, which inter alia can be characterised by subordinate footing of the related subjects.

54   See for this rule PCIJ, Case concerning the Payment of Various Serbian Loans issued in France (France v. Kingdom of the Serbs, Croats and Slovenes), Judgment of 12 July 1929, Publications of the Permanent Court of International Justice, Ser. A., No. 20, 1929, hereinafter Serbian Loans, p. 41: "any contract which is not a contract between States in their capacity of subjects of international law is based on the municipal law of some country".

55   Walter: Oil Concession Disputes, Arbitration on, in: Max Planck Encyclopaedia of Public International Law (eds. Wolfrum et al.), 2010, accessible online at <www.mpepil.com>, at 24 et seq.

guise of economic emergency to excuse non-payment of sovereign loans.[56] In these rather old cases, international tribunals and courts accepted the plea without articulating any concern about the private nature of the loan agreement. This was due to the fact those proceedings were traditional state to state proceedings or individual-state arbitrations where the state had conferred its right to a particular dispute to individuals.

Quite recently, the Bundesverfassungsgericht, the German constitutional court, had to deal with the issue of whether Argentina could invoke necessity to justify non-payment of coupons and nominal amounts. Basing its decision on an expert report of Professor Reinisch, the Bundesverfassungsgericht decided that international law does not allow for the plea of necessity to be invoked against private persons.[57] After an analysis of jurisprudence, the court concluded that Argentina could not invoke customary law necessity to justify its conduct.[58] The argument that states regularly invoked necessity in investment arbitration did not convince the court as it reasoned the basis of those arbitrations lay in a treaty and as such the international law defence of necessity could be invoked.[59] In a dissenting opinion Judge Lübbe-Wolff came to another conclusion.[60] She argued that, in accordance with Article 38 (1) (c) of the ICJ, it was a 'general principle of law recognised by civilized nations' that in all private law relationships, in terms of estoppel or principle, the breach of an obligation is excused in exceptional circumstances.[61] She did not see a difference for investment arbitration since in those proceedings the investor exercises its own right in its capacity as private person.[62] Moreover, domestic jurisprudence of other states does not indicate that necessity is only applicable between states.[63] It is clear that the application of necessity in investor state arbitration is conceptually a rather difficult undertaking and its invocation also may impact the development of the status of individuals in international law.

---

56   Serbian Loans; French Company of Venezuelan Railroads, Decision of the Mixed Claims Commission France-Venezuela of 31 July 1905, UNRIAA Vol. X, 1962, pp. 285 - 355; Affaire de l'indemnité russe (Russia, Turkey), Decision of 11 November 1912, UNRIAA Vol. XI 1962, pp. 421 - 447.

57   Bundesverfassungsgericht, 2 BvM 1-5/03, 1, 2/06, Order of the Second Senate of 8 May 2007, acessible at <www.bundesverfassungsgericht.de> (hereinafter Bundesverfassungsgericht); for a discussion see Rudolf/Hüfken: Argentinean State Bonds - Defence of Necessity in Relationship Between State and Private Debtor, AJIL 2007, pp. 857 - 865.

58   Bundesverfassungsgericht, at 64.

59   Ibid., at 52 - 53.

60   Bundesverfassungsgericht, 2 BvM 1-5/03, 1, 2/06, Dissenting Opinion of Judge Lübbe-Wolf concerning the Order of the Second Senate of 8 May 2007, accessible at <www.bundesverfassungsgericht.de> (hereinafter Bundesverfasungsgericht Dissent).

61   Bundesverfasungsgericht Dissent, 82.

62   Ibid., at 89.

63   Ibid., at 91 - 93.

The second development in international law purports that classic public international law as law exclusively designed for states no longer represents the full picture. International organisations and other non-state actors in the form of non-governmental organisations and multinational enterprises are creeping onto on the international plane.

The position of the individual in relation to human rights is the most well established in international law. For example, regional conventions establishing a human rights framework contain provisions that expressly confer subjective rights to the individuals.[64] Moreover, individuals can find legal relief for breaches of *their* rights directly before international courts such as the European Court of Human Rights (ECtHR).[65] As such, individuals in the field of human rights own subjective rights on the level of public international law. By vesting the individual with subjective international rights, individuals are to some extent elevated into the role of a subject of international law. In this position they are creditor of an international obligation.[66] Consequently, (it could be argued) that the state owing the international obligation may raise the defence of necessity for a violation of the convention. In human rights law, however, necessity has so far not been utilised. The reason would appear to be that human rights conventions themselves often contain provisions defining *in concreto* the specific cases in which the contracting states may deviate from its human rights obligations. Due to the particular nature and specific importance of human rights, the so-called emergency clauses contain very high thresholds for non-compliance. For example, Article 15 of the ECHR states under the heading of 'derogation in time of emergency':

"(1) In time of war or other public emergency threatening the life of the nation any High Contracting Party may take measures derogating from its obligations under this Convention to the extent strictly required by the exigencies of the situation, provided that such measures are not inconsistent with its other obligations under international law."

The jurisprudence of the ECtHR indicates that the Court, while being generally permissive in accepting derogations from the ECHR by states, applies a

---

64 See the wording of Articles 5, 8, 9, 10 ECHR „everyone has the right..."
65 Article 32 ECHR states: "The Court may receive applications from any person, non-governmental organisation or group of individuals claiming to be the victim of a violation by one of the High Contracting Parties of the rights set forth in the Convention or the protocols thereto. The High Contracting Parties undertake not to hinder in any way the effective exercise of this right." (Emphasis added).
66 This is also defined by Article 33 DASR.

high degree of scrutiny in defining when the derogation is 'strictly required'.[67] The narrow scope of Article 15 ECHR has precluded any recourse to customary law of necessity. As a result, one cannot draw persuasive from the field of human rights. However, the systemic structure of treaty-based defences and their relationship to defences of general international law provides some authority for IIA-based necessity defences, a point we will return to in due course.

2. Defining the Legal Relationship of Investors and Respondent States

The question of the nature of IIA rights and obligations has been comprehensively considered by Douglas and others.[68] Douglas distinguished the possible variations as derivative and direct approaches.[69] While the derivative approach, which included investors who merely received a mediated version of the state's right of diplomatic protection, was refused due to its incompatibility with the legal reality in the law of investment protection, the 'direct model' has found approval.[70] The direct model describes the rights and obligations in an IIA as 'original'. The investor receives through the IIA direct access to the content of the IIA. However, the scope of the investor's access to treaty rights needs further explanation. *Douglas* distinguished the approaches in two models. One model does not differentiate between the substantive and the procedural rights of the IIA. All rights of an IIA are conferred to the investor.[71] The other model distinguishes between 'substantive obligations of investment protection' and 'the obligation to submit to investor/state arbitration upon the filing of a notice of claim by the claimant investor'.[72]

Due to the nature of the IIA as a treaty between states, it can hardly be argued that all rights *in abstracto* belong to the investor. This view is supported by the fact that the majority of IIAs contain provisions concerning the settlement of disputes of the contracting states in matters of treaty interpretation, which is a general matter. On the other hand IIAs grant investors the right to commence arbitration proceedings only in specific disputes where their interests are violated

---

67   The Case of A. and Others v. the United Kingdom, Application no. 3455/05 v. 19 February 2009.

68   Douglas: The International Law of Investment Claims, Edition, Cambridge 2009; Douglas in: BYIL 2003; Paulsson: Arbitration Without Privity, ICSID Review 1995, at p. 256; Burdeau: Nouvelles Perspectives Pour L'Arbitrage Dans Le Contentieux Économique Intéressant Les Etats, Rev. Arb. 1995, at pp. 12 et seq; Wälde: Investment Arbitration Under the Energy Charter Treaty, Arb. Int.1996, at pp. 435 et seq.

69   Douglas: in: BYIL 2003, at pp. 182 et seq.

70   Douglas: The International Law of Investment Claims, at 32 et seq.

71   Ibid., at 72.

72   Ibid., at 73.

by the state. The existence of those clauses militates in favour of the second approach of Douglas's direct rights theory.

In order to avoid redundant systemic anomalies in international law, an alternative view of the legal relationship between investor and respondent state should be considered. Following Douglas, the rights and obligations of an IIA *in abstracto* are owed only between the contracting states since the treaty *in abstracto* can only be enforced by the contracting states. *In concreto,* however, after a particular dispute has arisen, the arbitration clause of the IIA contains an offer of the contracting state to commence arbitration proceedings. This offer is directed to any person who qualifies as an investor under the IIA definition. The IIA is thus not a traditional contract for the benefit of a third party since the third party (the investor) cannot directly enforce the obligations in the treaty as they are stipulated *in abstracto*. The offer to arbitrate includes that, in proceeding, investors can allege breaches of the IIA standards of treatment and protection only in their particular case. In offering the arbitration proceedings the state is not acting in its capacity as a subject of international law. Since individuals cannot regularly act as subjects of international law,[73] while states may easily act on a different level with private persons in the form of *acta iure gestinonis*, or as the ILC states, 'commercial',[74] the arbitration agreement may not be of a public international law nature. In accepting the offer by filing a request for arbitration, the investor and the state form in a legal relationship. The nature of this legal relationship cannot easily be qualified as mere private law since the state is acting in its public capacity. However, due to the fact that in the case of arbitrations investors and states act at arms length, the relationship has a strong perception of a private law relationship in commercial arbitration. The investor is not catapulted to the level of a subject of international law - rather the state and the individual meet on a neutral level.[75]

Regardless of the nature of the relationship between investor and respondent state, the governing law of arbitration is open to agreements between the parties. Many IIA contain provisions determining the applicable law for those proceedings and these provisions vary from designating the applicable law as the law of

---

73   In human rights issues this is different. The decision of the ICJ in LaGrand (Germany v. United States of America), Decision of 27 June 2001, I.C.J. Reports 2001, pp. 466 - 517, (hereinafter LaGrand) may be promising that individuals may generally rise to the level of international law subjects, however, such approach in the international investment law's sub-area of international investment arbitration is not intellectually unavoidable and thus may be conceptually flawed.

74   ILC Draft Articles on State Responsibility with Commentaries, at Art. 4, 6.

75   This is not different from arbitration clauses in concession or PPP agreements.

the IIA, the law of the host state or public international law.[76] This is the case despite the fact that even without direct stipulation in the IIA the applicable law of the dispute may still be the law of the IIA in combination with public international and host state law. The application of civil law interpretation techniques which seek to reveal the true will of the contracting state regardless of the wording point to only one conclusion: the state, when signing the IIA, expressed its will in an international legal sense, not merely domestically. Due to the interpretative flexibility of civil law relationships, it is possible to transfer and adopt rules of international law, which were originally designed for interstate relations into the relations between investors and individuals. Different from sovereign loans, where the application of public international law is neither explicitly defined nor ascertainable through interpretation, in investment arbitration, necessity, as an element of general international law, can rightly be invoked by respondent states.

Whether or not they do so with such a rationale in mind, investment tribunals are correct in permitting the use of the defence of necessity in such arbitrations. In relation to the threat of fragmentation discussed earlier, this approach would appear to be ambivalent. Investor state disputes offer a multitude of opportunities in which varying interpretations can be made. As such, inherent in the positive effect lies the peril; that arbitrators may wrongly apply or misinterpret the principle, giving rise to a higher degree of fragmentation. The absence of *stare decisis* and an appeal system in investment arbitration law multiplies the threat of a divergent interpretations and applications. Ultimately, however, the positive effects outweigh the negative though tribunals must of course exercise due care in applying necessity.

II. Art. 25 Elements Interpreted by Investment Tribunals

Tribunals have been faced with pleas of necessity based in customary international law. Respondent states pleaded this justification for treaty violations on grounds of the customary international law of necessity as it is articulated in Article 25 DASR. These tribunals have unanimously acknowledged Article 25 as reflecting 'the state of customary international law on the matter'.[77] Further,

---

76 United Nations Conference on Trade and Development: Dispute Settlement: Investor State, UNCTAD Series on Issues in International Investment Agreements 2003, UNCTAD/ITE/IIT/30, accessible at <www.unctad.org>, at p. 57.

77 CMS (2005), at 315; Enron (2007), at 303; Sempra (2007), at 344.

these tribunals were not reluctant to stress the exceptional nature of necessity and its potential for abuse.[78]

While some tribunals comprehensively discussed the different elements of Article 25, the tribunal in *BG*, although generally accepting the applicability of the defence, did not apply it due to the exceptional nature of necessity the tendency of tribunals to abuse it.[79] Instead of applying the law of Article 25 to the facts, it provided evidence as to how Argentina had acted abusively when invoking necessity. As evidence for Argentina's misconduct in relation to foreign investors, it referred to the adopted measures.[80] Similarly, before applying the law to the facts the tribunal in *CMS*, performed an "abuse test" which it answered negatively for Argentina's plea different from *BG*.[81] Fortunately for this study, the *BG* award – driven by pure equity concerns – is the only award so far that has neglected the application of necessity under Article 25 without even considering its written requirements.

Article 25 stipulates the elements which cumulatively must be fulfilled in order to preclude the wrongfulness of an act of a state.[82] Paragraph 1 sets forth requirements for the *situation of necessity* as well as the *act of necessity*, while paragraph 2 serves as a corrective which excludes invocation of necessity due to the prior conduct of the state. In what follows, the elements of Article 25 will be explained and illuminated by interpretations of international law scholars and general international case law. Those findings are then contrasted with interpretations of investment tribunals in order to conclude whether the elements of Article 25 are interpreted differently in investment arbitration.

1. The Situation of Necessity

The situation of necessity is defined as 'grave and imminent peril' for 'an essential interest'.[83] By using this wording, the ILC made clear that the situation of necessity is not limited to where the existence of a state itself is in danger but can

---

78 CMS (2005), at 317; Enron (2007), at 304; Sempra (2007), at 345.
79 BG (2007), at 411.
80 Ibid: "(i) luring BG and other investors to accept a temporary suspension of the dollar denominated tariff and the adjustment mechanism by indicating that the measures would be temporary; (ii) threatening companies that resorted to arbitration; (iii) attempting to force investors which commenced arbitration to withdraw these proceedings as a condition to negotiations; and (iv) setting up a mechanism for the revision of the concessions that was never intended to restore the conditions of Argentina's initial representations.".
81 CMS (2005), at 321.
82 Gabčíkovo-Nagymaros (1997), at 40 - 41.
83 Garcia Amador already used the same definition.

be established as early as when an essential interest is threatened.[84] The final commentary of the Article did not enumerate or define 'essential interests' due to the desire that any judgement on this be made on a case to case basis, depending on the nature of the interest at stake for the state, its people and the international community as a whole.[85] However, what may qualify as essential or particularly important interest of the state was succinctly defined by Special Rapporteur *Ago* as:

'the existence of the State itself, political or economical survival, the continued functioning of its essential services, the maintenance of internal peace, the survival of a sector or its population, the preservation of the environment of its territory or a part thereof'[86]

Importantly, the owner of the 'essential interest' is not defined, unlike paragraph (1) (b). As such, and given that the other elements are met, it may thus be feasible for a state to preclude the wrongfulness of its conduct by invoking an interest far removed from its own.[87] Apart from this wide, the ICJ decision in *Gabčíkovo-Nagymaros* indicated that an essential interest may also only focus on a particular region.[88]

The ICJ sought to define the threatening peril to the essential interest by referring to the term 'danger' in as much as it 'evokes the idea of "risk" more than 'material damage'.[89] 'Peril' has to be established objectively on the basis of reasonable evidence available *ex ante* and may not suffice if the peril is merely subjective.[90] Similarly, uncertain peril of a long-term nature does not preclude wrongfulness.[91] Concerning scientific uncertainty, Crawford suggested that since scientific experts may differ regarding the certainty of a particular threat the Article should include a precautionary element.[92] This element was discussed particularly in relation to environmental matters and may also be applicable in relation to a state's economic situation. Additionally, the peril has to fulfil the temporal and the substantial threshold of imminence and graveness respectively. The former does not require the peril to be existent; however, it is not enough for the

---

84   Third Report García Amador, at 19.
85   ILC Draft Articles on State Responsibility with Commentaries, at Art. 25, 15; it was stated that the peremptory norms of international law may constitute the core content of "essential interest", Viñuales: State of Necessity and Peremptory Norms in International Investment Law, Law & Bus. Rev. Am. 2008, pp. 79 - 105, at p. 82.
86   Third Report García Amador, at 2.
87   Bjorklund, in: Handbook of Investment Law, at p. 477 et seq.
88   Gabčíkovo-Nagymaros (1997), at 53.
89   Gabčíkovo-Nagymaros (1997), at 54.
90   ILC Draft Articles on State Responsibility with Commentaries, at Art. 25, 15.
91   Bjorklund, in: Handbook of Investment Law, at p. 482.
92   ILC Draft Articles on State Responsibility with Commentaries, at art. 25, 16.

peril to be merely 'apprehended or contingent'.[93] The ILC defined 'imminent' in the sense of proximate.[94] Furthermore, the ICJ held that imminence is synonymous with 'immediacy' or 'proximity' and goes far beyond the concept of 'possibility'.[95] Concerning the latter threshold, there is no gravity scale specified by the ILC. However, as *Ago* states, the danger has to be 'extremely grave'.[96]

Some investment tribunals in the cases of *CMS*, *Enron*, *Sempra* and *LG&E* elaborated whether Argentina's crisis fulfilled the element of a situation of necessity under Article 25. The situation of necessity in the majority of arbitrations was Argentina's economic crisis from the beginning of the millennium. In particular, the crisis was described as:

"the significant decreases in the Argentine Gross Domestic Product (GDP), consumption and investment during the crisis period, together with the deflation and the reduction in value of Argentine corporations, resulted in widespread unemployment and poverty, with dramatic consequences for health, nutrition and social policy. Public institutions were no longer functioning."[97]

Although the tribunals did not appropriately distinguish object (essential interest) and subject (grave and imminent peril) of the situation of necessity[98] and only gave a general analysis of the severity of the Argentine crisis, some of their findings in the awards give insight in to how the tribunals interpreted Article 25 (1)(a).

The term 'essential interest' was interpreted by some tribunals in a very narrow way. For instance, the tribunals in *Enron* and *Sempra*, in using Argentina's 'very existence' and independence as threshold for the 'essential interest' neglected to qualify the situation as necessity in Argentina.[99] *Enron* and *Sempra* indicate that the graveness of the peril was interpreted in accordance with the ease of its management. The respective tribunals neglected the sufficient gravity of the peril reasoning that events were not 'out of control' nor had they become 'unmanageable'.[100] Similarly in *CMS*, the tribunal stated that only a 'total breakdown of the economy' or 'disruption and disintegration of society' would qualify as a situation of necessity.[101]

93   Ibid..
94   Ibid., 15 .
95   Gabĉíkovo-Nagymaros (1997), at 54.
96   Third Report García Amador, at 13; 32nd ILC Report, at p. 49, 33.
97   Enron (2007), at 289; Sempra (2007), at 326.
98   Bjorklund, in: Handbook of Investment Law, at p. 481.
99   Enron (2007), at 306; Sempra (2007), at 348.
100   Enron (2007), at 307; Sempra (2007), at 349.
101   CMS (2005), at 354.

In contrast, the tribunal in *LG&E* decided that necessity was not only limited to interests of the state's existence.[102] By citing Crawford's second report on state responsibility the tribunal distinguished necessity from self-defence.[103] The tribunal observed that Argentina's 'existence, its political and economic survival, the possibility of maintaining its essential services in operation and the preservation of its internal peace' was endangered by an 'extremely serious threat'.[104]

These different approaches show the difficulties tribunals have had in applying the defence of necessity as a result of their equity considerations. All tribunals were aware of the exceptional nature of the defence of necessity as it was stressed by the ILC and they unanimously accepted that an economic emergency could give rise to the necessity plea. In order to interpret Article 25 the tribunal in *LG&E* used commentaries and preparation work of the ILC, while tribunals in *CMS, Sempra* and *Enron* argued with an outdated interpretation of 'essential interest'. This may be in favour of the interests of the investor; it is not in line with the meaning given by the ILC. These three decisions interpreted 'essential interest' as 'existence of the state' but their inconsistency with the rule of customary international law does not symbolise settled jurisprudence in investment arbitrations. Further, the lack of distinction between object and subject of the situation of necessity, if pursued in further jurisprudence, may lead to a fragmented approach in international investment law.

2. The Act of Necessity

The *act of necessity* must be 'the only way' to safeguard the essential interest. Additionally, the necessity action is reviewed against the background of whether it violates essential interests of the state to which the obligation is owed as well as the interests of the international community as a whole.

The *ultima ratio* nature of the act of necessity emphasises the exceptional nature of necessity most clearly. The commentary stresses that 'the plea is excluded if there are other (otherwise lawful) means available, even if they may be more costly or less convenient'.[105] This understanding was accepted by the ICJ in *Gabčíkovo-Nagymaros*, where it was stated that the cost of the possible alternatives was not a determinative factor for the state of necessity.[106] Though costs may not be the criterion to disqualify other possible ways of conduct, the *ultima*

---

102   LG&E (2006), at 251.
103   Ibid., at 252.
104   Ibid., at 257.
105   ILC Draft Articles on State Responsibility with Commentaries, at art. 25, 15.
106   Gabčíkovo-Nagymaros (1997), at 55.

ratio may not be judged on an absolute scale. For instance, an alternative action that itself threatens an 'essential interest' of the state may not be required.[107] In determining whether the action undertaken had been the only way there may be recourse to the remarks concerning the existence of an 'imminent peril' similarly. Hence, the application of an objective *ex ante* test may be logically and reasonably preferable. Moreover, it was pointed out that, in the field of economic emergencies, considerations of proportionality and adequacy may become required.[108]

Only if the *ultima ratio* act outweighs other interests is the claim for the necessity defence valid. It is self-evident that interests embodying peremptory norms of international law always outweigh the invoking states interests.[109] The formulation 'or of the international community as a whole' broadens the scope of the balancing test under Article 25 (1) (b) and thus may also include international human rights or even individual interests.[110]

Investment tribunals in *CMS, Enron, Sempra* and *LG&E* discussed whether Argentina's measures qualified as acts of necessity. The *ultima ratio* nature of Argentina's measures was neglected in *Enron* and *Sempra* on the grounds that experiences of other economic crises indicated that 'there are always many approaches to addressing and resolving such critical events'.[111] The tribunals limited their reasoning through stating that other ways potentially exist but neither mentioning nor discussing their suitability.[112] The subsequent annulment committee in *Enron* found that such approach constitutes a ground for annulment because the tribunal failed to apply the applicable law and failed to state reasons for its decision.[113] The committee stated that merely relying on an expert opinion, which shows that other options were available, does not meet the 'only way requirement' of article 25 DASR. The committee expressed that an interpretation of the requirement has to address the quality and likelihood of those potential 'other ways'.[114]

The tribunal in *CMS* stated that it is not the task of the tribunal to evaluate the different opportunities qualitatively and thus performed only a quantitative

---

107 Boed: State of Necessity as Justification for Internationally Wrongful Conduct, Yale Hum. Rts. & Dev. L.J. 2000, pp. 1 - 43, at 18.
108 Reinisch: Necessity in International Investment Arbitration - an Unnecessary Split of Opinions in Recent ICSID Cases? Comments on CMS v. Argentina and LG&E v. Argentina, TDM 2006, at p. 12.
109 Viñuales in: Law & Bus. Rev. Am. 2008, at 90 et seq.
110 Reinisch in: TDM 2006, at p. 12.
111 Enron (2007), at 309; Sempra (2007), at 350.
112 Enron (2007), at 310; Sempra (2007), at 351.
113 Enron Annulment, at 378.
114 Ibid., 370-372.

evaluation in deciding whether 'there was only one or various ways'.[115] It found reason for the quantitative approach in the ILC's commentary to Article 25 where it was stressed that cost cannot be a determination factor.[116]

Without defining the *ultima ratio* element specifically, the tribunal in *LG&E* found 'an economic recovery package' was the only way to answer to the situation of necessity.[117] Though the tribunal acknowledged that 'there may have been a number of ways to draft the economic recovery plan', it found the measures 'necessary'.[118]

The approach in *LG&E* indicates that the tribunal, unlike those in *CMS, Enron* and *Sempra*, performed a qualitative approach of this necessity element. Whether such approach can be derived from the wording 'other ways' cannot be answered unequivocally. Further cases may shine more light on this issue. On the other hand, the literal interpretation of the *ultima ratio* element, without implementing a quality check of those 'other ways', as performed in *CMS, Enron* and *Sempra*, may lead to a continuous inapplicability of customary necessity since alternatives are always imaginable (such as idleness). The annulment decision in *Enron* indicates a rather comprehensive interpretation of the 'other way' requirement is necessary. To speak of fragmentation, however, would seem to be an exaggeration.

In *CMS, Enron* and *Sempra*, the balancing test of Article 25 (1) (b) was not decided in favour of the international community as a whole 'as it is an interest of a general kind'.[119] Additionally, in *CMS* the tribunal neglected a violation of a peremptory norm of international law as carried out by Article 26 DASR.[120] Tribunals in *Enron* and *Sempra* held that Argentina's invocation of necessity does not 'generally' impair the interests of the other contracting state.[121] In *CMS*, the tribunal came to the same conclusion but distinguished the essential interest of investors from the interests of state parties.[122] In contrast, the tribunals in *Enron* and *Sempra* underlined that the interests of the 'ultimate beneficiaries', in other words private entities, had to be taken into consideration.[123] The annulment committee in *Enron* stated that such approach 'contrasts with the language of Article 25 (1) (b) of the ILC Articles'.[124]

---

115   CMS (2005), at 323.
116   Ibid., at 324.
117   LG&E (2006), at 257.
118   Ibid.
119   Enron (2007), at 310; Sempra (2007), at 352.
120   CMS (2005), at 325.
121   Enron (2007), at 341; Sempra (2007), at 390.
122   CMS (2005), at 358.
123   Sempra (2007), at 391.
124   Enron Annulment (2010), at 383.

The *LG&E*-tribunal understood the balancing test not as an element of the act of necessity but rather as a way to prevent invoking necessity for non-essential interests.[125] It came to the same conclusion as the tribunals in *CMS*, *Enron* and *Sempra*, that 'no other state's right was seriously impaired by the measures'.[126] However, it did not address the interests of investors.

Interpreting Article 25 (2) (b) as also including interests of investors, like in *Enron* and *Sempra*, is different from the understanding of the ILC. The *Enron* annulment committee expressed a rather sceptical view on the issue. However, the approach seems appropriate in order to perform the transformation of customary law in the field of investment arbitration properly. Such mutative adoption seems appropriate since, in signing the IIA with an investor-state arbitration clause, the contracting state expressed its will to protect rights of foreign investors. Those interests should be included in the balancing test. However, there might not be much deviation from the traditional rule because the interests of investors, as pointed out, are predominately of pecuniary nature, which in theory would regularly be outweighed by the more important interests of a whole state.[127]

3. The Limitations of Necessity

The second paragraph of Article 25 sets out two exceptions in which the plea of necessity is not applicable, even if the situation and the act of necessity may be validly established. The exceptions embody the reasoning that a state's plea may be denied due to two situations of prior conduct: first, the violated international obligation itself precludes necessity, and second, the state invoking necessity contributed to the situation of necessity.

a) Prohibition of Necessity due to the Obligation

This prohibition of the invocation can be stated explicitly or derived from the object and purpose of the obligation.[128] The ILC's commentary gives the example of a humanitarian convention explicitly not allowing recourse to military necessity.[129] Additionally, the object and purpose of the obligation may also prohibit

---

125   Ibid., at 254.
126   Ibid., at 257.
127   Bjorklund, in: Handbook of Investment Law, at p. 487.
128   Ibid., at p. 488.
129   ILC Draft Articles on State Responsibility with Commentaries, at art. 25, 19.

the preclusion of wrongfulness by invoking necessity. For instance, obligations which are purposely made for abnormal situations of emergency may not be breached and excused or justified by necessity.[130] Investment tribunals in *CMS*, *LG&E* and *Funnekotter* have discussed whether the IIA excludes the application of Article 25.

The tribunal in *CMS* pursued a relative approach to deciding whether the BIT excludes the plea of necessity under Article 25.[131] In answering this question, the tribunal referred to the object and purpose of the BIT which it defined as 'being designed to protect investments at a time of economic difficulties or other circumstances leading to the adoption of adverse measures by the Government'.[132] However, the tribunal did not apply an absolute test, but rather weighed the object and purpose of the BIT with the severity of the crisis. It came to the conclusion that, in the absence of 'profoundly serious conditions', the BIT would exclude the application of Article 25.[133]

In contrast, the *LG&E* tribunal used the existence of the treaty clause for necessity as evidence against prohibition of necessity under customary law. It reasoned that if the parties to the BIT agreed to the clause they simultaneously acknowledged the possibility 'that one of them may invoke the state of necessity'.[134]

In *Funnekotter* the tribunal seems to have neglected Zimbabwe's plea on the grounds of 25 (2) (a).[135] Article 6 of the Netherlands-Zimbabwe BIT attached legality of an expropriation to the requirements of public interest, non-discriminatory matter and payment of compensation. Zimbabwe did not pay compensation although it expropriated multiple farms. It argued its non-payment was justified by a state of necessity under customary international law.[136] The tribunal, in its award did not address explicitly the elements of necessity. However, it concluded that 'it [Zimbabwe] never explains why such a state of necessity prevented it from calculating and paying the compensation due to the farmers in conformity with the BIT'.[137] This may only be understood as the object and purpose of the duty to pay compensation for an expropriation in public interest does not allow recourse to necessity.

Analysing the different decisions, the difficulties become evident. On the one hand, IIA are made for protection in 'abnormal situations', on the other hand

---

130 Ibid.
131 CMS (2005), at 353.
132 Ibid., at 354.
133 Ibid.
134 LG&E (2006), at 255.
135 Funnekotter (2009), at 106.
136 Ibid., at 102.
137 Ibid., at 106.

they do not expressly stipulate non-application and moreover often seem to accept a situation of necessity in crisis-treatment clauses. The shrewd approach in *LG&E* does not work in situations where there is no emergency clause in the IIA, as is the case in the majority of cases. The approach in *CMS* is flexible but may be too arbitrary. In a detailed version, the same issue appeared in *Funnekotter*. Indeed, the conditional expropriation clause before the *Funnekotter* tribunal may be designed for abnormal situations. However, it is arguable whether the contractual prohibition of expropriation in the BIT as a whole and not its conditions may be excluded by necessity. The comprehensive stipulation in IIA of the specific elements under which an otherwise unlawful expropriation may be exceptionally lawful, may be understood as precluding any other exceptions of this rule. Concerning fragmentation issues, the law of investment arbitration has not further moved from the general international law rule. The issues discussed by tribunals are inherent in the cross-application of necessity in investment protection law.

b) Prohibition due to Significant Contribution

Of extremely high significance is the second exception in paragraph 2 (b) which stresses that a state who has contributed to the situation of necessity may not invoke necessity. Case law suggests the contribution does not require an action but can also be an omission.[138] The commentary of Article 25, however, makes clear that not every contribution of the state to the situation of necessity excludes its application. The contribution's threshold is described as having to be sufficiently substantial and not merely incidental or peripheral.[139] The rationale of the element derives clearly from good faith considerations such as the principle *venire contra factum proprium*.

Investment tribunals in *CMS, Enron, Sempra, LG&E, Continental Casualties* and *National Grid* discussed the issue of whether Argentina was excluded from invoking necessity because of its contribution to the crisis.

In the *CMS, Enron* and *Sempra* cases, the tribunals distinguished between endogenous and exogenous factors. They found the crisis was due to both factors.[140] Concerning the threshold of the contribution the tribunal in *CMS* found that 'evolving government policies and their shortcomings' contributed to the crisis sufficiently substantially.[141] The tribunals in *Sempra* and *Enron* came to

---

138 Gabčíkovo-Nagymaros (1997), at 57: "helped, by act or omission to bring about".
139 ILC Draft Articles on State Responsibility with Commentaries, at art. 25, 20.
140 CMS (2005), at 328; Enron (2007), at 311; Sempra (2007), at 353.
141 CMS (2005), at 329.

the same conclusion but without giving explicit reasons.[142] In conclusion, all three tribunals held Argentina as a whole state had contributed to the situation of necessity although no particular Argentinean administration may be held responsible for the crisis.[143] The annulment committee in *Enron* held that the tribunal in *Enron* had failed to apply the law. The committee stated that the tribunal based its decision merely on an expert economist and did not interpret the 'contribution' element of necessity.[144]

The *LG&E*-tribunal merely stated that there was no evidence of Argentina's contribution in the record.[145]

The tribunal in *National Grid* dismissed the necessity defence because Argentina had failed to establish it did not contribute to the crisis.[146] Different from the finding in *LG&E*, the burden of proof was allocated to the state invoking necessity. This different approach was explained by the lack of an emergency clause in the UK-Argentina BIT.[147] The tribunal held that the crisis was caused by internal and external factors, both of which both qualify the substantive and direct contribution threshold of Article 25 (2) (b).[148] The tribunal did not differentiate between the external and internal sources due to the gravity of their impact but rather exercised a historical distinction: internal factors such as external indebtedness, fiscal policies or labour market rigidity were held to have created the 'fertile ground for the crisis to develop'. External factors only came into play afterwards.[149]

In *Continental Casualties*, the tribunal, although not applying Article 25 (2) (b), considered the contribution element in its rationale when interpreting the treaty based necessity defence.[150]

The contribution element of necessity is very difficult to distinguish. Its importance is indicated by the fact that tribunals also consider its rationale when applying a treaty-based defence. In economic crises it is often impossible to determine who is victim or perpetrator of the crisis. Different scholars, following different schools of thought, come to different results. For instance, *Alvarez-Jiménez* compares the contribution requirement to the violation of the fair and equitable and national treatment standard. Since not every legislative failure amounts to a breach of the fair and equitable treatment standard not every contri-

---

142 Enron (2007), at 312; Sempra (2007), at 354.
143 CMS (2005), at 329; Enron (2007), at 312; Sempra (2007), at 354.
144 Enron Annulment (2010), at 392 et seq.
145 LG&E (2006), at 257.
146 National Grid (2008), at 261.
147 Ibid.
148 Ibid., at 260.
149 Ibid.
150 Continental Casualty (2008), at 234.

bution should preclude the application of necessity.[151] The annulment committee's decision in *Enron* shows it is not sufficient for a tribunal to merely base its decision on expert opinions of economists. This suggests that an interpretation of this element requires further considerations than mere economic data.

The substantiality test serves the purpose of showing that not every contribution disqualifies the application of necessity. The analysis of the tribunal's decisions does not signal a fragmentation of the necessity defence. Indefinite legal terms need to be interpreted case by case. Differing results dealing with the same issue have to be considered along with the diversity of arbitrator opinions and the nature of arbitration. Considering the burden of proof of whether the state has contributed to the situation of necessity, there is some fragile support for the allocation to the respondent state in the analysed cases. Such an approach does not contradict the draft of the ILC and serves the extraordinary nature of the necessity defence.

III. Necessity Applied in Conjunction with IIA Defences

The majority of arbitrations in which necessity was invoked involved necessity defences *ex contractu*. As an alternative to recourse to customary law, respondent states may invoke necessity (or a state described as in a state of emergency or national security) on the basis of a provision contained in IIAs. In 2009, UNCTAD issued a report on 'the protection of national security in IIAs'.[152] According to the study, only 12 % of the BITs reviewed contained a national security exception, although exceptions are widely used in Free Trade Agreements (FTA).[153] National security exceptions are only included in the BITs of a small group of states such as the USA. For instance, Article XI of the US-Argentina BIT sets forth:

"This Treaty shall not preclude the application by either Party of measures necessary for the maintenance of public order, the fulfilment of its obligations with respect to the maintenance or restoration of international peace or security, or the protection of its own essential security interests."

---

151 Alvarez-Jiménez: Foreign Investment Protection and Regulatory Failures as State's Contribution to the State of Necessity Under Customary International Law - a New Approach Based on the Complexity of Argentina's 2001 Crisis, 2010, pp. 141 - 177.
152 UNCTAD: The protection of national securtiy in IIAs.
153 Ibid., at p. 72.

Those necessity defences *ex contractu* have to be distinguished from clauses in IIA that grant investors substantial rights such as most favoured nation and national treatment in the event of a state of necessity. These 'national crisis clauses' are contained in the majority of IIA, for instance in all German BITs. Through their explicit wording, 'national crisis clauses' do not allow the respondent state to derogate from its treaty obligations,[154] but rather regulate its conduct under those circumstances.[155] They may also serve as an indicator that the IIA does not preclude the invocation of necessity as discussed above. The application of emergency clauses raises two issues, which will be discussed below: first, their systemic interplay with customary law defences of necessity and second, the interpretation of its elements.

1. Conceptual Interplay of Customary and Conventional Necessity

It is widely recognised that IIA represent a *lex specialis* concerning the treatment of investments and investor state arbitrations.[156] The existence of those explicit rules derogates rules of customary international law.[157] As such, the application of Article 25 may only be allowed if the IIA does not express the issue in a different way.[158] Thus, the specific regulation of a state of necessity in an IIA prohibits the right of a contracting state of that treaty to invoke the general doctrine of necessity as justification for non-compliance of their obligations in emergency situations.[159] Especially and obviously, this is correct when the treaty lays down a higher threshold than the defence in customary law (like in human rights conventions), however it must also be true in cases where the treaty stipulates a lower threshold. Authority may be found in Article 55 DASR[160] which manifests the general rule that *lex specialis derogat legi generali*.[161] Nevertheless, tribunals

---

154 In Funnekotter (2009), at 104, the Tribunal neglected such clause as the basis for BIT-based plea of necessity; see also Enron (2007), at 321; Sempra (2007), at 363.
155 CMS (2005), at 375; Enron (2007), at 320; Sempra (2007), at 362; LG&E (2006), at 244.
156 See the holding in the recent Ahmadou Sadio Diallo Case (Republic of Guinea v. Democratic Republic of the Congo), Judgment of 24 May 2007 on Preliminary Objections, ICJ General List No. 103, online accessible at www.icj-cij.org, at 88.
157 ILC Report on Fragmentation, 56, 66,
158 See McLachlan in: ICLQ 2008, at p. 391.
159 Kretzmer: State of Emergency, in: Max Planck Encyclopaedia of Public International Law (eds. Wolfrum et al.), 2010, accessible at <www.mpepil.com>, at 2. The lex specialis of the convention derogates the lex generalis of customary international law.
160 Article 55: "where and to the extent that the conditions for the existence of an international wrongful act or the content or implementation of the international responsibility of a State are governed by special rules of international law."
161 ILC Draft Articles on State Responsibility with Commentaries, at Art. 55, 2;

in *CMS, Enron, Sempra, LG&E,* and *Continental Casualties* as well as the ad hoc committees in the *CMS, Enron and Sempra* annulment decisions have dealt with the conceptual interplay of necessity *ex contractu* and Article 25 differently:

In *CMS* the tribunal inter-mixed the elements of Article 25 and Article XI of the relevant BIT. The tribunal's reasoning implies that it interpreted Article XI according to the customary law rules of necessity.[162] The tribunals in *Enron* and *Sempra* also neglected the predominant role of the BIT and applied customary law necessity within and across Article XI because Article XI 'did not deal with the legal elements necessary for legitimate invocation of a state of necessity'.[163] Thus, the tribunals found that Article XI does stipulate the same conditions as Article 25.[164]

The *LG&E*-tribunal followed the opposite approach and dealt first with the treaty-based defence in Article XI of the BIT. After having established necessity under Article XI, the tribunal considered necessity under Article 25 to 'support the tribunal's conclusion.'[165] The tribunal defined the consequences of Article XI as 'exclusion from wrongfulness of an act of the state'.[166]

The annulment committee in *CMS* expressed the opinion that Article XI is conceptually different from Article 25. If the conditions of Article XI were met, the substantive obligations under the BIT would not apply, whereas Article 25 precludes the wrongfulness of the violation of an international obligation.[167] Moreover, both rules are also substantially different since they consist of different elements.[168] In this context the committee evaluated the intermingling approach in *CMS* as 'manifest error of law'[169] and shed light on the relationship between treaty and custom based necessity. It stressed customary law necessity could only be subsidiary to necessity under Article XI.[170] If Article 25 symbolised a primary rule of international law its regulative conflict with Article XI had to be decided in favour of the latter according to the *lex specialis* rule.[171] If Article 25 is to be characterised as a secondary rule (as characterised by the ILC), its application required a breach of a primary rule such as the BIT. In considering whether there was a violation of the BIT the possible exclusion of a

---

162   CMS (2005), at 374
163   Sempra (2007), at 378; similar wording in Enron (2007), at 334
164   Ibid., at 339; at 388
165   LG&E (2006), at 245.
166   Ibid., at 261
167   CMS Annulment (2007), at 129.
168   Ibid., at 130.
169   Ibid.
170   Ibid., at 132.
171   Ibid., at 133.

breach by Article XI must also be considered.[172] Recourse to Article 25 was only permissible if one concluded a violation of the BIT.

The tribunal in *Continental Casualties* differentiated between the defence in the BIT and the customary defence based on their meaning and their content.[173] The tribunal qualified Article XI of the Argentina-US BIT as a *lex specialis* of primary nature not subject to the same conditions as the plea of necessity under general international law.[174] Thus it explicitly refused to apply the requirement under Article 25 (2) (b) when reviewing Article XI.[175]

The annulment committee in *Sempra* followed the approach of *CMS annulment* and *Continental Casualties*. It stipulated that Article XI 'differs in material respects' from Article 25.[176] Contrary to the annulment decision in *CMS*, however the annulment committee in *Sempra* established such lack of distinction as a manifest excess of powers. For this reason the committee annulled the former award in *Sempra*. The annulment committee in *Enron* came to a similar conclusion. It concurred with the annulment decision in *CMS* and held that Article 25 and Article XI have 'a different operation and content'.[177]

As stipulated in the annulment decision of *CMS*, the application of Article 25 has to be subsidiary to any treaty-based defence. It is hard to understand why the tribunals in *CMS*, *Enron*, and *Sempra* made such a mistake. The tribunals might have confused their approach with the interpretation of the fair and equitable treatment standard under NAFTA. There recourse to customary law (the minimum standard as defined in the holding in the *Neer*-arbitration) was deemed to be the appropriate interpretative approach since the stipulations in NAFTA were not expressive. However, the emergency clause in the US-Argentina BIT contains a different approach to necessity as does general international law. Although there is a tendency among scholars to include general international law in treaty regimes by interpreting in the course of so-called systemic integration it is undisputed that general international law may only play a supportive role. The flawed and nearly anarchic application of Article 25 in *CMS*, *Enron* and *Sempra* is a grave peril to a unified system of international law. However, to speak of an existing fragmentation may be exaggerating the case law. The decision in *LG&E* which was criticised by scholars mostly due to its investor-unfriendly outcome did reach the systemically correct direction. After the annulment committee in *CMS*, of which Crawford was a member, exposed the errors of the *CMS* decision

---

172   Ibid., at 134.
173   Continental Casualty (2008), at 161.
174   Ibid., at 167.
175   Ibid., at 234.
176   Sempra Annulment (2010), at 198.
177   Enron Annulment (2010), at 405.

the interaction between treaty and customary law gained higher scrutiny. The *Continental Casualties* award and the recent annulment decisions in *Enron* and *Sempra* give hope for further development. Thus, the threat of fragmentation was apparent but may have been overcome by prudent arbitrators. Further decisions will shine the required light on the question.

2. Interpretations of Emergency Clauses

The methods for interpretation of treaties are set forth in Articles 31 and 32 of the Vienna Convention on the Law of Treaties (VCLT). In the hierarchical order of the different approaches, the literal wording of the treaty takes the predominant role. It is followed by object and purpose of the clause in its context within the treaty. Recourse to general rules of international law is allowed according to Article 31 (3) (c) VCLT.

In *CMS, Enron* and *Sempra* a restrictive interpretation in accordance with object and purpose of the BIT (to guarantee the rights of investors in 'situations of economic difficulty and hardship'), was stressed as mandatory.[178] The tribunals interpreted the term 'essential security interest' of Article XI in the light of Article 25.[179] The tribunals followed a rather pragmatic reasoning for such an interpretative approach: the lack of comprehensive stipulations in the BIT and the presence of those in Article 25.[180] Furthermore, the reference to the UN Charter in the definition of 'peace and security' in the protocol of the BIT also favoured this approach, it was reasoned.[181] The tribunals concluded that since the elements of Article 25 were not met Article XI could not be fulfilled.[182] In *Sempra*, the tribunal further reasoned that the lack of reference to customary international law in Article XI as a source for interpretation did not limit the tribunal to applying customary international law because 'international law is not a fragmented body of law as far as basic principles are concerned and necessity is no doubt one such basic principle'.[183]

On the contrary, in *LG&E*, the tribunal gave priority to the wording of the BIT but also stated it would apply general international law 'to the extent required for

---

178 Enron (2007), at 331; Sempra (2007), at 373.
179 Enron (2007), at 333; Sempra (2007), at 375 et seq.
180 "the treaty provision is inseparable from the customary law standard insofar as the definition of necessity and the conditions for its operation are concerned, given that its is under customary law that such elements have been defined." Ibid., at 376; similar wording in Enron (2007), at 334
181 Ibid., at 333; at 376
182 Enron (2007), at 334, 339; Sempra (2007), at. 378, 388.
183 Ibid., at 378

interpretation and application of the treaty'.[184] In determining whether Article XI was fulfilled, the tribunal comprehensively stated the facts of the crisis. Finally it came to the conclusion that the 'protections afforded by Article XI have been triggered in this case'.[185] Later, after having established necessity under Article 25, the tribunal stated that this would 'support the tribunal's analysis' on the question of whether the measures were 'necessary' under Article XI.[186]

In interpreting whether the measures performed by Argentina were actually 'necessary' according to Article XI of the BIT, the tribunal in *Continental Casualties* referred to GATT and WTO case law, explicitly neglecting customary international law.[187] In doing so the tribunal neglected the finding in *Enron,* arguing that Article XI derived from parallel model clauses in FCN treaties which reflect the formulation of Article XX GATT 47.[188] Concerning the contribution of Argentina to the crisis, as alleged by claimants in *Continental Casualties*, the tribunal neither applied Article 25 (2) (b) nor did it interpret Article XI in light of it.[189] However, the tribunal stated that measures that contributed to the crisis may not be held 'necessary' under Article XI.[190]

The annulment committee in *Sempra* concluded that Article 25 offers no 'guide to interpretation of the terms used in Article XI'.[191]

The approaches in *CMS, Enron*, and *Sempra* may go beyond the appropriate supportive application of general international law when interpreting treaty clauses. However, as other investment arbitration decisions indicate, there is no clear jurisprudence in relation to tribunals who have defied the clear wording of the IIA; rather the opposite.[192] The innovative, interpretative approach in *Continental Casualties* may be a just solution but is far from standard investment arbitration practice.[193]

184   LG&E (2006), at 206
185   Ibid., at 245.
186   Ibid., at 258.
187   Continental Casualty (2008), at 192.
188   Ibid.
189   Ibid., at 234
190   Ibid.
191   Sempra Annulment (2010), at 199.
192   For instance, Waste Management Inc. v. United Mexican States, ICSID Case No. ARB(AF)/00/3, Final Award of 30 April 2004, Crawford/ Magallón Gómez/ Civiletti, at para. 85: "Where a treaty spells out in detail and with precision the requirements for maintaining a claim, there is no room for implying into the treaty additional requirements, whether based on alleged requirements of general international law in the field of diplomatic protection or otherwise."
193   The approach was also subject of some criticism, see Alvarez/Brink: Revisiting the Necessity Defence: Continental Casualty v. Argentina, IILJ Working Paper 2010/03, accessible at <www.iilj.org>

IV. Necessity and Compensation

Perhaps the most crucial aspect of the defence of necessity is the legal consequences that flow from it. The goal of a state pleading the necessity defence is to parry the investor's claim and in doing so to avoid the payment of compensation. The investor's intention, on the other hand, is to recover its losses under the IIA. Different tribunals have taken different approaches to dealing with legal consequences though arbitrators often seem to forget they can only decide *ex aquo et bono* if the parties have explicitly agreed to this.[194] The scope of the different approaches to legal consequences ranges from full compensation to no compensation at all. Only the tribunals in *LG&E* and *Continental Casualties* (and to some extent the ad hoc committee in *CMS Annulment*) accepted the necessity defence under the Argentina-US BIT. In those cases the tribunals denied the duty to compensate during the situation of necessity. However, the tribunals which did not ascertain a state of necessity also dealt with issues of compensation. For instance in *National Grid*, although not accepting the plea of necessity, the tribunal considered Argentina's crisis when calculating damages.[195] Further, the *Sempra* tribunal stated that as a 'measure of justice' it had to take into account 'the crisis conditions' when determining damages.[196] Similarly, the *CMS* tribunal held that even though Argentina's plea would not preclude the wrongfulness 'from a legal point of view', it had to be considered when determining compensation.[197] Those decisions show that in relation to the issue of compensation, legal logic is confronted with considerations of equity.

The following analysis focuses on two issues. Firstly, the analysis focuses on whether violations of treaty standards that occurred before or after the situation of necessity may trigger the duty for compensation. Inherent in this issue is the determination of the period of time in which the situation of necessity exists. Secondly, the crucial question will be addressed of whether the respondent state has a duty to compensate the losses of the investor which have occurred during the existence of the situation of necessity.

194   See 42 (3) ICSID.
195   National Grid (2008), at 274.
196   Sempra (2007), at 397.
197   CMS (2005), at 356.

1. Compensation outside the Existence of Necessity

Under customary international law the successful invocation of the defence of necessity precludes the wrongfulness of a violation of an international obligation. It is stated above that necessity neither terminates nor annuls an international obligation. This was stressed by the ICJ in *Gabcikovo-Nagymaros* where it stated:

'Even if found justified [the state of necessity], it *does not terminate* a Treaty. The Treaty may be ineffective as long as the condition of necessity continues to exist; it may in fact be dormant, but - unless the parties by mutual agreement terminate the Treaty - it continues to exist. As soon as the state of necessity ceases to exist, the duty to comply with treaty obligations revives'.[198]

Investment tribunals have widely adhered to the rule.[199] The clarity of the rule, however, must not distract one from the fact that the determination of the time period of the situation of necessity is often less than clear.

In *LG&E* the tribunal refused to determine the dates of the period of necessity the same as the domestic emergency law.[200] The enactment of domestic emergency legislation is only a reaction to the situation of necessity and thus cannot be its starting point. Nor can the closing date of the domestic emergency legislation be held as the end of the situation of necessity since it was still in force at the date of the arbitration. The tribunal thus set as its starting point 1 December 2001 when major economic indicators reached their low point and the Government issued a decree of necessity and emergency.[201] As the final date of the necessity situation the tribunal determined 25 April 2002 when President *Kirchner* was elected.[202]

The beginning of the situation of necessity (i.e. when the grave and imminent peril starts to threaten the essential interest) may be fixed by the date on which the state issues its domestic emergency legislation. However, the end of the state of necessity cannot always be sharply be distinguished. Tribunals will always perform case-by-case decisions depending on the particular facts of each case. However, in determining the final date tribunals may have a certain scope of discretion that should be used in favour of the investor due to the exceptional nature of the defence of necessity and the threat of abuse inherent in its operation.

---

198 Gabĉíkovo-Nagymaros (1997), at 101, emphasis added.
199 LG&E (2006), at 261.
200 Ibid., at 227.
201 Ibid., at 235.
202 Ibid., at 228.

Guidance for tribunals may be the duration of the domestic state of necessity, as well as statistical data, depending on the nature of the threat.

2. Compensation within the Existence of Necessity

During the situation of necessity the duty to compensate losses is treated ambivalently by tribunals. Before discussing the holdings of tribunals, one has to understand the different variations in theory.

a) Theoretical Approach

First, one has to determine the basis for the defence of necessity (treaty or custom) and secondly the basis for the obligation for compensation (treaty or custom). Thus, there are four distinct possibilities logically applicable.

After a state has successfully invoked the customary necessity defence under Article 25, the investor has two options: seek compensation under the treaty or under customary international law. As Article 27 (b) sets out, the invocation of a state defence is without prejudice to the other party if compensation for the material loss caused by the violating act in question has to be paid. Some IIA contain clauses that explicitly stress the duty to compensate an investor's losses during a situation of necessity.[203] Whether there is a duty under customary international law for compensation cannot be answered unequivocally.

If the state successfully invokes a state of necessity under the IIA, the investor may receive compensation under a provision of the IIA, as stated above. However, depending on the extent of the IIA emergency clause, access to IIA-based compensation may be entirely precluded since the applicability of the IIA as a whole may be derogated by the emergency clause. Similarly, recourse to customary rules for compensation, in whatever form, may not be accessible. For example, in circumstances of necessity *ex contractu* a violation of an interna-

---

203 For instance see the Agreement between the Federal Republic of Germany and Brunei Darussalam concerning the Encouragement and Reciprocal Protection of Foreign Investments, German Law Gazette, Part Two 2004, p. 41 – 47, Article 5:
Without prejudice to Paragraph 1 of this Article ["national crisis clause"], nationals and companies of one Contracting Party who in any of the situations referred to in that Paragraph suffer damages or losses in the territory of the other contracting Party resulting from:
(a) requisitioning of their property by its forces or authorities, or
(b) destruction of their property by its forces or authorities which was not caused in combat action or was not required by the necessity of the situation,
shall be accorded restitution or fair and adequate compensation.

tional obligation in terms of the Draft Articles on State responsibility does not exist. Hence, there is no case of state responsibility, which may trigger a duty for customary reparation as stipulated in Article 34 DASR. Only if one could ascertain a rule of customary international law that contains a duty to compensate for losses which occur in absence of a violation of an international obligation would the investor may have recourse to compensation in absence of a treaty provision. However, at this stage there exists no such rule of customary international law.

b) Case Law in Investor State Arbitration

There is a fair amount of case law on the issue of compensation. Due to the fact that some tribunals neglected the application of the defence of necessity, the position of these tribunals on this matter are *obiter dicta*.

The tribunals in *CMS*, *Enron* and *Sempra*, although having neglected the application of necessity, considered Article 27 DASR in establishing the payment of compensation.[204] The Tribunal in *CMS* and *Enron* held that since Article 27 DASR did not exclude an agreement on compensation between the parties, the lack of such agreement allowed the tribunal to decide upon the question of compensation.[205]

In *LG&E*, in which the tribunal established treaty-based and custom-based necessity, it found Argentina exempt from liability during the situation of necessity.[206] The tribunal stressed that neither Article 27 DASR nor Article XI defined a duty to pay compensation and held that 'the damages suffered during the state of necessity should be borne by the investor'.[207]

In similarly clear fashion, the annulment committee in *CMS* stated that if treaty based-necessity applied the operation of the substantive provisions of the BIT were excluded and thus there could be 'no possibility for compensation being payable during that period'.[208] The violation of the BIT in the case of the non-applicability of necessity defences from custom and *ex contractu* results in an internationally wrongful act. In this case, Article 27 DASR is not applicable and still less cannot serve as basis for compensation.[209]

In *Continental Casualties*, the tribunal accepted the plea of necessity under Article XI and held that as far as Argentina could invoke the defence of necessity

---

204 CMS (2005), at 379 et. seq; Enron (2007), at 343 et seq; Sempra (2007), at 392 et seq.
205 CMS (2005), at 394; Enron (2007), at 345.
206 LG&E (2006), at 261.
207 Ibid., at 264.
208 CMS Annulment (2007), at 146.
209 Ibid., at 148.

it did not have to fulfil the obligations in the BIT. As such, it did not violate substantive BIT rights during the period of the crisis.[210] The tribunal only considered compensation for those violations outside the scope of the necessity defence.[211]

The *Funnekotter* case discussed above gives an opposite point of view of the issue. In this case the tribunal neglected the application of necessity because Zimbabwe did not obey its duty to pay compensation under the BIT within the alleged time of necessity.[212] The tribunal's reasoning can be understood as above, in other words that the contractual duty to pay compensation cannot be justified by necessity as dictated by Article 25 (2) (a) DASR. By the same token, however, the reasoning of the tribunal may serve as authority for the opinion that even during the situation of necessity there may be a duty to pay compensation under the BIT.

3. Summary

The issue of compensation distinctly shows the important legal consequences of the defence of necessity in investment arbitration. If applied systemically correctly the investor (unless the treaty contains a clause to the contrary) has no chance of receiving compensation for violating substantive IIA rights. Bearing in mind the fact that the object and purpose of the IIA is to foster foreign investment by implementing a stable legal framework distinct from the domestic legal system it is questionable whether the burden of risk of unstable situations should be carried only by the investor. On the other hand, when making investment decisions in politically unstable regions, investors should reasonably include political risks in their risk management considerations. It has been regularly held by investment tribunals that a bad business decision should not be compensated by the recourse to investor state arbitration.[213]

If tribunals were to give compensation to investors for losses incurred during the situation of necessity the customary rule of necessity would be considerably altered, probably to the extent of systemic misapplication. There are scholars who favour such a duty to compensate such as Bjorklund who argues that the duty to pay compensation is only 'temporarily suspended, rather than extinguished'.[214] Such an approach echoes the ILC's concept of necessity's effect as

---

210 Continental Casualty (2008), at 304.
211 Ibid., at 305.
212 Funnekotter (2009), at 106.
213 For an overview see Ripinsky/Williams, Damages in International Investment law, 2008, p. 329.
214 Bjorklund, in: Handbook of Investment Law, at p. 515.

suspension not termination of the international obligation. Reinisch points out that the ILC itself presumes the need for an adjustment of the losses since it stipulates a duty to compensate material losses of innocent third parties.[215]

These approaches favour an investment friendly climate. However, the approach followed here does not consider maximizing equitable treatment of investors but consistency in a united system of international law. Tribunals should rather consider the elements of the necessity defence more carefully before inventing a corrective which balances out drastic consequences of necessity's application. Ripinsky correctly stresses that, in the absence of clear stipulations of the law, tribunals will base their decision on considerations of equity and fairness depending on the particularities of each case.[216] Although a lower level of legal certainty is inherent to investment arbitration without the doctrine of precedent, one should not encourage mere equity decisions. The only means to solve the apparent conflict of interests in a systemically correct way is to draft IIAs with more precise wording concerning the duty to pay compensation. Otherwise, the need for an equitable solution results in fragmentation of investment arbitration law.

D. Conclusion and Outlook

The preceding analysis has attempted to shed some light on the application of necessity in investment arbitration. Although the nature of investment arbitration cannot easily be specified in traditional terms of international law the defence of necessity in arbitration proceedings against investors is empirically and systemically applicable. Such a situation is desirable due to the fact that investment tribunals may generate case law that further illuminates the different elements of the defence of necessity. As far as one can discern from the limited case law to date, generally there does not appear to be substantially different understandings of the elements of Article 25 DASR in the jurisprudence of investment proceedings. The biggest threat in terms of fragmentation of international law derives from the misapplication in *CMS*, *Enron* and *Sempra* in context of the treaty-based necessity defence. However, the inconsistency of those three decisions has not yet created a discrete sub-system of international law and at most indicated the beginning of a trend towards fragmentation. Furthermore, the annulment decisions in those three cases represent an extremely strong argument contrary to the position held by Orrego Vicuña's in relation to Article XI of the US-Argentina BIT. It is easily predictable that those annulment decisions will have a

---

215   Reinisch in: TDM 2006, at p. 19.
216   Ripinski: State of Necessity: Effect on Compensation, TDM Vol. 4, 2007, p. 17.

great impact on subsequent cases (at least in such cases based on the US-Argentina BIT) similar to the influence already discernable in the award of *Continental Casualties*.

In cases where a necessity defence *ex contractu* is raised the invocation of Article 25 DASR will be limited. The multitude of pending cases against Argentina will produce further case law.[217] Moreover, annulment proceedings in the necessity cases of *LG&E* and *Continental Casualties* are expected with interest.[218] In relation to disputes regarding IIAs that do not contain a necessity clause the application of Article 25 may be argued by respondent states. The recent world financial crisis may have at least the positive side effect of giving opportunity for further development of the defence of necessity in this regard.[219] The politically and economically critical situations in Greece and Iceland may also offer opportunity for further investment disputes in which the respondent state relies on the defence of economic necessity. Whether investment law establishes its own custom of necessity is in the hands of the contracting states. More distinct stipulations in IIAs can help to prevent merely equitable awards that threaten the unified system of international law.

217 For the cases currently pending see: <www.worldbank.org/icsid/cases/pending.htm>.
218 See for further awards see: <www.worldbank.org/icsid>.
219 Fellenbaum/Klein: Investment Arbitration and Fincanial Crisis: The global financial crisis and BITs, GAR Vol. 3, 2008.

Restitution and Compensation – Reconstructing the Relationship in Investment Treaty Law

Steffen Hindelang[*]

A. *Introduction*

Stay or leave? Restitution or compensation? Perhaps in this admittedly simplified way one could sketch strikingly the choice to be made when deciding between the two forms of reparation in investment arbitration. While the restitution of, e.g., unlawfully taken property means continued presence and perhaps retention of business activities in a host State, compensation often opens up the possibility to seek new investment opportunities beyond the borders of the host State.

This paper intends to shed light on the rules governing the abovementioned choice in investment treaty law. Starting point of this elaboration will be the "general" rules governing the consequences of the commitment of an international wrong. These rules are contained in the International Law Commission's ("ILC") Articles on Responsibility of States for Internationally Wrongful Acts ("ASR" or "ILC Articles") and basically mirror customary international law (below B.). Thereafter it will turn to the rules applicable to investment treaties, hereby answering the question of whether and to what extent the "general" rules on the relationship between restitution and compensation are also valid within this specific area of investment treaty law (below C.). A review of recent arbitral awards (below C. I.) will form the basis for a normative construction of the relationship in investment treaty law (below C. II.). This construction will proceed from the assumption that the purposes State parties pursue with the conclusion of investment treaties essentially remain in an inter-State sphere (below C. II. 1. b (1)) and, hence, *substantive* treatment rights in respect of foreign investment accrue to the host State of the investor (below C. II. 1. b (2)). Based on such understanding of the purposes pursued with the conclusion of investment treaties, this paper comes to an end with suggesting to strictly "prioritise" restitution among the forms of reparation available in the area of investment treaty law (below C. II. 3.).

[*]   Dr *Steffen Hindelang*, LL.M.; Senior Research Associate and Lecturer at Humboldt-University Berlin.

B. The Content of the International Responsibility of a State in "General" Public International Law

Once an internationally wrongful act has been committed, questions as to the restoration and future of the legal relationship thereby affected arise.

The obligation breached – the so-called primary obligation – is not affected by the legal consequences of an internationally wrongful act. The responsible or author State is, consequently, bound to the continued duty to perform the (primary) obligation breached. This general rule is stated in Article 29 ASR, which is commonly perceived as reflecting the current situation under customary international law.[1]

Furthermore, there are two general – additional, secondary – obligations of the author State *consequent* upon the commission of an internationally wrongful act. That is, first, the obligation of cessation[2] and non-repetition[3] of the wrongful act, also found in Article 30 ASR. This rule aims at protecting and restoring the ongoing relationships or situations of continuing value and shows that State responsibility is not just backward-looking.[4]

Second, there is the obligation to make full reparation for the injury caused by the internationally wrongful act, whereby injury includes any damage, whether material or moral, caused by the internationally wrongful act. The latter obligation, the obligation to make full reparation, was included by the ILC in Article 31 ASR. This provision was based upon the judgement of the Permanent Court of International Justice ("PCIJ") in the *Factory at Chorzow* case[5] where the Court stated:

"It is a principle of international law that the breach of an engagement involves an obligation to make reparation in an adequate form."[6]

---

1   Cf., for the situation under customary international law pre-ASR, e. g. Čepelka, Les conséquences juridiques du délit en droit international contemporain, 1965, p. 18.
2   Cf. for the distinction of cessation and reparation: Arangio-Ruiz, Preliminary Report on State Responsibility, Yearbook of the International Law Commission 1988, Vol. II (Part One), Document A/CN.4/416 & Corr. 1 & 2 and Add. 1 & Corr. 1, p. 6, para. 39 – 41; Cf. for the distinction between cessation and restitution in kind: idem, para. 48 – 52.
3   Cf., e.g., LaGrand (Germany v. United States of America), Judgement, ICJ Rep. 2001, p. 466, para. 124.
4   Crawford/Olleson, in: Evans (ed.), International Law, 2. ed. 2006, p. 470.
5   Judgement of 13.9.1928, PCIJ Series A, No. 17; for a display of judgements and awards granting non-pecuniary remedies see also Schreuer, Non-Pecuniary Remedies in ICSID Arbitration, 20 Arbitration International 2004, p. 325 et seqq.
6   Judgement of 13.9.1928, PCIJ Series A, No. 17, p. 29.

The Court specified in more detail the content of the obligation *"to make reparation in an adequate form"* as follows:

"...reparation must, as far as possible, wipe out all the consequences of the illegal act and re-establish the situation which would, in all probability, have exis-ted if that act had not been committed. Restitution in kind, or, if this is not possible, payment of a sum corresponding to the value which a restitution in kind would bear; the award, if need be, of damages for loss sustained which would not be covered by restitution in kind or payment in place of it – such are the principles which should serve to determine the amount of compensation due for an act contrary to international law."[7]

While the Court in the specific case mentioned only two forms of reparation – i.e. restitution (in kind) (below I.) and compensation (below II.) – in certain cases, satisfaction[8] – the third form of reparation – may be called for. All those three forms of reparation – either granted separately or in combination – are also reflected in Article 34 ASR. The provision of each of the forms of reparation described in Article 34 ASR is subject to further specification in Articles 35 to 39 ASR. In principle, restitution is the very first remedy to be sought among the three forms of reparation as it most closely conforms to the general rule of the law of responsibility according to which the author State is obliged to "wipe out" all consequences with the view to re-establishing the original situation.[9] This clear legal priority is also reflected in the ILC Articles which allow for compensation in Article 36 (1) ASR only insofar as damages cannot be made good by restitution (below III.). Considering the relationship between the forms of reparation Articles 33 and 55 ASR also need to be addressed. The former regulates, *inter alia*, the application of ASR rules on the form of reparation to non-State actors (below IV.), the latter refers to *leges speciales* which could replace the ASR rules (below V.)

---

7   Judgement of 13.9.1928, PCIJ Series A, No. 17, p. 47.
8   Wyler/Papaux, in: Parlett/Crawford/Pellet/Olleson (eds.), The Law of International Responsibility, 2010, p. 623 et seqq.
9   Cf. Arangio-Ruiz, Preliminary Report on State Responsibility, Yearbook of the International Law Commission 1988, Vol. II (Part One), Document A/CN.4/416 & Corr. 1 & 2 and Add. 1 & Corr. 1, p. 6, para. 114 - 118. The relationship between restitution and compensation is discussed in detail further below, cf. B. III.

I. Restitution

1. The Breadth of the Concept of Restitution

Turning to the concept of restitution in more detail, one is faced with the problem of definition. Broadly speaking, two different readings of reparation were historically offered in literature. Probably the most common view referred to restitution in kind as re-establishing the *status quo ante*, namely the situation that existed prior to the occurrence of the wrongful act, in order to bring the parties' relationship back to its original state.[10] The other reading was to understand restitution in kind as the establishment or re-establishment of the situation that would exist, or would have existed, if the wrongful act had not been committed.[11]

Arangio-Ruiz, Special Rapporteur of the International Law Commission on State Responsibility, explained the differences between the two readings in his Preliminary Report as follows:

"The two concepts cover different areas. In the first place, it is obvious that the first definition refers, for the purposes of restitutio, to a factual and/or juridical situation which has really existed in the past and has been altered additionally or principally as a consequence of the violation. The second definition refers instead to a theoretical legal/factual state of affairs which at no time has been a part of reality but could presumably be a part of reality if the wrongful act had not interfered in the course of events. [... The first] definition views restitution in kind stricto sensu and per se. It leaves outside the concept of compensation which presumably will be due to the injured party for the loss suffered during the period elapsed during the completion of the wrongful act and thereafter until the time when the remedial action is taken. [The second] definition seems instead [...] to absorb into that concept not just the re-establishment of the status quo ante [...] but also the integrative compensation. In other words, [the first definition] separates the purely restitutive from the compensatory function of reparation, while [the second one] presents, so to speak, an 'integrated' concept of restitution in kind within which the restitutive and compensatory elements are fused."[12]

---

10 E. g. de Visscher, La responsibilité des Etats, Bibliotheca Visseriana, 1924, vol. II, p. 118 ; Verdross, Völkerrecht, 5. ed. 1964, p. 399.

11 E. g. Anzilotti, Cours de droit international, French translation of 3.Italian ed. 1929, p. 526; Strupp, in: Stier-Somlo (ed.), Handbuch des Völkerrechts, vol. III, 1.part, 1920, p. 209.

12 Arangio-Ruiz, Preliminary Report on State Responsibility, Yearbook of the International Law Commission 1988, Vol. II (Part One), Document A/CN.4/416 & Corr. 1 & 2 and Add. 1 & Corr. 1, p. 6, para. 67.

Article 35 ASR adopts the narrower definition which has the advantage of not having to deal with a hypothetic inquiry into what the situation would have been if the wrongful act had not been committed. Applying the narrow definition however does not mean that the injured State is placed in a worse situation. Restitution may of course be completed by compensation.[13]

2. Material and Legal Restitution

For systematic reasons, a distinction can be drawn according to the kind of injury for which reparation is due. Material restitution means that the injury takes the form of material damage proper. Good examples of material restitution would therefore be the restitution of confiscated property, the release of a detained individual, or the restitution of an arrested ship.[14] Legal restitution refers to cases where implementation of restitution involves the modification of a legal situation either within the legal system of the author State or on the international plane. Legal restitution can, thus, require *inter alia* annulling certain national laws or court decisions or even annulling an international treaty.[15]

With regard to legal restitution in the domestic law of the author State an additional point should be addressed in respect of this doctrinal distinction. The distinction between material and legal restitution in the domestic law of the author State "*should be viewed not so much as different remedies but as distinct aspects of one and the same remedy.*"[16] This follows from the fact that one can hardly conceive a State effecting restitution which would involve purely material operations. Under the rule of law,

"it is hardly thinkable that the Government responsible for an internationally wrongful act could accomplish any restitution without something 'legal' happe-ning within its system. ...

---

13   See further below B. II.

14   Cf., e.g. Temple of Preah Vihear case, ICJ Rep. 1962, p. 6, p. 36 – 37. For more references see Arangio-Ruiz, Preliminary Report on State Responsibility, Yearbook of the International Law Commission 1988, Vol. II (Part One), Document A/CN.4/416 & Corr. 1 & 2 and Add. 1 & Corr. 1, p. 6, para. 74 - 75.

15   Cf. e.g. Bryan-Chamorro Treaty case, Anales de la Corte de Justicia Centroamericana (San José, Costa Rica), vol. VI, Nos. 16 - 18, p. 7 = 11 AJIL (1917), p. 674 et seqq; Martini case, United Nations, Reports of International Arbitral Awards, vol. II. p. 975 et seqq; for more references see Arangio-Ruiz, Preliminary Report on State Responsibility, Yearbook of the International Law Commission 1988, Vol. II (Part One), Document A/CN.4/416 & Corr. 1 & 2 and Add. 1 & Corr. 1, p. 6, para. 76.

16   Arangio-Ruiz, Preliminary Report on State Responsibility, Yearbook of the International Law Commission 1988, Vol. II (Part One), Document A/CN.4/416 & Corr. 1 & 2 and Add. 1 & Corr. 1, p. 6, para. 82.

[Hence restitution will in any way] be essentially legal [...], accompanying or preceding material restitutio."[17]

II. Compensation

Compensation constitutes the second secondary obligation consequent of a breach of a primary obligation in international law, either completing or replacing restitution. Article 36 ASR restates this as follows:

"1. The State responsible for an internationally wrongful act is under an obligation to compensate for the damage caused thereby, insofar as such damage is not made good by restitution.
2. The compensation shall cover any financially assessable damage including loss of profits insofar as it is established."

The damage compensated for is the financial harm caused by the breach, established by measuring the difference between the actual financial position resulting from the breach and that which otherwise would have obtained. This assessment of the compensable damage does not only involve a challenging fact-finding mission but a complex

"fact-specific delineation exercise in which the freedoms, rights, and prerogatives of actors in both public and private spheres are defined not only by reference to their competing interests, but in light of additional procedural and governance obligations calculated to raise the standards of conduct of all parties and to secure peaceful enjoyment of property".[18]

Hence, rules and methods may vary depending on whether compensation is sought for personal injury, incidental loss, claims to money, property, business and income-producing assets, or lost profits.[19] In any case, however, the way in

---

17 Arangio-Ruiz, Preliminary Report on State Responsibility, Yearbook of the International Law Commission 1988, Vol. II (Part One), Document A/CN.4/416 & Corr. 1 & 2 and Add. 1 & Corr. 1, p. 6, para. 80.
18 Barker, in: Parlett/Crawford/Pellet/Olleson (eds.), The Law of International Responsibility, 2010, p. 599, p. 603. In respect of interest see: Lauterpacht/Nevill, in: Parlett/Crawford/Pellet/Olleson (eds.), The Law of International Responsibility, 2010, p. 613.
19 Barker, in: Parlett/Crawford/Pellet/Olleson (eds.), The Law of International Responsibility, 2010, p. 599, p. 604 - 610. On the ILC Articles see: Shelton, Righting Wrongs: Reparation in the Articles on State Responsibility, 96 AJIL (2002), p. 833, p. 851 - 863. See in respect of international investment law also: Marboe, Calculation of Compensation and Damages in International Investment Law, 2009; Ripinsky/Williams, Damages in Inter-

which compensation is calculated has a significant impact on public policy and carries the immanent hazard that either ordinary commercial risk or legitimate private rights or market positions respectively are illicitly socialised or public goods or interests are secretly privatised.[20]

III. The Relationship between Restitution and Compensation

The relationship between the two forms of reparation is – at first sight – resolved in a straightforward fashion. What can be described by and large as a codification of customary international law[21], in the absence of an election,[22] pursuant to Article 36 (1) ASR restitution is the primary form of restitution, followed – *to the extent* restitution is impossible or excessively onerous – by compensation (and then, to the extent restitution and compensation are impossible, by satisfaction).[23] What can be drawn from the aforesaid is that the three forms are not mutually exclusive within the context of an award. Apparently, they can be granted either separately or in combination, which can be derived from Article 34 ASR.

Within this hierarchy, restitution is placed first because it most closely conforms to the general rule of the law of responsibility according to which the author State is obliged to "wipe out"[24] all consequences with the view to re-establishing the original situation.[25]

It is, furthermore, claimed that *prioritising* restitution serves the purpose of justifying a specific method of calculating compensation, i.e. compensation must

national Investment Law, 2009; For commercial arbitration see: Kantor, Valuation for Arbitration, 2008.

20 Barker, in: Parlett/Crawford/Pellet/Olleson (eds.), The Law of International Responsibility, 2010, p. 599, p. 610.

21 For further references cf. Arangio-Ruiz, Preliminary Report on State Responsibility, Yearbook of the International Law Commission 1988, Vol. II (Part One), Document A/CN.4/416 & Corr. 1 & 2 and Add. 1 & Corr. 1, p. 6, para. 114 et seqq.

22 In this respect, Article 43 paragraph 2 lit. (b) ASR indicates that the injured State invoking the responsibility of another State "may specify in particular what form reparation should take in accordance with the provisions of part two."

23 Article 37 (1) reads "…insofar as it cannot be made good by restitution or compensation". Note, however, that the prioritisation of restitution and compensation over satisfaction is hardly supported by international practice. Cf. Kerbrat, in: Parlett/Crawford/Pellet/Olleson (eds.), The Law of International Responsibility, 2010, p. 573, p. 581.

24 Factory at Charzów case, Judgement of 13.9.1928, PCIJ Series A, No. 17, p. 47.

25 Arangio-Ruiz, Preliminary Report on State Responsibility, Yearbook of the International Law Commission 1988, Vol. II (Part One), Document A/CN.4/416 & Corr. 1 & 2 and Add. 1 & Corr. 1, p. 6, para. 114.

cover both, *damnum emergens* and *lucrum cessans*.[26] Such reasoning is, however, not convincing. It is neither the priority given to restitution nor the concept of restitution itself which would justify such standard of calculation as restitution as embodied in Article 35 ASR – contrary to the view taken in the *Factory of Charzów* case – does not contain "hypothetical elements" of *lucrum cessans* but adopts a narrower definition as stated above. What does justify adopting a standard of compensation including *lucrum cessans* is the general rule of responsibility "to wipe out" all consequences of a wrongful act which indeed contains also "hypothetical elements".

Turning to practice, while courts[27] and – albeit to a lesser extent – tribunals[28] generally affirm the existence of the rule of priority, restitution is granted only very rarely. Within the area of law on the protection of alien property, a survey of the case law in respect of the rule of priority of restitution reveals that its existence is, although confirmed, greeted with some more reluctance and applied equally seldom. The PCIL in its *Factory at Charzów*[29] case again laid down the foundations for subsequent rulings. Arbitral tribunals also followed suit. However, the reference to the *Factory of Charzów* judgement is less common than in juridical practice.[30] In *Texaco v. Libya*[31] and in the *Amoco* case[32] of the Iran-US Claims Tribunal the rule was followed. However, some awards also demonstrate a different attitude, for example the *Walter Fletcher Smith* award, and in particu-

---

26 Cf. Kerbrat, in: Parlett/Crawford/Pellet/Olleson (eds.), The Law of International Responsibility, 2010, p. 573, p. 585 et seq.

27 Factory at Charzów case, Judgement of 13.9.1928, PCIJ Series A, No. 17, p. 48. Further references are found by Arangio-Ruiz, Preliminary Report on State Responsibility, Yearbook of the International Law Commission 1988, Vol. II (Part One), Document A/CN.4/416 & Corr. 1 & 2 and Add. 1 & Corr. 1, p. 6, para.116, esp. footnote 243.

28 Cf. British claims in the Spanish zone of Morocco case, Decision of 01.5.1925, United Nations, Reports of International Arbitral Awards, vol. II. p. 621 - 625, p. 651 - 742; Religious Property expropriated by Portugal case, Decision of 04.9.1920, United Nations, Reports of International Arbitral Awards, vol. I, pp. 7 et seq; Walter Fletcher Smith case , United Nations, Reports of International Arbitral Awards, vol. III, p. 856; Heirs of Lebas de Courmont case, Decision No. 213 of 21.6.1957 of the Franco-Italian Conciliation Commission, United Nations, Reports of International Arbitral Awards, vol. XIII, p. 764; Kerbrat, in: Parlett/Crawford/Pellet/Olleson (eds.), The Law of International Responsibility, 2010, p. 573, p. 585.; Arangio-Ruiz, Preliminary Report on State Responsibility, Yearbook of the International Law Commission 1988, Vol. II (Part One), Document A/CN.4/416 & Corr. 1 & 2 and Add. 1 & Corr. 1, p. 6, para. 116.

29 Judgement of 13.9.1928, PCIJ Series A, No. 17, p. 47.

30 Cf. Kerbrat, in: Parlett/Crawford/Pellet/Olleson (eds.), The Law of International Responsibility, 2010, p. 573, p. 583.

31 Texaco v. Libyan Arab Republic, 17 ILM, p. 1, p. 36, para. 109.

32 Amoco International Finance Corp. V. Iran, Partial Award of 14.7.1987, 15 Iran-US CTR, p. 189, p. 246 et seqq.

lar the *BP v. Libya* award,[33] which contested that the priority rule applied in case of expropriation and unlawful nationalisation.

All in all, the case law seems to confront us with a paradox: the validity of the priority rule being regularly confirmed but restitution granted only infrequently. Thisappears to be grounded in the fact the State parties either exclude by consensus the form of restitution or the injured party restricts its claim to compensation (1.) or restitution is impossible or disproportionate (2.).

1. Election

Article 43 (2) lit. (b) ASR indicates that the injured State invoking the responsibility of another State *"may specify in particular what form reparation should take in accordance with the provisions of part two."*[34] Taken literally, in the absence of an agreement between the State parties[35], it appears to be for the injured State party to choose the suitable form of reparation.

However, State practice does not unequivocally embrace that the explicit choice or intentions inferred from unilateral acts adopted by the injured State party throughout the proceedings determine the (only) admissible form of reparation. Except for the situation that the responding State party does not object to an explicit or implicit election amounting to a *solo consensu* agreement between the State parties, the question of whether the reaction of the responding State can fully be ignored by the tribunal appears unsettled.[36] Clearly, the possibility of an election always inherits the possibility of abuse. Nevertheless, two observations should not be disregarded in this respect. It was the respondent State in the first place which inflicted the wrong and it should consequently also bear any negative consequences accruing from this wrong. And, while compensation is always possible and the issue of excessive onerousness may be dealt with within the question of *quantum*, the election of a State party in favour of restitution was interpreted by the tribunals as implicitly entailing a request for compensation or satisfaction whenever restitution was impossible or disproportionate.[37]

33   BP Exploration Co. v. Libyan Arab Republic, 53 ILR, p. 297, p. 332 - 354.
34   Cf. Germany's election in the Factory at Charzów case and Finland's election in the Passage through the Great Belt case.
35   Cf. compromis in Aminoil v. Kuweit, 66 ILR p. 533, compromis in Oberlander and Messenger case (United States/Mexico) in: Fontaine, Pasicrisie Internationale 1794 - 1900, reprint 1997, p. 558 - 568.
36   Cf. Arangio-Ruiz, Preliminary Report on State Responsibility, Yearbook of the International Law Commission 1988, Vol. II (Part One), Document A/CN.4/416 & Corr. 1 & 2 and Add. 1 & Corr. 1, p. 6, para. 112.
37   Cf. Corfu Chanel case (United Kingdom v. Albania), Merits, ICJ Rep. 1949, p. 4, p. 35 cited Application of the Convention for the Prevention and Punishment of the Crime of

2. Possibility and Proportionality

If there is no election, it is for international courts and tribunals to determine the appropriate form of reparation in accordance with international law. As already stated previously, in principle restitution is the very first remedy to be sought. The principle meets, however, its limits, first, in case of factual or material impossibility of restitution (Article 35 lit (a) ASR) and, secondly, in a situation where restitution would constitute an excessive onerousness on the side of the author State (Article 35 lit (b) ASR).

The notion of factual or material impossibility does usually not cause much of a problem. An illustrative example would be that the ship to be returned sank and cannot be recovered by any means. In such situations restitution is obviously impossible. Material impossibility covers, though, more complex situations going beyond physical destruction. *The Forests of Central Rhodope* case, for example, demonstrates that partial change of conditions of an illicit expropriated forest coupled with the existence of municipal third party rights to the forest acquired in good faith after the expropriation have a bearing on the possibility of restitution.[38]

Some controversy in the proceedings of the International Law Commission surrounded the question of whether impossibility on the grounds of legal or practical difficulties flowing from the municipal legal[39] system of the author State would constitute a valid plea to evade restitution. With respect to the general rule of non-interference with internal matters of a State it was argued that restitution must be replaced by compensation in case restitution would involve interference in or violation of domestic jurisdiction. In particular, the injured State would be denied restitution where the application of such remedy would entail the annulment or the non-application of legislative provisions, of administrative acts or final judgments within the municipal legal system of the author State.[40]

Genocide case (Bosnia-Herzegovina v. Serbia), Judgement, para. 463. This is a moderation of the non ultra petita rule: Kerbrat, in: Parlett/Crawford/Pellet/Olleson (eds.), The Law of International Responsibility, 2010, p. 573, p. 578.

38 Restitution was in the end denied: cf. United Nations, Reports of International Arbitral Awards, vol. III, p. 1405, p. 1432.

39 „Legal impossibility" is perceivable in a situation in which restitution meets obstacles in the UN Charter (cf. Article 103) or other prevailing norms of international law. Cf. Arangio-Ruiz, Preliminary Report on State Responsibility, Yearbook of the International Law Commission 1988, Vol. II (Part One), Document A/CN.4/416 & Corr. 1 & 2 and Add. 1 & Corr. 1, p. 6, para. 87.

40 Cf. Riphagen, Second Report of the Special Rapporteur, Yearbook of the International Law Commission 1981, Vol. II (Part One), Document A/CN.4/344 & Corr. 1 & 2, p. 79, para. 156 – 157.

In the end, impossibility on the grounds of legal (or practical) difficulties flowing from the municipal legal system of the author State was not included in the ASR and, thus, is not covered by Article 35 lit (a) ASR.[41] This is underscored by Article 31 ASR which states:

"The responsible State may not rely on the provisions of its internal law as justification for failure to comply with its obligations under this part."

The approach taken by the ILC in concurrence with prevailing doctrine is that difficulties which a State may encounter within its own legal system in discharging its international obligations are not decisive as a legal justification for failure to discharge such international obligations. Otherwise restitution would practically be almost always impossible as there is hardly any international rule compliance with does not imply some impact on the municipal law of the State bound by the rule.[42]

While, in general, obstacles in municipal law will not lead to impossibility of restitution, this, however, does not mean that there are no foreseeable situations in which compensation would be the more appropriate form of reparation. It is conceivable that legal restitution involves a burden out of proportion to the benefit deriving from that restitution. However, any plea of excessive onerousness on the part of an author State in order to escape a claim of restitution should be the object of strict evaluation on the basis of equity and reasonableness.

As just mentioned, the duty of the author State to provide for restitution is also limited by excessive onerousness or, in other words, by proportionality. This has been confirmed by State practice[43] and is evidenced in Article 35 lit. (b) ASR which states that restitution may not

"involve a burden out of all proportion to the benefit deriving from restitution instead of compensation".

---

41 Draft Articles on Responsibility of States for Internationally Wrongful Acts, with Commentaries, Yearbook of the International Law Commission 2001, vol. II. (Part Two), p. 31, Art.35, para. 8.

42 Cf. Arangio-Ruiz, Preliminary Report on State Responsibility, Yearbook of the International Law Commission 1988, Vol. II (Part One), Document A/CN.4/416 & Corr. 1 & 2 and Add. 1 & Corr. 1, p. 6, para. 90 – 98 with further references.

43 Cf. Arangio-Ruiz, Preliminary Report on State Responsibility, Yearbook of the International Law Commission 1988, Vol. II (Part One), Document A/CN.4/416 & Corr. 1 & 2 and Add. 1 & Corr. 1, p. 6, para. 99 et seqq with further references.

Although the ASR do generally not provide for determination of the form of reparation by the primary obligation breached[44] but the focus is on the nature of injury,under this heading the primary obligation breached may play a role with respect to the form and extent of reparation.[45]

IV. Applicability of the ILC Rules on the Form of Reparation to non – State Actors?

Speaking about the relationship between restitution and compensation, Article 33 ASR is to be addressed, stating in its first paragraph that the obligations mentioned above are essentially owed to States. In respect of non-State actors paragraph 2 of Article 33 ASR provides that the provisions on the content of State responsibility are without prejudice to any right, arising from the international responsibility of a State, which may accrue directly to any person or entity other than a State.

Hence, the ILC Articles on State Responsibility recognize that the primary rule may provide rights for non-State entities. The commentary to Article 33 paragraph 2 adds that in such cases,

44 Rainbow Warrior case, United Nations, Reports of International Arbitral Awards, vol. XX, p. 215, para. 111; see also: Kerbrat, in: Parlett/Crawford/Pellet/Olleson (eds.), The Law of International Responsibility, 2010, p. 573, p. 578. There is, hence, neither reason to differentiate in respect of responsibility deriving from contractual and delicious wrongs [Cf. Stern, Le préjudice dans la théorie de la responsabilité internationale, 1973, p. 13] nor between the breach of peremptory norms and the breach of other rules. Cf. Arangio-Ruiz, Preliminary Report on State Responsibility, Yearbook of the International Law Commission 1988, Vol. II (Part One), Document A/CN.4/416 & Corr. 1 & 2 and Add. 1 & Corr. 1, p. 6, para. 113.

45 Probably even broader: Draft Articles on Responsibility of States for Internationally Wrongful Acts, with Commentaries, Yearbook of the International Law Commission 2001, vol. II. (Part Two), p. 31, Art.34, para. 3; Gray, in: Parlett/Crawford/Pellet/Olleson (eds.), The Law of International Responsibility, 2010, p. 589, p. 594; More restrictive: Kerbrat, in: Parlett/Crawford/Pellet/Olleson (eds.), The Law of International Responsibility, 2010, p. 573, p. 578; cited in support: Rainbow Warrior case, United Nations, Reports of International Arbitral Awards, vol. XX, p. 215, para. 111; Draft Articles on Responsibility of States for Internationally Wrongful Acts, with Commentaries, Yearbook of the International Law Commission 2001, vol. II.(Part Two), p. 31, Art.35, para. 3: "[I]n certain cases, especially those involving the application of peremptory norms, restitution may be required as an aspect of compliance with the primary rules". Kerbrat holds, hence, the view that there is neither reason to differentiate in respect of responsibility deriving from contractual and delicious wrongs [Cf. Stern, Le préjudice dans la théorie de la responsabilité internationale, 1973, p. 13] nor between the breach of peremptory norms and the breach of other rules. Cf. Arangio-Ruiz, Preliminary Report on State Responsibility, Yearbook of the International Law Commission 1988, Vol. II (Part One), Document A/CN.4/416 & Corr. 1 & 2 and Add. 1 & Corr. 1, p. 6, para. 113.

"it will be a matter for the particular primary rule to determine *whether* and *to what extent* persons or entities other than States are entitled to invoke responsibility on their own account".[46]

In other words, primary rules creating obligations owed to non-State actors can have their own set of secondary obligations, *inter alia*, on the form of reparation. When this is the case and which secondary rules are to be applied, was intentionally left open by the International Law Commission, therewith avoiding a debate[47] which probably would have prolonged the discussion process within the Commission significantly.

In this context it is also worth glancing at the customary international law governing the treatment of property of aliens and its enforcement by the way of the concept of diplomatic protection. The traditional view in international law [48] – though not undisputed in legal writing[49] – is to perceive individuals and corporate entities as objects of international law. In respect of the protection of alien property this means that rights and obligations exist exclusively between sovereign States. The injured individual is not privy to this legal relationship and he cannot claim the customary international law obligations in his own right.[50]

This position was concisely formulated by the PCIJ in its *Mavrommatis* judgement[51]:

---

46   Emphasis added.
47   Cf Arangio-Ruiz, Preliminary Report on State Responsibility, Yearbook of the International Law Commission 1988, Vol. II (Part One), Document A/CN.4/416 & Corr. 1 & 2 & Add. 1 & Corr. 1, p. 6, para.121, para.115, citing para. 76 et seqq: "The practice discussed ... does not seem to justify the identification of special rules concerning the treatment of aliens except in the 'neutral' sense of showing a merely numerical prevalence of cases concerning the treatment of aliens over cases concerning other areas of State responsibility."; Garcia-Amador, Sixth Report on State Responsibility, Yearbook of the International Law Commission 1961, Vol. II, Document A/CN.4/134 & Add. 1, p. 1, para. 177: "It would, nevertheless, be feasible and desirable to formulate a number of general principles that have served to limit the extent of reparation or to define more precisely the forms or measures applicable in the case of injuries sustained by aliens."
48   Janis, Individuals as Subjects of International Law, 17 Cornell Int'l L J 1984, p. 61 et seqq.
49   Opposing: de Vischer, Cours général de droit international public (1954 II), 86 Hague Recueil, 507; see in this respect also Garcia-Amador, Sixth Report on State Responsibility, Yearbook of the International Law Commission 1961, Vol. II, Document A/CN.4/134 & Add. 1, p. 1, para. 176: "The 'injury' or 'damage' should be considered in terms of the subject in fact harmed — i.e., the alien — and reparation should be considered in terms of its real and only object — i.e., not as reparation 'due to the State', but as reparation due to the individual in whose behalf diplomatic protection is being exercised."
50   "Anyone who mistreats a citizen directly offends the State." Cf. de Vattel, Le droit des gens ou les principes de la loi naturelle, vol. I, 1789, 309.
51   Judgement of 30.8.1924, PCIJ Rep. Series A, No. 2, confirmed and applied in cases before the PCIJ, the ICJ and other international tribunals; for further references refer to

"By taking up the case of one of its subjects and by resorting to diplomatic action or international juridical proceedings on his behalf, a State is in reality asserting its own rights – its rights to ensure, in the person of its subjects, respect for the rules of international law."[52]

Hence, the injury caused to the property of a foreign individual constitutes a "moral injury" to the State to which the individual is attached to by the bond of nationality. The application of Articles 28 ASR et seqq. in case of the violation of the rules on the protection of alien property would, therefore, not be limited by Article 33 ASR.

V. Leges Speciales to the ILC Regime

Article 55 ASR can also have a potential impact on the relationship between restitution and compensation. It provides for the case that States make, *inter alia*, special provisions for the legal consequences of breaches of primary obligations. The ILC Articles on State Responsibility

"do not apply where and to the extent that [...] the content or implementation of the international responsibility of a State are governed by special rules of international law."

Hence, a treaty provision may, for example, exclude restitution or change the provisions on the forms of reparation and their hierarchical relationship. If not expressly providing for its relationship with the general rules, the question often arisingwill be whether the specific treaty provision excludes the general rules or coexists, at least partially. In this situation, it is for the specific rule to establish whether and to what extent the general rules are not to be applied.[53]

Douglas, The Hybrid Foundations of Investment Treaty Arbitration, 74 BYIL 2004, p. 151, p. 165, footnote 67.

52 Judgement of 30.8.1924, PCIJ Rep. Series A, No. 2, p. 12; see also Garcia-Amador, Sixth Report on State Responsibility, Yearbook of the International Law Commission 1961, Vol. II, Document A/CN.4/134 & Add. 1, p. 1, para. 41.

53 Draft Articles on Responsibility of States for Internationally Wrongful Acts, with Commentaries, Yearbook of the International Law Commission 2001, vol. II. (Part Two), p. 31, Art.55, para. 1 - 5. As a matter of interpretation, for the lex specialis principle to apply the same subject matter must be covered by the two provisions, the one more specific than the other. Furthermore, there must be some actual inconsistency between them or, at least, a discernable intention that one provision shall prevail over the other.

C. Investment Treaty Law

After having summarised the situation under "general" public international law we shall now turn to investment treaty law. In a first step of analysis, the operation of the rules on the content of international responsibility and, more particular, on the relationship between restitution and compensation in the context of investment arbitration is brought in focus (below I.) Against the background of the conclusions arrived at this paper sets forth a normative construction of the relationship between the two aforementioned forms of reparation in investment treaty law (below II.).

I. The Relationship between Restitution and Compensation through the Eyes of Arbitral Tribunals Constituted on the Basis of an Investment Treaty

When looking at the more recent arbitral awards, decisions and orders rendered on the basis of investment treaties, one can observe that the vast majority of them does not discuss – indeed, not even mention – different forms of reparation but turns straight to compensation. This is at first sight somewhat surprising since most investment treaties – NAFTA[54] and the Energy Charter Treaty ("ECT")[55], for example, are notable exceptions – do not set out the content of international responsibility including the forms of preparation and, therefore, apparently leave room for examining the governing rules.

To some extent, this phenomenon might be explained by the fact that claimants frequently ask the tribunal to award compensation only and hence de-elect any other form of reparation. Any reference to Article 43 (2) lit. (b) ASR or any other "justification" for the admissibility of such (de-)election is frequently omittedthough.Such modus operandi can perhaps be "explained" by some sort of commercial-arbitration-mindset in which party autonomy constitutes a paramount overarching principle, rendering any further explanation dispensable.

However, even from a public international law point of view there is indeed not much reason to discuss this point in detail in an award as long as the claimant's choice constitutes a valid, especially by the respondent unopposed election. Nevertheless, an election should be made transparent. Remarkable examples of

---

54 See Article 1135 (1) NAFTA; restated below C. II. 2.
55 See Article 12 (2) and Article 26 (8) 2. sentence ECT; restated below footnote 124.

awards where an election was discussed are *Duke Energy v. Ecuador*[56], *Rumeli Telekom and Telsim v. Kazakhstan*[57] and *CMS v. Argentina*[58].

In particular the tribunal in the last mentioned case – *CMS v Argentina* – made some effort in this respect. In fact – without any need – it went even further: The tribunal, in some length, discussed customary international law governing reparation including its "restatement" in the Articles on State Responsibility making, *inter alia*, reference to Article 35 ASR and the *Factory of Charzów* case.[59]

The tribunal characterised restitution – in broad accord with general public international law – as

"by far the most reliable choice to make the injured party whole as it aims at the reestablishment of the situation existing prior to the wrongful act".[60]

Without referring to the tests in Article 35 lit. (a) and (b) ASR the tribunal went on stating:

"In a situation such as that characterising this dispute and the complex issues associated with the crisis in Argentina, it would be utterly unrealistic for the Tribunal to order the Respondent to turn back to the regulatory framework existing before the emergency measures were adopted, *nor has this been requested*."[61]

In its further discussion of the possibility of restitution[62], while rejecting the option of re-establishing the regulatory framework existing before the Argentina crisis, the Tribunal, suggested "restitution by negotiation of the parties" in order to rebalance contractual relations between Argentina and the foreign investors as its favoured way of restitution.[63]

---

56 Duke Energy Electroquil Partners & Electroquil S.A. v. Ecuador, ICSID Case No.ARB/04/19, Award of 18.8.2008.
57 Rumeli Telekom A.S. and Telsim Mobil A.S. v. Kazakhstan, ICSID Case No ARB/05/16, Award of 29.7.2008.
58 CMS Gas Transmission Company v. Argentina, ICSID Case No.ARB/01/8, Award of 12.5.2005.
59 CMS Gas Transmission Company v. Argentina, ICSID Case No.ARB/01/8, Award of 12.5.2005, para. 399 - 405.
60 CMS Gas Transmission Company v. Argentina, ICSID Case No.ARB/01/8, Award of 12.5.2005, para. 406.
61 [Emphasis added] CMS Gas Transmission Company v. Argentina, ICSID Case No.ARB/01/8, Award of 12.5.2005, para. 406.
62 One could ask whether the Tribunal attributed binding force to the Claimant's choice of reparation or whether its statement on impossibility was an obiter dictum.
63 CMS Gas Transmission Company v. Argentina, ICSID Case No.ARB/01/8, Award of 12.5.2005, para. 407.

While this is certainly not restitution *sensu stricto* as it would not lead to the re-establishment of the *status quo ante*, it appears to be a "mixture" of the obligation to cease the wrongful act as envisaged in Article 30 lit. (a) ASR[64] and a suggestion of conflict resolution by amicable settlement.[65]

Ultimately, the Tribunal ended up awarding compensation as it did not want to let the claimant wait until a settlement had eventually been reached between the parties to the dispute.[66]

The conclusions in respect of the available form of reparationin *CMS v. Argentina* were quickly adopted by some other tribunals dealing also with the aftermaths of the Argentina crisis. In *Enron v. Argentina*, for example, the Tribunal found that the respective bilateral investment treaty ("BIT") did not contain any provision on the "standard of reparation". It then continued stating rather cryptically:

"Absent an agreed form of restitution by means of renegotiation of contracts or otherwise, the appropriate standard of reparation under international law is compensation [...]".[67]

The reasoning in *Sempra v. Argentina* slightly deviated from that in *CMS v. Argentina*, perhaps acknowledging that "restitution by negotiation" actually does not constitute restitution *sensu stricto*. The Tribunal stated:

"In the absence of restitution *or* agreed renegotiation of contracts *or* other measures of redress, the appropriate standard of reparation under international law is compensation for the losses suffered by the affected party."[68]

---

64 Cf. CMS Gas Transmission Company v. Argentina, ICSID Case No.ARB/01/8, Award of 12.5.2005, para. 245: "The Government has the duty to redress this abnormal situation, first, by putting an end to what by definition should be a temporary situation, a step that might be adequately taken in the context of the continuing negotiations between the parties, and next by paying compensation for the damage caused."

65 Cf. CMS Gas Transmission Company v. Argentina, ICSID Case No.ARB/01/8, Award of 12.5.2005, para. 407: "As long as the parties were to agree to new terms governing their relations, this would be considered as a form of restitution as both sides to the equation would have accepted that a rebalancing had been achieved." [Emphasis added]

66 CMS Gas Transmission Company v. Argentina, ICSID Case No.ARB/01/8, Award of 12.5.2005, para. 407 - 408.

67 Enron Corporation and Ponderosa Assets, L.P. v. Argentina, ICSID Case No.ARB/01/3, Award of 22.5.2007, para. 359. Compare: Enron Corporation and Ponderosa Assets, L.P. v. Argentina, ICSID Case No. ARB/01/3, Decision on Jurisdiction, 14.01.2004, para. 75-81.

68 [Emphasis added] Cf. Sempra Energy International v. Argentina, ICSID Case No.ARB/02/16, Award of 28.9.2007, para. 401.

Unfortunately, however, the Tribunal did not feel obliged to go into further detail why restitution was – in the words of the Tribunal – "absent".

In its award in *Nykomb v. Latvia* the tribunal[69] made reference to Articles 34 and 35 ASR and the *Factory of Chorzow case* which would – in the absence of any *lex specialis* – govern the content of State responsibility. The tribunal confirmed that restitution constitutes the primary form of reparation. It stated:

"[E]ven if damage or losses to an investment may be inflicted indirectly through loss-creating actions towards a subsidiary in the country of a Contracting State, restitution must primarily be seen as an appropriate remedy in a situation where the Contracting State has instituted actions directly against the investor."[70]

In the eyes of the tribunal, restitution was conceivable in the case at hand by the way of juridical restitution of provisions of Latvian law ensuring the claimant's right to double tariff for the purchase of electric power or compensation, i.e. the payment of a certain sum of money which the claimant would have received if the contract for purchase of power between the respondent and claimant had been properly executed.

In the end the tribunal opted for compensation with the argument that ultimately it would not matter for the claimant – in any way "only" entitled to a certain sum of money – whether the tribunal ordered legal restitution or compensation.[71]

Certainly, such reasoning is difficult to bring in line with orthodox reasoning on the basis of the general rules on State responsibility. It is hard to say whether the tribunal actually meant that granting restitution in such a case would have been disproportionate and, therefore, went for compensation or that there was no hierarchy among the forms of reparation.

LG&E v. Argentina constitutes a case where the claimants explicitly requested compensation only in case no restitution would be available.[72] Already in its *Decision on Liability* the Tribunal pointed out – though, at that point in time it did

---

69   Nykomb Synergetics Technology Holding AB v. Latvia, Arbitration Institute of the Stockholm Chamber of Commerce, Award of 16.12.2003, Section 5.1.
70   Nykomb Synergetics Technology Holding AB v. Latvia, Arbitration Institute of the Stockholm Chamber of Commerce, Award of 16.12.2003, Section 5.1.
71   "An award obliging the Republic to make payments to Windau in accordance with the Contract would also in effect be equivalent to ordering payment under Contract No. 16/07 [- which would amount to the juridical restitution of the contract -] in the present Treaty arbitration. The Arbitral Tribunal therefore finds the appropriate approach, for the time up to the time of this award, to be an assessment of compensation for the losses or damages inflicted on the Claimant's investments." Cf. Nykomb Synergetics Technology Holding AB v. Latvia, Arbitration Institute of the Stockholm Chamber of Commerce, Award of 16.12.2003, Section 5.1.
72   LG&E v. Argentina, ICSID Case No.ARB/02/1, Award of 25.7.2007, para. 32 in connection with footnote 7.

not order it – that Argentina was under the principle duty to restore the initial legal framework which existed prior to the crisis. It explained

"… what Argentina should have done, once the state of necessity was over on 26 April 2003. The very following day (27 April), Argentina's obligations were once again effective. Therefore, *Respondent should have re-established the tariff scheme offered to LG&E* or, at least, it should have compensated Claimants for the losses incurred on account of the measures adopted before and after the state of necessity."[73]

Again, it is not fully clear whether the tribunal acted on the assumption that there is a hierarchy among the forms of reparation.

In its final Award the Tribunal became even more cautious and ultimately refused to grant restitution. It held:

"The judicial restitution required in this case would imply modification of the current legal situation by annulling or enacting legislative and administrative measures that make over the effect of the legislation in breach. The Tribunal cannot compel Argentina to do so without *a sentiment of undue interference with its sovereignty*."[74]

While sentiment of arbitrators surely is nota valid reason under public international law to deny a claimant reparation taking the form of restitution, the underlying message is nevertheless clear: as soon as an author State has brought about the wrongful act by legislative or administrative acts, the possibility of restitution is seriously called in question – allegedly due to an illegitimate interfe-rence with its sovereignty. In this respect the reasoning also differs from the other Argentina cases mentioned above as the Tribunal in *LG&E v. Argentina* did not – at least not explicitly – look at impossibility or excessive onerousness.

The same underlying sovereignty argument – though with references to impossibility and excessive onerousness[75]– can be found in *Occidental v. Ecuador* where theclaimants sought provisional measures in relation to Ecuador's termination of a participation contract for the exploration of hydrocarbon reserves. Provisional measures would have amounted to the preservation of rights enjoyed under the participation contract. The Tribunal took the view that it

---

73   [Emphasis added] LG&E v. Argentina, ICSID Case No.ARB/02/1, Decision on Liability of 3.10.2006, para. 86; NB: para. 265.

74   [Emphasis added] LG&E v. Argentina, ICSID Case No.ARB/02/1, Award of 25.7.2007, para. 87.

75   Occidental Petroleum Corporation, Occidental Exploration and Production Company v. Ecuador, ICSID Case No.ARB/06/11, Award of 17.8.2007, para. 75 et seqq.

"is well established that where a State has, in the exercise of its sovereign powers, put an end to a contract or a license, or any other foreign investor's entitlement, specific performance must be deemed legally impossible."[76]

It continued:

"The adequate remedy where an internationally illegal act has been committed is compensation deemed to be equivalent with restitution in kind. Such solution strikes the required balance between the need to protect the foreign investor's right and the right of the host State to claim control over natural resources"[77]

Put in a broader perspective, such calls to revert the priority rule and deny restitution on principle in case a respondent State is required to effect such restitution by some internal legal act are not new. They featured high in the proceedings of the International Law Commission as discussed above.[78]

The last case which shall be mentioned here is the ICSID case *Micula v. Romania* which could turn into a *Nykomb v. Latvia*-type approach to the issue of the relationship between restitution and compensation. In *Micula v. Romania* the investor alleged a breach of investment treaty provisions when Romania dismantled policies or regulations that were deemed by the European Commission to run counter to the terms of European Union ("EU") law in the course of the EU accession process. In the case at hand Romania withdrew investment incentives – including exemptions from customs duties and certain taxes – which were contrary to EU State aid law.

In the proceedings the investor asked for "restitution of the legal framework" which had prevailed prior Romania's alignment with the European *acquis communautaire*. Already on the jurisdictional level Romania tried to challenge the claimant's request on the grounds that the tribunal lacked the power to order the restoration of old laws which would breach EU law. However, in its jurisdictional ruling, the tribunal noted that it did not lack such power and would determine the appropriateness of restitution in the merits phase of the proceedings.[79] Looking at the case from the perspective of the Articles on State Responsibility such reasoning appears to be in line with orthodox reasoning.[80]

---

76 Occidental Petroleum Corporation, Occidental Exploration and Production Company v. Ecuador, ICSID Case No.ARB/06/11, Award of 17.8.2007, para. 79.
77 Occidental Petroleum Corporation, Occidental Exploration and Production Company v. Ecuador, ICSID Case No.ARB/06/11, Award of 17.8.2007, para. 85.
78 See above 0 III. 2.
79 2 (8) IA Reporter 2009, 11.5.2009.
80 A completely different question is the one of whether the tribunal lost jurisdiction – partially or in full – on the basis of the Sweden-Romania BIT due to the conclusion of sub-

If one wants to sum up and attempt a rough categorisation of the case law referred to above, one could form two broad groups. The first and larger one comprises all those cases in which the claimant opted for compensation. The validity of such election – when accompanied by some reasoning – was justified by the tribunals by taking recourse to the general law of State responsibility.

The second group relates to those cases where there was no election or an election which referred to the "hierarchy of the forms of reparation". The tribunals equally tried to base their reasoning – more or less closely – on the general rules on State responsibility thereby affirming – in principle – their continuing validity and applicability within the context of investment treaties. However, some awards seem to deviate from the general rules on State responsibility insofar as legal restitution is involved. Decisions display patterns of arguments put forward to restrict or even rule out the admissibility of restitution in favour of compensation as the preferred form of reparation within the context of international responsibility flowing from the breach of an investment treaty. Those overly sovereignty-oriented arguments were previously successfully refuted in the course of the proceedings of the International Law Commission, especially by preventing special provisions on foreign investment in respect of reparation to be included in the International Law Commission's Articles on State Responsibility.[81] The critical point in the reasoning of the arbitral awards which display an intent of putting the author State in a more favourable situation is that ultimately it would generally rule out restitution as a the primary form of reparation as any restitution in a State governed by the rule of law would require some sort of legal action within the domestic legal system. It furthermore erodes the general principle that an author State may not rely on internal law in order to justify failure to comply with its obligations.

One final observation should be made: As far as one can see, in the course of the elaboration on the issue of available forms of reparation, none of the examined arbitral awards or decisions discussed the preliminary question of applicability of the Articles on State Responsibility in the context of investment treaties. The issue to whom the substantive rights contained in an investment treaty accrue to was left untouched. No reference was, hence, made to Articles 33 and 55 ASR. Not wanting to overly interpret such treatment of the issue, it nevertheless seems to show that investment tribunals hold the view that the rules – or at

sequent treaties, i.e. the so-called Europe agreement and the accession agreement to the EU, by the State parties concerned. Cf. for an account of the incompatibility of intra-EU BITs with EU law: Hindelang, Member State BITs - There's Still (Some) Life in the Old Dog Yet - Incompatibility of Existing Member State BITs with EU Law and Possible Remedies, in: Sauvant (ed.), Yearbook on International Investment Law & Policy 2010-2011, forthcoming 2011.

81 See above B. III. 2.

least the guiding principles – on the form of reparation matter to investment treaties. The question is though whether those rules apply directly or "indirectly".

II. A Normative Construction of the Relationship between Restitution and Compensation

After having reviewed more recent awards dealing with the form of reparation, in this section we shall turn to a normative construction of the relationship between restitution and compensation. As the ILC Articles on the form of reparation apply directly only to States, the question which has to be answered first in this respect is the one of the applicability of the ILC Articles to investment treaty law, a field significantly characterised by the presence of non-State actors (below 1.). Another issue to be addressed is that of Article 55 ASR. According to this provision the ILC Articles apply only if investment treaty law does not constitute *lex specialis* (below 2.). Subsequently, the results gained are summarised and distinct features of the applicable rules on the forms of reparation in the context of investment treaty law are highlighted (below 3.)

1. The Applicability of the Articles on State Responsibility or: To whom Accrue the Substantive Rights Contained in Investment Treaties?

Article 33 ASR states that Part twoof the ILC Articles on State responsibility – including the Articles on the forms of reparation – essentially applies to States only and

"is without prejudice to any right, arising from the international responsibility of a State, which may accrue directly to any person or entity other than a State."

Investment treaties contain, on the one hand, substantive rights, such as the fair and equitable treatment standard, non-discrimination, full protection and security as well as rules on expropriation. On the other, they provide for procedural rights and duties in the form of investor-State (and State-State) arbitration. The crucial question is, hence, to which those rights directly accrue to.

As individuals or corporate entities established under a municipal law ("investors") have often accepted offers of State parties contained in investment treaties to submit a dispute to impartial arbitration and have acted in hundreds of investment arbitrations under their names as claimant und party to the dispute, independently conducting proceedings against States, it appears less critical to perceive the *investor* as the *holder of the procedural rights* in the context of an investor-State arbitration.[82] While it is beyond doubt that the direct *beneficiary* of the substantive rights contained in an investment treaty is an investor, the crucial question is whether the investor is the "owner", i.e. the *direct holder* of the substantive rights under an investment treaty or "merely" the "*nominal claimant*" in a dispute over rights ultimately held by his home State. Obviously –recalling Article 33 ASR – the ILC Articles on the form of reparation would only apply *directly* if the investor was to be perceived as a "normative claimant" and the true holder of the rights were the State parties to the investment treaty.

As mentioned previously, the traditional view in international law is to perceive individuals and corporate entities as objects of international law. According to the *Mavrommatis*-formula rights and obligations in respect of the property of foreign investors exist in the context of the concept of diplomatic protection exclusively between sovereign States.[83] The question which arises is whether the vast network of multi- as well as bilateral investment treaties has changed this position. When glancing at arbitral awards and scholarly writing one quickly notices a considerable disagreement on this point. In the following the two major "theories" are depicted by reference to pertinent arbitral awards (below a.) and critically reviewed (below b.) against the background of the objective and purpose pursued with the conclusion of investment treaties.

a. Derivative and Direct Rights "Theory"

One view perceives investment treaties as institutionalising and reinforcing the law on the protection of alien property within a modified system of diplomatic protection.[84] The substantive obligations of the treatment of foreign investment contained in investment treaties are owed to the contracting States, just as in customary international law, and those States confer *standing* upon their national investors to enforce such obligations before international arbitral tribunals. Such view has been labelled "derivative (rights) theory".[85]

Such perception is also mirrored in a number of investment tribunal awards, most prominently in *Loewen*, where the NAFTA tribunal stated:

---

82 Spiermann, Individual Rights, State Interests and the Power to Waive ICSID Jurisdiction under Bilateral Investment Treaties, 20 Arbitration International 2004, p. 179, p. 185 et seq. For further references see idem, p. 186, footnotes 31, 32.

83 See above B. IV.

84 Sornarajah, State Responsibility and Bilateral Investment Treaties, 20 J of World Trade L 1986, p. 79, p. 93; Crawford, Retrospect, 96 AJIL 2002, p. 874, p. 888 mentioning it as a possibility, without taking a clear own position though.

85 Cf. for such label Douglas, The Hybrid Foundations of Investment Treaty Arbitration, 74 BYIL 2004, p. 151, p. 163.

"claimants are permitted for convenience to enforce what are in origin the rights of Party states".[86]

Equally, in the *Archer Daniels* award, the majority of arbitrators concluded in respect of the question of rights contained in NAFTA:

„[T]he proper interpretation of the NAFTA does not substantiate that investors have individual rights as alleged by the Claimants. Nor is the nature of investors' rights under Chapter Eleven comparable with the protections conferred by human rights treaties. Chapter Eleven may share (under Section B [, which refers to the investor-State arbitration mechanism]) with human rights treaties the possibility of granting to non-State actors a procedural right to invoke the responsibility of a sovereign State before an international dispute settlement body. But the fundamental difference between Chapter Eleven of the NAFTA and human rights treaties in this regard is, besides a procedural right of action under Section B, that Chapter Eleven does not provide individual substantive rights for investors, but rather complements the promotion and protection standards of the rules regarding the protection of aliens under customary international law."[87]

Such position has also been taken in unison by all three State parties to NAFTA.[88] The recent statement by Mexico in the *Archer Daniels* proceedings can serve as an example:

[...] [T]he substantive obligations are obligations that each NAFTA Party has assumed vis-à-vis the other Parties. They do not cease to be interstate obligations just because an investor has been granted a right of action. [...] [I]nvestment treaties provide a set of obligations which

---

86 Loewen v. USA, ICSID Case No.ARB(AF)/98/3, Award of 26.6.2003, para. 233.
87 Archer Daniels Midland Company and Tate & Lyle Ingredients Americas, Inc v. Mexico, ICSID Case No ARB(AF)/04/05, Award and Separate Opinion of 26.9.2007, para. 171.
88 Canada in: The Attorney General of Canada v. S.D. Myers Inc. Challenge of the Award, Amended Memorandum of Fact and Law of the Applicant, para. 67 (for reference see Douglas, The Hybrid Foundations of Investment Treaty Arbitration, 74 BYIL 2004, p. 151, p. 164, footnote 55): "The obligations listed in Section A of NAFTA Chapter Eleven are not owed directly to individual investors. Rather, the disputing investor must prove that the NAFTA Party claimed against has breached an obligation owed to another NAFTA Party under Section A and that the investor had incurred loss or damage by reason of or arising out of that breach."; USA: in its Reply to the Counter-Memorial on Jurisdiction of the Loewen Group, Inc., p. 33 et seq. (for reference see Douglas, The Hybrid Foundations of Investment Treaty Arbitration, 74 BYIL 2004, p. 151, p. 164, footnote 56) "Mexico is correct that 'the right of direct access conferred by Section B of the NAFTA does not in any way alter the interpretation of the Treaty's substantive rights and obligations, which exist at the international plane between the States inter se."; Mexico: for reference see Douglas, The Hybrid Foundations of Investment Treaty Arbitration, 74 BYIL 2004, p. 151, p. 164, footnote 362.

require the State to treat investments of qualified investors in accordance with the standards of the treaty, but [...] these obligations are owed only to the State of the investors' nationality."[89]

The opposite view holds that investors are recognised to be in a *direct* legal relationship with the host State and they are given procedural means to enforce their *own* substantial rights.[90] Investment tribunals – equally split over the issue – have lent a voice to such perception. In *Corn Products International v. Mexico*, for example, the arbitral tribunal stated:

"[C]laims [under NAFTA chapter 11] are brought by investors, not by States... In the case of Chapter XI of the NAFTA, the Tribunal considers that the intention of the Parties was to confer substantive rights directly upon investors. That follows from the language used and is confirmed by the fact that Chapter XI confers procedural rights upon them."[91]

b. Critical Appraisal

Arbitral tribunals, in discharging their duty to decide a particular dispute presented to them, frequently chose to limit themselves to some apodictic-style statements in respect of the question of the ownership of the substantive rights contained in investment treaties. This might occasionally convey the impression

89   Archer Daniels Midland Company and Tate & Lyle Ingredients Americas, Inc v. Mexico, ICSID Case No ARB(AF)/04/05, Award and Separate Opinion of 26.9.2007, para. 163-4.
90   Spiermann, Individual Rights, State Interests and the Power to Waive ICSID Jurisdiction under Bilateral Investment Treaties, 20 Arbitration International 2004, p. 179, p. 206 et seq; with further references at p. 185, footnote 24, Schwartmann, Private im Wirtschaftsvölkerrecht, 2005, p. 93; In consequence probably also Douglas, The Hybrid Foundations of Investment Treaty Arbitration, 74 BYIL 2004, p. 151, p. 189; summarising the views in German literature Braun, in: Kaushal, et al. (eds.), The Backlash against Investment Arbitration, Proceedings of a Harvard Law School conference, 2009, p. 491, p. 496 et seqq. See also Draft Articles on Responsibility of States for Internationally Wrongful Acts, with Commentaries, Yearbook of the International Law Commission 2001, vol. II. (Part Two), p. 31, Art.33, para. 4 reads "Part Two deals with the secondary obligations of States in relation to cessation and reparation, and those obligations may be owed, inter alia, to one or several States or to the international community as a whole. In cases where the primary obligation is owed to a non-State entity, it may be that some procedure is available whereby that entity can invoke the responsibility on its own account and without the intermediation of any State. This is true, for example ... in the case of rights under bilateral or regional investment protection agreements."
91   Corn Products International, Inc. v. The United Mexican States, ICSID Case No. ARB(AF)/04/01 (Additional Facility), Decision on Responsibility of 15.01.2008, para. para. 164 - 165, 167, 176; note also para. 12.; see also MTD Equity Sdn. Bhd. and MTD Chile S. A. v. Republic of Chile, ICSID Case No ARB/01/07, Decision on Annulment, 21.3.2007, para. 99.

that the issue can be decided in a clear-cut and straightforward fashion. However, already when looking at the text of investment treaties or – putting it in the words of the tribunal in *Corn Products International v. Mexico* – at the "language used" therein, one encounters problems – similar to those when looking at the text of the WTO agreements[92] – to identify *conclusively* the ultimate holder of the substantive rights contained in investment treaties. Such treaties, furthermore, do not address the status of a tribunal hearing investor-State claims.[93]

It therefore appears that the text in itself, as well as the *travaux préparatoires,* is insufficient to identify conclusively the ultimate holder of the rights contained in investment treaties. An interpretation must consequently focus on the context and on object and purpose of the treaties which can be derived from the overall architecture of the investment treaties (below(1))in order to identify the holder of the substantive rights (below (2)).

(1) Object and Purpose: Establishing a Healthy Investment Climate, Depoliticisation, and a Legal System Based on the Rule of Law

Which aims do State parties pursue with the conclusion of an investment treaty which contains both, substantive treatment rights in respect of an investment of a foreign investor and procedural means to enforce the aforesaid? In their preamble BITs usually refer to the aim of intensifying economic cooperation, creating favourable conditions for investments, promoting and protecting investments and furthering development and prosperity of the contracting State parties. Thus, the State parties reciprocally promise to create a *long-term and stable investment environment* in their territory for investments made by investors of the other contracting State party on the basis of the rule of law.[94] In short: they aim at establishing and maintaining a *"healthy investment climate"* in the territory of the respective other State party.[95]

---

92 Cf. ECJ, T-174/00 (Biret/Council), ECJ Rep. 2002, p. II-17, para. 61 et seq.; AG Alber in: ECJ, C-93/02 P, ECJ Rep. 2003, p. I-10497, para. 116 - 118; see also Panel Report on United States Sections 301-310 of The Trade Act of 1974, WT /DS152R, para. 7.71-7.92.

93 Douglas, The Hybrid Foundations of Investment Treaty Arbitration, 74 BYIL 2004, p. 151, p. 164, p. 167.

94 Critical in respect of advancement of the rule of law by investment treaties: Van Harten, Five Justifications for Investment Treaties: A Critical Discussion (June 9, 2010). Trade, Law & Development, vol. 2, no. 1, p. 1, 2010, available at SSRN: http://ssrn.com/abstract =1622928.

95 See for this notion in the context of customary international law on foreign investment: Hindelang, Bilateral Investment Treaties, Custom and a Healthy Investment Climate, 5 JWIT 2004, 789 et seqq.

Not conclusive, but certainly notable: the substantive treatment standards in investment treaties are frequently formulated in respect of an investment and not an investor.[96] Hence, there is no clear focus on the investor who is protected in his peaceful enjoyment of his property as in human rights agreements[97] but it appears to be the property to which the legal protection is attached. This regulatory approach seems to be in line with the aforesaid overall aim of erecting and maintaining a healthy investment climate which looks on investment treaties more in terms of regulatory stability and predictability of legal orders and economic development and prosperity of State economies instead of fundamental rights of an individual to be protected from the State.

Two constitutive elements appear to be central to such perception of investment treaties. That is, *first*, the predictability, foreseeability and limitation of the exercise of sovereign powers in respect of the treatment of foreign property which is effectuated in the investment treaties' description of *basic treatment standards* in regard to foreign investment. Those obligations under international law limit the exercise of the host State's regulatory and administrative powers with the consequence that any dispute about those obligations essentially constitutes a public law dispute about the conformity of their exercise.[98] Therefore, the interest of a State party in the application and interpretation of the basic treatment standards in the course of investor-State arbitration goes beyond allowing its nationals to clarify the meaning of law, remitting the parties to privately ordering their affairs. By regulating the interactions of sovereign powers with foreign property within their territory now and in the future,[99] State parties aim at

---

96   Cf., e.g., Article 2 (2) German-Chinese BIT „Investments ... shall enjoy constant protection and security in the territory of the other Contracting Party."; Article 3 (1) German-Chinese BIT „Investments ... shall at all times be accorded fair and equitable treatment in the territory of the other Contracting Party."; Article 4 (2) German-Chinese BIT „Investments ... shall not directly or indirectly be expropriated, nationalized or subjected to any other measure the effects of which would be tantamount to expropriation or nationalization in the territory of the other Contracting Party (hereinafter referred to as expropriation) except for the public benefit and against compensation."

97   Cf. Article 1 of Protocol to the Convention for the Protection of Human Rights and Fundamental Freedoms as amended by Protocol No. 11 "Every natural or legal person is entitled to the peaceful enjoyment of his possessions."

98   Schill, Crafting the International Economic Order: The Public Function of Investment Treaty Arbitration and Its Significance for the Role of the Arbitrator, 23 LJIL 2010, p. 404, p. 410.

99   This future oriented, "systemic interest" of States in investor-State arbitration is highlighted by the generalised and prospective consent to arbitration contained in BITs; quite in contrast to other treaty-based mechanisms providing for investor-State dispute settlement like the United States-Mexican General Claims Commission or the Iran-United States Claims Tribunal where subject matter jurisdiction was more limited and retrospective. Cf. Schill, Crafting the International Economic Order: The Public Function

establishing and developing a *legal system* which involves difficult balancing and delineation processes, having impactswhich go beyond the individual case, between the common good taking the form of national security, social welfare, the protection of cultural heritage or environmental protection and private interests. It can, thus, be said that investment treaties fulfil

"a governance function in influencing the behaviour of foreign investors, States, and civil society more generally by crafting and concretising international standards of investment protection"[100]

beyond individual investor-State disputes. Viewed from such a perspective one can argue that State parties have (retained) an own, a *"systemic interest"* in the well-functioning of such legal system in a way envisaged by the State parties.[101] Whether, in the context of setting up such a system, the individual investor was sufficiently in the contemplation of States can therefore be doubted with some reason.[102]

Such a rule based system, by definition, to a large extent requires the absence of diplomatic discretion and political arbitration, two properties characteristic to the traditional concept of diplomatic protection. This requirement plays into the hands of the *second* constitutive element for achieving a "healthy investment climate" as envisaged by the State parties to the investment treaty: the "depoliticisation" of a possible investment dispute to the extent possible. Pursuing and resolving investment disputes under the concept of diplomatic protection carries with it potential spillover effects into other, unrelated policy areas as the host State in particular will aim at expanding its bargaining powers on the diplomatic stage. It also involves "diplomatic humiliation" by the way of being exposed to a claim in traditional international judicial *fora*, such as the International Court of Justice ("ICJ"). If the individual investment dispute is "de-

of Investment Treaty Arbitration and Its Significance for the Role of the Arbitrator, 23 LJIL 2010, p. 404, p. 411 as well as footnotes 40, 42.

100 Schill, Crafting the International Economic Order: The Public Function of Investment Treaty Arbitration and Its Significance for the Role of the Arbitrator, 23 LJIL 2010, p. 404, p. 409.

101 Schill, Crafting the International Economic Order: The Public Function of Investment Treaty Arbitration and Its Significance for the Role of the Arbitrator, 23 LJIL 2010, p. 404, p. 408 et seqq, footnote. 25; Idem, p. 408: „By promoting and protecting foreign investment, enhancing the rule of law, creating employment, and enhancing trade opportunities, in particular in developing countries, investment treaty arbitration assumes a public function in backing up the international order created by international investment treaties."

102 Douglas, The Hybrid Foundations of Investment Treaty Arbitration, 74 BYIL 2004, p. 151, p. 184.

politicised" – i.e. relegated from the diplomatic stage or traditional international judicial *fora* – it helps preventing the individual investment disputes straining general inter-State relations and, in turn, it promotes the intended stability in the economic and non-economic inter-State relations.[103] However, due to the nature of conflict a complete "de-politicisation" remains and, indeed, must remain wishful thinking.[104]

The "de-politicisation" of investment relations was effectuated by nominating the investor, an "international law lightweight" if contrasted with a State, as claimant in a possible arbitration over the basic treatment rights contained in investment treaties.

However, the main concern of the State parties to an investment treaty was not to relieve the individual investor of its home-State-dependence– common to the concept of diplomatic protection in customary law – but to "de-politicise" their *inter-State* bilateral relations. Article 27 (1) ICSID, which reads

"No Contracting State shall give diplomatic protection, or bring an international claim, in respect of a dispute which one of its nationals and another Contracting State shall have consented to submit or shall have submitted to arbitration under this Convention, unless such other Contracting State shall have failed to abide by and comply with the award rendered in such dispute."

can be understood in this sense as a safeguard mechanism for the respondent State – and for the respondent State only – to ensure that a "de-politicised" arbitration is not suddenly politicised by a parallel claim on the basis of the traditional concept of diplomatic protection. Relieving the investor from political negotiations with his home State could therefore be viewed as an unavoidable, not

103 Shihata, Towards a Greater Depoliticization of Investment Disputes: The Roles of ICSID and MIGA, in: The World Bank in a Changing World, 1991, p. 309 et seqq; Schreuer, The ICSID Convention: A Commentary, 2001, p. 398.
104 Note, for example, the still existing tensions in the German-Philippine bilateral relations due to Fraport's expropriated investment in the Philippines: Fraport AG Frankfurt Airport Services Worldwide v. Philippines, ICSID Case No. ARB/03/25, Award of 16.8.2007; Decision on Annulment, 23.12.2010 (not public). Despite the (initial) defeat of the investor in an – although not uncontroversial – investment arbitration the Auswärtiges Amt (German Federal Foreign Office) declares on its website: „Die deutsch-philippinischen Wirtschaftsbeziehungen sind jedoch getrübt, nachdem die philippinische Regierung im Dezember 2004 den von einem deutsch-philippinischen Konsortium im Dezember 2002 fertig gestellten neuen internationalen Flughafenterminal Manila enteignet hat; bislang wurde erst eine relativ kleine Anzahlung auf die Enteignungsentschädigung geleistet." (Auswärtiges Amt, Website, http://www.auswaertiges-amt.de/diplo/de/Laenderinforma tionen/Philippinen/Bilateral.html, last visited: 02.9.2010).

necessarily intended, but by the investor certainly appreciated side – effect of the change of the (nominal) claimant.

(2) The Owner of the Substantive Rights

Having outlined the purposesState parties pursue with the conclusion of an investment treaty, those shall now form the basis for an interpretationof an investment treatywith the view to decide on the question of the ownership of substantive rights. This interpretation is conducted in the spirit of *in dubio mitius*.[105]

With that said it appears that the referral of procedural rights on the investor which includes the right of standing as *nominal claimant*[106] in investor-State arbitrations seems to suffice to effectuate all purposes pursued with the conclusion of an investment treaty.

While States are apparently under *no compelling need* to additionally limit their sovereignty by also transferring substantive rights upon individuals, one can in fact even bring forward the argument that such transfer would *run counter to the aims pursued* with the conclusion of investment treaties. It was stated above that State parties hold a "systemic interest" in the well-functioning of the legal system they established to order the interactions of State parties with foreign property. They are, furthermore, interested in possible investment disputes not being needlessly politicised. In light of the aforesaid it is suggested that the State parties have retained means to defend their "systemic interest" they hold if threatened by claims of a normative claimant which runs counter to the purposes pursued with by the investment treaty.

Granting the investor the right of a normative claimant entails the danger of misuse and abuse of the position as he is only driven – and this is by no means understood negatively – by self-interest. For example, a claim could run contrary to the ends pursued with the investment treaty if the true purpose of the claim were not to secure conformity of the exercise of the host State's regulatory and administrative powers with its obligations under international law but to recover loss sustained by bad, illegal or even criminal business practice or loss suffered

---

105 Von Heinegg, in: Ipsen, Völkerrecht, 4. ed. 1999, § 11 mn. 20; see also SGS Société Générale de Surveillance S.A. v. Pakistan, ICSID Case No. ARB/01/13, Decision on Objections to Jurisdiction of 06.8.2003, para. 171: "The appropriate interpretive approach is the prudential one summed up in the literature as in dubio pars mitior est sequenda, or more tersely, in dubio mitius."

106 In contrast, the referral of a position of an agent upon the investor would not suffice for the attainment of the aim of "de-politicisation" as this would not change the parties to the dispute. The two State parties would still be claimant and defendant; a situation actually to be avoided.

by obviously legitimate regulatory measures of the host State and if, as a consequence, such a claim were to significantly strain the bilateral relations of the two State parties. Equally, merely bringing claims to pressure a host State to make "illegitimate" concessions by hoping that governments will wish to avoid the negative publicity of being the recipient of investment claims does not serve the ends pursued with the conclusion of an investment treaty but discredits the instruments used to implement those ends.

While it is not just difficult but also unwanted against the background of the aim of "de-politicisation" for a home State to meaningfully intervene *by procedural means* in investor-State arbitration[107] and recourse to the classic procedural enforcement mechanism of diplomatic protection – *cf.* Article 27 (1) ICSID – is usually foreclosed, a workable way of securing its interests in the well-functioning of the system it created appears to be by keeping control over substantive rights.

If the home State of the investor is of the opinion that a claim is ill-founded in the aforesaid manner and if there is the danger that "misdirected" self-interest of an individual would discredit the whole system, then the home State should be able to intervene *on the level of substantive law* in a "systemic interest", recalling that "de-politicisation" was not undertaken in favour of the investor but to the advantage of the bilateral relations of the State parties to the investment treaty. This intervention would take the simple form of a waiver of substantive rights in respect of an individual investor *vis-à-vis* the host State which – without taking recourse to any procedural means – would pull out the rug from under an investor-State arbitration.[108]

Such perception is, though, not shared by those who champion the so-called "direct rights theory". Those who favour perceiving investment treaties as conferring direct substantive rights upon an investor mainly build their argument on the difference between the enforcement of (substantive rights in) investment treaties and the enforcement of the rules on protection of alien property. While

---

107 A certain exception in this respect constitutes Article 1128 NAFTA and BITs on the basis of the 2004 US Model BIT (cf. Article 28 (2)). Notable is also the US submission in 2008 on the interpretation of Articles 53 and 54 ICSID in the Siemens v. Argentina annulment proceeding. The submission relied on the amicus curiae authority provided under the recently adopted Article 37 (2) of the ICSID Arbitration Rules, as well as on the authority under Article 44 ICSID to accept amicus submissions found under prior ICSID practice in the event that the new arbitration rules were not applicable to that proceeding.

108 See for an outline of consequences of the differing perceptions on the issue of the holder of substantive rights in investment treaties: Bjorklund, Private Rights and Public International Law: Why Competition Among International Economic Law Tribunals Is Not Working, 59 HASTINGS L.J. 2007, p. 241, p. 263 - 70. See also Roberts, Power and Persuasion in Investment Treaty Interpretation: The Dual Role of States, 104 AJIL 2010, p. 179, p. 184 et seqq.

the latter are made effective by the way of diplomatic protection, investment treaties have installed investor-State-arbitration mechanisms which heavily rely on elements borrowed from commercial arbitration.

While it is neither possible nor suitable in the context of this paper to discuss the whole of the arguments advanced in favour of the "direct rights theory" in detail, in the following three major arguments relating to the applicable law in investment arbitration (below (a)), to the non-applicability of the doctrines of continuous nationality and effective/genuine link (below (b)), and to the non-applicability of the exhaustion of local remedies rule (below (c)) shall be addressed in all necessary brevity. Those arguments allegedly evidence that

"the national State of the investor retains no interest in an investment treaty arbitration instituted against another contracting State".[109]

(a) The Applicable Law

Public international law governs diplomatic protection claims in State-State adjudication. The situation in investor-State-arbitration is less clear: if an investor opts for an arbitration administered by rules designed for commercial disputes, such as the rules of the International Chamber of Commerce ("ICC"), the United Nations Commission on International Trade Law ("UNCITRAL") or the Stockholm Chamber of Commerce ("SCC"), the ultimately governing law – the *lex arbitri* – is the municipal law of the seat of arbitration. Some draw from that that

"[i]f an investor was in essence bringing a claim on behalf of its national State, the logical consequence would be that public international law would govern the arbitration by default as the rights of the two States under an international treaty would be the ratione materiae of the dispute."[110]

While it is certainly correct to perceive public international law as default law in case of investment disputes, this paper however submits that States in their sovereign capacity deviated from this default rule by the way of allowing for the use of commercial arbitration bodies with their choice of law clauses contained in their arbitration rules. Although it might look peculiar turning – figuratively speaking– the hierarchy of norms upside downand although one may identify good reasons to perceive commercial arbitration bodies as ill– fitting with the public law nature of investment arbitration, States are free to resolve their disputes by the law they deem suitable. Whether one can draw the conclusion from an (implicit) choice of law made by the State parties to an investment treaty that

109 Douglas, The Hybrid Foundations of Investment Treaty Arbitration, 74 BYIL 2004, p. 151, p. 170.
110 Idem., p. 178.

"the general application of municipal law of the seat of arbitration to investment treaty arbitrations once again refutes the derivative theory for investment treaty claims"

remains therefore doubtful. It is not just that an investor-State dispute is rarely resolved by complete neglect of public international law, but also the logical deduction of the holder of a right from the question of applicable law appears not compelling.

(b) Doctrines of Continuous Nationality and Effective/Genuine Link

In contrast to diplomatic protection investment treaty arbitration does not seem overly anxious avoiding forum shopping and competing claims by way of claims based on indirect holdings; hence the doctrines of continuous nationality and effective/genuine link do not play a significant role. Does this imply that a home State has lost its interest in investment claims just because they can be brought by investors which do not unfold significant business activities in a home State's territory?[111] Indeed, the degree of interest of the home State of an investor in a claim against a host State may vary depending on the nature and extent of the business activities of the investor in the home State and the consequential contributions to the community. However, it can be doubted that the home State completely lost its interest in such claims. Again, it is suggested that the home State holds a "systemic interest": each well-founded claim of an investor reinforces and strengthens the rule of law in bilateral investment relations and ultimately furthers an overall healthy investment climate for all investors of the home State in the host State's territory. Moreover, the possibility of forum shopping and competing claims,originating from a broad definition of BIT protected investments, might be owed to the desire to protect indirect shareholdings better by overcoming the *Barcelona Traction*[112] and *Diallo*[113] rulings which by and large advocated a test of incorporation and, therefore, foreclosed indirect claims by shareholders.

---

111 Arguing in such direction: Douglas, The Hybrid Foundations of Investment Treaty Arbitration, 74 BYIL 2004, p. 151, p. 175.

112 Barcelona Traction, Light and Power Company, Limited, Judgment, ICJ Reports 1970, p. 3.

113 Ahmadou Sadio Diallo (Republic of Guinea v. Democratic Republic of the Congo), Judgement (Preliminary Objections) of 24.5.2007, para. 86 et seqq.

(c) The Exhaustion of Local Remedies Rule

Before a diplomatic protection claim can be brought on behalf of a national, the national needs to exhaust local remedies in order to give the host State the chance to redress the wrongdoing by its own means, within the framework of its own domestic legal system.[114] This serves not just the interests of the host but also of the home State of the national. Conflicts on the level of the individual with its host State are prevented from being transformed too quickly into an international dispute between two States.[115]

Without a special provision in an investment treaty, investment tribunals do not require an investor to exhaust local remedies before bringing his case.[116] This allegedly shows that

> "[b]y dispensing with the local remedies rule as a procedural requirement for the investor's treaty claims, the contracting States have also abandoned their interests that are protected by the rules. If they had a legal interest at stake in an investment treaty claim then this would be a surprising concession."[117]

This conclusion, however, appears not compelling. The home State's interest – i.e. avoiding the politicisation of an investment dispute as long as possible – in the context of an investment treaty is by far better served by the fact that the investor has taken over the role of the nominative claimant. Viewed from this perspective, the local remedies rule has become superfluous. Also from the perspective of the host State, compromising the local remedies rule might not at all be a surprising concession but the prize to be paid for the attraction of investment.

c. Summary So Far

After having glanced at some major arguments in favour of a "direct rights theory" it can be doubted that

> "[t]he fundamental assumption underlying the investment treaty regime is clearly that the investor is bringing a cause of action upon the vindication of its own rights rather than those of its national State."[118]

---

114 Cf. Interhandel Case, Judgment, I.C.J . Reports 1959, p. 6, p. 27.
115 McNair, International Law Opinions, vol. 2, 1956, p. 197.
116 Cf. Douglas, The Hybrid Foundations of Investment Treaty Arbitration, 74 BYIL 2004, p. 151, p. 179, footnote 145.
117 Idem., p. 179.
118 Idem., p. 182; but see also Idem, p. 184.

The state of play, it is respectfully submitted, is neither clear nor is there – as of yet – any assumption in respect of the holder of the substantive rights contained in an investment treaty which deserves to be labelled fundamental. The purpose of the preceding discussion was to demonstrate that a prudent teleological interpretation of investment treaties in the spirit of *indubio mitius* also allows for a conclusion that the State parties did *not* confer substantive rights on the investor in order to effectuate their purposes pursued with the conclusion of an investment treaty; rather the referral of procedural rights seems to suffice to meet their ends.

Much confusion results from the recourse in investment treaties to commercial arbitration-type adjudication which also leads to the peculiar choice of law by the State parties to the investment treaty which partially turned – figuratively speaking – the conventional hierarchy of norms upside down. The question of whether this regulatory approach justifies the conclusion that the State parties intended to create a system fundamentally different from the one of diplomatic protection with which the rules on protection of alien property are enforced remains open. It is not unlikely that State parties employed such mechanisms due to of a lack of alternative or/and practicability considerations and otherwise wanted to remain in the "old order of things".

Tying in with *Douglas'* observation that "[i]n deciding between the competing 'derivative' and 'direct' theories, the starting point must be that international legal theory allows for both possibilities"[119], the author of this paper would add that not just legal theory but also practice currently allows for both conclusions.

Coming back to the starting point of this section, i.e. the question of whether Part twoof the ILC Articles on State Responsibility – including those Articles on the forms of reparation – also apply in the context of investment treaties: for the purpose of the subsequent discussion, this paper proceeds from the assumption that the question can be answered in the affirmative in respect of the substantive rights flowing from investment agreements. Such conclusion seems to be justified against the background of an *in dubio mitius* interpretation which implies that the aims attached to investment agreements can be (better) achieved if substantive rights remain with the States.

2. Investment Treaty Law as a Subsystem within the Meaning of Article 55 ILC?

As explained in detail above,[120] Article 55 ASR provides for the case that States, when defining the primary obligations that apply between them, also make spe-

119 Idem., p. 168.
120 See B. V.

cial provision for the legal consequences of breaches of these obligations or for determining whether there has been such a breach. In such a case the ILC Articles do not apply to the extent that the conditions for the existence of an internationally wrongful act or its legal consequences are determined by special rules of international law. However, except when explicitly provided for, controversy sparks off the question of whether the specific provision is to coexist with or exclude the general rule that would otherwise apply.[121]

Those who hold that investment treaties confer substantive rights upon individuals also argue – most likely in the sense of a "moreover-argument"[122] – that Article 55 ILC must apply as the ILC Articles are preoccupied with the consequences flowing from the breach of inter-State obligations and, hence, *"[t]he sub-system created by investment treaties is by definition sui generis"*.[123]

As this paper however proceeds from a different assumption in respect of the holder of substantive rights, there is no room for a "general sub-system created by investment treaties" and, hence, Article 55 ASR does generally not apply in the case of investment treaties as they rarely contain secondary rules. One notable exception[124] in respect of the content of international responsibility constitutes Article 1135 (1) NAFTA which states:

"Where a Tribunal makes a final award against a Party, the Tribunal may award, separately or in combination, only:

(a)   monetary damages and any applicable interest;

---

121   Draft Articles on Responsibility of States for Internationally Wrongful Acts, with Commentaries, Yearbook of the International Law Commission 2001, vol. II. (Part Two), p. 31, Art.55, para.1 - 2.

122   In fact, if Article 33 ASR was to apply and investment treaties were outside the scope of application of the ASR, Article 55 ASR does not play any role anymore.

123   Douglas, The Hybrid Foundations of Investment Treaty Arbitration, 74 BYIL 2004, p. 151, p. 189; Douglas appears to operate with some kind of "hybrid" perception of lex specialis. It is true that some international treaties which confer rights upon individuals – e.g. the Treaty on European Union ("TEU") and the Treaty on the Functioning of the European Union ("TFEU") – create a "sub-system" which, although sharing many of the secondary rules contained in the inter-State system, must be analysed independently. However, these treaties contain their own complex sets of secondary rules; investment treaties are usually silent on this point. One must ask the question of whether it is possible to derogate the general rules without having a lex specialis in an investment treaty.

124   See also Article 12 (2) ECT, applicable to loss suffered owing to war or other armed conflict, state of national emergency, civil disturbance, or other similar event, which reads "[…] an Investor of a Contracting Party which, […], suffers a loss in the Area of another Contracting Party […] shall be accorded restitution or compensation which in either case shall be prompt, adequate and effective." Note also Article 26 (8) 2. sentence ECT which reads "An award of arbitration concerning a measure of a sub-national government or authority of the disputing Contracting Party shall provide that the Contracting Party may pay monetary damages in lieu of any other remedy granted."

(b)   restitution of property, in which case the award shall provide that the disputing Party may pay monetary damages and any applicable interest in lieu of restitution".

3. Appreciation

The previous discussion revealed that there is sufficient reason to argue that the ILC Articles on State Responsibility *directly* apply to breaches of substantive obligations contained in investment treaties. Turning to the rules on the forms of reparation their validity in the context of investment treaties is additionally confirmed by and large by arbitral practice. Some arbitral rulings, however, question the general rule of prioritising restitution in case the legal order of the author State causes obstacles. Such interpretation, as explained above, is hardly reconcilable with the general principle that States may not rely on internal law to justify the failure to comply with international obligations.

Apart from that, in the area of investment treaty law restitution constitutes – like in the ambit of general public international law – the very first form of reparation, replaced by compensation only in case of de-election, impossibility or dis-proportionality. State practice witnesses that such view is shared by many States: If States felt the need to deviate from the aforementioned principle they explicitly included clauses in their treaties stating that restitution is no available form of reparation or restitution is limited to certain situations, or restitution is not the first remedy to be sought by an investor.[125] One can therefore safely conclude that the rules on the form of reparation in the area of investment treaty law, thus, exist in broad systemic integration with general rules as embodied in the ILC Articles on State Responsibility.

Prioritising restitution, it is recalled, is on principle justified by the argument that it

"conforms most closely to the general principle of the law on responsibility according to which the author State is bound to 'wipe out' all the legal and material consequences of its wrongful act by re-establishing the situation that would exist if the wrongful act had not been committed".[126]

---

125 Cf., e.g., Article 1135 (1) NAFTA, Art. 26 (8) ECT; apparently of a different view: Kriebaum, in this volume.
126 Arangio-Ruiz, Preliminary Report on State Responsibility, in: International Law Commission (ed.) Yearbook of the International Law Commission, vol. II (1) 1988; UN Document No. A/CN.4/416 & Corr. 1 & 2 and Add.1 & Corr.1, para. 114.

This paper suggests that in the area of investment treaty law the justification to prioritise restitution is even stronger compared to general public international law. Prioritising restitution contributes to the overall aim of the contracting State parties to the investment treaty to establish and maintain *long term* and *stable* investment relations on the basis of the rule of law and it would further strengthen their "juridification". This is because it would – to some extent – render it less attractive for a host State to employ (internationally) wrongful means to rid itself of a "disliked" foreign investor due to the fact that the possibility of simply "buying oneself out" of the investment relationship by the way of paying compensation would be restricted. Turned positively, prioritising restitution would give the host State a second chance to present itself as being committed to establishing and maintaining long term and stable investment relations on the basis of the rule of law. Already by knowing that it might see the foreign investor "again", the host State has an increased interest in constantly working on the relationship.

Of course, restitution must not be de-elected by the claimant, still be possible and not constitute an excessive onerousness. Material impossibility and excessive onerousness should, however, be assessed in a very strict sense in order to achieve the ends pursued with the conclusion of the investment treaty.

While one could doubt whether such reasoning would be appropriate if an individual were the holder of the substantive rights contained in an investment treaty, if the injured State is perceived as their holder prioritising restitution suits well the State parties' abovementioned "systemic interest" in concluding the investment treaty. Furthermore, from the perspective of the author State the continued cooperation with the foreign investor after having lost arbitration can also be understood as evidence of a matured political and legal system.

D. Summary

"General" international law and investment treaty law do not form two isolated sets of rules. Far from it. This paper demonstrated that Articles 28 *et seqq.* ASR, which set out the content of the international responsibility of a State, can claim validity and are applied in practice in the context of investment treaty law. Since the substantive rights contained in investment treaties accrue to the State parties, the ILC Articles on State Responsibility apply *directly*. The rules on the forms of reparation – including the rule of priority of restitution – contained in the ILC Articles unreservedly govern also the international responsibility caused by the violation of a substantive treatment standard contained in an investment treaty.

This paper further suggested that within investment treaty law the claim to prioritise restitution is a strong one as it contributes to the overall aim of the contracting State parties to the investment treaty to establish and maintain long term and stable investment relations on the basis of the rule of law and it would further strengthen their "juridification". Closing the circle, the choice to be made in investment arbitration between restitution and compensation or between "stay" or "leave", as it was sketched in the introduction, it can be said to contain a slight spin in favour of "staying", a spin which might contribute to the strengthening of a long term perspective on foreign investment relations in investment arbitration.

Restitution in International Investment Law

Comments by *Ursula Kriebaum*[*]

Steffen Hindelang suggested in his presentation that restitution should be given preference over compensation in investment awards unless the former would cause an «excessive onerouseness».[1] For that purpose he relied primarily on the ILC's Articles on State Responsibility[2] and on the judgement of the PCIJ in the Chorzów case.[3]

Should restitution really be the primary form of reparation in investment cases? What do the ILC's Articles say on the matter? Are there limitations to the power of investment tribunals to provide for non-pecuniary remedies in investment protection treaties or the ICSID Convention? What has the practice of investment tribunals concerning pecuniary and non-pecuniary remedies been so far?

A. Parts II and III of the ILC-Articles Articles Are Not Applicable in Investor State Disputes

In interstate cases, including those where a State exercises diplomatic protection, the content of state responsibility is set out in Part II of the ILC's Articles on State Responsibility. Articles 34, 35 and 36 of the ILC's Articles on State Responsibility, which are located in Part II, provide that restitution, compensation and satisfaction are the three forms of reparation provided for in international

---

[*]   Professor Dr Ursula Kriebaum, Professor of Public International Law, University of Vienna.
[1]   The following comments are based on the oral presentation on 13 March 2010.
[2]   http://untreaty.un.org/ilc/publications/yearbooks/Ybkvolumes%28e%29/ILC_2001_v2_p2_e.pdf.
[3]   «The essential principle contained in the actual notion of an illegal act – a principle which seems to be established by international practice and in particular by decision of arbitral tribunals – is that reparation must, as far as possible, wipe out all the consequences of the illegal act and re-establish the situation which would, in all probability, have existed if that act had not been committed.»
(PCIJ, Case Concerning the Factory at Chorzów (Indemnity), Judgment No. 13, 1928 PCIJ, Serie A No. 17, Order, 13 September 1928, p. 47).

law. Restitution is the primary form of reparation. Compensation is due subsidiarily if the damage is not made good by restitution.[4]

However, the rules prevailing in the realm of interstate cases are not as such applicable in investor-State cases.[5] Part II of the ILC's articles only address the consequences flowing from the breach of international obligations between States. This is pointed out in the commentary to Article 28. Article 28 is the first article of Part II of the ILC's articles.

The commentary states that although Part I is applicable with regard to all wrongful acts by states, Parts II and III are only applicable to the international responsibility of a State accruing to another State:

> (3) Article 28 does not exclude the possibility that an internationally wrongful act may involve legal consequences in the relations between the State responsible for that act and persons or entities other than States. This follows from article 1, which covers all international obligations *of* the State and not only those owed *to* other States. Thus, State responsibility extends, for example, to human rights violations and other breaches of international law where the primary beneficiary of the obligation breached is not a State. However, while Part One applies to all the cases in which an internationally wrongful act may be committed by a State, Part Two has a more limited scope. It does not apply to obligations of reparation to the extent that these arise towards or are invoked by a person or entity other than a State. In other words, the provisions of Part Two are without prejudice to any right, arising from the international responsibility of a State, which may accrue directly to any person or entity other than a State, and article 33 makes this clear.

Article 33(1) provides:

> Article 33. Scope of international obligations set out in this Part

---

4   Article 34. Forms of reparation
     Full reparation for the injury caused by the internationally wrongful act shall take the form of restitution, compensation and satisfaction, either singly or in combination, in accordance with the provisions of this chapter.
     Article 35. Restitution
     A State responsible for an internationally wrongful act is under an obligation to make restitution, that is, to re-establish the situation which existed before the wrongful act was committed, provided and to the extent that restitution:
     (a) is not materially impossible;
     (b) does not involve a burden out of all proportion to the benefit deriving from restitution instead of compensation.
     Article 36. Compensation
     1. The State responsible for an internationally wrongful act is under an obligation to compensate for the damage caused thereby, insofar as such damage is not made good by restitution.
     2. The compensation shall cover any financially assessable damage including loss of profits insofar as it is established.
5   Z. Douglas, Other Specific Regimes of Responsibility: Investment Treaty Arbitration and ICSID, in: J. Crawford/ A. Pellet/ S. Olleson, The Law of International Responsibility, 2010, 829 et seq.

1. The obligations of the responsible State set out in this Part may be owed to another State, to several States, or to the international community as a whole, depending in particular on the character and content of the international obligation and on the circumstances of the breach.

Therefore, Article 33(1) only refers to obligations owed to States and the international community. Article 33(2) carves out the problem of secondary obligations owed to non-State actors in the form of a reservation:

2. This Part is without prejudice to any right, arising from the international responsibility of a State, which may accrue directly to any person or entity other than a State.

The commentary to Article 33 confirms this interpretation.[6] It explicitly refers to rights accruing to non-State entities under bilateral or regional investment protection treaties.

It follows that Articles 34-36 deal with reparation owed to States. The commentary to Article 36 nevertheless refers to ICSID tribunals and points out in a footnote that ICSID tribunals have jurisdiction to award damages or other remedies.[7] It does, however, not point out what these other remedies are.

Therefore, the ILC's Articles do not address the consequences arising out of State responsibility with regard to non-State actors. They leave it to the primary rules applicable or to general international law to solve the issue. Therefore, a preference for restitution cannot be based on the ILC's Articles. Articles 34 to 36 do not apply to obligations of reparation arising towards investors or invoked by investors.

The *ad hoc* Committee in *MTD*[8] addressed the issue of applicability of Part II of the ILC's Articles in investor-State arbitration. It discussed the applicability of

---

6   (4) ... Part Two deals with the secondary obligations of States in relation to cessation and reparation, and those obligations may be owed, inter alia, to one or several States ... . In cases where the primary obligation is owed to a non- State entity, it may be that some procedure is available whereby that entity can invoke the responsibility on its own account and without the intermediation of any State. ... It is also true in the case of rights under bilateral or regional investment protection agreements. Part Three is concerned with the invocation of responsibility by other States, whether they are to be considered «injured States" under article 42, or other interested States under article 48, or whether they may be exercising specific rights to invoke responsibility under some special rule (art. 55). The articles do not deal with the possibility of the invocation of responsibility by persons or entities other than States, and paragraph 2 makes this clear. It will be a matter for the particular primary rule to determine whether and to what extent persons or entities other than States are entitled to invoke responsibility on their own account. Paragraph 2 merely recognizes the possibility: hence the phrase «which may accrue directly to any person or entity other than a State».

7   See footnote 522. (This footnote appears as footnote 555 in J. Crawford, The International Law Commission's Articles on State Responsibility, 2002.)

8   MTD Equity Sdn. Bhd. and MTD Chile S. A. v. Republic of Chile, Decision on Annulment, 21 March 2007.

Part II of the ILC's Articles when it analysed whether it had to take into account a contribution to the injury by the injured party in the determination of reparation. It said:

> Part II of the ILC Articles, in which Article 39 is located, is concerned with claims between States, though it includes claims brought on behalf of individuals, e.g., within the framework of diplomatic protection. There is no reason not to apply the same principle of contribution to claims for breach of treaty brought by individuals.[9]

The *Ad hoc* Committee noted that Part II of the ILC's Articles is concerned with claims between States. It applied the principles laid down in them by analogy to claims brought by investors.

B. Investment Protection Treaties and Pecuniary and Non-Pecuniary Remedies

Investment treaties are typically silent on the matter of available remedies in case of a breach of the obligations contained in the treaty. However, some treaties such as NAFTA,[10] CAFTA,[11] the ECT,[12] the ACIA[13] and a number of BITs and

---

9   Ibid., para. 99.
10   Article 1135 NAFTA: Final Award
1. Where a Tribunal makes a final award against a Party, the Tribunal may award, separately or in combination, only:
(a) monetary damages and any applicable interest;
(b) restitution of property, in which case the award shall provide that the disputing Party may pay monetary damages and any applicable interest in lieu of restitution.
11   Article 10.26 CAFTA: Awards
1. Where a tribunal makes a final award against a respondent, the tribunal may award, separately or in combination, only:
(a) monetary damages and any applicable interest;
(b) restitution of property, in which case the award shall provide that the respondent may pay monetary damages and any applicable interest in lieu of restitution.
12   Article 26(8) Energy Charter Treaty (ECT)
(8) The awards of arbitration, which may include an award of interest, shall be final and binding upon the parties to the dispute. An award of arbitration concerning a measure of a sub-national government or authority of the disputing Contracting Party shall provide that the Contracting Party may pay monetary damages in lieu of any other remedy granted. Each Contracting Party shall carry out without delay any such award and shall make provision for the effective enforcement in its Area of such awards.
13   Asean Comprehensive Investment Agreement adopted in Thailand 26 February 2009.
Article 41 ACIA: Awards
2. Where a Tribunal makes a final award against either of the disputing parties, the tribunal may award, separately or in combination, only:
(a) monetary damages and any applicable interest; and
(b) restitution of property, in which case the award shall provide that the disputing Member State may pay monetary damages and any applicable interest in lieu of restitution.

FTAs concluded by the US and Canada[14] do limit available remedies. Some limit the remedies to monetary damages and restitution. Some provide the State with a choice between other granted remedies and monetary damages.

NAFTA, CAFTA and ACIA allow for monetary damages or restitution and give a choice to be made by the State. The Energy Charter Treaty apparently is based on the assumption that specific performances can be ordered in an award. In case of a sub-national government or authority the State may pay monetary damages in lieu of any other remedy granted.

Therefore, in those treaties which do contain rules on the matter a clear preference for monetary damages instead of restitution is visible. They all provide the debtor State with a choice.

C. Practice of Investment Tribunals Concerning Pecuniary and Non-Pecuniary Remedies

Investment tribunals have dealt with the issue of the implementation of international responsibility in several disparate ways.[15] The vast majority of tribunals acceded to the investor's request for monetary relief, if appropriate, and awarded just compensation without discussing other forms of reparation. In cases where investors seek only monetary damages it would be *ultra petita* for a tribunal to order specific performances.

In most cases parties simply ask for monetary relief and the tribunals accede to this request if appropriate without discussing other forms of reparation.

Some tribunals decided that they are competent to order pecuniary and non-pecuniary remedies. They relied on Part II of the articles without addressing the

---

14 See e.g. Canada /South Africa BIT
Article XIII Settlement of Disputes between an Investor and the Host Contracting Party
...
(9) A tribunal may award, separately or in combination, only:
(a) monetary damages and any applicable interest;
(b) restitution of property, in which case the award shall provide that the disputing Contracting Party may pay monetary damages and any applicable interest in lieu of restitution.
US/Peru FTA
Article 10.26: Awards
1. Where a tribunal makes a final award against a respondent, the tribunal may award, separately or in combination, only:
(a) monetary damages and any applicable interest; and
(b) restitution of property, in which case the award shall provide that the respondent may pay monetary damages and any applicable interest in lieu of restitution.
15 See also: C. Schreuer, Non-Pecuniary Remedies in ICSID Arbitration, 20 Arbitration International 2004, no. 4, 325.

issue of their applicability. An example of such an approach is the Tribunal in *Nycomb*.[16] The investor had undertaken to construct a power plant. In turn a State entity had promised a higher than usual price for the electricity generated there.

The Tribunal found that Latvia had violated the fair and equitable treatment clause as well as subjected the investor to a discriminatory measure. When determining the amount of compensation due it relied on the ILC's Articles as reflecting customary law without discussing their applicability in investor-State cases. The Tribunal stated:

> The Arbitral Tribunal holds, and it seems to be agreed between the parties, that the question of remedies to compensate for losses or damages caused by the Respondent's violation of its obligations under Article 10 of the Treaty must primarily find its solution in accordance with established principles of customary international law. Such principles have authoritatively been restated in The International Law Commission's Draft Articles on State Responsibility adopted in November 2001 (hereinafter referred to as the «Articles ILC"). According to Articles 34 and 35 ILC restitution is considered to be the primary remedy for reparation.[17]

The Tribunal found that compensation was the appropriate approach for the losses incurred during the time up to the award. For the time after the award it ordered the performance of the contract:

> As specifically regards the asserted losses on delivery of electric power to Latvenergo for the remainder of the eight year period, the Tribunal considers this potential loss to be too uncertain and speculative to form the basis for an award of monetary compensation. But the Tribunal considers it to be a continuing obligation upon the Republic to ensure the payment at the double tariff for electric power delivered under the Contract for the rest of the eight year period, and therefore gives an order for the Republic to fulfill its obligation under the Treaty to protect the Claimant's investment.[18]

In *Micula*, the claimant had asked for restitution of the legal situation prevailing before the interference of the defending State. The Tribunal found that it had the power to order pecuniary and non-pecuniary remedies. It stated that:

> 166. Under the ICSID Convention, a tribunal has the power to order pecuniary or nonpecuniary remedies, including restitution, …28. … The fact that restitution is a rarely ordered remedy is not relevant at this stage of the proceedings. Similarly, and contrary to Respondent's argument, the fact that such a remedy might not be enforceable pursuant to Article 54 of the ICSID Convention should not preclude a tribunal from ordering it. Remedies and enforcement are two distinct concepts.

> 167. In addition, the Tribunal finds no limitation to its powers to order restitution in the BIT, the instrument on which the consent of the parties is based. …

---

16   Nycomb v. Latvia, Award, 16 December 2003, 5.1., 5.2. See also Micula v. Romania, Decision on Jurisdiction, 28 September 2008, paras. 166-168; ADC v. Hungary, Award, 2 October 2006, paras. 479-500.

17   Nycomb v. Latvia, Award, 16 December 2003, 5.1.

18   Nycomb v. Latvia, Award, 16 December 2003, 5.2.

168. The Tribunal therefore does have the powers to order restitution, both under the ICSID Convention and the BIT, ...

28 International Law Commission, Articles on Responsibility of States for Internationally Wrongful Acts, annexed to the General Assembly Resolution 56/83, UN Doc A/RES/56/83, 12 December 2001, Article 35. See Enron Corporation and Ponderosa Assets, L.P. v. Argentine Republic (ICSID Case No. ARB/01/3), Decision on Jurisdiction of 14 January 2004, ¶¶ 79 to 81, Exh. RL-64.

The defendant, Romania, admitted that «restitution is, in theory, a remedy that is available under the ICSID Convention».[19] Whether restitution was appropriate in that particular case, had to be left to the decisions on the merits.[20]

Another group of tribunals ordered non-pecuniary remedies without relying on Part II of the ILC Articles. The Tribunal in *Enron* can serve as example for this approach.[21] The claimants argued that stamp taxes assessed but not yet collected by several provinces of Argentina were tantamount to an expropriation. They asked for an injunctive relief:

77. ... the Claimants have indeed requested that the taxes assessed be declared expropriatory and in breach of the Treaty and unlawful, and that they be annulled and their collection permanently enjoined.

Argentina argued that the Tribunal lacked the power to order injunctive relief. The government asserted that the Tribunal could only either issue a declaratory statement that might satisfy the investor or else determine the payment of compensation based on a finding that an expropriation had occurred or a certain measure was wrongful.

However, the Tribunal held that it had the power to order specific performance:

79. An examination of the powers of international courts and tribunals to order measures concerning performance or injunction and of the ample practice that is available in this respect, leaves this Tribunal in no doubt about the fact that these powers are indeed available.

It found that the claimants had convincingly invoked the authority of the *Rainbow Warrior*. It referred to *Rainbow Warrior*, *Goetz* v. *Burundi* and Professor Schreuer's Commentary. The Tribunal concluded that it had the power to order specific performances or injunctions:

The Claimants have convincingly invoked the authority of the *Rainbow Warrior*, where it was held:

19   Micula v. Romania, Decision on Jurisdiction and Admissibility, 24 September 2008, para. 166.
20   Ibid., para. 168.
21   Enron, Decision on Jurisdiction, 14 January 2004, paras. 77-81; see also e.g.: ATA Construction, International Trading Company v. Jordan, Award, 18 May 2010, paras. 129-132; Société d'Exploitation des Mines d'Or de Sadiola SA (Semos) v. Mali, p. 129.

«The authority to issue an order for the cessation or discontinuance of a wrongful act or omission results from the inherent powers of a competent tribunal which is confronted with the continuous breach of an international obligation which is in force and continues to be in force. The delivery of such an order requires, therefore, two essential conditions intimately linked, namely that the wrongful act has a continuing character and that the violated rule is still in force at the time in which the order is issued».

80. The same holds true under the ICSID Convention. In *Goetz v. Burundi* such a power was indeed resorted to by the Tribunal, and the fact that it was based on a settlement agreement between the parties does not deprive the decision of the Tribunal of its own legal force and standing. A scholarly opinion invoked by the Claimants is also relevant in this context, having an author concluding that it is

«...entirely possible that future cases will involve disputes arising from ongoing relationships in which awards providing for specific performance or injunctions become relevant».

81. The Tribunal accordingly concludes that, in addition to declaratory powers, it has the power to order measures involving performance or injunction of certain acts. Jurisdiction is therefore also affirmed on this ground. What kind of measures might or might not be justified, whether the acts complained of meet the standards set out in the *Rainbow Warrior*, and how the issue of implementation that the parties have also discussed would be handled, if appropriate, are all matters that belong to the merits.[22]

Therefore, the Tribunal found that it was competent to order specific performance and affirmed jurisdiction on this ground. But it stated that it would be for the merits to decide whether the requested injunctions were appropriate. In the end the Tribunal did not order specific performance but awarded compensation.[23]

The Tribunal in *LG&E*[24] adopted yet another approach and denied its competence to order the restoration of the legal situation prior to the government's interference with the foreign investment. The case arose from the attractive framework of laws and regulations for foreign investors in the field of gas transportation that the Argentinean government had created to attract foreign investors. These guarantees were subsequently revoked. Claimants asked the Tribunal to «invite" the government to restore the legal system in place before the government's various interferences:

Firstly, that the Tribunal «*invite*» the Respondent to give formal assurances that it will fully restore the basic guarantees of the gas regulatory framework by a given date.[25]

22 Enron, Decision on Jurisdiction, 14 January 2004, para. 79-81, footnotes omitted. Critical, Z. Douglas, Other Specific Regimes of Responsibility: Investment Treaty Arbitration and ICSID, in: J. Crawford/ A. Pellet/ S. Olleson, The Law of International Responsibility, 2010, p. 830 et seq.
23 Enron, Award, para. 453.
24 LG&E v. Argentina, Award, 25 July 2007.
25 Ibid., para. 81.

The Tribunal decided not to express such an «invitation" and found that it cannot order judicial restitution without violating Argentina's sovereignty. It said:

> 87. Likewise, if approached as restitution, the Tribunal cannot go beyond its fiat in the Decision on Liability. The judicial restitution required in this case would imply modification of the current legal situation by annulling or enacting legislative and administrative measures that make over the effect of the legislation in breach. The Tribunal cannot compel Argentina to do so without a sentiment of undue interference with its sovereignty. Consequently, the Tribunal arrives at the same conclusion: the need to order and quantify compensation.[26]

Therefore, with the exception of the Tribunal in *LG&E*, investment tribunals found that their powers were not limited to ordering pecuniary relief or to make a declaratory statement but that they may also order specific performance.

D. The ICSID Convention – Article 54

The ICSID Convention does not provide for any particular form of reparation. It does not exclude non-pecuniary relief.[27] This interpretation is also supported by the *travaux préparatoires*.[28] Article 54(1) only provides for enforcement of pecuniary obligations imposed by arbitral awards. This does not mean that a tribunal may not order non-pecuniary relief such as specific performance or restitution. However, this remedy cannot be enforced in other States parties to the Convention.

Non-enforceability does not automatically imply that the Tribunal is not competent to order non-pecuniary relief. However, it would be wise for a claimant to also request the Tribunal to specify an alternative amount of damages in case the debtor State does not comply with the award.

---

26 Ibid., para. 87.
27 See C. Schreuer, Non-Pecuniary Remedies in ICSID Arbitration, 20 Arbitration International, no. 4, 325.
    Article 54
    (1) Each Contracting State shall recognize an award rendered pursuant to this Convention as binding and enforce the pecuniary obligations imposed by that award within its territories as if it were a final judgment of a court in that State.
    See also: C. Schreuer et al., The ICSID Convention, A Commentary, 2ed. 2010, 72-80.
28 See History, vol. I, pp. 246, 248; vol. II 344, 346, 347, 425, 903, 990, 991, 1019.1026, 1029; C. Schreuer, Non-Pecuniary Remedies in ICSID Arbitration, 20 Arbitration International, no. 4, 325.

E. Conclusions

Investment Tribunals enjoy the power to order also non-pecuniary remedies unless the parties have limited their power in the instrument of consent to compensation or claimants have only asked for pecuniary relief. In most cases parties simply ask for monetary relief and the tribunals accede to this request if appropriate without discussing other forms of reparation.

In many cases, especially if the investor lost confidence in the host State because of the latter's interferences with the investment, pecuniary remedies will be the preferable remedy. However, there might also be situations where an order of specific performance, like the continuation of contractual obligations, would be an appropriate remedy.[29] This is particularly so where it is difficult to estimate the pecuniary consequences of future damage incurred by the investor as a consequence of the non-performance of a contract.

In light of the possibility of non-compliance with such an order for specific performance and the non-enforceability of non-pecuniary remedies in third States, awards should provide for a pecuniary alternative in case of non-compliance. This may be in the form of liquidated damages.

---

29 See e.g. the approach of the Tribunals in Goetz v. Burundi, Award, 10 February 1999, 15 ICSID Review 516 and Nycomb v. Latvia, Award, 16 December 2003, 5.2.

Diplomatic Protection and Investment Arbitration

Kate Parlett[*]

A. Introduction

Investment arbitration is now generally acknowledged as a burgeoning field, rapidly expanding since the first investment treaty claim was referred to arbitration in 1987. The widespread inclusion of substantive investment protection provisions in investment treaties, together with procedural provisions for the submission of investment disputes to arbitration, has fostered the growth of investment treaty arbitration. During the same period, the inclusion of dispute resolution provisions in investment contracts concluded with the state has accorded contracting investors the possibility of direct-recourse international arbitration in the event of a contractual dispute. While 30 years ago a foreign investor might only have a slim chance of inducing its state of nationality to espouse a diplomatic protection claim on its behalf, it could now be in a position to pursue such a claim directly, without the assistance or approval of its state of nationality. Such a claim might be based on a multilateral or bilateral investment treaty (*BIT*), or on the basis of an investment contract concluded with a host state.

Investment arbitration has usurped, to a large extent, the role of diplomatic protection in relation to foreign investment. In 2007, in its decision on preliminary objections in *Case Concerning Ahma-dou Sadio Diallo*, the International Court of Justice suggested that the role of diplomatic protection in investment disputes had diminished, referring to the settlement of investment disputes under bilateral or multilateral treaty arrangements. The Court noted:

…in contemporary international law, the protection of the rights of companies and the rights of their shareholders, and the settlement of the associated disputes, are essentially governed by bilateral or multilateral agreements for the protection of foreign investments, such as the treaties for the promotion and protection of foreign investments, and the Washington Convention of 18 March 1965 on the Settlement of Investment Disputes between States and Nationals of Other States, which created an International Centre for Settlement of Investment Disputes (IC-SID), and also by contracts between States and foreign investors. In that context, the role of

[*]   Dr Kate Parlett, Associate, Freshfields Bruckhaus Deringer LLP, Paris.

diplomatic protection somewhat faded, as in practice recourse is only made to it in rare cases where treaty régimes do not exist or have proved inoperative.[1]

The relationship between the law of diplomatic protection and the investment protection regime can be considered through at least three broad questions. First, one could consider whether investment claims are a form of diplomatic protection claim or whether they represent a different form of international claim. Second, one could consider the influence of the rules of diplomatic protection on the international investment regime, and the extent to which the rules of diplomatic protection are applied in investment arbitration. Third, there is a question whether the international investment regime might influence the rules of diplomatic protection under general international law, or whether it must be dismissed entirely as a separate, *lex specialis* regime. Each of these questions will be considered in turn, before drawing some broad conclusions about the relationship between international investment law and general international law.

B. The Character of Investment Arbitration

It will be useful to recall the definition of diplomatic protection. Diplomatic protection claims permit one state to take action against a second state to vindicate an injury which is caused by an internationally wrongful act committed by the second state against a national of the first state. The basic premise of diplomatic protection is traced to Vattel, who wrote:

> Whoever uses a citizen ill, indirectly offends the state, which is bound to protect this citizen; and the sovereign of the latter should avenge his wrongs, punish the aggressor, and, if possible, oblige him to make full reparation; since otherwise the citizen would not obtain the great end of the civil association, which is safety.[2]

The classical formulation of the doctrine is to be found in the decision of the Permanent Court in 1924 in the *Mavrommatis* case. The Court recognised Greece as a proper claimant against Great Britain in respect of a claim that Ma-

---

1   *Case Concerning Ahmadou Sadio Diallo (Republic of Guinea v Democratic Republic of the Congo)*, Preliminary Objections, ICJ, 24 May 2007, para 88.
2   E de Vattel, *The Law of Nations or, Principles of the Law of Nature Applied to the Conduct and Affairs of Nations and Sovereigns* (1758, B. Kapossy and R. Whatmore (eds)) (Indianapolis, Liberty Fund, 2008), Book II, Chapter VI, §71 (p. 298). Vattel's formulation joined the view that it was the duty of the sending state to protect its citizens injured abroad to the view that the sending state was thereby vindicating its own rights: see §71 (p. 298).

vrommatis, a Greek subject, had been treated by the British authorities in Palestine in a matter incompatible with certain international obligations they were bound to observe. Thus the dispute fell within the jurisdiction of the Court which, pursuant to Article 34 of the Court's Statute, was limited to disputes between states or members of the League. The Court said:

> It is true that the dispute was at first between a private person and a State – i.e., between M. Mavrommatis and Great Britain. Subsequently the Greek Go-vernment took up the case. The dispute then entered upon a new phase; it entered the domain of international law, and became a dispute between two States. Henceforward therefore it is a dispute which may or may not fall under the jurisdiction of the Permanent Court of International Justice.[3]

The Court stated further, in point of principle:

> It is an elementary principle of international law that a State is entitled to protect its subjects, when injured by acts contrary to international law committed by another State, from which they have been unable to obtain satisfaction through ordinary channels. By taking up the case of one of its subjects and by resorting to diplomatic protection or international judicial proceedings on his behalf, a State is in reality asserting its own rights – its right to ensure, in the person of its subjects, respect for the rules of international law.[4]

The *Mavrommatis* formulation of diplomatic protection has been affirmed by the ICJ in several cases.[5] The suggestion that a state was obliged to exercise its

---

3   *Mavrommatis Palestine Concessions, Judgment No 2*, PCIJ ser A no 2 (1924), at p. 12.
4   *Ibid*. The PCIJ elaborated this principle in other cases, notably: *Case Concerning the Payment of Various Serbian Loans Issued in France / Case Concerning the Payment in Gold of Brazilian Federal Loans Issued in France*, PCIJ ser A nos 20/21 (1929); and *The Panevezys-Saldutiskis Railway Case (Estonia v Latvia)*, PCIJ ser A/B no 76 (1939). In other decisions the Permanent Court indirectly affirmed the doctrine of diplomatic protection. For example, in 1933 the Court affirmed that the dispute between the two states was distinct from the dispute between an injured individual and the respondent state (*Appeal from a Judgment of the Hungaro-Czechoslovak Mixed Arbitral Tribunal (The Peter Pázmány University v The State of Czechoslovakia)*, PCIJ ser A/B no 61 (1933), at p. 221); and in *Case Concerning the Factory at Chorzów (Claim for Indemnity) (Merits)*, PCIJ ser A no 17 (1928), at pp. 26-28, the PCIJ affirmed that, in a diplomatic protection claim, the rights at issue are states' rights, not rights of individuals.
5   See for example, *Interhandel Case (Switzerland v United States of America), Preliminary Objections*, ICJ Rep 1959, p. 6 at 27; *Case Concerning United States Diplomatic and Consular Staff in Tehran (USA v Iran)*, ICJ Rep 1980 p. 3, at 5-6 (para 8); *Case Concerning Elettronica Sicula SPA (ELSI) (USA v Italy)*, ICJ Rep 1980 p. 15; *Case Concerning the Vienna Convention on Consular Relations (Paraguay v USA)*, ICJ Rep 1998 p. 248, at 250 (para 5); *LaGrand Case (Germany v USA)*, ICJ Rep 2001 p. 466, at 472 (para 10); *Oil Platforms case (Iran v USA)*, Separate Opinion, Judge Rigaux, ICJ Rep 2003 p. 161, at 369-70 (para 10); *Case Concerning Ahmadou Sadio Diallo (Republic of Guinea v*

right to diplomatic protection in a particular case was rejected firmly in *Barcelona Traction*: in that case the Court emphasised the discretionary character of the right of diplomatic protection.[6] In 2006, the ILC adopted Draft Articles on Diplomatic Protection[7] which, by large, confirmed the traditional parameters of the doctrine.[8] Article 1 of the Draft Articles defines diplomatic protection as:

the invocation by a State, through diplomatic action or other means of peaceful settlement, of the responsibility of another State for an injury caused by an internationally wrongful act of

Democratic Republic of the Congo), Preliminary Objections, ICJ, 24 May 2007, para 86. In *Case Concerning Avena and Other Mexican Nationals (Mexico v USA)*, Mexico brought the case by way, *inter alia,* of diplomatic protection, but the Court declined to address the case as such: ICJ Rep 2004 p. 12 at 36 (para 40). Belgium, in the *Case Concerning the Arrest Warrant of 11 April 2000*, took the position that the case was transformed into one of diplomatic protection after the Foreign Minister of the DRC left office. But the DRC had not brought the case by way of diplomatic protection and the Court rejected the Belgian position: ICJ Rep 2002, p. 3, at 16-7 (paras 37-40). Cf, implying that the Court (mistakenly) treated Spain's case as one brought by way of diplomatic protection, Dissenting Opinion, Judge Torres Bernárdez, *Fisheries Jurisdiction case (Spain v Canada),* ICJ Rep 1998, p. 432, at 589 (paras 20-2).

6   *Barcelona Traction, Light and Power Co Ltd (Belgium v Spain)*, ICJ Rep 1970 p. 4, at 44 (para 79).

7   For Dugard's work on the subject see First Report on Diplomatic Protection, ILC, 52nd Session, 2000: A/CN.4/506 & Addendum 1; Second Report on Diplomatic Protection, ILC, 53rd Session, 2001; A/CN.4/514; Third Report on Diplomatic Protection. ILC, 54th Session, 2002; A/CN/523 & Addendum 1; Fourth Report on Diplomatic Protection, ILC, 55th Session, 2003.A/CN.4/530 & Addendum 1; Fifth Report on Diplomatic Protection, ILC, 56th Session, 2004, A/CN.4/538; Sixth Report on Diplomatic Protection, ILC, 57th Session, 2005, A/CN.4/546; Seventh Report on Diplomatic Protection, ILC, 58th Session, 2006, A/CN.4/567. See also J Dugard, "Diplomatic Protection and Human Rights: The Draft Articles of the International Law Commission" (2005) 24 *Australian YIL* 75. The final Draft Articles on Diplomatic Protection with commentaries are atILC, *Report of the Fifty-eighth Session* (2006), A/CN.4/L.684. The ILC had taken up the topic of diplomatic protection in 1996: *Official Records of the General Assembly, Fifty-first Session, Supplement No. 1* (A/51/10), para. 249, and annex II, addendum 1; before that it had formed part of the extended study of state responsibility commencing in 1956: First Report of FV García Amador, *ILC Ybk* 1956/II, 173, 192ff (A/CN.4/96).

8   This approach was encouraged by Special Rapporteur Dugard, who noted: ...diplomatic protection, albeit premised on a fiction, is an accepted institution of customary international law, and one which continues to serve as a valuable instrument for the protection of human rights. It provides a potential remedy for the protection of millions of aliens who have no access to remedies before international bodies and it provides a more effective remedy to those who have access to the often ineffectual remedies contained in international human rights instruments.
First Report on Diplomatic Protection, ILC, 52nd Session, 2000: A/CN.4/506 & Addendum 1, 25, para 64, references omitted.

that State to a natural or legal person that is a national of the former State with a view to the implementation of such responsibility.[9]

In *Diallo*, the ICJ acknowledged that this formulation reflected the content of customary international law.[10]

It is generally accepted, in international practice[11] and by commentators,[12] that investment claims are not diplomatic protection claims. A key distinction is that diplomatic protection claims are presented by and at the discretion of the state of nationality of the wronged person, whereas investment claims may be presented by the investor directly, without the consent of their state of nationality. In some cases the state of nationality has intervened in proceedings to oppose the investor's claim:[13] an eventuality which could not be explained if the claim was in reality a claim brought by the state. A second significant difference is that damages awards are paid directly to the claimant investor, unlike awards for diplomatic protection claims, which are paid to the state of nationality. That state has no international law obligation to distribute the proceeds of the claim to its national.[14] Moreover, damages are calculated solely on the basis of the harm caused to

9 ILC, *Report of the Fifty-eighth Session* (2006), A/CN.4/L.684, Article 1.

10 *Case Concerning Amhamdou Sadio Diallo (Republic of Guinea v Democratic Republic of the Congo)*, Preliminary Objections, ICJ, 24 May 2007, para 39.

11 See for example *The Republic of Ecuador v Occidental Exploration and Production Company, Court of Appeal (Civil Division)* [2006] 1 QB 432; *The Republic of Ecuador v Occidental Exploration and Production Company, High Court Queen's Bench Division* [2005] EWHC 774 (Comm), para. 61; *The Loewen Group Inc and Raymond L Loewen v United States of America* (Award, 26 June 2003), 7 ICSID Reports 421, paras 222-3. Further, The ICJ implied that investment treaty claims were not diplomatic protection claims when it concluded that practice of the former could not contribute to the creation of a rule of customary international law applicable to diplomatic protection claims: *Case Concerning Ahmadou Sadio Diallo (Republic of Guinea v Democratic Republic of the Congo), Preliminary Objections*, ICJ, 24 May 2007, para 86.

12 Z Douglas, *The International Law of Investment Claims* (Cambridge, CUP, 2009), pp 32-33, paras 65-67; T Wälde, "Investment Arbitration under the Energy Charter Treaty" (1996) *Arbitration International* 429, 435-437.

13 In *GAMI Inc v United States of Mexico*, the US intervened pursuant to Article 1128 of NAFTA to argue that the Tribunal had no jurisdiction to hear the claims of its national (*GAMI Inc v United States of Mexico*, see submission of the United States of America, 30 June 2003, available at www.state.gov/documents/organization/22212.pdf); and in *Mondev International Ltd v United States of America*, Canada made submissions to the Tribunal which supported the conclusion that the its national investor's claims ought to be dismissed on the merits (*Mondev International Ltd v United States of America* (Award, 11 October 2002), 6 *ICSID Reports* 192).

14 In Article 19 of the ILC Articles, entitled "Recommended practice", the ILC suggested that a state entitled to exercise diplomatic protection should transfer any compensation, less reasonable deductions, to the injured person: see ILC, *Report of the Fifty-eighth Session* (2006), A/CN.4/L.684, Commentary to Article 19, 94-95. Any individual right to

the interests of the investor and do not take into account other consi-derations which may be taken into account in the calculation of damages in a diplomatic protection claim brought on an inter-state basis.[15]

This conclusion is confirmed, at least in respect of investment disputes submitted to ICSID, by Article 27 of the ICSID Convention, which provides:

(1)   No Contracting State shall give diplomatic protection, or bring an international claim, in respect of a dispute which one of its nationals and another Contracting State shall have consented to submit or shall have submitted to arbitration under this Convention, unless such other Contracting State shall have failed to abide by and comply with the award rendered in such dispute.

(2)   Diplomatic protection, for the purposes of paragraph (1), shall not include informal diplomatic exchanges for the sole purpose of facilitating a settlement of the dispute.

Thus, where an investor and host state have consented to submit a dispute to ICSID arbitration, the state of nationality of the investor is prohibited from bringing a diplomatic protection claim.[16] Similar provisions are found in a number of model BITs and some BITs which are in force.[17] These provisions suggest that investment claims brought by investors are not diplomatic protection claims.

compensation in respect of a diplomatic protection claim will ordinarily only arise as a matter of domestic law, but it might also engage international human rights law. In 1994 the European Court of Human Rights held that an international agreement making provi-sion for compensation for claims espoused on the basis of diplomatic protection could give rise to an enforceable right on the part of the injured nationals to compensation. It held that Article 6 of the European Convention on Human Rights was engaged where the French Government settled claims of French citizens against the Moroccan Government relating to the nationalisation of assets by a lump sum agreement incorporated in a treaty, and subsequently by decree established a national administrative committee to distribute the proceeds of the settlement. The right to compensation was held to be a pecuniary right which was susceptible to determination in accordance with the standards of the Eu-ropean Convention: *Case of Beaumartin v France* (Application no. 15287/89), 25 No-vember 1994, [1994] ECHR 40.

15   This can be contrasted with awards in diplomatic protection claims: while the loss to the national most commonly forms the basis for an assessment of damages, other considera-tions may be taken into account, including the character of the breached international ob-ligation: *Case Concerning the Factory at Chorzów (Claim for Indemnity) (Merits)*, PCIJ ser A no 17 (1928), 28.

16   See *Banro American Resources v Democratic Republic of the Congo*, ICSID Case No ARB/98/7, Award, 1 September 2000, 17 ICSID Rev.-FILJ 232 (2002), paras 15-21; CH Schreuer, *The ICSID Convention: A Commentary*, 2nd ed (Cambridge, CUP, 2009), paras 27-6 and 27-7 (pp 416-417).

17   For a detailed discussion of these provisions and Article 27 of the ICSID Convention, see B Juratowitch, "The Relationship between Diplomatic Protection and Investment Trea-ties" (2008) 23 *ICSID Review* 10, 14-22.

A more controversial question is whether the underlying rights being vindicated in international investment claims belong to the investor, or to its state of nationality.[18] It seems clear that either construct is a theoretical possibility in the framework of the modern international legal system, in which individuals can derive substantive rights from international treaties.[19] For present purposes, it is not necessary to resolve the question whether the relevant substantive rights belong to the investor, or whether investors are "permitted for convenience to enforce what are in origin the rights of [states]."[20] Even if the substantive rights are rights belonging to the state of nationality of the investor, the claim itself is not brought on the basis of diplomatic protection, but rather as a direct claim by the investor against the host state.[21]

C. Rules of Diplomatic Protection in Investment Arbitration

Since investment claims are to be distinguished from diplomatic protection claims, it is unsurprising that the rules applicable to diplomatic protection claims are not considered to be automatically applicable to investment claims.[22] Whether a particular rule applies to an investment claim is rather to be determined by the parties' arbitration agreement, which may be constituted by the BIT or the relevant contract (or both, in a case involving an umbrella clause) and the agreed applicable rules (including, where relevant, the ICSID Convention and Rules). Traces of the rules applicable to diplomatic protection claims can be found in investment claims, but these rules are applied in a modified form. Moreover, they are not applied because they reflect customary principles applicable to the investment regime; rather they are applied because they are required by the relevant arbitration agreement. It is not a question of the investment regime opting out of the applicable rules of diplomatic protection claims, because in reality those rules never applied wholesale in the first place. Rather it is the case that the rules applicable to diplomatic protection claims may apply to in-

---

18   For a discussion of the positions, see Z Douglas, *The International Law of Investment Claims* (Cambridge, CUP, 2009), 1-38; Z Douglas, "The Hybrid Foundations of Investment Treaty Arbitration" (2003) 74 *BYIL* 151, esp. 162-164.

19   K Parlett, "The PCIJ's Opinion in *Jurisdiction of the Courts of Danzig*: Individual Rights under Treaties"(2008) 10 *JHIL* 119; K Parlett, *The Individual in the International Legal System* (Cambridge, CUP, 2011 *forthcoming*).

20   *The Loewen Group Inc and Raymond L Loewen v United States of America* (Award, 26 June 2003), 7 *ICSID Reports* 421, para. 233.

21   K Parlett, *The Individual in the International Legal System: Continuity and Change in International Law* (Cambridge, CUP, 2011), Chapter 2.

22   See F Berman, "The Relevance of the Law on Diplomatic Protection in Investment Arbitration", in in F Ortino et al (eds), *Investment Treaty Law: Current Issues II* (2007), 67.

vestment claims, whether in the form applicable directly to diplomatic protection claims or in some modified form, for the reason that the arbitration agreement requires their application.

I. The Critical Date for Nationality

For diplomatic protection claims, the nationality of claims rule requires that the injured national must have the nationality of the claimant state at the time of the injury through to when notice of the claim is presented, or to the date of the award or judgment.[23] The ILC considered that the established rule was that nationality was required at the date of injury and at the date of the official presentation of the claim, noting that this was "most frequently used in treaties, judicial decisions and doctrine".[24] The ILC declined to require continuity of nationality to the date of the award, suggesting that it would be "contrary to the interests of the individual, as many years may pass between the presentation of the claim and its final resolution".[25] "In an exercise in progressive development of the law", the ILC drafted the rule to require that the relevant individual be a national continuously between the date of the injury and presentation of the claim, suggesting that it would be incongruous to require nationality at those two dates, but not continuously.[26] The Draft Articles as adopted create a presumption of continuity if nationality existed at both relevant dates.[27]

---

23 See for example J Dugard, Fourth Report on Diplomatic Protection, ILC, 55th Session, 2003. A/CN.4/530 & Addendum 1, para 931; J Dugard, Fifth Report on Diplomatic Protection, ILC, 56th Session, 2004, A/CN.4/538, para 10; J Dugard, Seventh Report on Diplomatic Protection, ILC, 58th Session, 2006, A/CN.4/567, paras 31-47; cf I Brownlie, *Principles of Public International Law*, 6th ed (2003), p 460; E Borchard, "The Protection of Citizens Abroad and Change of Original Nationality" (1933-1934) 43 *Yale LJ* 359, 372.

24 ILC, *Report of the Fifty-eighth Session* (2006), A/CN.4/L.684, Commentary to Article 5, para 4, 37. In 1965 the Institute of International Law had adopted a resolution which reaffirmed the traditional rule by requiring nationality at both the date of presentation and of injury, but did not specifically require continuity between those dates: Institute of International Law, "Resolution on the National Character of an International Claim Presented by a State for Injury Suffered by an Individual, Warsaw Session, 1965", *Resolutions de l'Institut de Droit International, 1957-1991* (1992), 55-56.

25 ILC, *Report of the Fifty-eighth Session* (2006), A/CN.4/L.684, Commentary to Article 5, para 5, 37-38.

26 *Ibid.*, 36.

27 The Draft Articles introduced some limited exceptions to the requirement that the espousing state be the national state at the time of the injury. Paragraph 2 of Article 5 accordingly provides that a state may exercise diplomatic protection in respect of a person who was a national at the date of official presentation of the claim but not at the date of injury provided that three conditions are met: first, the injured person had the nationality of a

In contrast, a claimant in investment arbitration is commonly required only to demonstrate that it has requisite nationality at the time the notice of claim is filed. It is not necessary to demonstrate that the claimant had the relevant nationality at the time of injury. Article 25(2)(b) of the ICSID Convention defines a "National of another Contracting State" as "any juridical person which had the nationality of a Contracting State other than the State party to the dispute on the date on which the parties consented to submit such dispute to conciliation or arbitration".[28] Where a claim is brought on the basis of an investment treaty, and the claimant takes up the host state's offer to arbitrate by filing a claim, the critical date is the date of the request for arbitration.[29] Whether the investor continues to hold the relevant nationality after that date is irrelevant for the purposes of establishing the tribunal's jurisdiction.[30]

In the absence of a specific provision of NAFTA specifying when a claimant need satisfy the nationality of claims requirement, the Tribunal in *Loewen v United States* required the claimant to demonstrate continuous nationality in accordance with what it perceived to be the rule applicable under general international law. On that basis the Tribunal required the claimant to demonstrate continuous nationality from the time of the injury through to the date of the award.[31] This conclusion was consistent with the *Loewen* tribunal's view that NAFTA arbitration permitted individuals "for convenience to enforce what in origin are the

---

predecessor state or had lost his or her previous nationality; second, that the injured person acquired the new nationality for a reason unrelated to the bringing of the claim; and third, the new nationality had been acquired in a manner not inconsistent with international law: *ibid.*, Article 5. These exceptions do not apply in the case of a claim against the state of which the individual was a national at the time of the injury: *ibid.*, Article 5, para 3. These exceptions, the ILC noted, were intended to introduce an element of flexibility into the continuity rule to avoid unfairness, while retaining safeguards which prevent abuse by individuals and states. The Special Rapporteur had suggested that the continuity rule should be abolished altogether: see First Report on Diplomatic Protection, ILC, 52nd Session, 2000: A/CN.4/506 & Addendum 1, 15, para 24.

28 ICSID Convention, Article 25(2)(b).

29 CH Schreuer, *The ICSID Convention: A Commentary*, 2nd ed (Cambridge, CUP, 2009), para 25-754 (pp 294-295); *Rompetrol v Romania*, Decision on Jurisdiction, 18 April 2008, para 79. See also *Ceskoslovenska Obchodni Banka, A.S. v The Slovak Republic* (ICSID Case No ARB/97/4) Decision of the Tribunal on Objections to Jurisdiction, 24 May 1999, paras 31-32; *Société Ouest Africaine des Bétons Industriels [SOABI] v State of Senegal*, ICSID Case No ARB/82/1, Decision on Jurisdiction, 1 August 1984, 2 ICSID Rep 164, para 29.

30 See, for example, *Vivendi v Argentina*, Resubmitted Case: Decision on Jurisdiction, 14 November 2004, para 63.

31 *The Loewen Group Inc and Raymond L Loewen v United States of America* (Award, 26 June 2003), 7 *ICSID Reports* 421, paras 220-240.

rights of Party states"[32] – that is, that NAFTA claims were diplomatic protection claims which could be brought by investors directly. The decision has been subjected to criticism on several grounds, including that general international law does not require nationality to be demonstrated continuously to the date of the award.[33]

In general, the investment regime applies a rule which represents a modified form of the rule applicable to diplomatic protection claims in respect of continuity of nationality. In investment claims the claimant need only demonstrate nationality at the time the notice of claim is filed.

II. Exhaustion of Local Remedies

A diplomatic protection claim is subject to the rule requiring exhaustion of local remedies: the injured national must first exhaust available remedies in the host state before a diplomatic protection claim is made on its behalf.[34] The local remedies rule serves a dual purpose: it is a concession to the sovereign independence of the host state, which must be permitted an opportunity to render justice through its own courts; and it gives effect to the principle that foreign nationals are subject to the municipal law of the host state.[35]

In the absence of a specific provision in a treaty requiring an investor claimant to exhaust local remedies,[36] investment treaty tribunals have not applied the local remedies rule.[37] In this way the investment regime does not apply the rule appli-

---

32   *The Loewen Group Inc and Raymond L Loewen v United States of America* (Award, 26 June 2003), 7 *ICSID Reports* 421, at para 233.

33   See for example J Paulsson "Continuous Nationality in *Loewen*" (2004) 20 Arbitration International 213; N Rubins, "The Burial of an Investor-State Arbitration Claim" (2005) 21 Arbitration International 1; M Mendelson, "The Requirement for Continuous Nationality"in F Ortino ed al (eds), *Investment Treaty Law: Current Issues II* (2007), 41. See also CH Schreuer, *The ICSID Convention: A Commentary*, 2nd ed (Cambridge, CUP, 2009), para 25-756 (p 295).

34   ILC, *Report of the Fifty-eighth Session* (2006), A/CN.4/L.684, Article 14; C Amerasinghe, *Local Remedies in International Law* (199), 69-72.

35   See *Interhandel Case (Switzerland v United States of America), Preliminary Objections*, ICJ Rep 1959, p. 6, 27; *Case Concerning Elettronica Sicula SPA (ELSI) (USA v Italy)*,ICJ Rep 1980 p. 15, at 42, para 50; E Borchard, *The Diplomatic Protection of Citizens Abroad or the Law of International Claims* (1915), 817-818; Z Douglas, *The International Law of Investment Claims* (Cambridge, CUP, 2009), p 29; ILC, *Report of the Fifty-eighth Session* (2006), A/CN.4/L.684, Article 14.

36   See CF Amerasinghe, "Whither the Local Remedies Rule?" (1990) 5 ICSID Rev-FILJ 292, 294; CH Schreuer, *The ICSID Convention: A Commentary*, 2nd ed (Cambridge, CUP, 2009), para 27-4 (p 416).

37   See for example *Generation Ukraine v Ukraine*, Award, 16 September 2003, paras 13.1-13.6; *AES v Argentina*, Decision on Jurisdiction, 26 April 2005, para 69.

cable to diplomatic protection rules. Where the claim is for a denial of justice in the judicial system of the host state, the claimant may be required to exhaust local remedies, although there it is for the reason of proving a breach rather than to satisfy the requirements of the local remedies rule as such.[38]

III. Standing: Claims by Shareholders

Investment arbitration claims may be brought by any investor, and the investment need not be held directly, so that claims may be brought by shareholders, even of a company incorporated in the host state.[39] On first blush, it appears that the rules on standing applicable in investment claims are much less restrictive than those applicable to diplomatic protection claims, which traditionally can only be brought by the state where the corporation has registered office and is incorporated.

The question of standing to bring a diplomatic protection claim in respect of injury suffered by a corporation has been dominated by the seminal decision of the ICJ in *Barcelona Traction*. In that case, a claim was brought by Belgium against Spain, in respect of injury suffered by a company incorporated in Canada, with 88% of its shares held by Belgian nationals.[40] Spain raised an objection to jurisdiction concerning the right of Belgium to exercise diplomatic protection on behalf of shareholders in a company incorporated in Canada. The Court upheld the objection, finding that the right of diplomatic protection in respect of an injury to a corporation belongs to the state under the laws of which the corporation is incorporated and in whose territory it has its registered office, and not to the national state(s) of the shareholders.[41] The Court suggested that the state of nationality of a shareholder might be able to exercise diplomatic protection in circumstances where either the corporation had ceased to exist in its place of incorporation, or where the state of incorporation was itself responsible for in-

---

38 See for example *Rompetrol v Romania*, Decision on Jurisdiction, 18 April 2008, paras 58, 111, 114; *Loewen v United States*, Award, 26 June 2003, para 168; *Waste Management v Mexico II*, Award, 30 April 2004, paras 97, 116.

39 See for example *CMS v Argentina* (ICSID Case NO ARB/01/8), Decision on Jurisdiction, 17 July 2003, pars 66, 68; *Siemens v Argentina* (ICSID Case No ARB/02/8), Decision on Jurisdiction, 3 August 2004, para 150. This can and has given rise to criticisms where different tribunals constituted to determine claims brought by a shareholder and a company in respect of the same subject matter have reached different conclusions: *CME v Czech Republic*, Merits, 9 ICSID Rep 121; *Lauder v Czech Republic*, Merits, 9 ICSID Rep 66.

40 *Case Concerning the Barcelona Traction, Light and Power Company Limited*, 1970 ICJ Reports, p 3.

41 Ibid., p 42 (para 70), p 46 (para 88); p 39 (para 60).

flicting injury on the company.[42] However, neither of these circumstances existed in *Barcelona Traction*, and hence the Court left open whether in such circumstances the state of nationality of the shareholders would be entitled to bring a claim.[43]

The rules of standing to bring a diplomatic protection claim under customary international law may now be less restrictive than that set out in the *Barcelona Traction* decision. The ILC's Draft Articles on Diplomatic Protection provided for the direct protection of shareholders in two circumstances. The first (which was averred to in *Barcelona Traction*), permits a state of nationality of the shareholder to bring a claim in circumstances where the corporation has ceased to exist in the state of incorporation for reasons unrelated to the injury, and in circumstances where (a) the corporation had, at the date of injury, the nationality of the state causing the injury and (b) incorporation in that state was a precondition for doing business there.[44] The second permits a state of nationality of a shareholder to exercise diplomatic protection in circumstances where the rights of the shareholder are directly injured.[45] This is characterised as an "exception" but it may be better characterised as following from first principle: since the claim is for direct injury to the direct rights of a national, such a claim can properly be brought by the state of nationality of the shareholder. The second exception was affirmed by the ICJ in the *Diallo* case;[46] in the circumstances that the other exception did not apply on the facts, the Court left open whether it reflected customary international law.[47]

In its decision on the merits in *Diallo*, rendered in November 2010, the International Court implicitly upheld the *Barcelona Traction* rules of standing, affirming its decision on preliminary objections and only examining claims relating to direct rights held by Mr Diallo as *associé*, and not other claims relating to the contractual rights of his company against the state of Zaire and other enti-

---

42   Ibid., pp 40-41 (paras 65-68); p 48 (para 92).
43   For criticism of the Court's decision on preliminary objections in *Diallo*, see the Joint Dissenting Opinion of Judges Al-Khasawneh and Yusuf, *Case Concerning Ahmadou Sadio Diallo (Republic of Guinea v Democratic Republic of the Congo)*, Merits, ICJ, 30 November 2010, esp pp. 2-4. See also the Dissenting Opinion of Judge Bennouna, *Case Concerning Ahmadou Sadio Diallo (Republic of Guinea v Democratic Republic of the Congo)*, Merits, ICJ, 30 November 2010, para 18.
44   ILC, *Report of the Fifty-eighth Session* (2006), A/CN.4/L.684, Article 11.
45   ILC, *Report of the Fifty-eighth Session* (2006), A/CN.4/L.684, Article 12.
46   *Case Concerning Ahmadou Sadio Diallo (Republic of Guinea v Democratic Republic of the Congo)*, Preliminary Objections, ICJ, 24 May 2007, para 64.
47   The Court left open whether Article 11(b) reflected customary international law: ibid., para 91.

ties.[48] The Court noted that this distinction might appear artificial but nevertheless considered that this was the correct approach. It stated:

> In the following paragraphs, the Court is careful to maintain the strict distinction between the alleged infringements of the rights of the two SPRLs at issue and the alleged infringements of Mr. Diallo's direct rights as *associé* of these latter. The Court understands that such a distinction could appear artificial in the case of an SPRL in which the *parts sociales* are held in practice by a single *associé*. It is nonetheless well-founded juridically, and it is essential rigorously to observe it in the present case. Guinea itself accepts this distinction in the present stage of the proceedings, and most of its arguments are indeed based on it. The Court has to deal with the claims as they were presented by the Applicant.[49]

In this respect the Court rejected the argument presented by Guinea that in expropriating his companies, the DRC infringed Diallo's ownership rights in his *part sociales*, since from the factual perspective, the property of the two companies merges with his.[50] The Court emphasised that there is a distinction between the property of a corporation and that of the shareholder, even in the case of a single shareholder.

> The Court observes that international law has repeatedly acknowledged the principle of domestic law that a company has a legal personality distinct from that of its shareholders. This remains true even in the case of an SPRL which may have become unipersonal in the present case. Therefore, the rights and assets of a company must be distinguished from the rights and assets of an *associé*. In this respect, it is legally untenable to consider, as Guinea argues, that the property of the corporation merges with the property of the shareholder. Furthermore, it must be recognized that the liabilities of the company are not the liabilities of the shareholder....[51]

The Court then referred to *Barcelona Traction*, noting that even where a wrong done to a company causes prejudice to its shareholders, it is the companies' rights that are infringed and the company which must institute appropriate action.[52]

The International Court's application of its 2007 decision on preliminary objections on the merits was criticised by several judges in dissenting opinions.

---

48 *Case Concerning Ahmadou Sadio Diallo (Republic of Guinea v Democratic Republic of the Congo)*, Merits, ICJ, 30 November 2010, p 37 (para 114).
49 Ibid, p 38 (para 115) (references omitted).
50 Ibid, p 46 (para 151).
51 Ibid, p 47 (para 155). See also ibid, p 47 (para 157).
52 Ibid, p 47 (para 156).

Judge Bennouna suggested that the Court had first distinguished between the rights of *associés* and those of the companies in its decision on preliminary objections and then had refused to take account of Diallo's right to exercise his rights as *associé* on the merits, effectively leaving his rights devoid of any real scope.[53] In their joint dissenting opinion, Judges Al-Khasawneh and Yusuf went even further, implying that the Court's decision on preliminary objections had been wrongly decided. Referring to the decision in *Barcelona Traction*, the joint dissenting opinion noted that the Court:

> ...never precluded, as a matter of principle, the operation of diplomatic protection of shareholders when there is no protecting State. We cannot think of a situation where considerations of equity would have been more appropriate than in the present case, all the more so since there was no danger of "confusion and insecurity in international economic relations" as a result of "opening the door to competing diplomatic claims".[54]

Referring to paragraph 115 of the Court's judgment, extracted above, the joint dissenting opinion suggested that the Court had been "patently apologetic",[55] stating:

> Of course Guinea had to accept this distinction in view of the *res judicata* of the 2007 Judgment. However, we believe it was well within the Court's power to take cognizance of the reality of the situation, in particular that where there is in effect one *associé/gérant* the infringement of the company rights is *ipso facto* infringement of the direct rights of the owner.

By insisting on a dogmatic application of the approach taken in *Barcelona Traction* (or rather on a narrow interpretation of *Barcelona Traction* that did not take account of the absence of a protecting State), the Court missed a chance to provide redress to Mr. Diallo as a matter of equity without at the same time detracting from the formal force of its 2007 Judgment. Equally importantly, the Court missed a chance to bring into line the standard of protection of investors like Mr. Diallo with the standard now found in jurisprudence emanating from regional courts and arbitral tribunals. This latter standard, as had been previously alluded to, has arguably become an international minimum standard to which even those investors not covered by bilateral or multilateral investment treaties may be entitled.[56]

53   Ibid, Dissenting Opinion of Judge Bennouna, esp para 18.
54   Ibid, Joint Dissenting Opinion of Judges Al-Khasawneh and Yusuf, p 4 (references omitted).
55   Ibid, Joint Dissenting Opinion of Judges Al-Khasawneh and Yusuf, p 6.
56   Ibid, Joint Dissenting Opinion of Judges Al-Khasawneh and Yusuf, p 7.

The opinion had in an earlier part lamented the discrepancies between customary international law on diplomatic protection and the standards in investment treaties, noting:

> Luckily, those foreign investors whose investments in foreign States are protected by bilateral or multilateral investment treaties would be shielded from [a risk of having no redress]. These treaties typically go much further than what Guinea has asked for in this case, namely in affording protection through well-established techniques such as compulsory arbitration, dispensing with the need to exhaust local remedies, broadening the scope of the term "investment", incorporating in the State of nationality of shareholders or in a third State, etc. These developments in the field of foreign investments have led to the wholesale abandonment of the distinction between the corporate personality of the company on the one hand and that of the shareholders on the other, resulting in a wide discrepancy between the customary international law standard and the standard contained in most investment treaties, with the customary law standard (if at all represented by what is contained in *Barcelona Traction*) being significantly lower than the one existing in the realm of investment treaties. The least that can be said about the state of customary international law given this discrepancy is that it is unsatisfactory.[57]

In contrast to the *Barcelona Traction* approach applied by the majority of the ICJ in *Diallo*, in investment claims, there is no specific restriction on the standing of a shareholder to bring a claim in its own right. That claim will be for injury to the shareholder's "investment", that investment being the shares in a company. A shareholder will be entitled to investment treaty protection for its investment in a foreign state. As noted by the tribunal in *Total v Argentina*

> The protection that BITs afford to... investors is... not limited to the free enjoyment of their shares but extends to the respect of the treaty standards as to the substance of their investments.[58]

While claims by shareholders are clearly admissible before investment tribunals, there is a separate question as to the scope of protection which is afforded to shareholders, under investment treaties or investment contracts. In respect of the latter, the annulment committee in *CMS v Argentina* clearly distinguished between the capacity of a shareholder to bring a claim against the host state and the admissibility of the substance of that claim, stating:

---

57   Ibid, Joint Dissenting Opinion of Judges Al-Khasawneh and Yusuf, p 2.
58   *Total S.A.v Argentina* (ICSID Case No ARB/04/01), Preliminary Objections, 25 August 2006, para 74.

CMS must be considered an investor within the meaning of the BIT. It asserted causes of action under the BIT in connection with that protected investment. Its claims for violations of its rights under the BIT were accordingly within the jurisdiction of the Tribunal. This is without prejudice to the determination of the *extent* of those rights, a question to which the Committee will return.[59]

If the extent of the rights which can form the basis of a claim by a shareholder relate only to their direct rights, then the scope of admissible claims by shareholders under the investment regime does not differ significantly from the scope of claims which may be brought under the rules of diplomatic protection. The difference between the two regimes in respect of claims in respect of shareholders would then only be formal, since, as the ICJ affirmed in *Diallo*, a claim can be brought in respect of direct injury to the rights of a shareholder by the shareholder's state of nationality.[60] But the practice of investment tribunals does not clearly reflect the distinction between rights of shareholders and those of the company. In respect of claims which relate to contract, whether brought under a treaty on the basis of an umbrella clause or under the contract itself, the decision of the annulment committee in *CMS v Argentina* provides clear indication that it is only the shareholders' direct rights which can form the basis of a claim; but where the claims relate to more generalised standards of treatment applicable under a BIT, tribunals have not made a clear distinction between claims based on shareholders' direct rights and claims based on the company's rights. The "more realistic" assessment of the practice of investment treaty tribunals is that "[t]he investment treaty regime recognises for the shareholders in the company a separate and independent right or interest in respect of damage done to the company by a foreign government to any extent and in all circumstances."[61] The current

59   *CMS v Argentina* (ICSID Case No ARB/01/8, Decision on Annulment, 25 September 2007, para 75 (emphasis in original). The annulment committee annulled the tribunal's decision on the umbrella clause for a failure to state reasons, and gave a number of reasons why the shareholder could not rely on the obligations entered into by the company: ibid, paras 95, 97.
60   *Case Concerning Ahmadou Sadio Diallo (Republic of Guinea v Democratic Republic of the Congo)*, Preliminary Objections, ICJ, 24 May 2007, para 64.
61   Z Douglas, *The International Law of Investment Claims* (Cambridge, CUP, 2009), para 756. See *AES v Argentina*, Preliminary Objections, 12 ICSID Rep 312, paras 85-9; *CMS v Argentina*, Preliminary Objections, 7 ICSID Rep 494, paras 9, 68; *Siemens v Argentina*, Preliminary Objections, 12 ICSID Rep 74, paras 141-142; *National Grid v Argentina*, Preliminary Objections, para 169; *LG&E v Argentina*, Preliminary Objections, 11 ICSID Rep 414, para 63; *Gas Natural v Argentina*, Preliminary Objections, paras 34-35; *Continental Casualty v Argentina*, Preliminary Objections, paras 79, 87; *Pan American Energy v Argentina*, Preliminary Objections, para 218; *Sue v Argentina*, Preliminary Objections, para 51; *Total v Argentina*, Preliminary Objections, para 74; *Noble Energy v Ecuador*, Preliminary Objections, para 77.

state of practice cannot be said to reflect the distinction urged by the *CMS* annulment committee, nor can it be reconciled with the rules applicable to diplomatic protection claims.

Thus it can be seen that the investment regime has adopted a less restrictive approach to standing than that applicable under the rules of diplomatic protection in relation to claims by shareholders.

D. The Influence of the Investment Regime on Diplomatic Protection

The International Court has been reluctant to find that the rules applicable to investment claims have impacted on the rules applicable to diplomatic protection claims under general international law, characterising investment claims practice as *lex specialis*. In *Barcelona Traction* the ICJ noted the existence of special regimes which permitted claims to be brought in respect of injury to shareholders, noting that the protection of shareholders in international law was only achieved by reference to those special regimes:

> Thus, in the present state of the law, the protection of shareholders requires that recourse be had to treaty stipulations or special agreements directly concluded between the private investor and the State in which the investment is placed. States ever more frequently provide for such protection, in both bilateral and multilateral relations, either by means of special instruments or within the framework of wider economic arrangements. Indeed, whether in the form of multilateral or bilateral treaties between States, or in that of agreements between States and companies, there has since the Second World War been considerable development in the protection of foreign investments. The instruments in question contain provisions as to jurisdiction and procedure in case of disputes concerning the treatment of investing companies by the States in which they invest capital. Sometimes companies are themselves vested with a direct right to defend their interests against States through prescribed procedures. No such instrument is in force between the Parties to the present case.[62]

The Court characterised such regimes as *lex specialis* and did not consider that this practice had an impact on the customary international law rules applicable to diplomatic protection claims.[63]

The ILC, in its Draft Articles on Diplomatic Protection, confirmed that the international investment regime constitute a *lex specialis* regime and the rules applicable in that context do not govern diplomatic protection claims or contribute

---

62 *Case Concerning the Barcelona Traction, Light and Power Company Limited*, 1970 ICJ Reports, p 3, p 47 (para 90).
63 Ibid, pp 40-41 (paras 62-63).

to the development of customary rules applicable to diplomatic protection claims.[64] The same point was made by the ICJ in *Diallo* in 2007, distinguishing between direct claims by investors under ICSID and diplomatic protection claims,[65] and as explained above, the majority of the Court upheld that approach in the Court's decision on the merits in 2010. That the investment regime constitutes a *lex specialis* regime has also been acknowledged by a number of investment tribunals.[66]

To the extent that investment claims are distinct from diplomatic protection claims, and are not subject to the rules governing diplomatic protection claims, it is not clear that the investment regime can or should have an influence on the rules governing diplomatic protection claims. The discrepancies between the two regimes referred to in the joint dissenting opinion in *Diallo* may be lamentable, but the fact remains that the majority of the Court demonstrated an unwillingness to depart from the decision in *Barcelona Traction*. The joint dissenting opinion asserted that the standard now found in the jurisprudence of arbitral tribunals "has arguably become an international minimum standard to which even those investors not covered by bilateral or multilateral investment treaties may be entitled"[67] but – perhaps lamentably itself – did not address the question of *lex specialis* of the investment treaty regime. This is not to detract from its convincing arguments on the interpretation of *Barcelona Traction* and its reference to equitable considerations; but this stands apart from the direct applicability of rules derived from the investment regime, the juridical foundation for which is less clear. The Court may very well have "missed a chance to do justice to Mr. Diallo", as the joint dissenting opinion asserts,[68] but this may be due to its failure to properly apply and confine *Barcelona Traction* rather than its failure to apply the standards applicable in the investment regime.

Nevertheless, the investment regime has a very real potential to influence the rules governing diplomatic protection in a less overt way. For example, where the rule on exhaustion of local remedies is incorporated in a BIT, an investment treaty tribunal's decision applying that rule and defining its content could pro-

---

64 ILC, *Report of the Fifty-eighth Session* (2006), A/CN.4/L.684, Article 17. See also *Case Concerning Amhamdou Sadio Diallo (Republic of Guinea v Democratic Republic of the Congo)*, Preliminary Objections, ICJ, 24 May 2007, para 88.

65 *Case Concerning Amhamdou Sadio Diallo (Republic of Guinea v Democratic Republic of the Congo)*, Preliminary Objections, ICJ, 24 May 2007, para 88.

66 See for example *Camuzzi v Argentina I*, Decision on Jurisdiction, 11 May 2005, para 145; CH Schreuer, *The ICSID Convention: A Commentary*, 2nd ed (Cambridge, CUP, 2009), para 27-9 (p 417).

67 *Case Concerning Ahmadou Sadio Diallo (Republic of Guinea v Democratic Republic of the Congo)*, Merits, ICJ, 30 November 2010, Joint Dissenting Opinion of Judges Al-Khasawneh and Yusuf, p 7.

68 Ibid, p 9.

vide guidance as to the scope of the same rule applicable to diplomatic protection claims.[69] The investment regime cannot be supplanted wholesale, but it might have influence in a more nuanced way. Given the sheer number of investment claims now being decided, and the relative (and increasing) scarcity of diplomatic protection claims, it is likely that the investment regime will have an influence – albeit in a piecemeal way – on the elucidation of the rules of diplomatic protection applicable under general international law.

E. Investment Claims and Diplomatic Protection: Merely Parallel Regimes?

The investment regime is still in an infantile stage of development, a fact which might be obscured by its rapid development in recent times. There are many unanswered questions about its juridical and theoretical foundations,[70] and tribunals and scholars are only just beginning to recognise and confront these questions. A consensus seems to be forming that investment claims are distinct from diplomatic protection claims, that investment claims are not governed by the rules governing diplomatic protection claims under general international law. This positions the investment regime as one parallel to, rather than intersecting with, diplomatic protection under general international law. But to view these as parallel regimes is an oversimplification and risks undermining the potential for cross-fertilization. There is a possibility of the practice of investment tribunals exerting influence on the content of the rules applicable to diplomatic protection claims, but that influence will occur at the micro-level, in the application of specific rules which are relevant to and applicable in both regimes. At this level, the investment regime cannot be dismissed on the mere basis of *lex specialis*, and has a role to play in the development of general international law.

---

69   Z Douglas, "Nothing if Not Critical for Investment Treaty Arbitration: *Occidental, Eureko* and *Methanex*" (2006) 22 *Arbitration International* 27.

70   See for example Z Douglas, "The Hybrid Foundations of Investment Treaty Arbitration" (2003) 74 *BYIL* 151; A Roberts, "Power and Persuasion in Investment Treaty Interpretation: The Dual Role of States" (2010) 104 *AJIL* 179.

International Investment Law and the Law of State Immunity: Antagonists or Two Sides of the Same Coin?

*Stephan W. Schill**

A. Introduction: Towards a Dynamic and Contextual Perspective

Examining the relationship between international investment law and the law of State immunity is part of the more general quest of the present book to understand the relationship between international investment law and general international law. For the general international lawyer, one of the main concerns in this context is the fragmentation of international law, that is, its loss of unity as a system of law which is capable of providing order for international relations.[1] Given the proliferation of international investment treaties[2] and the phenomenal growth of investment treaty arbitrations since the end of the Cold War,[3] one core question becomes not only whether international investment law is itself a system of law,[4] but whether it conforms to, or diverges from, the architecture, methods, notions, and concepts of general international law.[5]

Dr Stephan W. Schill, LL.M., Senior Research Fellow, Max Planck Institute for Comparative Public Law and International Law, Heidelberg; Rechtsanwalt, Attorney-at-Law (New York).

1 See Martti Koskenniemi, 'Fragmentation of International Law: Difficulties Arising from the Diversification and Expansion of International Law', Report of the Study Group of the International Law Commission, International Law Commission, 13 April 2006, UN Doc A/CN.4/L.682, paras. 1-15.

2 See UNCTAD, 'Recent Developments in International Investment Agreements (2008-June 2009)' (2009) IIA Monitor No. 3, 2, at http://www.unctad.org/en/docs//webdi aeia20098_en.pdf (recording an aggregate of 2,676 bilateral investment treaties by the end of 2008). On the development of international investment law see Kenneth J. Vandevelde, 'A Brief History of International Investment Agreements' (2005) 12 UC Davis JLP 157.

3 See UNCTAD, 'Latest Developments in Investor-State Dispute Settlement' (2010) IIA Issues Note No. 1, 2-3, at http://www.unctad.org/en/docs//webdiaeia20103_en.pdf (recording an aggregate of 357 treaty-based investment disputes by the end of 2009).

4 For the argument that international investment law is a proper system of law see Stephan Schill, The Multilateralization of International Investment Law (2009); similarly Santiago Montt, State Liablity in Investment Treaty Arbitration (2009) 86 (describing current in-

Determining the relationship between two bodies of international law – one general, one specific – requires a static snapshot of the present doctrinal interactions of two fields. Regarding the relation between international investment law and the law of State immunity such an approach is rather straightforward: from a doctrinal perspective both areas of international law interlock neatly, thus raising few, if any, concerns about fragmentation. Thus, immunity from jurisdiction, as the first element of State immunity,[6] plays no role in investment arbitrations: just as in other international courts or tribunals, State immunity is not available as a defense to the jurisdiction of an investment treaty tribunal because the respondent State does not submit to the jurisdiction of the courts of another State.[7] Im-

ternational investment law as a «BIT system» and proposing to approach it with a new theory: «the BIT generation as a virtual network»).

5   On the relationship between international investment law and general international law see Campbell McLachlan, 'Investment Treaties and General International Law' (2008) 58 ICLQ 361; Jürgen Bering et al, General Public International Law and International Investment Law, The International Law Association German Branch, Sub-Committee on Investment Law (2009), at http://www.50yearsofbits.com/docs/0912211342_ILA_Working_Group_IIL_PIL.pdf. In addition, the relationship between international investment law and other specific areas of international law is of increasing concern. See, for example, Bruno Simma and Theodore Kill, 'Harmonizing Investment Protection and International Human Rights: First Steps Towards a Methodology' in Christina Binder et al (eds), International Investment Law for the 21st Century – Essays in Honour of Christoph Schreuer (2009) 678; Moshe Hirsch, 'Interactions between Investment and Non-investment Obligations' in Peter Muchlinski et al (eds), The Oxford Handbook of International Investment Law (2008) 154; and the contributions in Pierre-Marie Dupuy et al (eds), Human Rights in International Investment Law and Arbitration (2009).

6   Comprehensively on State immunity from jurisdiction Hazel Fox, The Law of State Immunity (2nd edn 2008) 68-99.

7   Albert J. van den Berg, 'The New York Arbitration Convention and State Immunity' in Karl-Heinz Böckstiegel (ed), Acts of State and Arbitration (1997) 41, 49; KI Vibhute, International Commercial Arbitration and State Immunity (1999) 63-67; Dhisadee Chamlongrasdr, Foreign State Immunity and Arbitration (2007) 81-85. Cf also United Nations Convention on Jurisdictional Immunities of States and Their Property, adopted 2 December 2008, not yet in force, GA Res 59/38, annex, Official Records of the General Assembly, Fifty-ninth Session, Supplement No. 49 (A/59/49) ('hereinafter UN Convention'), Art. 1, limiting the scope of application of the Convention «to the immunity of a State and its property from the jurisdiction of the courts of another State.» A different issue is whether immunity from jurisdiction applies when domestic courts are seized in their ancillary role of compelling and aiding arbitration; see Christoph Schreuer, State Immunity: Some Recent Developments (1988) 71-75; Fox (supra note 6) 495-501. Under UN Convention, Art. 17 a State cannot invoke immunity against the exercise of jurisdiction in such cases. This issue, however, will not be dealt with further as it is of only minor practical importance in investment treaty arbitrations and concerns an issue of the division of competences between arbitral tribunals and domestic courts rather than the relations between international investment law and the law of State immunity.

munity from enforcement, as the second element of State immunity,[8] by contrast, is left unscathed: the legal framework governing investment treaty arbitrations, either explicitly or implicitly, allows States to invoke State immunity against enforcement of awards made by investment treaty tribunals.[9] Under Article 55 of the ICSID Convention, States are expressly permitted to refuse enforcement of an ICSID award based on their respective domestic sovereign immunity doctrine.[10] Similarly, the New York Convention allows States to resist enforcement of non-ICSID investment awards for reasons of sovereign immunity.[11]

A purely doctrinal perspective, however, is necessarily limited. Above all, it does not allow us to understand the relation between two areas of international as a dynamic process, in which both general and special bodies of international law interact and influence each other.[12] Taking such a dynamic perspective allows us not only to determine to what extent international investment law is in conformity with, or opts out of, general international law. It also allows us to look at the reverse process by which international investment law has repercussions on the development of general international law.[13] This perspective is dynamic in focus-

8   Fox (supra note 6) 599-662. See also James Crawford, 'Execution of Judgments and Foreign Sovereign Immunity' (1981) 75 AJIL 820.

9   Cf Alexis Blane, 'Sovereign Immunity as a Bar to the Execution of International Arbitral Awards' (2009) NYU JILP 453, 454; Okezie Chukwumerije, 'ICSID Arbitration and Sovereign Immunity' (1990) Anglo-Am L Rev 166, 178-182.

10   ICSID Convention, Art. 55 provides: «Nothing in Article 54 [ie the obligation to recognize and enforce ICSID awards] shall be construed as derogating from the law in force in any Contracting State relating to immunity of that State or of any foreign State from execution.» Notwithstanding, the respondent State is obliged under ICSID Convention, Art. 53(1) to comply with an ICSID award, even if State immunity is invoked as a bar to execution; see Christoph Schreuer et al, The ICSID Convention – A Commentary (2nd edn 2009) Art. 55, para. 7. As a consequence of non-compliance, the right of the investor's home State to grant diplomatic protection revives; see ICSID Convention, Art. 27(1). In particular, the home State can institute proceedings in the International Court of Justice under ICSID Convention, Art. 64. This right is also not affected by the invocation of immunity in enforcement proceedings; Schreuer et al, ibid, Art. 64, para. 14.

11   Although not explicitly mentioned as grounds for refusing enforcement of an award against a State, enforcement immunity can form part of the public policy exception in Article V(2)(b) New York Convention or apply under Article III of the Convention as a rule of domestic procedure applicable to enforcement. See Andrea K Bjorklund, 'State Immunity and the Enforcement of Investor-State Arbitral Awards' in Binder et al (supra note 5) 302, 308-9; August Reinisch, 'Enforcement of Investment Awards' in Katia Yannaca-Small (ed), Arbitration under International Investment Agreements (2010) 671, 681-682 (referring to a case decided by the German Supreme Court, BGH, NJW-RR 2006, 198); van den Berg (supra note 7) 41, 56.

12   For a similar perspective as regards human rights and humanitarian law and their influence on general international law see Theodor Meron, The Humanization of International Law (2006).

13   For this dual perspective regarding international investment law and general international law see Bering et al (supra note 5) 7-8.

ing on the mutual interaction between two bodies of law over time; it also is contextual in assessing how the interests protected by different bodies of international law develop in relation to each other. As regards the relations between international investment law and the law of State immunity, these interests are the protection of private economic rights, on the one hand, and State sovereignty, on the other.

A dynamic and contextual perspective helps to understand the development both international investment law and the law of State immunity have undergone during the past decades, and are still undergoing today. This development is characterized by the rapid growth of international investment treaties and investor-State arbitration,[14] on the one hand, and the wide-spread transition from absolute towards more limited forms of State immunity, on the other.[15] These developments are interrelated because, as will be argued in this chapter, rigid forms of jurisdictional immunity were one factor precipitating the emergence of international investment law and investor-State arbitration. Notwithstanding, the common core of the development in international investment law and the law of State immunity is the increasing recognition of the importance of protecting private economic interests under international law in an increasingly globalized economy.[16] In that respect, the rise of investor-State arbitration and the retreat of absolute forms of State immunity form part of the same trend away from the sovereignty-centered international law of Westphalian imprint, which was exclusively concerned with delineating different public spheres as a *ius inter gentes*, towards a rule of law-based international law that takes individuals and their protection seriously.[17] In that regard, international investment law and the law of State immunity are but two sides of the same coin.

The continued recognition of enforcement immunity, by contrast, stresses that States and their international law do not accord unconditional primacy to the economic interests of foreign investors, but ensure the availability of procedural

---

14   See supra notes 2 and 3.
15   On the development of the law of State immunity from absolute to restrictive forms see Schreuer (supra note 7) 1-9; Fox (supra note 6) 201-236; Chamlongrasdr (supra note 7) 65-77. A rich historic perspective is also offered by Ernest K. Bankas, The State Immunity Controversy in International Law (2005).
16   For the view that international investment law is an important building block for the global economy see Schill (supra note 4) 3-6. On the impact of globalization on international law more generelly see, for example, Stephan Hobe, 'Die Zukunft des Völkerrechts im Zeitalter der Globalisierung' (2000) 37 Archiv für Völkerrecht, 253; David J. Bederman, Globalization and International Law (2008); see also the contributions in Stephan Hobe (ed), Globalisation – the State and International Law (2009).
17   There is now a vast amount of literature on the rise of the individual in international law and the effects this development has on international law more generally. See comprehensively Meron (supra note 12).

means to protect State interests against enforcement of investment treaty awards. This can serve the legitimate purpose of shielding assets from attachment and seizure that States need in order to act in the public interest, such as the protection of property used by diplomatic or consular missions as a precondition for States to cooperate with other States and to assist their own citizens abroad,[18] or even help States fend off payment of damages in times of dire financial crisis.[19] In that respect, the ability to prevent enforcement of investment treaty awards can be seen as a safety valve for States to protect legitimate public interests against the interests of foreign investors.

At the same time, the balance that the procedural framework on investor-State arbitrations strikes between private and public interests by leaving enforcement immunity untouched also allows States to refuse enforcement of investment treaty awards for purely opportunistic motives. This can effectively eviscerate claims by foreign investors for damages that have been validly determined in the arbitral process. In that regard, enforcement immunity is antagonistic to the objective of international investment law to promote and protect foreign investors. For that reason, it aptly has been designated as the «Achilles' heel in the body of investor-State dispute settlement.»[20]

In spite of the limitations to effective investment protection in the procedural framework of investor-State arbitration, one needs to be mindful, however, of the substantive standards of investment protection. These standards, such as fair and equitable treatment and full protection and security, could increase the protection of foreign investors against State immunity if the invocation of sovereign im-

---

18   Accordingly, under the prevalent practice assets are immune from enforcement in a foreign State if they serve a public purpose or pertain to the category of property specifically protected under international law, such as diplomatic property, military property, central bank property, and cultural heritage. See Chamlongrasdr (supra note 7) 259-315.

19   In this regard, enforcement immunity could be a means for debtor States to implement a defense against payment of debt based on necessity in economic crises. This defense has been accepted in a number of older cases before international courts and tribunals; it entitles States to suspend, but not to release it of, its payment obligations in severe economic crises. See August Reinisch, 'Sachverständigengutachten zur Frage des Bestehens und der Wirkung des völkerrechtlichen Rechtfertigungsgrundes «Staatsnotstand»' (2008) 68 ZaöRV 3, 10-16. Similarly, in modern investment treaty arbitration, arbitral tribunals have recognized that necessity can become operative in case of economic crises. See Stephan Schill, 'International Investment Law and the Host State's Power to Handle Economic Crises' (2007) 24 J Int Arb 265, 279-284. It is debated, however, whether a State can also invoke necessity under international law against claims by private parties. The German Constitutional Court, in particular, has declined in one of the Argentine bondholder cases that Argentina could rely on necessity under customary international law to suspend payment obligations under bonds issued in Germany. See German Constitutional, 2 BvM 1-5/03, 1-2/06, Decision, 8 May 2007, BVerfGE 118, 124.

20   Bjorklund (supra note 11) 321; see also Schreuer et al (supra note 10) Art. 55, para. 8.

munity is contrary to such substantive investment treaty obligations. This could contribute to a more appropriate balance of private and public interests than the one struck under the procedural rules governing investor-State arbitration, in particular one that prevents States from relying on enforcement immunity for any, including purely opportunistic reasons.

The effect of substantive investment treaty obligations on issues of immunities is, however, far from settled: investment treaty tribunals deal with issues of sovereign immunity as seldom as domestic courts consider investment treaty obligations when applying domestic sovereign immunity law. Notwithstanding, substantive standards of international investment law arguably have a significant potential in affecting the sovereign immunity law applied by courts at the domestic level. This potential crystallizes when drawing parallels between investment treaty arbitration and human rights adjudication, in particular the jurisprudence of the European Court of Human Rights (ECtHR). Unlike investment tribunals, the ECtHR has had ample opportunities to pronounce on the tension between sovereign immunity and the right to property and access to justice protected under the European Convention on Human Rights and Fundamental Freedoms (ECHR) and its Protocols. This jurisprudence, and the interpretative methods the ECtHR applies, above all proportionality analysis for resolving tensions between private and public interests, arguably could serve as a yardstick for conceptualizing the relationship between international investment law and the law of State immunity. This cross-fertilization could not only further the harmonious development of investment law and human rights law, but also push for the development of a legal framework that protects foreign investment more effectively, while leaving sufficient leeway for States to act in the public interests and protect the property necessary for that purpose.

Against this background, Part B of the present chapter adopts a historic perspective and shows how the rise of international investment law and the erosion of absolute immunity of States concerning jurisdiction and enforcement are closely connected to the changing role of the State and of international law in an increasingly global economy. It argues that the development of both bodies of law centers around a recognition of the need for international law to protect private interests against undue State interference. Part C focuses on the impact substantive investment treaty obligations can have on the law of sovereign immunity as it is applied in the domestic context. It suggests that concepts of sovereign immunity applied in domestic settings, both to decline jurisdiction and to refuse enforcement of judicial and arbitral decisions, can constitute a breach of the substantive principles of international investment law, if the application of immunity is overly broad and does not further a legitimate public interest in a proportionate manner. Part D then explores the potential of cross-fertilization between international investment law and human rights law by turning to proportionality analysis used in ECtHR jurisprudence to deal with the relation between sovereign immunity and rights granted under the ECHR. Part E concludes.

B. A Historical Perspective: International Investment Law, State Immunity, and the Recognition of the Individual in International Law

Both international investment law and the law of State immunity have undergone fundamental changes compared to their encapsulations in what was considered traditional international law, that is, the law governing the relations between States, and States only.[21] These changes, as will be argued in this section, are a reaction to an evolution in the understanding of the role of the State in its relation to the economy, in particular the emerging global economy. In it, States not only act as regulators of private economic activity, but have themselves become important economic actors that engage in various transborder economic activities, including the procurement of goods, services, and capital on foreign markets, and cooperate with foreign traders and investors at home. The changes in the patterns of economic activities affected international investment law and the law of State immunity. Accordingly, this section first gives an overview of the evolution of international investment law and the law of State immunity (I.), before arguing that this development can be understood as driven by new economic realities, most importantly the emergence of a global economy (II.).

I. The Evolution of International Investment Law and the Law of State Immunity

International investment law has developed, accelerated by the end of the Cold War, through the proliferation of bilateral, regional, and sectoral investment treaties, and the rise of investor-State arbitration.[22] At the core of its evolution is, on the one hand, the treatification of substantive standards for the protection of foreign investors[23] and, on the other, the creation of a right of foreign investors to

---

21 For this classical view of international law see Lassa Oppenheim, International Law (1905) Vol I, § 13, p. 19 («States solely and exclusively are the subjects of International Law.»); ibid, § 20, p. 26 («Municipal Law regulates relations between the individuals under the sway of the respective State and the relations between this State and the respective individuals. International Law, on the other hand, regulates relations between the member States of the Family of Nations.»); similarly Heinrich Triepel, Völkerrecht und Landesrecht (1899) 9, 11-26.

22 See supra notes 2 and 3.

23 Cf Jeswald Salacuse, 'The Treatification of International Investment Law' (2007) 13 L & Bus Rev of the Americas 155.

initiate arbitration directly against the host State, without having to rely on the mechanism of diplomatic protection.[24] Foreign investors, in consequence, have seen an expansion of the legal protection they receive under international law, both substantively and procedurally. Host States, in turn, face increasingly effective means by which foreign investors can make them comply with their international obligations. The evolution of international investment law, therefore, marks the emancipation of foreign investors from mere objects of State regulation to actors who dispose of their own rights and remedies under international law and, on that basis, can cooperate with States more efficiently.

The law of State immunity also has seen major developments during the past decades: numerous common law countries have passed statutes codifying their domestic laws on foreign sovereign immunity, including the United States and the United Kingdom;[25] and domestic courts, primarily in civil law countries, have rendered important decisions on issues of foreign sovereign immunity.[26] Furthermore, relying on the Draft Articles prepared by the International Law Commission in 1991,[27] the UN General Assembly adopted, on 2 December 2004, the United Nations Convention on Jurisdictional Immunities of States and Their Property.[28] Preceded by international conventions with a more limited ambit, such as the 1972 European Convention on State Immunity,[29] the UN Convention marks the first universal instrument to codify the international law of State immunity. Although it has not yet entered into force, but is expected to do so in the near future, domestic and international courts already have referred to the UN

---

24 See Stephan Schill, 'Private Enforcement of International Investment Law: Why We Need Investor Standing in BIT Dispute Settlement' in Michael Waibel et al (eds), The Backlash against Investment Arbitration (2010) 29, 31 (arguing that «the foreign investor's right to initiate arbitration against the host state for a violation of investment treaty obligations is the most central feature of such treaties and an important institutional arrangement in order to promote and protect foreign investment»).

25 See Schreuer (supra note 7) 2-4.

26 See August Reinisch, 'European Court Practice Concerning State Immunity from Enforcement Measures' (2006) 17 EJIL 803.

27 See Draft Articles on Jurisdictional Immunities of States and Their Property (1991) ILC Ybk., Vol. II, Part Two 13; on the draft see Catherine Kessedjian and Christoph Schreuer, 'Le Projet d´Articles de la Commission du Droit International des Nations Unies sur les immunités des Etats' (1992) 96 RGDIP 299; Burkhard Heß, 'The International Law Commission's Draft Convention on Jurisdictional Immunities of States and Their Property' (1993) 4 EJIL 269.

28 For the full reference see supra note 7. On the UN Convention see also Gerhard Hafner and Ulrike Köhler, 'The United Nations Convention on Jurisdictional Immunities of States and Their Property' (2004) 35 Neth YBIL 3; David P. Stewart, 'The UN Convention on Jurisdictional Immunities of States and Their Property' (2005) 99 AJIL 194.

29 European Convention on State Immunity 1972, signed 16 May 1972, entered into force 11 June 1976, ETS No. 74, (1972) 11 ILM 470.

Convention as an expression of customary international law, including the ECtHR.[30]

As regards substance, the central evolution of the law of State immunity, both at the domestic and the international level, is the erosion of doctrines of absolute immunity and the turn towards more restrictive forms of immunity.[31] Thus, today the domestic courts of the large majority of States distinguish, in respect of jurisdictional immunity, between public acts (*acta iure imperii*) of foreign States and commercial acts (*acta iure gestionis*), and regularly limit sovereign immunity to the former.[32] In parallel, in respect of enforcement immunity, most States limit sovereign immunity to assets of a foreign State serving a public purpose and permit enforcement into commercially used assets.[33] This increases the power of domestic courts to exercise jurisdiction over foreign States and to enforce judicial and arbitral decisions against them. It equally exposes States hosting foreign investors to increasingly effective means of implementing liability for breaches of their rights within domestic legal orders. In that regard, the development of international investment law and the law of State immunity displays important parallels.

II. New Economic Realities as the Driving Force for the Adaptation of International Investment Law and the Law of State Immunity

Both the rise of international investment law and the erosion of absolute doctrines of immunity can be seen as reactions to new patterns of economic activities, namely the increase in transborder trade and investment, and a changed role of the State in relation to the economy. These changes coincide with the general development of international law away from State-centered conceptions towards an international law that furnishes a legal framework for an international society and a truly global market economy. In particular, modern international law provides private economic actors with mechanisms allowing them to ensure that host States live up to commitments they made. Most importantly, these mechanisms encompass, compared to the reign of traditional international law, broader possibilities of third-party dispute settlement and enforcement of awards and

---

30 See Cudak v. Lithuania, Judgment, 23 March 2010, para. 67 (regarding UN Convention, Art. 11). Mentioning domestic cases that considered provisions of the UN Convention as customary international law Reinisch (supra note 11) 683-685.

31 See references supra note 15.

32 See Fox (supra note 6) 502-530. See also UN Convention, Art. 10.

33 See Schreuer (supra note 7) 134-137; Reinisch (supra note 11) 683-688; comprehensively also Fox (supra note) 599-662; Chamlongrasdr (supra note 7) 259-298. See also UN Convention, Art. 19.

judgments against States.[34] This allows foreign investors to curtail arbitrary behavior of States and to reduce the political risk inherent in foreign investment activities more effectively.

This section therefore shows how international law more generally, as well as international investment law and the law of State immunity in particular, developed in reaction to changing economic patterns. After describing how the Westphalian model of international law and its underlying economic model construed international investment law and the law of State immunity (1.), this section points to the shortcomings of such a model for a global economy (2.). It is these shortcomings that precipitated changes to both international investment law and the law of State immunity as compared to Westphalian times. In that perspective, the rise of international investment law and the decline of absolute State immunity strengthen the position of private economic actors vis-à-vis abuses of public power and can be understood as part of the emergence of a rule of law framework for investor-State relations (3.).

1. The Westphalian System, its Concept of National Economies, and Classical International Law

International law, as it was initially conceived in the Westphalian system was insufficient to furnish the legal framework that was necessary for the efficient functioning of a global economic system. Most importantly, classical international law neither offered independent and effective third-party dispute settlement for disputes between investors and States, nor did it provide uniform rules necessary for a global market economy to function. Instead, conceived of as solely governing the relations between sovereign States, and focusing on the notion of sovereignty, the main function of international law under the Westphalian model was to protect States against interferences by other States and to delineate, in an exclusive inter-State system, spheres of sovereignty between them.[35] Private economic actors, in contrast, were alien to this concept of international law: they were neither considered as subjects of international law with individual rights vis-à-vis foreign sovereigns, nor was the content of international law con-

---

34   On the connection between the possibility to make credible commitments and the existence of third-party dispute settlement and enforcement see Alan Schwartz and Robert E. Scott, 'Contract Theory and the Limits of Contract Law' (2003) 113 Yale LJ 541, 556–562; see also Andrew T. Guzman, 'Why LDCs Sign Treaties That Hurt Them: Explaining the Popularity of Bilateral Investment Treaties' (1998) 38 Va JIL 639, 658 et seq. For a game-theoretic reconstruction see Robert Cooter and Thomas Ulen, Law and Economics (4th edn 2004) 195 et seq.

35   Fox (supra note 6) 57-59.

cerned with regulating, let alone sustaining or even promoting, cross-border economic activities.

Instead, the economic model underlying the Westphalian system of international law was one of national economies that were separated, both legally and economically, from other national economies. Accordingly, from the point of view of domestic law, cross-border trading and foreign investment often were not subject to the same legal regime as purely internal economic relations, but governed by a body of (domestic and international) law pertaining to external trade and foreign investment. Cross-border trade and foreign investment, in other words, were not conceived of as part of one global economic system transcending the economies of nation-States, but as an external, and incidental, aspect of domestic economies.

Whether this model actually represented the economic reality of the international economy in early modernity, is open to debate.[36] What is crucial from a conceptual perspective, however, is that the rise of the nation-State and its claim to absolute internal and external sovereignty, resulted in a specific blueprint for domestic regulation of economic activities, which was based on the model that the economic space corresponded to politically divided spheres of sovereignty of different nation-States. The nation-States' interaction with the economy, therefore, was one in which the question was not how to design rules that could enhance economic activity based on the needs of economic actors, but one in which economic activities had to conform to the State's claim for absolute internal and external sovereignty.[37] Essentially, the economic model underlying the Westphalian system of international law followed the political differentiation into separate sovereign entities and did not depart from a sociological understanding of the reality of (cross-border) economic exchange. The State and its public power, in other words, defined the economic space rather than were defined by it: eco-

---

36   After all, cross-border trading has been a significant aspect of merchant activities since the Middle Ages and was regulated by a body of rules designated as lex mercatoria. This body of rules had gained some independence from national laws based on the usages and customs of the merchant community itself and often was enforced outside the State court system by special commercial courts established in the major European maritime and land-trading centers. See Richard J. Howarth, 'Lex Mercatoria: Can General Principles of Law Govern International Commercial Contracts?' (2004) 10 Canterbury LR 36, 40. See also Armin von Bogdandy and Sergio Dellavalle, 'Die Lex mercatoria der Systemtheorie' in Gralf-Peter Callies et al (eds), Soziologische Jurisprudenz – Festschrift für Gunther Teubner (2009) 695 (putting the lex merctoria into perspective as an ordering paradigm for the global economy).

37   On this classical view of sovereignty see Alfred Verdross and Bruno Simma, Universelles Völkerrecht (3rd edn 1984) 25 et seq.; Malcolm N. Shaw, International Law (6th edn 2008) 21-22; Jean Combacau and Serge Sur, Droit international public (8th edn 2008) 236-237.

nomics followed politics, rather than vice versa. Or, as *Carl Schmitt* put it: *cujus regio ejus economia.*[38]

This constructivist conception of the relation of States and their economies also founds its reflection in the law of State immunity and the traditional mechanism for resolving investor-State disputes. Thus, the law of State immunity was conceived of in absolute terms and found its justification in the principle that one sovereign could not exercise power over another sovereign: *par in parem non habet imperium.* The classical expression of the conceptual foundations of the principle of absolute State immunity can be found in the 1812 US Supreme Court decision in *The Schooner Exchange v. McFaddon*:

> This full and absolute territorial jurisdiction being alike the attribute of every sovereign ... would not seem to contemplate foreign sovereigns nor their sovereign rights as its objects. One sovereign being in no respect amenable to another; and being bound by obligations of the highest character not to degrade the dignity of his nation, by placing himself or its sovereign rights within the jurisdiction of another, can be supposed to enter a foreign territory only under an express license, or in the confidence that the immunities belonging to his independent sovereign station, though not expressly stipulated, are reserved by implication, and will be extended to him.

> This perfect and absolute independence of sovereigns, and this common interest impelling them to mutual intercourse, and an interchange of good offices with each other, have given rise to a class of cases in which every sovereign is understood to waive the exercise of a part of that complete exclusive territorial jurisdiction, which has been stated to be the attribute of every nation.[39]

Absolute sovereign immunity also applied in respect of enforcement of judicial decisions against foreign sovereigns. The House of Lords, for example, stated as follows in *Compania Naviera Vascongado v. SS Cristina*:

> the courts of a country ... will not by their process, whether the sovereign is a party to the proceedings or not, seize or detain property which is his or of which he is in possession or control. There has been some difference in the practice of nations as to possible limitations of this second principle as to whether is extends to property only used for the commercial proposes of the sovereign or to personal private property. In this country it is in my opinion well settled that it applies to both.[40]

Based on this understanding of absolute immunity, disputes with a foreign sovereign only could be entertained in the domestic courts of the foreign sovereign itself; and awards could only be enforced in its territory. The courts of any other State, including those of the home State of an individual negatively affected by acts of a foreign sovereign could not have jurisdiction as this would have inter-

---

38   Carl Schmitt, Der Nomos der Erde im Völkerrecht des Jus Publicum Europaeum (1950) 229. Similarly already Johann Gottlieb Fichte, Der Geschlossene Handelsstaat (1800).
39   The Schooner Exchange v. McFaddon & Others, 11 U.S. 116, 137 (1812).
40   Compania Naviera Vascongado v. SS Cristina [1938] AC 485, 490.

fered with the foreign State's sovereignty. In consequence, the protection of private interests was relegated to the internal affairs of each State.

This model equally informed customary international law concerning the protection of alien property.Whileproviding some protection to foreign investment against uncompensated expropriations and other breaches of the international minimum standard of treatment,[41] customary international law mediated foreign investors through an inter-State prism. It only allowed the investor's home State to espouse the investor's claim vis-à-vis the host State and take the dispute to the international level through the instrument of diplomatic protection.

The classical expression of this position can be found in the *Mavrommatis Palestine Concessions* case decided by the Permanent Court of International Justice (PCIJ) in 1924. In that case, the Greek Government brought a claim against the United Kingdom for breach of a concession granted to a Greek national for the construction and operation of an electric tramway and the supply of electric light, power, and drinking water in Jerusalem. With respect to the relationship between the Greek investor, the United Kingdom as the sovereign over the host State territory, and Greece as the investor's home country, the PCIJ stated:

> In the case of the Mavrommatis concessions it is true that the dispute was at first between a private person and a State – i.e. between M. Mavrommatis and Great Britain. Subsequently, the Greek Government took up the case. The dispute then entered upon on new phase; it entered the domain of international law, and became a dispute between two States. ... It is an elementary principle of international law that a State is entitled to protect its subjects, when injured by acts contrary to international law committed by another State, from whom they have been unable to obtain satisfaction through the ordinary channels. By taking up the case of one of its subjects and by resorting to diplomatic action or international judicial proceedings on his behalf, a State is in reality asserting its own rights – its right to ensure, in the person of its subjects, respect for the rules of international law.[42]

While allowing some protection of interests of individuals when harmed by a foreign State, customary international law and the instrument of diplomatic pro-

---

41   On the historical development of customary international law relating to the protection of foreign property see Rudolf Dolzer, Eigentum, Enteignung und Entschädigung im geltenden Völkerrecht (1985) 13 et seq.; Andreas Lowenfeld, International Economic Law (2nd edn 2008) 467 et seq. On the international minimum standard of treatment see Andreas H. Roth, The Minimum Standard of International Law Applied to Aliens (1949).

42   The Mavrommatis Palestine Concessions (Greece v. Britain), Judgment, 30 August 1924, PCIJ Series A, No. 2 (1924) 12. Similarly, The Factory at Chorzów (Claim for Indemnity) (Germany v. Poland), Merits, Judgment, 13 September 1928, PCIJ Series A, No. 17 (1928) 28; Payment of Various Serbian Loans Issued in France (France v. Kingdom of the Serbs, Croats and Slovenes), Judgment, 12 July 1929, PCIJ Series A, No. 20/21 (1929) 17; The Panevezys-Saldutiskis Railway Case (Estonia v. Lithuania), Judgment, 28 February 1939, PCIJ Series A/B, No. 76 (1939) 16; Nottebohm (Liechtenstein v. Guatemala), Judgment, 6 April 1955, ICJ Reports 1955, 24; Barcelona Traction, Light and Power Company, Limited(Belgium v. Spain), Judgment, 5 February 1970, ICJ Reports 1970, 45-46, para. 85.

tection ensured that international law remained a governance mechanism for inter-State relations in line with the Westphalian model of international law and economics. Private interests as such found no place in that system.

Yet, entrusting dispute settlement between foreign investors and host States almost entirely to the domestic courts of the host State made the development of rules for a global economy virtually impossible, as the resolution of disputes between individuals and States at the domestic level enabled States to implement a primarily domestic vision of the regulation of national economies. A global economy that transcends national economies, by contrast, could hardly take shape given that dispute settlement in the domestic courts of various nation-States followed domestic rather than global rationales. International law, at the time, buttressed this vision and ensured that States could assert absolute sovereignty over their respective territories and shield themselves from interferences by foreign powers, both politically as well as economically. Both the law of State immunity and the customary law on the protection of aliens relegated the relations between economic and State interests primarily to the domestic level.[43] Quite tragically, however, many domestic legal systems also exempted the State from liability towards private economic actors under domestic law. The doctrine that the «king can do no wrong», and therefore could not be held liable for damage caused to individuals, was a concept common to many common and civil law countries, often far into the 20th century.[44]

2. The Insufficiencies of the Westphalian System for a Global Economy

From an economic perspective the primacy of politics over economics, and its ramifications in absolute immunity and diplomatic protection, could only inadequately protect the interests of foreign investors against interference by host

---

43   See Fox (supra note 6) 42 («Immunity can be seen as a useful device to reconcile these two aspects, insulating the power to administer and to operate the public service of one State [free] from interference by another State and its courts. There can be little doubt that the early American and English decisions are based on the Westphalian model of the State, and of the international community as an inter-State society; they reflect the view of Bodin and Austin of the sovereign legislative power vested in the State and the consequent inability of another State to subject it to scrutiny.»).

44   See Irmgard Marboe, 'State Responsibility and Comparative State Liability for Administrative and Legislative Harm to Economic Interests' in Stephan Schill (ed), International Investment Law and Comparative Public Law (2010) 377 (showing how domestic legal system initially often exempted the State from liability for harm caused to private interests but during the 19th and 20th centuries developed a State liability law); for a comparative analysis see also Duncan Fairgrieve, State Liability in Tort. A Comparative Law Study (2003).

States and, therefore, constituted significant obstacles in an increasingly globalized economy. While the Westphalian model may still have been adequate for economic systems in which cross-border trade and investment played but a marginal role, it proved insufficient to accommodate economic reality as soon as certain transborder economic activities that are specifically exposed to interference by foreign States became more wide-spread. At that point, absolute doctrines of State immunity could hardly accommodate the need of private parties for legal protection before courts other than the courts of the host State.[45] This need arose when States appeared as borrowers from private parties on the international capital markets and purchaser of goods and services, but also with the increase of foreign investment and the exposure of foreign investors to the sovereign powers of host States. The courts of those States, however, were often considered as affording insufficient protection against the State because foreign traders and investors often have reservations regarding the neutrality of those courts vis-à-vis foreign parties, if not even their independence and impartiality in reviewing acts of their own governments.[46]

Dispute settlement in the domestic courts of a third State was one possible reaction to these concerns. Consequently, the law of State immunity reacted to the need of economic investors for legal protection, by introducing the distinction between commercial acts (*acta iure gestionis*) and acts of a sovereign nature (*acta iure imperii*), and by allowing enforcement against assets serving a commercial purpose. Similarly, at the level of domestic law, immunity of the State from suit for regulatory activity increasingly gave way to accountability in many common and civil law countries.[47]

Notwithstanding the evolution towards more restrictive forms of jurisdictional immunity, foreign sovereign immunity still constituted a considerable obstacle for foreign investors to seek redress against many of the host State's acts outside

---

45 On insufficiencies in settling disputes in the domestic courts of the State who has interfered with a private party's interest in the setting of investment dispute see Schill (supra note 24) 33-34.

46 The institutional dependence of courts vis-à-vis the executive, both on the local as well as the national level, and the at times active interference of political interests in judicial proceedings compromise the ability of courts in a number of countries to settle investor-State disputes efficiently and impartially. This influence can stem from the power of a political party or from other government or political influence over the outcome of a specific dispute. The often insufficient financial support and lack of manpower in many developing countries further compromise efficient dispute settlement in the host State's courts. Corruption in the courts of many countries add further complications. See Eduardo Buscaglia and Maria Dakolias, 'An Analysis of the Causes of Corruption in the Judiciary' (1999) 30 Law & Pol'y Int'l Bus 95; Maria Dakolias and Kimberley L. Thachuk, 'The Problem of Eradicating Corruption from the Judiciary: Attacking Corruption in the Judiciary: A Critical Process in Judicial Reform' (2000) 18 Wis ILJ 353.

47 See references supra 44.

that State's domestic courts. Most importantly, regulatory acts of host States affecting foreign investors, including expropriations for a public purpose or administrative decisions rescinding an investment contract, constitute public acts (*acta iure imperii*), that consequently continue to benefit from sovereign immunity in third-country courts. Moreover, even if domestic courts outside the host State assume jurisdiction over foreign sovereigns, they often hesitate to review sovereign acts of foreign States.[48] For example, domestic courts often apply doctrines of judicial restraint, such as the act of State-doctrine, when it comes to determining whether the acts of a foreign sovereign were in conformity with the international commitments made by that State. Under the act of State-doctrine, for example, the US Supreme Court in *Banco Nacional de Cuba v. Sabbatino*, refused to

> [E]xamine the validity of a taking of property within its own territory by a foreign sovereign government … in the absence of a treaty or other unambiguous agreement regarding controlling legal principles, even if the complaint alleges that the taking violates customary international law.[49]

The rationale behind the act of State-doctrine, and comparable doctrines applied by domestic courts outside the United States,[50] is similar to that of the law of State immunity.[51] On the one hand, it is a consequence of the principle of State sovereignty that required mutual respect among sovereigns and thus prevented one sovereign from judging the acts of another sovereign passed in the latter's territory.[52] On the other hand, it can also be explained by the domestic separation of powers. In *Sabbatino*, for example, the US Supreme Court specifically referred to the primacy of the executive branch in matters of diplomacy and foreign affairs as a reason for exercising judicial restraint,[53] and considered that redress for violations of customary international law had to be sought primarily through traditional inter-State channels, given that domestic courts usually are not empowered to make foreign policy choices independently from the executive.[54] In view of foreign sovereign immunity doctrines, the domestic courts of the investor's home State, as well as the courts of any third State, therefore could not afford sufficient protection to foreign investors against sovereign acts of the host State.

---

48 For the State-friendly application of the Foreign Sovereign Immunities Act by the US Supreme Court see Ronald Mok, 'Expropriation Claims in United States Courts: The Act of State Doctrine, the Sovereign Immunity Doctrine, and the Foreign Sovereign Immunities Act. A Roadmap for the Expropriated Victim' (1996) 8 Pace ILR 199.
49 See Banco Nacional de Cuba v. Sabbatino, 376 U.S. 398, 428 (1964).
50 See Muthucumaraswamy Sornarajah, The Pursuit of Nationalized Property (1986) 291-299 (discussing the application of similar concepts before European Courts).
51 Ibid 279 - 282 (discussing the rationale of the act of State - doctrine).
52 See Banco Nacional de Cuba v. Sabbatino, 376 U.S. 398, 416 (1964).
53 Ibid 423.
54 See ibid 427 - 433.

At the same time, the increasing engagement of private individuals in investment activities on the territory of foreign States also cast the effectiveness of the system of diplomatic protection to afford protection to foreign investors into doubt. Diplomatic protection suffered from several shortcomings. First, diplomatic protection is a right of a State vis-à-vis another State to «ensure in the person of its nationals respect for the rules of international law»[55] without a corresponding duty of the home States to grant diplomatic protection.[56] Second, as a consequence of the distinction between domestic and international law, the home State is vested, under international law, with the exclusive control over the rights of their nationals on the international level and is entitled to settle, waive or modify the rights of their nationals by an international agreement with the host State.[57] Third, in view of the distinction between the rights of the investor and the rights of its home State any compensation received by the home State did not have to be passed on, as a matter of international law, to the damaged investor.[58] Finally, diplomatic protection required the exhaustion of local remedies by the foreign investor. This also constituted a limit to effective investment protection,

---

55 See supra note 42.
56 See already Edwin Borchard, The Diplomatic Protection of Citizens Abroad (1915) 29-30, 354, 356, 363-365; Barcelona Traction, Light and Power Company, Limited (Belgium v. Spain), Judgment, 5 February 1970, ICJ Reports 1970, 44, para. 79 (stressing the discretion States enjoy as a matter of international law in espousing claims of their nationals). Likewise, most domestic legal systems do not oblige the State to pursue claims of their nationals by means of diplomatic protection, see, for example, Rainer Hofmann, Grundrechte und grenzüberschreitende Sachverhalte (1994) 107 et seq. (regarding the situation in Germany); Abbasi v. Secretary of State for the Home Department, [2002] EWCA Civ 1598 (regarding the situation in the United Kingdom); Kaunda v. President of the Republic of South Africa, (2005) 44 ILM 173 (regarding the situation in South Africa). See also Annemarieke Vermeer-Künzli, 'Restricting Discretion: Judicial Review of Diplomatic Protection' (2006) 75 Nordic JIL 279 (2006) (discussing national jurisprudence and developments on the international level and observing an emerging development towards a State's obligation to exercise diplomatic protection in case of serious violations of human rights law). Ultimately, this discretion is the expression of the difference in the legal relation between the investor and the host State, on the one hand, and the relationship between the two States, on the other.
57 Borchard (supra note 56) 366-375. See also Juliane Hagelberg, Die völkerrechtliche Verfügungsbefugnis des Staates über Rechtsansprüche von Privatpersonen (2006) 49-52 (arguing, however, that human rights law restricts the home State's disposition over claims of its nationals, ibid 147 et seq.); similarly, Dolzer (supra note 41) 136 et seq. In practice, this entitlement has led to the settlement of international claims concerning the violation of the rights of foreigners by lump-sum agreements. See Richard B. Lillich and Burns H. Weston, International Claims: Their Settlement by Lump-Sum Agreements (1975); Burns H. Weston et al, International Claims: Their Settlement by Lump-Sum Agreements 1975-1995 (1999).
58 Borchard (supra note 56), 356-359. 383-388; Hagelberg (supra note 57) 51.

in particular when the host State's courts are not sufficiently impartial and independent in affording protection against actions of their own State.

The conclusion of international investment treaties and, in particular, access to investor-State arbitration can thus be seen as a reaction to the insufficiencies of both diplomatic protection and sovereign immunity law to afford private investors protection that is independent from the investor's home State against sovereign acts by host States. The establishment of investor-State arbitration and the rise of investment treaty arbitration are therefore *inter alia* due to the obstacles posed by the law of State immunity to efficient investment protection in domestic courts outside the host State and the insufficiencies of investment protection under traditional customary international law.

3. Towards an International Rule of Law Framework for Investor-State Relations

Both the erosion of absolute immunity and the rise of international investment law and arbitration are a reaction to changes in the underlying economic realities brought about by increasing transborder economic activities of investors and States and the multiplied potential that State conduct can be a threat to private economic activity. Both the rise of international investment law and the erosion of absolute immunity have the purpose of protecting individuals and embedding States into a system that is based on the rule of law and that aims at protecting private parties by granting access to third-party dispute resolution. Although international investment law protects the private interests of foreign investors, and the law of State immunity serves to protect the State, the common concern underlying the developments in both fields was the insufficient structure traditional international law provided for the efficient functioning of transborder economic activity and, in particular, cooperation between States and private economic actors in a global economy.

In fact, both international investment law and the law of State immunity reflect a changed understanding of sovereignty and the role of the State in relation to the individual. Both have adapted to the need to strengthen the protection of private interests vis-à-vis public power. Instead of a rigid delimitation between public spheres in inter-State relations as under the Westphalian system, both bodies of law now recognize that public and private interests require adequate protection, and that the solution to enhancing global economic exchange cannot lie in giving unconditional primacy to the determination of public interests by States in purely inter-State relations. In this sense, the rise of international investment law, on the one hand, and the erosion of State immunity are not antagonist developments, but merely two sides of the same coin in adapting international law to the needs of a truly global economy.[59] This coincides with a change of paradigm in international law from backing up sovereign equality towards more effective control of the use of public powers vis-à-vis private individuals and by embedding the exercise of that power into a framework based on the rule of law.

C. Looking at State Immunity from the Perspective of International Investment Law

Despite a common trajectory in the development of international investment law and the law of State immunity towards embedding States into a rule of law-framework for investor-State cooperation, international investment law still falls short of providing efficient investment protection in one important aspect: the enforcement of arbitral awards. Indeed, while investor-State arbitration provides a mechanism to determine whether the conduct of host States was in conformity with the commitments made to foreign investors in investment treaties or investor-State contracts, the enforcement of the decisions of investment treaty tribunals themselves is severely limited.

Although non-compliance with an ICSID award constitutes breach of Art. 53(1) of the ISCID Convention, such breach is unenforceable for the foreign investor, as Art. 55 ICSID Convention, as well as the New York Convention, completely defer to domestic law regarding enforcement immunity.[60] An investor thus remains dependent on its home State to exercise diplomatic protection in case the host State does not comply with an investment treaty award.[61] Although

---

59   For a similar argument that both State immunity and investor-State arbitration share the common thrust to move the law concerning international trade and investment from a power-based to a rules-based system of international relations with a stronger focus on the doctrinal structures of investor-State arbitration and State immunity under the US Foreign Sovereign Immunities Act, Charles H. Brower, 'Mitsubishi, Investor-State Arbitration, and the Law of State Immunity' (2005) 20 Am U ILR 907 (2005).

60   Schreuer et al (supra note 10) Art. 55, para. 13. The only way enforcement immunity under domestic law can be overcome is through a waiver of immunity by the respondent State. See Schreuer et al (supra note 10) Art. 55, paras. 72 et seq. Participation in the IC-SID Convention and consent to ICSID arbitration per se, without more, can, however, not be construed as a waiver of enforcement immunity. Cf Schreuer et al (supra note 10) Art. 55, paras. 75. See also UN Convention, Arts. 19 and 20 (requiring express consent to measures of constraint in addition to consent to jurisdiction). Some domestic courts, by contrast, have treated consent to arbitration by States as an implicit waiver of enforcement immunity. See, for example, in the context of consent to ICC arbitration the decision by the French Cour de cassation, 1e civ., 6 July 2000, Creighton v. Ministère des Finances de l'Etat du Qatar, 127 JDI 1054, 1055 (2000).

61   See supra note 9.

enforcement in third States is possible, it is equally limited because States often only maintain assets abroad that serve a public purpose, such as property belonging to diplomatic or consular missions, which is exempt from execution under State immunity doctrines.

Thus, enforcement immunity as «the last bastion of State immunity»[62] creates a loophole in the efficient protection of foreign investors. Although most States voluntarily comply with arbitral rulings against them,[63] that loophole is amply illustrated by cases of investors struggling for years to enforce an award against assets not protected by enforcement immunity. A prominent example of this struggle is the «Sedelmayer saga»,[64] involving a German investor who, after having obtained an award against the Russian Federation for breach of the German-Russian BIT in 1998, has made numerous, partly successful, partly unsuccessful, attempts at enforcement of the award. In this endeavor, he was refused satisfaction on several occasions based on foreign sovereign immunity accorded to assets he had tried to attach.[65] This illustrates how significant enforcement immunity can vitiate the aspiration of international investment law to protect foreign investors efficiently.[66]

---

62 See Draft Articles on Jurisdictional Immunities of States and Their Property, Commentary to Article 18, para. 2 (1991) ILC Ybk., Vol. II, Part Two 13, 56.
63 It is widely assumed that voluntary compliance with investment treaty awards is the rule. See Blane (supra note 9) 464 - 465 (with further references).
64 Bjorklund (supra note 11) 314 -316.
65 For the various attempts at enforcement in the Sedelmayer case see Reinisch (supra note 11) 681, 685-688. The Sedelmayer case, however, is not a singular case: according to a 2008 survey conducted by the School of International Arbitration at Queen Mary University of London out of the 19% of participants in the survey – all major corporations – who had to go through enforcement of an award against a State, 46% experienced difficulties; in 13% of these cases sovereign immunity was the reason for difficulties. See Loukas Mistelis and Crina Baltag, 'Recognition and Enforcement of Arbitral Awards and Settlement in International Arbitration: Corporate Attitudes and Practices' (2009) 19 Am Rev Int'l Arb319, 354 - 61; see also Crina Baltag, 'Enforcement of Arbitral Awards against States' (2009) 19 Am Rev Int'l Arb 391. On problems of enforcement of ICSID awards against Argentina see also Bjorklund (supra note 11) 310-314; Charity L. Goodman, 'Unchartered Waters: Financial Crisis and Enforcement of ICSID Awards in Argentina' (2007) 28 U Pa JIEL 449.
66 For the same conclusion regarding litigation in domestic courts against foreign sovereigns see Schreuer (supra note 7) 125 («Enforcement is an important corollary to jurisdiction. The assumption of jurisdiction by domestic courts over foreign States without any prospect of having the resulting decisions made effective would not only be rather half-hearted but would also largely nullify the progress made in the protection of the private claimant. In fact, allowing plaintiffs to proceed against foreign States and then to withhold from them the fruits of successful litigation through immunity from execution may put them into the doubly frustrating position of having been lured into expensive and seemingly successful lawsuits only to be left with an unenforceable judgment plus legal

There are several reactions to difficulties with the law of State immunity concerning efficient investor-State dispute settlement and enforcement.[67] Investors could simply change their expectation that successful dispute settlement does not necessarily allow them to enforce a favorable award; or conversely States may agree to waive sovereign immunity in investment treaties or investor-State contracts. The first view is rather cynic, the second at most a project for future investment treaty negotiations. The more immediate, and more practical avenue might be that domestic sovereign immunity doctrines are reinterpreted so as to meet the need for more effective investment protection. While economic incentives can pressure States to reduce the scope of their sovereign immunity doctrines applied at the domestic level, the question also arises whether substantive investment treaty obligations may have a legal impact on the law of foreign sovereign immunity applied in domestic courts.

This Part therefore analyzes whether the application of sovereign immunity to protect a State's interest at the domestic level can result in breach of substantive investment treaty obligations (I.). It concludes by suggesting that the relationship between investment protection and State immunity can be conceptualized within a framework of proportionality reasoning that is increasingly used by investment treaty tribunals (II.).

I. Application of State Immunity as Breach of Investment Treaty Obligations

Four substantive standards of international investment law could affect sovereign immunity doctrines applied in domestic courts: (1) the obligation to treat foreign investors fairly and equitably, which includes the prohibition of denial of justice;[68] (2) the obligation to provide full protection and security, which is increasingly often interpreted as requiring host States to provide, beyond physical safe-

---

costs. Voluntary compliance with foreign court decisions can be expected no more than voluntary compliance with obligations in the face of immunity from jurisdiction.»).

67 See Blane (supra note 9) 495-505.
68 Stephan Schill, 'Fair and Equitable Treatment as an Embodiment of the Rule of Law', in Rainer Hofmann and Christian J Tams (eds), The International Convention for the Settlement of Investment Disputes (ICSID): Taking Stock After 40 Years (2007) 31, 49-50, 58-59; Ali Ehsassi, 'Cain and Abel: Congruence and Conflict in the Application of the Denial of Justice Principle' in Schill (supra note 44) 213; Don Wallace, 'Fair and Equitable Treatment and Denial of Justice: Loewen v. U.S. and Chattin v. Mexico' in Todd Weiler (ed), International Investment Law and Arbitration: Leading Cases from the ICSID, NAFTA, Bilateral Treaties and Customary International Law (2005) 669. See generally on denial of justice Jan Paulsson, Denial of Justice in International Law (2005).

ty, a legal infrastructure for the effective protection of foreign investment;[69] (3) the prohibition of expropriations without compensation, which can be affected if rights are rendered worthless, even if the property title remains intact;[70] and (4) provisions in investment treaties, such as Article 10(12) of the Energy Charter Treaty (ECT), that expressly requires that «[e]ach Contracting Party shall ensure that its domestic law provides effective means for the assertion of claims and the enforcement of rights with respect to investments, investment agreements, and investment authorizations.»[71]

The precise scope of many of these investor's rights, however, is still unsettled, given that investment treaties and investor-State arbitration are a relatively novel phenomenon. In particular, the issue of whether the grant of foreign sovereign immunity constitutes breach of an investment treaty has not been raised or decided in an investment treaty arbitration or in domestic court proceedings.[72] Nevertheless, there is arbitral jurisprudence dealing with questions of access to domestic courts and enforcement of commercial arbitration awards that may give an indication of how substantive investment law can affect questions of foreign

---

69 See Helge Zeitler, 'Full Protection and Security' in Schill (supra note 44) 183, 196-198; Andrew Newcombe and Lluís Paradell, Law and Practice of Investment Treaties – Standards of Treatment (2009) § 6.45.

70 In international law it is generally recognized that an unreasonable destruction of the value of an investment, even without affecting the property title, can constitute an indirect or de facto expropriation. See George C. Christie, 'What Constitutes a Taking of Property Under International Law?' (1962) 38 BYBIL 307; Burns H. Weston, '«Constructive Takings» under International Law' (1975) 16 Va JIL 103; Rosalyn Higgins, 'The Taking of Property by the State: Recent Developments in International Law' (1982) 176 Recueil des Cours 259, 322 et seq.; Rudolf Dolzer, 'Indirect Expropriation of Alien Property' (1986) 1 ICSID Rev - FILJ 41; Thomas W. Wälde and Abba Kolo, 'Environmental Regulation, Investment Protection and «Regulatory Taking» in International Law' (2001) 50 ICLQ 811; L. Yves Fortier and Stephen L. Drymer, 'Indirect Expropriation in the Law of International Investment' (2004) 19 ICSID Rev - FILJ 293; Andrew Newcombe, 'The Boundaries of Regulatory Expropriation' (2005) 20 ICSID Rev - FILJ 1; Campbell McLachlan et al, International Investment Arbitration – Substantive Principles (2007) 291-313; Markus Perkams, 'The Concept of Indirect Expropriation in Comparative Public Law - Searching for Light in the Dark', in Schill (supra note 44) 107.

71 A similar provision is contained in Article II(7) of the Treaty between the United States of America and the Republic of Ecuador concerning the Encouragement and Reciprocal Protection of Investment, signed 27 August 1993, entered into force 11 May 1997 («Each Party shall provide effective means of asserting claims and enforcing rights with respect to investment, investment agreements, and investment authorizations.»).

72 Problems that have arisen in the enforcement of investment treaty awards so far have not concerned the question of how investment treaty obligations may influence enforcement, but have only concerned the interrelations between the procedural framework, namely the ICSID Convention, and enforcement. In all, only four cases have arisen in domestic courts so far concerning enforcement of ICSID awards. See Edward Baldwin et al, 'Limits to Enforcement of ICSID Awards' (2006) 23 J Int Arb 1, 5 - 9.

sovereign immunity. This arbitral jurisprudence will be examined in this section, starting with questions relating to jurisdictional immunity (1.), and turning to enforcement immunity thereafter (2.).

It is, however, important to realize the limitations of the direct impact investment treaty obligations can have on the application of State immunity at the domestic level. First, awards for damages rendered on the basis that State immunity doctrines are in breach of investment treaty obligations face itself the enforcement limitations under the ICSID or the New York Convention. Second, and more importantly, the impact of substantive investment treaty obligations will regularly be limited to the application of immunity from jurisdiction and enforcement in host States themselves. The reason for this is that the application of State immunity by third States regularly would not come under the scope of application of an investment treaty as no investment has been made in that third State.

Nevertheless, investment treaty obligations requiring the reduction in scope of immunity doctrines with respect to the host State itself could nevertheless pressure States more generally to bring their domestic legal orders in line with investment treaty obligations as all States are potential respondents in investment treaty arbitrations. Furthermore, investment treaty obligations may also indirectly impact the law of foreign sovereign immunity as applied by domestic courts because in many States foreign sovereign immunity doctrines and domestic sovereign immunity doctrines align.[73]

1. Jurisdictional Immunities in Investment Treaty Arbitration

Jurisdictional immunities played a role in the NAFTA arbitration in *Mondev v. United States*.[74] The tribunal was faced with the question of whether a statutory immunity granted under Massachussetts law to certain public bodies for various intentional torts was in breach of the obligation to grant full protection and security contained in Art. 1105(1) of NAFTA. It observed:

> In the Tribunal's opinion, circumstances can be envisaged where the conferral of a general immunity from suit for conduct of a public authority affecting a NAFTA investment could amount to a breach of Article 1105(1) of NAFTA. Indeed the United States implicitly accepted as much. It did not argue that public authorities could, for example, be given immunity in contract vis-à-vis NAFTA investors and investments.[75]

---

73   See Fox (supra note 6) 59-61.
74   Mondev International Ltd. v. United States of America, ICSID Case No.ARB(AF)/99/2 (NAFTA), Award, 11 October 2002, paras. 139-156.
75   Ibid para. 151.

The tribunal therefore accepted that full protection and security was affected when States applied sovereign immunity doctrines to prevent access to its domestic courts. It also observed, however, that

> [R]easons can well be imagined why a legislature might decide to immunize a regulatory authority, mandated to deal with commercial redevelopment plans, from potential liability for tortious interference. Such an authority will necessarily have both detailed knowledge of the relevant contractual relations and the power to interfere in those relations by granting or not granting permissions. If sued, it will be able to plead that it was acting in good faith and in the exercise of a legitimate mandate – but such a claim may well not justify summary dismissal and will thus be a triable issue, with consequent distraction to the work of the Authority.[76]

The tribunal therefore accepted that considerations relating to the effectiveness of governmental regulation and administration could justify restricting access to domestic courts in specific cases. While holding that the grant of sovereign immunity in the case at hand did not breach Art. 1105(1) of NAFTA, the tribunal also stressed that the statutory immunity in question would not apply in NAFTA arbitration and could not shield the host State from investor-State arbitration.[77] This reasoning suggests that the fact that the investor had a remedy available in investor-State arbitration, and therefore could enforce its rights in a forum outside domestic courts, had a positive impact on the assessment of the statutory immunity under the obligation to grant full protection and security to foreign investors.

The tribunal's reasoning therefore suggests that the obligation to provide full protection and security requires States to grant access to justice to foreign investors, be it at the domestic or the international level.[78] This right is affected when States apply sovereign immunity doctrines to prevent access to their courts. The tribunal's reasoning, however, also shows that access to domestic courts is not

---

76   Ibid para. 153.

77   Ibid para. 154 (stating that «such an immunity could not protect a NAFTA State Party from a claim for conduct which was substantively in breach of NAFTA standards – but for this NAFTA provides its own remedy, since it gives an investor the right to go directly to international arbitration in respect of conduct occurring after NAFTA's entry into force. In a Chapter 11 arbitration, no local statutory immunity would apply.»).

78   This reasoning is also in line with customary international law on denial of justice. A prohibition of suits against the treasury, for example, was held to constitute a denial of justice under customary international law Case of Ruden & Co (US v. Peru), Decision, 18 January 1870 (1898) 2 Moore Int'l Arb 1653, 1655; Case of R.T. Johnson (US v. Peru) (1898) 2 Moore Int'l Arb 1656, 1657. The same obligation, that is to grant access to domestic courts, also derives from the fair and equitable treatment standard. This standard, inter alia, can be violated «if Claimants were denied access to [domestic] courts . . . or if the Claimants were treated unfairly in those courts (denial of procedural justice) or if the judgment of those courts were substantively unfair (denial of substantive justice).». See Compañía de Aguas del Aconquija SA & Compagnie Générale des Eaux v Argentine Republic ICSID Case No. ARB/97/3, Award, 21 November 2000, para. 80.

unconditional; instead, host States can limit access to their courts to pursue legitimate public policy grounds. Although the case related to domestic sovereign immunity, there is no reason not to apply the same conceptual framework also to foreign sovereign immunity cases. However, just as in domestic immunity cases, the questionwould need to be asked if granting foreign sovereign immunity pursues a legitimate aim in the case at hand.

2. Obstacles to Enforcement as a Breach of Investment Treaty Obligations

Not only immunity from jurisdiction can breach investment treaty obligations, but also the application of immunity as a defense against the enforcement of arbitral awards. Thus, in *Desert Line v. Yemen*, the tribunal found a violation of a provision of the Yemen-Oman BIT containing the obligation to provide fair and equitable treatment and the prohibition of discriminatory and legally unjustified measures because the Respondent had pressured the Claimant to accept lesser payment in satisfaction of the sums due under an arbitral award, which the Claimant had obtained against the respondent State.[79] In consequence, in the tribunal's reasoning, the obligation to provide fair and equitable treatment and not to subject investors to discriminatory and legally unjustified measures required the host State to comply with and enforce the arbitral award in question.[80] While the award in question was an award rendered in the context of a commercial arbitration, the same would seem to apply, mutatis mutandis, to the enforcement of an investment treaty award.

79 Desert Line Projects LLC v. The Republic of Yemen, ICSID Case No.ARB/05/17, Award, 5 February 2008, para. 193 (stating that «the conduct of the Respondent, by inadmissibly pressuring the Claimant to accept and execute the Settlement Agreement instead of the final and binding Yemeni Arbitral Award, amounted to a breach of Art. 3 of the BIT»). Similarly, the Claimant in Romak v. Uzbekistan argued that the nonenforcement by Ukranian courts of a commercial arbitration award entered into against a State-owned company constituted breach of the provisions of the Swiss-Uzbek BIT, notably the prohibition of expropriation without compensation, fair and equitable treatment and the treaty's umbrella clause; see Romak S.A. v. The Republic of Uzbekistan, PCA Case No. AA280, UNCITRAL, Award, 26 November 2009, paras. 12 - 70, 133 - 138). The tribunal, however, declined jurisdiction ratione materiae because it considered that Claimant in the case at hand had not made an investment in Ukraine. Non-execution of domestic court judgments was also considered as a denial of justice in Waguih Elie George Siag and Clorinda Vecchi v. The Arab Republic of Egypt, ICSID Case No.ARB/05/15, Award, 1 June 2009, para. 454.

80 Also under customary international law the concept of denial of justice included the obligation of State authorities not to refuse execution of judgments or to postpone execution indefinitely Montano Case (Peru v. US), Opinion, 27 May 1855 (1898) 2 Moore Int'l Arb 1630, 1635); Fabiani case (France v. Venzuela), Award, 30 December 1896 (1898) 5 Moore Int'l Arb 4878, 4893 - 4897.

Similarly, in *Saipem v. Bangladesh,* the issue arose whether conduct of the domestic courts of the host State that interfered with an ICC arbitration between a foreign investor and an entity owned by the respondent State, and which ultimately compromised the enforcement of the arbitral award, constituted breach of the prohibition of expropriation without compensation in the Italy-Bangladesh BIT.[81] In the case at hand, Bangladeshi courts had issued not only an injunction restraining Claimant from continuing the arbitration, but also revoked the authority of the arbitral tribunal to entertain the case. When the arbitral tribunal proceeded with issuing a final award in favor of claimant for approx. US$ 6 million, stating that the authority to challenge and replace arbitrators fell into the exclusive jurisdiction of the ICC, the Bangladeshi court declared the award to be a nullity and unenforceable.

The ICSID tribunal seized of the matter found that the measures of the Bangladeshi courts constituted an expropriation because the investor was prevented from enforcing the award against assets of the Respondent located in Bangladesh. The tribunal found this to constitute an expropriation «[b]ecause, by the Respondent's own admission, the ICC Award could not be enforced outside Bangladesh.»[82] Even though the issue at hand did not concern a decision of domestic courts refusing enforcement of an enforceable award as such, its effects were comparable. The tribunal's reasoning, in principle, therefore would equally apply when a domestic court refuses enforcement of an enforceable arbitral award based on sovereign immunity.

Finally, applying enforcement immunity at the domestic level could also contravene provisions, such as Article II(7) of the United States-Ecuador BIT, or Article 10(12) ECT, that requires «[e]ach Party [to] provide effective means of asserting claims and enforcing rights with respect to investment, investment agreements, and investment authorizations.» While one tribunal considered that such provisions only impose systemic obligations on States to «provide an effective framework or system for the enforcement of rights, but does not offer guarantees in individual cases,»[83] other tribunals faced with interpreting similar provisions considered that such an obligation required that remedies in domestic

---

81 For the facts of the case see Saipem S.p.A. v. The People's Republic of Bangladesh, ICSID Case No.ARB/05/7, Award, 30 June 2009, paras. 6 – 51. The issue was framed in terms of expropriation because the dispute settlement clause in the Italian-Bangladesh BIT was restricted to «disputes arising between a Contracting Party and the investors of the other, relating to compensation for expropriation, nationalization, requisition or similar measures including disputes relating to the amount of the relevant payments.» See ibid para. 97.

82 Ibid para. 130.

83 Limited Liability Company Amto v. Ukraine, SCC Case No. 080/2005, Final Award, 26 March 2008, para. 88 (continuing that «[i]ndividual failures might be evidence of systematic inadequacies, but are not themselves a breach of Article 10(12) [ECT]»).

courts were available to foreign investors and that rights could be effectively enforced in every individual case.[84] The tribunal in *Chevron v. Ecuador*, for example, considered that such a provision «applie[d] to a variety of State conduct that has an effect on the ability of an investor to assert claims or enforce rights.»[85] Similarly, in *Petrobart v. Kyrgyz Republic*, the tribunal found a breach of Article 10(12) ECT because a domestic court in the respondent State had stayed the execution of a domestic judgment following an *ex parte* communication from the Vice Prime Minister asking for a stay of enforcement of a court decision against a State-owned company in order to allow debt restructuring.[86] A comparable reasoning, in principle, would also apply when sovereign immunity is applied to avoid enforcement of an arbitral award. At the same time, however, a tribunal would need to consider whether a legitimate public interest was pursued in refusing enforcement of an arbitral award based on sovereign immunity.

II. Proportionality Analysis as an Overarching Framework for Balancing Private and Public Interests in International Investment Law

The above mentioned decisions of investment treaty tribunals illustrate that the application of enforcement immunity and immunity from jurisdiction at the domestic level may touch upon various investment treaty standards. Although, none of the decisions concerned the application of foreign sovereign immunity doctrines, they deal with situations in which the attempt of an investor to access domestic courts or to have a judicial or arbitral decision enforced was effectively eviscerated by various executive, legislative, or judicial measures. From an economic perspective such conduct is equivalent in its effects to the application of foreign sovereign immunity doctrines as a bar to jurisdiction and enforcement.

---

84 Petrobart Limited v. Kyrgyz Republic, SCC Arb No. 126/2003, 77; Chevron Corporation (USA) and Texaco Petroleum Company (USA) v.The Republic of Ecuador, PCA Case No. 34877; UNCITRAL, Partial Award on the Merits, 30 March 2010, paras. 247; see also Duke Energy Electroquil Partners & Electroquil S.A. v. Republic of Ecuador, ICSID Case No. ARB/04/19, Award, 18 August 2008, paras. 390 - 403.

85 Chevron v. Ecuador (supra note 84), para. 248.

86 Petrobart v. Kyrgyz Republic (supra note 84) 77 (for the facts of the case see ibid 4 - 8). Even if provisions like Art. 10(12) ECT are only viewed as requiring States to provide a legislative framework for the effective protection of rights of foreign investors, such a reading would equally affect how States fashion their sovereign immunity doctrines, as these doctrines are of general application in the whole of the domestic court system. To the extent that sovereign immunity doctrines applied at the domestic level constitute a systemic deficiency in the enforcement of rights, provisions such as Art. 10(12) ECT would require a State to «tak[e] the appropriate steps to identify and address deficiencies in its legislation» and to «moderniz[e] and adap[t] [its legislation] from time to time.» See Amto v. Ukraine (supra note 83), p. 88.

As regards the rights granted under investment treaties, sovereign immunity, in principle, should be treated no differently from other instruments resulting in a denial of access to courts or other obstacles to enforcement.

Yet, treating sovereign immunity and other bars to jurisdiction and enforcement prima facie alike, does not mean that sovereign immunity doctrines could not be viewed as justified departures from investors' rights laid down in investment treaties and, in consequence, would not trigger the State's liability for breach of an investment treaty. Arguably, the same conceptual framework would apply to a State invoking immunity as would to a State invoking any other public interest to defend against a claim for damages. Reliance by a State on immunity, in others words, should be analyzed according to the same legal framework as that used by arbitral tribunals to determine a State's liability under investment treaties for any other measure that interferes with a foreign investment.

In that context, it bears noting that most of the standard rights granted under investment treaties, in particular fair and equitable treatment, full protection and security, or the prohibition of expropriations without compensation, are not understood by arbitral tribunals as absolute guarantees. Rather, most investment-treaty tribunals recognize that, in interpreting investment treaty standards, a balance needs to be struck between the private interests of foreign investors and the public interests of host States, for example by applying proportionality analysis.[87] In doing so, they recognize that interferences with interests of foreign investors based on legitimate public policy grounds, which are applied in a non-discriminatory manner and are proportional to the impact on the foreign investors, in principle, do not entitle the investor to damages.

The underlying idea of balancing private and public interests arguably could also be used in order to resolve the tension between international investment law and the effective protection of foreign investments, on the one hand, and the law of State immunity and the protection of interests of States, on the other. Proportionality analysis arguably helps to curtail abuses of State powers in invoking State immunity, while allowing to defendthe public interest against claims for protection of private interests. Under a proportionality framework, the relation between international investment law and the law of State immunity becomes less a question of how two bodies of international law relate to each other, but how the interests protected by the respective bodies of law relate to each other.

---

87 See Benedict Kingsbury and Stephan Schill, 'Investor-State Arbitration, Fair and Equitable Treatment, Proportionality, and the Emerging Administrative Law of Global Governance' (2009) IILJ Working Paper 2009/6 (Global Administrative Law Series) 30 - 40, at http://www.iilj.org/publications/documents/2009-6.KingsburySchill.pdf; Alec Stone Sweet, 'Investor-State Arbitration: Proportionality's New Frontier' (2010) 4(1) Law & Ethics of Human Rights 47, at http://www.bepress.com/lehr/vol4/iss1/art4.

Proportionality analysis thus also becomes a tool of defragmentation of international law.

In order to further develop this argument and to illustrate how precisely proportionality analysis can be applied as an interpretative tool to balance the interests of foreign investors and States in the context of sovereign immunity, this paper now turns to analyzing the jurisprudence of the ECtHR on how rights granted under the ECHR interact with public interests protected by sovereign immunity, including foreign sovereign immunity in a number of cases.

D. Taking a Human Rights Perspective on State Immunity: Proportionality Analysis in the Jurisprudence of the ECtHR

So far investment treaty arbitration has not directly dealt with the law of State immunity, and domestic courts have not looked towards international investment law when applying sovereign immunity at the domestic level as a bar either to jurisdiction or to enforcement of judicial and arbitral decisions. In other international legal regimes, by contrast, in particular under the ECtHR, the tension between sovereign immunity and the protection of individual rights has been dealt with in more detail. This section, therefore, analyzes the jurisprudence of the ECtHR on matters of immunity as potential guidance for how the relationship between sovereign immunity and international investment law could be conceptualized and concretized and whether, and under what circumstances, the application of sovereign immunity at the domestic level results in a breach of investment treaty standards.

Such a cross-regime analysis between international investment law and human rights relies on the conviction that both bodies of law are functionally comparable: they are both public law disciplines that aim at limiting governmental power in light of rights granted to private actors and that are implemented by means of international dispute settlement to which affected individuals have direct access.[88] Both international investment law and human rights therefore share the

---

88 See on the understanding of international investment law as a public law discipline and on investor-State arbitration as a mechanism similar to administrative or constitutional review Stephan Schill, 'International Investment Law and Comparative Public Law – An Introduction' in Schill (supra note 44) 3, 10-17. On this conceptualization of international investment law and the appropriateness of drawing inspiration from human rights law see also International Thunderbird Gaming Corp v. United Mexican States, UNCITRAL/NAFTA, Arbitral Award, 26 January 2006, Separate Opinion by Thomas Wälde, para. 13 («. . . more appropriate for investor-state arbitration are analogies with judicial review relating to governmental conduct—be it international judicial review (as carried out by the WTO dispute panels and Appellate Body, by the European- or Inter-American Human Rights Courts or the European Court of Justice) or national administrative courts

common aim of holding governments to rule of law standards and of sanctioning the abuse of public powers. In light of these commonalities, the potential for mutual learning between both bodies of international law is considerable.[89] A cross-regime analysis also appears useful, because, as will be shown in this Part, there are undeniable parallels between the principles of international investment law and the rights granted under the ECHR concerning access to justice in domestic courts and enforcement of arbitral decisions.

Against this background, this Part first analyzes the jurisprudence of the ECtHR concerning issues of State immunity (I.), and then focuses on the Court's proportionality reasoning as a framework for harmonizing human rights and State immunity (II.). This cross-regime analysis suggests that international investment law can draw inspiration from the interpretative methods and concepts used by the ECtHR, whose jurisprudence in many fields is further advanced and more mature than the arbitral jurisprudence in the rather young field of investment treaty arbitration. Certainly, human rights jurisprudence can only directly be relevant for the interpretation of investment treaties to the extent it is applicable law between the parties to the proceedings. Yet, even independent of the applicability of human rights law in investor-State arbitrations, human rights law can provide «guidance by analogy»[90] as to possible interpretations of rights granted under investment treaties, including fair and equitable treatment or full protection and security, as regards State immunity law.

judging the disputes of individual citizens' [sic] over alleged abuse by public bodies of their governmental powers. In all those situations, at issue is the abuse of governmental power towards a private party that did and could legitimately trust in governmental assurances it received; in commercial arbitration on the other hand it is rather a good-faith interpretation of contractual provisions that is at stake. Abuse of governmental powers is not an issue in commercial arbitration, but it is at the core of the good-governance standards embodied in investment protection treaties. The issue is to keep a government from abusing its role as sovereign and regulator after having made commitments.»).

89   For this reason cross-regime analyses of international investment law and human rights law are on the rise. Their aim is mostly to concretize the understanding of the often vague concepts of international investment law, or even reform international investment law so that it can deal more adequately with the conflicts between private and public interests. See, for example, Ursula Kriebaum, Eigentumsschutz im Völkerrecht (2008) 549-573; Freya Baetens, 'Discrimination on the Basis of Nationality: Determining Likeness in Human Rights and Investment Law' in Schill (supra note 44) 279; Ehsassi (supra note 68); William Burke-White and Andreas von Staden, 'The Need for Public Law Standards of Review in Investor-State Arbitrations' in Schill (supra note 44) 689; see also the contributions in Dupuy (supra note 5).

90   Mondev v. United States (supra note 74), para. 144.

I. Immunity as a Breach of Rights Granted under the Convention

Issues, including the application of State immunity, that international investment law deals with under the headings of fair and equitable treatment, full protection and security, the prohibition of expropriation without compensation, and special clauses requiring effective means for enforcing rights, are dealt with under the ECHR Convention as matters affecting the right to property in Art. 1 of Protocol 1 and the fair trial-principle in Art.6(1) ECHR. Both of these rights have also been applied by the ECtHR to deal with matters of immunity.

In order to draw parallels between international investment law and human rights law, this section first discusses the substantive standards in the ECHR that are affected when jurisdictional or enforcement immunities are applied (1.). It then turns to the ECtHR's jurisprudence on jurisdictional immunities (2.), before discussing the Court's specific case law concerning sovereign immunity and its relations to the rights granted under the ECHR (3.). The Court's jurisprudence is particularly instructive as regards the methodology applied by the Court.

1. Access to Justice and Protection of Property in ECtHR Jurisprudence

Since its landmark decision in *Golder v. United Kingdom* the ECtHR consistently interprets Art. 6(1) ECHR as guaranteeing individuals access to a domestic court, even though that right does not appear expressly in the text of the Convention.[91] Yet, the Court argued, a guarantee to access to courts was necessarily implied as otherwise the procedural guarantees laid down in Art. 6(1) ECHR concerning fairness, publicity, and promptness in the decision-making of courts would be meaningless.[92] Similarly, the ECtHR considers that Art. 6(1) ECHR grants a right to individuals to have judicial decisions enforced, as otherwise the right to access to a court «would be illusory if a Contracting State's domestic legal system allowed a final, binding judicial decision to remain inoperative to the

---

91   ECHR, Art. 6(1) provides:
    In the determination of his civil rights and obligations or of any criminal charge against him, everyone is entitled to a fair and public hearing within a reasonable time by an independent and impartial tribunal established by law. Judgment shall be pronounced publicly but the press and public may be excluded from all or part of the trial in the interests of morals, public order or national security in a democratic society, where the interests of juveniles or the protection of the private life of the parties so require, or to the extent strictly necessary in the opinion of the court in special circumstances where publicity would prejudice the interests of justice.

92   Golder v. United Kingdom, Judgment, 21 February 1975, ECHR Series A No. 18, paras. 28-36; most recently confirmed in Cudak v. Lithuania (supra note 30) para. 54.

detriment of one party.»[93] In consequence, a State is required under Art. 6(1) ECHR «to make use of all available legal means at its disposal in order to enforce a final court decision ... and that the overall enforcement system is effective both in law and in practice.»[94] Likewise, the ECtHR held that the non-execution of judgments constituted breach of Art. 1 of Protocol 1.[95]

Art. 6(1) ECHR also has been applied in relation to arbitration. Thus, the ECtHR considers that access to arbitration satisfies the obligations of Member States to grant individuals access to justice.[96] Likewise, the Court has held that a State that declares an arbitral award void by subsequent legislation and thereby changes the effects of an arbitral award rendered against it breached Art. 6(1) ECHR.[97] Finally, in *Regent v. Ukraine*, the ECtHR considered that continued non-enforcement of an arbitration award against a Ukrainian company, which was 99.9%-owned by the State, constituted breach of Art. 6(1) ECHR.[98] In *Regent v. Ukraine*, the Court also found that non-enforcement of a commercial arbitration award constituted breach of Art. 1 of Protocol 1.[99] In consequence, a Member State of the ECHR is required, not only as regards judicial decisions, but also in relation to arbitral awards, «to make use of all available legal means at its disposal in order to enforce a binding arbitration award providing it contains a sufficiently established claim amounting to a possession [and] must make sure that ... the overall system [for enforcement] is effective both in law and in practice.»[100] The parallels to the investment treaty decisions in *Desert Line v. Yemen*,[101] *Saipem v. Bangladesh*,[102] or *Mondev v. United States*[103] regarding access to justice and enforcement of awards are undeniable.

93   Hornsby v. Greece, Judgment, 19 March 1997, ECHR 1997-II, para. 40; see also Immobiliare Saffi v. Italy, Judgment, 28 July 1999, ECHR 1999-V, paras. 69-75 (unduly long stay of execution violates Art. 6(1) ECHR); Jasiūnienė v. Lithuania, Judgment, 6 March 2003, paras. 28-31; Satka and Others v. Greece, Judgment, 27 March 2003, para. 57.
94   Marčić and Others v. Serbia, Judgment, 30 October 2007, para. 56.
95   Immobiliare Saffi v. Italy (supra note 93) paras. 49-59.
96   Lithgow and Others v. United Kingdom, Judgment, 8 July 1986, ECHR Series A No. 102, para. 201; reiterated in Regent v. Ukraine, Judgment, 3 April 2008, para. 54.
97   Stran Greek Refineries and Stratis Andreadis v. Greece, Judgment, 9 December 1994, ECHR Series A No. 301-B, paras. 46-50.
98   Regent v. Ukraine (supra note 96) paras. 59-60.
99   Ibid para. 61.
100 Kin-Stib and Majkić v. Serbia, Judgment, 20 April 2010, para. 83.
101 See supra notes 79-80.
102 See supra notes 81-82.
103 See supra notes 74-77.

2. Immunity from Jurisdiction in ECtHR Jurisprudence

The ECtHR has also had a chance to consider whether the grant of immunity from jurisdiction in domestic courts breached Art. 6(1) ECHR. In *Fayed v. United Kingdom*,[104] the applicants were barred in the United Kingdom from bringing libel actions against inspectors appointed under the Companies Act 1985 who had delivered a report on the takeover of a major group of department stores. The inspectors' report contained statements that the applicants considered as damaging to their reputation.[105] They did not, however, dispose of a judicial remedy under English law, because domestic courts could only review the report for illegality, irrationality, and procedural impropriety, but, in principle, not for mistake of facts.[106] Libel actions against the inspectors, in turn, were entirely excluded because of an immunity granted under English law.[107]

In determining the conformity of this immunity, the ECtHR observed that

> [I]t would not be consistent with the rule of law in a democratic society or with the basic principle underlying Article 6 para. 1 (art. 6-1) ... if ... a State could, without restraint or control by the Convention enforcement bodies, remove from the jurisdiction of the courts a whole range of civil claims or confer immunities from civil liability on large groups or categories of persons.[108]

At the same time, however, the Court emphasized that the rights granted under Art. 6(1) ECHR were not absolute, but left room for States to impose restrictions that reflect «a fair balance between the demands of the general interest of the community and the requirements of the protection of the individual's fundamental rights.»[109]

For the Court, this balance referred to the proportionality of an interference with the applicants' right to access to court in light of the purpose of the interference pursued; at the same time, the ECtHR granted a margin of appreciation to the Contracting State. Thus, in *Fayed*, the Court observed that

---

104 Fayed v. United Kingdom, Judgment, 21 September 1990, ECHR Series A No. 294-B.
105 Ibid para. 64.
106 Ibid paras. 44 - 45.
107 Ibid para. 42. The Court regularly also stresses that jurisdictional immunity needs to be distinguished from the lack of a cause of action under the domestic law of the respondent State. Only proper immunities touch upon Art. 6(1) ECHR, while the lack of a cause of action does not. Z and Others v. United Kingdom, Judgment, 10 May 2001, paras.94 - 100; Roche v. United Kingdom, Judgment, 10 October 2005, para. 124. Under Art. 6(1) ECHR the Court therefore may not create a substantive right which has no legal basis in the State concerned. See Roche v. United Kingdom, ibid, paras. 116 - 117; Markovic and Others v. Italy, Judgment, 14 December 2006, para. 93.
108 Fayed v. United Kingdom (supra note 104) para. 65 (internal citation omitted); similarly, Markovic and Others v. Italy (supra note 107) para. 97; Cudak v. Lithuania (supra note 30) para. 58.
109 Fayed v. United Kingdom (supra note 104) para. 65.

> [T]he Contracting States enjoy a certain margin of appreciation, but the final decision as to observance of the Convention's requirements rests with the Court. It must be satisfied that the limitations applied do not restrict or reduce the access left to the individual in such a way or to such an extent that the very essence of the right is impaired.
>
> Furthermore, a limitation will not be compatible with Article 6 para. 1 (art. 6-1) if it does not pursue a legitimate aim and if there is not a reasonable relationship of proportionality between the means employed and the aim sought to be achieved.[110]

In applying this proportionality analysis to the case at hand, the Court found that protecting inspectors, whose mandate under the Companies Act aimed at «ensuring the overall soundness and credibility of the country's company law structures,»[111] from libel actions was justified by an «overriding interest of social importance.»[112] The Court also considered that the rights and reputational interests of companies subject to inspection, and of their shareholders, were sufficiently protected because the investigations under the Companies Act had to conform to a strict legal framework, which also included procedural safeguards during the inspection proceedings.[113]

Furthermore, the Court stressed the margin of appreciation accorded to the State:

> It is not, however, for the Court to substitute its own view for that of the national legislature as to what would be the most appropriate policy in this regard. The risk of some uncompensated damage to reputation is inevitable if independent investigators in circumstances such as those of the present case are to have the necessary freedom to report without fear, not only to the authorities but also in the final resort to the public. It is in the first place for the national authorities to determine the extent to which the individual's interest in full protection of his or her reputation should yield to the requirements of the community's interest in independent investigation of the affairs of large public companies.[114]

Proportionality analysis also figured prominently in other cases before the Court relating to immunities, Thus, the Court in several other cases found that immunity for members of parliament from suit by persons who considered they had been wronged by the words or deeds of such members, in principle, constituted a proportional restriction of the right to access to court that «pursued the legitimate aims of protecting free speech in Parliament and maintaining the separation of powers between the legislature and the judiciary.»[115] Such an immunity,

---

110   Ibid (quoting Lithgow and Others v. UnitedKingdom (supra note 96) para. 194). The Court already had set out proportionality analysis combined with the margin of appreciation doctrine in Ashingdane v. United Kingdom, Judgment, 28 May 1985, para. 57.

111   Fayed v. United Kingdom (supra note 104) para. 69.

112   Ibid para. 70.

113   Ibid para. 78.

114   Ibid para. 81.

115   A v. United Kingdom, Judgment, 17 December 2002, ECHR 2002-X 294-B, paras. 75-87 (quote at para. 77). See most recently also Kart v. Turkey, Judgment, 3 December 2009, paras. 49-114.

however, could not encompass cases where no clear link existed between the parliamentarian's conduct and a parliamentary activity, as this would result in a disproportionate restriction of the right to access to courts.[116]

There are also other instances in which the Court found that domestic immunity from jurisdiction breached Art. 6(1) ECHR because it was overly broad and did not allow for a differentiated application to the circumstances of each individual case. Thus, in *Osman v. United Kingdom* the Court found a general immunity of the police from suit for negligence in connection with the investigation and suppression of crime to be disproportional because the immunity did not permit to take into account the circumstances of each individual case.[117] Similarly, the Court found that Art. 6(1) ECHR was breached in case a government could block individuals from accessing courts simply by issuing national security certificates. In the Court's view «[t]he right guaranteed to an applicant under Article 6 § 1 of the Convention to submit a dispute to a court or tribunal in order to have a determination of questions of both fact and law cannot be displaced by the *ipse dixit* of the executive.»[118]

Overall, the cases dealing with various forms of domestic immunities as a bar to access to courts illustrate that proportionality analysis can be a way to reach balanced decisions, allowing States to protect public interests and to accord them primacy over the rights of individuals, while limiting such interferences to measures that pursue a legitimate aim and do not restrict individual rights more than necessary.

3. Foreign Sovereign Immunity in ECtHR Jurisprudence

Unlike investment treaty tribunals, the ECtHR has entertained several cases in which the applicants invoked that the application of foreign sovereign immunity to bar jurisdiction and enforcement of judicial decisions breached Art. 6(1) ECHR and Art. 1 of Protocol 1. Like in the domestic immunity cases discussed above, the ECtHR applied a proportionality test to balance the right of the indi-

---

116 In consequence, the Court found breach of Art. 6(1) ECHR in a number of cases despite because of parliamentary immunity under domestic law. See Cordova v. Italy (No. 1), Judgment, 30 January 2003, ECHR 2003-I, paras. 48-66; Cordova v. Italy (No. 2), Judgment, 30 January 2003, ECHR 2003-I, paras.58-67; Tsalkitzis v. Greece, Judgment, 16 November 2006, paras.45-51; C.G.I.L. and Cofferati v. Italy, Judgment, 24 February 2009, paras. 62-80.

117 Osman v. United Kingdom, Judgment, 28 October 1998, para. 151.

118 Tinnelly & Sons Ltd. And Others and McElduff and Others v. United Kingdom, Judgment, 10 July 1998, ECHR 1998-IV, para. 77. Similarly, Devlin v. United Kingdom, Judgment, 30 January 2001, para. 31.

vidual to access to justice with the interest protected by the law of State immunity, asking whether the immunity served a legitimate purpose and was proportional in the case at hand. Unlike in domestic immunity cases, the Court, however, supplemented its analysis on foreign sovereign immunity with a reference to the international law aspects of sovereign immunity. In case of foreign sovereign immunity the Court thus added that

> [t]he Convention, including Article 6, cannot be interpreted in a vacuum. The Court must be mindful of the Convention's special character as a human rights treaty, and it must also take the relevant rules of international law into account. The Convention should so far as possible be interpreted in harmony with other rules of international law of which it forms part, including those relating to the grant of State immunity.[119]

In doing so, the Court considered that granting foreign sovereign immunity as a bar to jurisdiction or enforcement, in principle, pursued the legitimate aim of complying with international law and of promoting comity and good relations between States.

Thus, in a first set of cases, the Court accepted that the grant of immunity from jurisdiction in domestic courts to an international organization in Germany was not a breach of Art. 6(1) ECHR. Applying the proportionality framework developed under Art. 6(1) ECHR in the context of domestic immunity cases, the Court considered that «the attribution of privileges and immunities to international organisations is an essential means of ensuring the proper functioning of such organisations free from unilateral interference by individual governments.»[120] Such grant, however, also needed to be proportional in the circumstances of the particular case.[121] The Court thus stressed that by attributing competences to an international organization, the Contracting States were not absolved from their responsibility to ensure the fundamental rights granted by the ECHR.[122] In the context of Art. 6(1) ECHR, however, this did not necessarily mean that applicants had to have access to domestic courts when affected by measures of that international organization. Instead, in the Court's view it was

---

119 See Al-Adsani v. United Kingdom, Judgment, 21 November 2001, ECHR 2001-XI, para. 55 (citing Loizidou v. Turkey, Judgment, 18 December 1996, ECHR 1996-VI, para. 43); Fogarty v. United Kingdom, Judgment, 21 November 2001, ECHR 2001-XI, para. 35; McElhinney v. Ireland, Judgment, 21 November 2001, ECHR 2001-XI, para. 36. For discussion of these cases see Emmanuel Voyiakis, 'Access to Court v State Immunity' (2003) 52 ICLQ 297; Alastair Mowbray, 'European Convention on Human Rights: Report of the Evaluation Group and Recent Cases' (2002) 2 Human Rights Law Review 127, 131-140; Ed Bates, 'The Al-Adsani Case, State Immunity and the International Legal Prohibition on Torture' (2003) 3 Human Rights Law Review 193.

120 Waite and Kennedy v. Germany, Judgment, 18 February 1999, ECHR 1999-I, para. 63. See also the parallel case Beer and Regan v. Germany, Judgment, 18 February 1999.

121 Waite and Kennedy (supra note 120) para. 64.

122 Ibid para. 67.

sufficient if applicants disposed of reasonable alternative means to protect their Convention rights, such as access to dispute settlement mechanisms established under the framework of the international organization itself.[123]

In a second set of cases, the Court extended these considerations to the relations between States. Thus, in *McElhinney v. Ireland*, the Court accepted that Ireland's grant of jurisdictional immunity to the United Kingdom for a tort committed by a UK border guard on Irish territory did not breach Art. 6 ECHR.[124] It reasoned that such grant constituted a proportional restriction on the applicant's right to have access to an Irish court which served to protect the diplomatic relations between the two States. In particular, the Court pointed out that despite a trend in international and comparative law towards limiting State immunity in respect of personal injury caused by an act or omission of a foreign State within the forum State, Ireland was not «alone in holding that immunity attaches to suits in respect of such torts committed by *acta jure imperii* or that, in affording this immunity, Ireland falls outside any currently accepted international standards.»[125] Moreover, the Court observed that there was no reason why suit could not have been brought in the United Kingdom.[126] Quite similarly, in *Fogarty v. United Kingdom*, the Court accepted that the United Kingdom's grant of jurisdictional immunity to the United States in an action in UK courts against the US embassy for alleged discrimination in the embassy's recruitment process was not «outside any currently accepted international standards.»[127]

Both *McElhinney* and *Fogarty* concerned situations where, in the view of the parties, international law did not require the forum State to grant immunity to a foreign State, but where immunity was extended as a discretionary act in order to protect the diplomatic relations of the forum State and the third State. While the Court accepted that the underlying policy constituted a sufficient public interest to limit the applicants' right to access to court, the Court did not view this discretion as granting a *carte blanche* to the States in question. Instead, the Court controlled the decision of the respondent States under a proportionality test that weighed the interests of the applicants against the interests of the State to protect its diplomatic relations.

By referring to currently accepted international standards, however, the Court indicated that the standards were subject to change. Furthermore, it determined whether granting sovereign immunity was acceptable internationally based on the subject matter of the claim pernding in domestic courts. This is an indication

---

123 Ibid paras. 68 - 69.
124 McElhinney v. Ireland (supra note 119) paras. 33 - 40.
125 Ibid para. 38.
126 Ibid para. 39.
127 Fogarty v. United Kingdom (supra note 119) para. 37.

that absolute immunities attaching to the status of the respondent in domestic proceedings as a foreign sovereign as such would not be a sufficient justification to prevent individuals from bringing suit against a foreign State in the domestic courts of another State. Finally, one important factor militating for the proportionality of the restriction to access to courts, at least in *McElhinney*, was the availability for the applicant of remedies in the courts of the third State that enjoyed immunity in the forum State.[128]

Whereas *Fogarty* and *McElhinney* concerned cases, in which granting foreign sovereign immunity was presented to the Court as a discretionary decision of the forum State, in *Al-Adsani v. United Kingdom*, the respondent State argued that international law required it to confer sovereign immunity to the third State.[129] The case concerned a claim in UK courts against the State of Kuwait for damages resulting from personal injury that the applicant allegedly had suffered when tortured by Kuwaiti police guards in Kuwait. In this case the Court, like in *Fogarty* and *McElhinney*, denied that the application of foreign sovereign immunity by UK courts was in breach of Art. 6(1) ECHR. Responding to the argument by the United Kingdom that it was required to accord immunity to Kuwait, the Court stressed the need for a harmonious interpretation of the Convention in light of general international law relating to State immunity. It observed

> [t]hat measures taken by a High Contracting Party which reflect generally recognised rules of public international law on State immunity cannot in principle be regarded as imposing a disproportionate restriction on the right of access to a court as embodied in Article 6 § 1. Just as the right of access to a court is an inherent part of the fair trial guarantee in that Article, so some restrictions on access must likewise be regarded as inherent, an example being those limitations generally accepted by the community of nations as part of the doctrine of State immunity.[130]

After declining the applicant's argument, that the United Kingdom was under an obligation under international law not to grant immunity for alleged acts of torture in view of the *ius cogens* nature of the prohibition of torture,[131] the Court found that the grant of foreign sovereign immunity in the case at hand did not breach Art. 6(1) ECHR.

The ECtHR, however, did not only accept that foreign sovereign immunity could be invoked as a restriction to access to a court, but equally in respect of the enforcement of a domestic judgment against a foreign State. In *Kalogeropoulou and others v. Germany and Greece*, the Court accepted that Greece had not breached Art. 6(1) ECHR,nor Art.1 of Protocol 1, when refusing to enforce a Greek judgment against Germany for damages for crimes committed by the

128 McElhinney v. Ireland (supra note 119) para. 39.
129 Al-Adsani v. United Kingdom (supra note 119) para. 44.
130 Ibid para. 56.
131 Ibid paras. 57-66.

German army during World War II in Greece.[132] The Court reasoned that Art. 6(1) ECHR was not violated because Greece, by refusing enforcement, granted foreign sovereign immunity to Germany within the scope commonly accepted by the community of States. Likewise, the Court considered that refusing enforcement was a proportional restriction on the right to property because it could not be expected from Greece to violate commonly expected principles of the law of State immunity in order to protect good international relations with another State.

The Court's jurisprudence in *McElhinney*, *Fogarty*, and *Al-Adsani* have been criticized as unnecessarily deferential, given that the Court did not engage in an in-depth inquiry into the proportionality of the immunities in the cases at hand.[133] Yet, in the recent judgment in *Cudak v. Lithuania* the Court showed that its proportionality approach did not only play out in favor of States. In the case in question, the Court found that the grant of foreign sovereign immunity by Lithuanian courts concerning an employment-related dispute involving the dismissal by the Polish embassy in Vilnius of a locally hired employee was in breach of Art. 6(1) ECHR.[134] The Court noted that the grant of immunity in the specific case was essentially equivalent to applying an absolute form of sovereign immunity, which, as the Court noted, «has, for many years, clearly been eroded.»[135] Instead, the Court applied a provision of the UN Convention dealing with employment contracts with a State, as an expression of customary international law,[136] and determined that that provision would not have entitled Poland to immunity in Lithuanian courts. In consequence, the Court found that

> by upholding in the present case an objection based on State immunity and by declining jurisdiction to hear the applicant's claim, the Lithuanian courts, in failing to preserve a reasonable relationship of proportionality, overstepped their margin of appreciation and thus impaired the very essence of the applicant's right of access to a court.[137]

This case shows that the Court's proportionality analysis does not only work in one direction to protect interests of State, but can equally afford protection to the rights of individuals. The decision is further noteworthy as the Court applied the UN Convention as an expression of customary international law and made allusion to the fact that absolute immunity doctrines were problematic in view of

---

132 Kalogeropoulou and others v. Greece and Germany, Decision, 12 December 2002, ECHR 2002-X.
133 Reinisch (supra note 26) 816.
134 Cudak v. Lithuania (supra note 30) paras. 60-75. For discussion of this case see Lijana Štarienė 'Cudak v. Lithuania and the European Court of Human Rights Approach to the State Immunity Doctrine' (2010) 2 Jurisprudencija/Jurisprudence 159.
135 Ibid para. 64.
136 Ibid paras. 64-67.
137 Ibid para. 74.

the blanket restrictions they impose on the right of private individuals to access to courts under Art. 6(1) ECHR. This case therefore can be viewed as an example of the ECtHR actively using human rights law to influence and reduce the scope of State immunity, much like substantive investment treaty obligations could be used to reduce the scope of domestic State immunity doctrines.

II. Proportionality Analysis as a Means of Harmonizing Human Rights and State Immunity

The core of the ECtHR's approach to conceptualizing the relationship between the right to access to courts and the right to property, on the one hand, and (foreign) sovereign immunity, on the other, is proportionality reasoning combined with the granting of a certain margin of appreciation to the respondent State. In the Court's interpretative framework, restrictions on the right to access to courts and on enforcement of judicial and arbitral decisions must serve a legitimate purpose and constitute a proportional restriction to the rights granted to individuals under the Convention. Despite granting a margin of appreciation to the State, the question of whether a host State has struck a proportional balance, ultimately, is to be determined by the Court itself. Granting a margin of appreciation, however, is justified because the Court is not well-placed, in terms of expertise and mandate, to replace its own judgment for that of the State.

Overall, the Court's approach allows it to balance the private rights protected by the ECHR and the measures pursued by the respondent State to protect a certain public interest. This avoids granting unconditional primacy to either private or public interests, which would either prevent governments from effectively regulating in the public interest, if primacy was granted to private rights, or giving governments *carte blanche* to interfere with private rights, if granting immunity would go unscrutinized by the Court.

In applying its conceptual framework, the Court considers that grants of jurisdictional and enforcement immunities can be permissible. However, they cannot be an end in themselves, but only the means of protecting an underlying public interest. It is noteworthy in this context that the Court appears to draw no principled distinction based on whether immunity was granted to a domestic public body or to a foreign State. In both cases, proportionality analysis is the preferred method of analysis. The Court only compliments its analysis, when dealing with foreign sovereign immunity, by making reference to Art. 31(3)(c) of the Vienna Convention to stress that the ECHR needs to be interpreted in light of general public international law.

The Court, thus, does not perceive of general public international law as an independent framework that is dissolved from the ECHR but as one that needs to fit harmoniously with the obligations States undertook by acceding to the Convention. Hence, in the Court's view, living up to other obligations under international law, safeguarding diplomatic relations with other States, and exercising comity vis-à-vis acts of those States are all legitimate reasons for granting immunity. Yet, these considerations do not absolve States from taking into account the rights of individuals to access to courts and to enforcement of judicial and arbitral decisions. Instead, proportionality analysis becomes a method for harmonizing the relationship between special and general international law through interpretation.[138]

Such an idea of balancing is not only familiar from human rights law. It is also inherent to the law of State immunity itself. As Judges Higgins, Kooijmans and Buergenthal noted in a Separate Opinion in the *Arrest Warrant* case when discussing the evolution of international law on the relation between immunity of high State officials and peremptory norms of international criminal law:

> These trends reflect a balancing of interests. On the one scale, we find the interest of the community of mankind to prevent and stop impunity for perpetrators of grave crimes against its members; on the other, there is the interest of the community of States to allow them to act freely on the inter-State level without unwarranted interference. A balance must therefore be struck between the two sets of functions which are both valued by the international community. Reflecting these concerns, what is regarded as a permissible jurisdiction and what is regarded as the law on immunity are in constant evolution. The weights on the two scales are not set for all perpetuity. Moreover, a trend is discernible that in a world which increasingly rejects impunity for the most repugnant offences, the attribution of responsibility and accountability is becoming firmer, the possibility for the assertion of jurisdiction wider and the availability of immunity as a shield more limited. The law of privileges and immunities, however, retains its importance since immunities are granted to high State officials to guarantee the proper functioning of the network of mutual inter-State relations, which is of paramount importance for a well-ordered and harmonious international system.[139]

As arbitral tribunals in investment treaty arbitration increasingly also have recourse to proportionality-type reasoning to balance investor rights and the host State's interest to take action in the public interest,[140] they could follow the example of the ECtHR and apply the same type of reasoning in dealing with the tension between investment protection and domestic and foreign sovereign immunity.

In applying proportionality reasoning, investment treaty tribunalswould need, first,to determine whether immunity from jurisdiction and enforcement in a gi-

---

138 See further Anne van Aaken, 'Defragmentation of Public International Law Through Interpretation: A Methodological Proposal (2009) 16 Ind JGLS 483, 502-506.
139 Case Concerning the Arrest Warrant of 11 April 2000 (Democratic Republic of Congo v. Belgium), Judgment, 14 February 2002, Joint Separate Opinion of Judges Higgins, Kooijmans and Buergenthal, ICJ Reports 2002, 63, para.75.
140 See supra note 87.

ven case protect a legitimate public interest; and, second, to restrict a State's interference with the interest of foreign investors to what is necessary to protect the public interest at stake. Finally, the measure in question would also need to be proportional in the strict sense, meaning that there is a reasonable relationship between what is protected by the immunity in question and the degree of interference with what is at stake for the investor. A respondent State, in turn, would need to show that the immunity granted serves a legitimate public policy purpose and that the rights of the person affected nevertheless are sufficiently protected by other substantive, procedural, and institutional means.

This framework makes justifying absolute forms of sovereign immunity difficult because they do not allow domestic courts to react to the individual circumstances of each case and prevent them from scrutinizing whether an appropriate balance was struck between public and private interests. That is why absolute forms of immunity are adverse to the very concept of the rule of law as public interests are given unconditional primacy in relation to the private interests affected. Applying proportionality analysis in this context constitutes a change in paradigm from permitting States to exercise largely uncontrolled discretion as to what type of sovereign immunity doctrine to follow at the domestic level towards requiring them to choose a more restrictive one that allows the protection of legitimate public interests, while affording the best possible protection to foreign investors.

Thus, not only the emergence of a global economy, but also considerations of human rights, the rule of law, and court supervision of State behavior, pressure States to reduce the scope of State immunity they grant to foreign States. International investment law, therefore, would be no exception in pushing for a further restriction of jurisdictional and enforcement immunities at the domestic level. Instead, applying proportionality analysis to determining the impact substantive investment treaty obligations have on jurisdictional and enforcement immunity would be the logical continuation in respect of the developments in international investment law and the law of State immunity towards a rule of law-based framework for investor-State relations. In this sense, international investment law, human rights law, and the law of State immunity can co-exist peacefully in their common search for a more balanced relation between private and public interests.

E. Conclusion

This chapter has suggested that the rise of international investment law and the retreat of State immunity are part of the larger evolution of international law away from an exclusive inter-State system towards one that takes individuals and their protection seriously. Both the evolution in international investment law and in the law of State immunity, it was argued, can be explained by the increasing need in a global economy to provide effective protection under international law to interests of individuals against the abuse of public power. This also meant taking leave from an international law that governed the relation between States only and welcoming one in which individuals are recognized as subjects of international law.

The recognition of individuals as part of international law, however, does not mean that private interests trump public interests. Instead, States and the power they exercise remain crucial for providing a legal infrastructure and necessary ordering mechanisms for the global society in general and the global economy in particular. Apart from increasing the accountability of States vis-à-vis private individuals, including foreign investors, international law also needs to ensure that States can remain functional in using their powers to serve the public good and, in times of globalization, bring about public institutions for a global social system that do not only work in the interest of some States, or some groups of society, but that enhance welfare globally. States, in other words, remain central in providing global ordering structures, not only for non-economic interests that cannot be protected through market mechanisms, but also for the functioning of global markets themselves.

Thus, while international investment law can contribute to strengthening the protection of private interests against the abuse of governmental powers, it also needs to provide sufficient leeway for States to act in the public interest. It needs to ensure above all that States remain in a position to effectively cooperate internationally in order to establish institutions that can govern globalized proceeses effectively. Foreign sovereign immunities can have an important function in the protection of such interests, for example by protecting assets of States that are necessary to enable inter-State communication and cooperation. At the same time, it is important to ensure that State immunities are not misused to frustrate the legitimate expectation of foreign investors that States live up to the obligations they have entered into in international investment agreements and in the context of international arbitration.

While the law of State immunity has reacted to those demands by departing from absolute immunity and adopting more restrictive versions, it still struggles for the appropriate balance between public and private interests. As Hazel Fox observes, the contours of the post-modern law of State immunity, as she calls it,

> are not fully discoverable, but certain conflicting trends can be perceived. In one direction, the enhanced status of the individual presses for the lifting of immunity from all claims arising from conduct of the State; in another direction, the pooling of national powers in

non-State entities calls for their protection to enable their proper development in the public interest.[141]

Both international investment law and the law of State immunity need to share the concern for finding an appropriate balance between the protection of private economic interests and the obligation and responsibility of States to act in the public interest. While that balance has been found in opening access to investor-State arbitration, where jurisdictional immunity does not apply, enforcement immunity still leaves ample opportunities for States to avoid compliance with their obligations vis-à-vis foreign investors. Thus, while united with international investment law in its development towards ensuring more accountability of States, the law of State immunity still displays antagonistic traits to the objective of international investment law, above all as regards the enforcement of arbitral awards.

This antagonism, however, could be overcome by adopting the conceptual foundations laid down by the ECtHR in its jurisprudence on the relation between rights granted to individuals under the ECHR and State immunity: balancing the interest of individuals and States by proportionality analysis. Investment treaty tribunals, when dealing with whether the grant of immunity from jurisdiction and enforcement breaches investment treaty obligations, and domestic courts, when making decisions about the enforcement of investment treaty awards against States, should draw on the solutions and the conceptual framework used by the ECtHR. This allows enhancing investor-State cooperation by protecting reliance of foreign investors on commitments by States, while safeguarding sufficient leeway for States to regulate and to cooperate efficiently with other States to further the public interest.

Such a proportionality analysis suggests that absolute forms of immunity would need to be abandoned as they violate investment treaty provisions, such as full protection and security, fair and equitable treatment, the prohibition of un-compensated compensations, and the obligation to provide effective remedies and means of enforcement. Limited forms of enforcement immunity that protect, for example, assets and bank accounts of foreign missions against enforcement, by contrast, are acceptable as they protect assets States require to serve the public interest, namely to cooperate with other States at the international level. In that sense international investment law may serve as a body of law that further pushes for the reduction in scope of foreign sovereign immunity doctrines without questioning the principle that certain public interests need to be protected by sovereign immunities. In that perspective, both international investment law and the law of State immunity serve the protection of important interests that need to

---

141 Fox (supra note 6) 5.

converge, and are in the process of convergence, in a framework that aims at balancing and optimizing private and public interests.